ENGLISH WRITERS

English Writers. By Henry Morley.

Vol. I.—From the Beginning to Beowulf.
,,   II.—From Cædmon to the Conquest.
,, III.—From the Conquest to Chaucer.
,, IV.—The Literature of the Fourteenth Century (Part I.).
,,   V.—The Literature of the Fourteenth Century (Part II.).
,, VI.—From Chaucer to Caxton.
,, VII.—From Caxton to Coverdale.
,, VIII.—From Surrey to Spenser.
,, IX.—Spenser and his Time.
,,   X.—Shakespeare and his Time: Under Elizabeth.
,, XI.—Shakespeare and his Time: Under James I.

A First Sketch of English Literature.

From the Earliest Period to the Present Time. By Henry Morley. *Thirty-first Thousand.*

Library of English Literature. Edited by

Henry Morley. Complete in 5 Volumes. With 630 Illustrations from old MSS., Books, Pictures, and Sculptures.

Vol. I.—Shorter English Poems.
,, II.—Illustrations of English Religion.
,, III.—English Plays.
,, IV.—Shorter Works in English Prose.
,, V.—Sketches of Longer Works in English Verse and Prose.

CASSELL & COMPANY. Limited. *Ludgate Hill, London.*

ENGLISH WRITERS

AN ATTEMPT TOWARDS

A HISTORY OF ENGLISH LITERATURE

BY

HENRY MORLEY

LL.D. PROFESSOR OF ENGLISH LITERATURE AT UNIVERSITY COLLEGE
LONDON

I

INTRODUCTION   ORIGINS

OLD CELTIC LITERATURE

BEOWULF

CASSELL & COMPANY, Limited

LONDON, PARIS, NEW YORK & MELBOURNE

1898

1272

First Edition in this form February 1887.
Reprinted March 1887, 1891, 1898.

PREFACE.

———◆◇◆———

A FIRST volume of ENGLISH WRITERS was published in the year 1864, as an account of the Writers before Chaucer, with an introductory sketch of the Four Periods of English Literature. This was an octavo of about 800 pages, presently divided into half volumes, and followed, in 1867, by a third half volume, which brought the story down to the invention of printing. The design, then partly completed, had been to describe the course of English Literature with detail enough to make its meaning clear and give it interest to readers generally. But the volumes chiefly passed into the hands of students, and the book was credited with having hit a mark at which it did not aim.

While that generous estimate of the book made its writer the more conscious of deficiency, it was securing him admission to new fields of labour, in which study of Literature, until then the chief pleasure, became also the chief duty of his working life.

Under such conditions the book could not be reprinted or continued without very considerable change of plan. At that time also the labours of the Early English Text Society and of many good scholars in England and Germany were beginning to make large annual addition to the knowledge of our early literature. In research over the whole field there were new energies at work. Their issues were worth waiting for.

With a resolve, therefore, to recast the original design, ENGLISH WRITERS, as first published, was suffered to pass out of print. The book, so planned and begun, was part of the fulfilment of a young desire. But even that desire had for a long time been held in check, because it was necessary, before attempting a large book upon Literature, to give years of maturer life to study both of books and men, and books are men, or the best part of them. After waiting and working on through yet another twenty years, the labourer has learnt that he knows less and less. Little is much to us when young; time passes and proportions change. But, however small the harvest, it must be garnered. Scanty produce of the work of a whole life, it may yield grain to some one for a little of life's daily bread.

One result of the change of plan in the book is an enlargement of its scale.

There is a long story to tell, of English Literature regarded as expression of a nation's History throughout the sequence of its thought. It is intended to include notes of the literature of all offshoots of the English race. If life and health last, this work, issued in half-yearly volumes, of moderate compass and convenient size, will go on steadily towards its close. The writer will say all that he thinks ought to be said, and is not bound by any other

pledge.   But as no labourer plans in his afternoon for a
long day's work before nightfall, the proportions of the book
should be upon a scale that will not extend it beyond twenty
volumes.   The whole narrative will be continuous; the
whole book, one.   But the volumes will be grouped also in
sections, which may be read as distinct Histories of Periods.
Each volume will be separately indexed, and, from time to
time, extra title pages will be supplied for the use of
readers who may wish to place any one section as a
distinct work upon their shelves.

January, 1887.

CONTENTS.

———◆◇◆———

INTRODUCTION.   PAGE

The Full History of Literature ... ...   1—3

There can be no Full Historian of Literature   3

The Purpose of this Book   3

The Four Periods of English Literature   4

The one Mind in them All 4, 5

Sources of Literature 5, 6

In Pagan Times   6

In Early Christian Days 7, 8

Under the Normans...   8

The Influence of Nation upon Nation   9

In the Outset of Italian Literature... ... ...   9—11

In the Outset of German Literature 11, 12

In England under the Early Norman Kings 12, 13

Foundations of the Early Influence of Italy on European
    Literature   13

In Activity of Commerce 13, 14

In the Liberal and Busy Sense of Individual and Social
    Rights 14, 15

Relation to its Time of Dante's " Vita Nuova " ... ...   15—17

Relation to all Time of the " Divine Comedy "   17

Transmission of certain Forms of Poetry from the Trou-
    badours through Dante to Petrarch ... .   18—21

Boccaccio and his Decameron 21, 22

Italian Influence on Chaucer   23

The Native and the Foreign Elements in Chaucer's Verse   23, 24

Dark Days of English Literature   24

	PAGE
Spread of Petrarchan Poetry, and Rise of Platonism ...	25
Italian Pastoral	26
Influence of Petrarch and of Italian Pastoral on English Literature. The English Mind under the Italian Manner	26—28
Reflection of Italian Love-conceits in "Astrophel and Stella"	28, 29
Spenser and the Italian Romantic Poets	29
Foreign Influence on Italy. "Amadis of Gaul" ...	30, 31
Sources of the New Taste for Romance. The Pulci ...	31
Bojardo	31
Ariosto	31, 33
The Taste for Quotation	33
Growing Demand for Allegory. Tasso	33, 34
Social and Literary Predominance of the Italians ...	34, 35
The Social Influence of Italy on English Literature ...	35
Secondary Causes of the Spread of a Taste for Conceited Writing. Euphuism	35—40
The English Mind under it all. Out of Decay New Life	40—42
Duration of Lyly's Popularity	42
Lyly himself a practical Englishman	42—47
Influence of Lyly and the Italians on Robert Greene ...	47—49
"Love's Labour's Lost"—a Jest upon the Fashionable Style	49, 50
Duration of Italian Influence in the Taste for Conceits ...	50—52
Ridiculed by Ben Jonson in "Cynthia's Revels" ...	52
French Euphuism. The "Divine Weeks" of Du Bartas	52, 53
Great English Reputation of Du Bartas. Its Duration ...	53—55
Italian Influence in France	55, 56
Spanish Influence in France allied to the Italian... ...	56
Tendency of French Literary Conceit to Verbal Criticism. The Reason of it	57
Ronsard	57, 58
Malherbe	58
The Meetings at the Hôtel Rambouillet	58—60
The *Précieuses*	60

PAGE

The French Academy   60

Settlement of the French Language by the Forty Dictionary Makers 60, 61

Advance of French Writers from Verbal to Literary
Criticism 61, 62

Boileau   ...   .   62—64

Influence of Boileau on English Literature   ...   ...   64—66

The Period of French Influence on English Literature ...   66, 67

English Acceptance and Imitation of the French Classical
Critics 67, 68

What the Polite World and French polished Critics said
of Shakespeare ...   .   68—70

Shakespeare endorsed by Pope 71, 72

Under French Influence, The English Mind 72, 73

Milton endorsed by Addison 73, 74

Latin English 74, 75

Substance and Accidents of English Style   ...   ...   75—77

Purpose and Limits of Generalisation 77, 78

The Period of Popular Influence ...   .   78—80

Defoe's Service of the People 80, 81

Defoe in the Pillory ...   .   81—84

Defoe in Newgate sets up the *Review*   84

Addison in the way of Patronage 85, 86

Steele represents the People   ...   .   86—89

Decreased Influence of the People on the Stage 89, 90

The Tatler ...   .   90—92

Relation of *The Tatler* to the People   92

Addison, drawn by Steele into Co-operation, writes for
the People better than for Patrons. *Tatler, Spectator,*
Guardian   ...   .   92—95

Steele's *Englishman* ...   .   95—97

Pope   97

Development of Prose Fiction—" Robinson Crusoe " and
" Gulliver "   ...   .   97—99

Richardson's " Pamela " 99, 100

Fielding   100

	PAGE
"Tom Jones"	100—104
The French Taste of the Lesser Critics	104
Samuel Johnson	104—107
Goldsmith's Influence on Goethe	107, 108
Relations between English and German Literature ...	108—110
Germany fastens upon "Robinson Crusoe"	110
The Spirit of Milton is Abroad. Gottsched and Bodmer	110, 111
Klopstock	111
The Revolt against Despotism in Life or Literature ...	111, 112
The Revolt most violent in France	112
Goethe	112, 113
Schiller	113
Limits of the German Influence on English Literature	113
Wordsworth, Coleridge, and Southey	113—115
Walter Scott	115—117
Development of Journalism	117—119
Writers and Readers	119—121

Book I.

CHAPTER I.—THE FORMING OF THE PEOPLE.

Life and Growth	123, 124
Ethnology. Origin of the English	124—126
The Indo-European Family	126—132
Stone, Bronze, and Iron Periods	132, 133
The Stone Period	134—136
Cromlechs	136—138
The Bronze Period. Barrows	138—140
The Iron Period	140
Were the Gaels Hyperboreans ?	140—146
Were the Celts Cimmerians ?	146—149
The Celtic Britons	149, 150
The Belgæ	150—152
The Gaels	152—154
The Cymry	154—156
The Celtic Element in English	157

PAGE

Celtic in Local Names ... ... 157—159
The Celtic Element in Common English ... .. 159—161
Faint Traces of the Roman Occupation. Latin of the
    First Period 161, 162
Twilight before the Dawn of English Literature. Druids 162—164

CHAPTER II.—OLD LITERATURE OF THE GAEL.

Ancient Literature of the Gael in Britain ... ... 165—167
The Ogham 167
Poets' Staves 170
Old Gaelic Degrees in Literature 170, 171
Of History among the Ancient Gaels ... ... 171—179
Old Gaelic Poetry ... ... 179—187
Gaelic Tales in Prose and Verse... ... ... 187—189
The Celtic Influence on English Literature 189, 19c
The Fenian Tales... ... ... 190—196
Adornment of MSS. 196, 197
The Battle of Magh Grath ... ... 197—200
MS. Materials for a Study of Old Gaelic Literature ... 200—202

CHAPTER III.—OLD LITERATURE OF THE CYMRY.

The Cymry 303
Germanic Settlements in Britain before A.D. 449 ... 204—206
Pressure of the Cymry and the Saxons on the Gaels in
    Gwynedd or North Wales ... ... 206—208
Pressure of the Saxons on the Cymry. The Record of
    Six Settlements 208
Connection of the Ancient Literature of the Cymry
    with the Anglo-Saxon Conquests 209
Urien 209, 210
Taliesin ... ... 210—214
Llywarch Hen ... ... 214—218
Merlin, and other Bards of the Sixth Century 219
Aneurin. The Gododin... ... ... 219—235
Celtic Metres 236, 237
MS. Materials for Study of Old Cymric Literature ... 237—239

PAGE

CHAPTER IV.—OLD LITERATURE OF THE TEUTONS.

    Gildas 240, 241
    The Anglo-Saxon Settlements .. .. 241—244
    Jutes ... ... 244—247
    Angles ... ... 247—249
    Saxons ... ... 249—253
    Frisians and Saxons 253, 254
    The Romans in Germany 254, 255
    Ulfilas and the Mœsogoths. Bible Translation ... 255—258
    The Song of Hildebrand ... ... 258—261
    The Weissenbrunner Prayer ... ... 261—263

CHAPTER V.—SCANDINAVIA.

    Ultima Thule ... ... 264—266
    Runes 266, 267
    Scandinavian England ... ... 267—269
    Iceland 269, 270
    The Islendinga Bók 270, 271
    The Landnama Bók 271
    Irish Hermits in Iceland 271
    Iceland Peopled 272, 273
    The Eddas 273
    The Old Northern Ars Poetica 273, 274
    Relation of England to the Edda Myths 274, 275

CHAPTER VI.—BEOWULF.

    "Beowulf." The Poem and the Manuscript 276, 277
    The Substance of the Tale ... ... 277—310
    Interpretations of "Beowulf" 311
        Thorkelin 311, 312
        Grundtvig 312
        John Mitchell Kemble 313, 314
        Leo 314
        Ettmüller 314
        Wackerbath 314

PAGE

Thorpe 314, 315

Simrock 315

Grein ... ... 315—319

Rev. D. H. Haigh ... ... 319—326

Prof. John Earle ... ... 327—331

The Historical Hygelac ... ... 331—336

An Episode of a Shrew ... ... 336—339

Heremod ... ... 339—340

Scyld Scefing 340, 341

Prof. Skeat on Grendel ... ... 341—343

" Beowulf " as Mythical History 343, 344

Of other Myths in " Beowulf " : —

Jacob Grimm 344

J. M. Kemble, L. Ettmüller 345

Karl Müllenhoff 345, 346

Uhland, Laistner 346, 347

Who Wrote " Beowulf " ? 347, 348

Hermann Möller's Argument from the Analysis of

Metre 348

CHAPTER VII.—THE FIGHT AT FINNESBURG.

The Fight at Finnesburg... 349

The Finnesburg Episode in " Beowulf " ... ... 350—352

Historical Foundation of the Tale 352, 353

Waldhere 353, 354

Widsith, Deor 354

BIBLIOGRAPHY OF BEOWULF ... ... 355—358

INDEX TO THE INTRODUCTION ... ... 359—361

INDEX TO THE FIRST BOOK ... ... 362—367

ENGLISH WRITERS.

——◆◇◆——

INTRODUCTION.

THE FOUR PERIODS OF ENGLISH LITERATURE.

THE soul of Literature is the soul of man at work through his best mind under the conditions to which he is born, which are in part natural and unalterable, in part social and variable from age to age. In the Literature of any People we perceive, under all contrasts of form produced by variable social influences, the one national character from first to last.

The full History of Literature.

The mind has, like the body, its physiognomy determined in some measure by climate and race. Between the kindred minds of men who call each other foreigners, when they are equal in right influence upon the world's advancement, as between their faces when they are equal in beauty, there are strongly-marked and hereditary differences of expression. But the full mind of a nation is its literature ; and we may be very sure that to a true history of the literature of any country must belong a distinct recognition of the national character that underlies it, gives coherence to it all, and throughout marks with strength its individuality.

On the surface of the true character of a literature lie manifest to every eye the frequent changes in the fashion of its utterance. There is   reason for the form as well as for

B

the substance of every book man ever wrote ; and a history
of our Literature that does not even ask why there was an
especially strong body of dramatists in the days of Elizabeth, why satire prevailed after the Restoration, why dramatists are now converted into novelists, overlooks nearly the
most obvious part of its work. Again, it is not only by
conditions of society within a country itself that the form of
its literature is modified from age to age. No land can be
to itself a world. Neighbouring nations act and react
strongly upon each other, and Englishmen, being insular,
touch every coast. Whenever the literature of any country
in Europe has for a time become stronger than that of its
neighbours, its admitted strength has influenced them in a
very marked degree ; and nowhere has influence of this
kind been more complete and general than in England,
where the great epoch of Italian literature and the *siècle Louis
Quatorze* established two of the chief bends in the current of
our literary history. To a fair account, then, of the literature
of any land, and not only to a history of English Literature,
discussion of its relations with the literature of surrounding
countries is, to a certain extent, indispensable. A chronological series of authors' names, with biographical dates and
extracts, has its use, of course ; and so has a list of the
affluents of a great river, with their measured lengths and
their distances from one another,—nor is it altogether useless to produce bottles of water drawn from each. But if
we are told nothing of the river's banks, or of the feeding-
grounds of its affluents, but are left to infer what we can
from the fact that one water is clear, another sandy, and
another contains clay ; if nothing is told us of the bluffs and
mountain-chains that turn the main river's course, the valleys
into which it pours, here rushing impetuously between rocky
banks, there spread into a sluggish lake over the marsh-land,
the stream may have been industriously measured. but it has
not been surveyed.

Of no literature does there exist, or will there ever exist, from the hand of one man a complete survey. He who shall begin in his old age to write, what he may not then hope to complete—the large history of a Literature—should have lived long and tranquilly, much tried by various conflicts with the passions and prejudices that he has often overcome in others, but himself has never largely shared. Continued health of mind and body, an almost boundless range of daily study among books, freshening the gladness of his intercourse with many sorts of men, and quickening that habit of energetic action in affairs of moment which alone can make him read a man where the recluse reads print,—these are, indeed, needful preparations for his work. But grant him these, he must yet have a perceptive genius akin to that of Shakespeare, if he would really show not only the form and stir of mind in every generation, but also the mind of each writer whose genius he seeks to define. And after all, if ever the man be born who shall be able thus to write the History of any Literature, it is not a History of Literature that he will write.

There can be no full History of Literature.

Thus, since we are all very much left to the guidance of our own impressions, there are formed, and it is well for us that there should be formed, literary opinions diverse as the moods and life-relations out of which they spring. In these volumes I desire to tell the History of English Literature as fully as I can, well knowing that the studies of one life are insufficient for the setting forth even of the little that one man can see. Each reader within the limit of his different range of sight must have observed much that will, in his own mind, add fulness to my story, or serve to correct some of its errors, and he will also find in it some things that he himself has not before seen. Give and Take keep the gates of knowledge, where none but the dwarfs pass through with unbowed head.

The purpose of this book.

B 2

In our national life there are no breaks. But as outward accidents affect the dress of our bodies so they affect the dress of thought. A student of costume could, by observation of those outward changes, come very near to the exact date of a picture representing life of its own time ; so might an approach be made to the dating of books, by observation of their language and their outward accidents of style. Upon historical accidents affecting fashions of speech, and not upon changes of the fixed natural character, we found, therefore, a division of this History into four periods, namely :—

The Four Periods of English Literature.

That of THE FORMATION OF THE LANGUAGE, during which English obviously and substantially differs from the English we now speak.

That of ITALIAN INFLUENCE, felt in Chaucer's day as influence of great writers on great writers, but first coming in as an influence of people upon people, with the "company of courtly makers" who preceded the age of Elizabeth.

That of FRENCH INFLUENCE, of which the beginning is marked strongly by a change in the style of Dryden subsequent to the "Annus Mirabilis."

And that of English POPULAR INFLUENCE, which was established gradually, but which may be dated from Defoe.

To the last-named there was added slight admixture of a *German Influence.*

Before adopting these divisions in a survey of the course of English Literature let me be permitted to explain more fully what they mean.

The student of English Literature who looks for the characteristic mind of the nation underlying through all generations for more than a thousand years the most distinct diversities of manner should found his divisions of the study upon such diversities of manner, but refuse to recognise division in the life itself.

The One Mind in them all.

Of every change of taste and style, marking a period, he should seek the origin in many influences—as of public events or struggles at home or abroad; of the personal character of the sovereign in the days of patronage; of the humour of the sovereign's court, which would colour the humours of all lesser patrons; of the genius of great writers, or the fashionable extravagances of small writers who were at the time in high repute. But at every turn it is to be remembered that those superficial differences do not change the mind within. An honest, earnest man may in a day so accommodate himself to the taste of his company that— with the same meaning to express—for one he shall be a warm attacker of abuses, for another a calm moralist, for another a jester, for another a satirist, for another a retailer of flat small talk; and with each companion he shall, by change of mood, have come into such honest sympathy that he shall have carried one and the same thought fairly home to all. Far more easy it is for the unity of a substantial English character to be maintained in variety of utterance by the different voices of many men, speaking at different times, but always straight from English lips to English ears.

Yet another consideration has to be applied constantly to the study of a literature. It is the expression of the best mind of the country. But why so ex- Sources of pressed? Books are produced either to uphold Literature. right for its own sake, or to procure credit and gain to their authors, or for the two reasons combined. The desire of gain never could mean for any honest English author, if he were not rich,—at any rate, down to the close of the last century,—more than labour for a livelihood; and if he were rich, it certainly was not by writing books that it would easily have occurred to anybody that he might increase his wealth. But the man without hereditary store who gave his labour to his pen has at all times been forced by the conditions of life to study how he might subsist by it. Money, that some affect to despise in the gross, means food, clothes, health—nay, the very lives—of wife and children ; power to be honest, power to be just, power to be merciful. Common truths as these are, they help to make many things clear when fairly and habitually applied to the analysis of Literature.

Thus, for example, in the old British and Pagan or half-Pagan times there were men who sang deeds of a chief and his forefathers. The rude civilisation hardly gave birth to high spiritual aspirations, and there was no bread for an author except what he ate at the table of such a patron. For what he received he paid with cunning words of flattery, and battle-songs to stir his master's followers to valour. The desire of gifts was never concealed by the bard. Thus Taliesin—in one of the few songs to Urien which may be as old as all pretend to be, and may really carry us back to the days when the Celts were contending against the invasion of the English—Taliesin is very explicit to his master. "The broad spoils of the spear," he says, "are given to my fair song delivered before the bright smiling hero. The most resolute of chieftains is Urien. . . . . Eagle of the land, very keen is thy sight. I have made a request for a mettled steed, the price of the spoils of Taliesin." The same aid to appreciation of the chieftain from whom came the minstrel's bread opens another of these songs, " Urien of the plain, most generous of baptized men ; much has he bestowed on skilful men. Like to the heaping together of scattered corn is the abundance of Christian bards." In the earlier days of English possession, when Christianity had not yet touched the hearts of our forefathers, still the military chief was the sole patron by whom an author could be fed, and battle-stories pleasant to his ear were all the literature he would pay for

Then followed the Christian days, when in the great monasteries there was a more peaceful life, with more honour and more assurance of bread to the scholar. The Church paid only for a religious literature. The earnest English mind was, as it still is, freely open to religious influence, and was practical then as it is now. Until there came some fusion with the Celts, the English were not only as serious and industrious as the Dutch, but quite as much deficient in the sense of fun. They gave philosophers and teachers to the Court of Charlemagne ; through that to Europe. Their best religious houses were great factories, into which loose material of knowledge was imported from abroad, often at great cost, to be worked up into compact epitomes. The higher motive of exertion was developed in men's hearts, and if the authors now supported by the Church worked for their sustenance, they worked also with all their minds for love of God. The dream of Cædmon, and a simple faith in the direct interposition from heaven that gave to his noble paraphrase of Scripture stories into English verse a stronger hold on the surrounding peasantry for whose instruction it was made, had in them no touch of untruth. To all secular knowledge the nature of the patronage gave also at that period a religious application. Knowledge was thought to be useless that did not serve directly to promote the glory of God : even arithmetic connected its number two with Adam and Eve, its three with the Trinity, its four with the Evangelists, and so forth. Only such knowledge was in the highest degree practical, and to diffuse practical knowledge was the only labour of the Church. The writings of Bede are an Encyclopædia, and his life at Jarrow was one uniform act of work and worship. "All my life I spent," he says, "in that monastery ; and in the intervals between the hours of regular discipline and the duties of singing in the church I always took pleasure in learning, or teaching, or writing something."

In early Christian days.

The religious mind and that quiet spirit of work in Bede were English. Outside the monasteries the fields were being tilled, and by successive colonisation the land had been occupied by an industrious race, willingly attentive to the teaching of an honest clergy. And in these respects the coming of the Normans did not change them.

The Normans were but a new race in France. It was only in the days of Alfred, when the First English had achieved their best, and were about to lapse into stolidity of character, that those bold Northmen settled in France, and became fathers of a mixed race that knew not whence it had come; supposing, indeed, its old home to be somewhere upon the Danube. When their chief joined to his rich dukedom in France the throne of England he became the richest prince of whom a bard could seek reward. French song, Arabic learning sought in Spain by busy scholars, the ready jest, soon familiarised to the whole English people in the miracle play that imparted its half-profane liveliness to religious teaching—such influences stirred English wits. The reckless rule of Norman feudal lords and the scandals often raised among their God-fearing flocks by the excess that had been common, even in Normandy, among the clergy—such influences stirred English temper. Song and romance found friends; but there began at once, and rose gradually in intensity, the determined protest against wrong, which forms the bone and marrow of our literature. There was reason now why men should speak from their hearts; there was reason also why the people should support their spokesman. Even at Court the Norman wits were as earnest in their Latin satires as the men of the soil in their own mother tongue. At last we have the whole religious soul of England centred about Wyclif; and the author of "Piers Plowman," with the old English religious seriousness, is urging with direct moralities, what Chaucer, in the more altered English and with his own

Under the Normans.

livelier wit brightened among the Normans in the capital, was urging with an equal earnestness of heart.

Meanwhile there had been transition, varying in different parts of England in extent and character, from first English towards the English we now speak. Into the reasons for the differences in Transition English, as well as the facts of them, the student *Influence of nation upon nation.* of the English language must needs enter fully. All English of this Period is known at once by its use of grammatical forms that have passed away, and many words that are now obsolete. But with Chaucer we draw towards the close of what we have called the Period of the Formation of the Language, while the Period of Italian Influence begins.

———————

At the source of modern European literature the chief spring is represented by the genius of Dante, which descends from a sublime height, as one pure and mighty column, to blend with the noisier and broader streams running from those two other fountains of abundant song and story, Petrarch and Boccaccio. But whence the strength and fulness of these headwaters? What morning dew of poetry, what obscure tricklings of verse, caused, in days barren of wit, the genius of Dante to leap forth from the dry rock?

After the confusion and darkness of the last days of the Ancient Literature, in the south of Europe there was rhyming of love-verses or devotional songs, feeble and rude until stirred into quicker life by conflict with *In the outset of Italian Literature.* a warm-witted Oriental people. Against this people the Spaniards had to maintain in their own land a daily strife, awakening devotional and patriotic chivalry, and giving soul to song and ballad—and against them the men of southern France went out to fight upon the sacred soil of Palestine. Italy, or the contending cities by which Italy was represented, stayed at home, every man eager to fight with his neighbour and trade profitably with the world. The provincial tongues of the old Roman Empire within the peninsula were marked by hundreds of conflicting local forms ; each city scorned its neighbour's dialect ; classical Latin was a neutral ground of speech, on which a writer for more than the circle of his townspeople could tread without offence. There was little Italian prose before the middle of the fourteenth century ; and the first Italian poem — a Dialogue between Lover and Lady, by Ciullo d'Alcamo—dates only from the years 1172-78, when the new stir of poetic life, south of the Loire and in Spain, had transmitted to Italy the impulse derived by others from their contest with the Moor.   D'Alcamo was a Sicilian. Folcachiero, whose Canzone upon his Condition through Love is almost, or altogether, contemporary, was a Tuscan.

It was at Palermo, in the thirteenth century, under the Emperor Frederic II. and his natural son Manfredi, both kings of Naples, that the true beginning was made of an Italian literature.   In the men who preceded this period, when Italian poetry was even known as "the Sicilian language," there is no very strong trace of direct influence from Provence.   The troubadours on one side of the Alps were but a livelier and more numerous body, kindred even in language to the few rhymers on the other. The boundary line was not strongly drawn between the Romance dialects on either side of Alps or Pyrenees.   When the Sicilian Court became a haunt of poets, although troubadours were tempted thither, it was rather from Spain than from France that the chief influence proceeded. The Italian sonnets by the earlier precursors of Dante do not greatly resemble poems of the troubadours, but are far more kindred in versification to the Spanish poems of the "Cid," written a century before the marriage of Frederic of Sicily with Constance of Aragon.

When Frederic II., at Palermo, married to Constance of Aragon, made the Sicilian Court the haunt of poets, it was through Aragon, or from the Mediterranean coast of Spain, that stray murmurs of the Castilian music penetrated. But the dialects of Aragon and Castile were almost two languages; the Aragonese, spoken along the whole Mediterranean coast of Spain, from Cape Palos northward, being in close relation to the Provençal. Unsettled variations, indeed, of the same Occitanian tongue of the troubadours, differing in Provence itself from Italian and Spanish no more than the Tuscan dialect from the Lombard and Venetian, were the language of song along the whole line of Mediterranean coast westward of Genoa, and almost to the Straits of Gibraltar. Thus, for example, with an air to modern readers of the most intelligible polyglot, begins one of the songs of Bernat de Ventadorn, born of the people of the Limousin :—

> " Non es meravelha s'ieu can
> Meils de nul autre cantador. "

The second or " Sicilian " period of early Italian literature received, then, some of its inspiration from a Spanish province, but in the days of Dante, and the generations next before him, they were the poets of Provence itself who gave the law of song to Italy.

Not Italy alone was influenced thus from without. The concourse and conflict of mind in the Crusades had infected courtly wits in Germany also—where the rug- *In the outset* gedly grand poem of the " Nibelungen " be- *of German* longed to the true mind of the people—with *Literature.* the epidemic of the *gai saber*. The Suabian Minnesänger in the generations before Dante were rivalling the troubadours of Provence in the fanciful delicacy of their praise of women. Emperor Barbarossa had been crowned King of Provence in 1133, and after the land of song was thus parted from France as a fief of the German empire, the Court of the Suabian Emperors cherished among its own minstrels the artifices of Provençal poetry. The reign of Barbarossa's grandson, Frederic II., not only established around his Italian throne a golden day of Italian song before the age of Dante ; in his own land also he was surrounded by the minstrelsy of such great chiefs of the minnesänger as Wolfram von Eschenbach and Walther von der Vogelweide, who went with Frederic to the Crusades— men without equals in Italy.

To England also there passed through Northern France the same spirit of southern song and story, not unaffected by the adventurous and busy temper of the thriving Normans, who found work and pay for Chroniclers in verse and prose. They liked well that the history they made should be written by cunning scholars who, being priests, must have licence to mingle histories of abbeys with the stories of the rise and fall of thrones. Old British tales that had passed out of mind came home again in song from Brittany, ever a distinct stronghold of fiction, yielding the true fairyland of Northern France. Out of such impulse arose also in England, during the generation or two before Dante, little or nothing indeed in imitation of the fantastic and courtly southern love-song which the earnest men of the soil, and the adventurous Normans, with the blood of the Sea Kings in their veins, were alike inapt to invent—but the first English metrical imitations of the cunningly invented narrative lays and fabliaux, or of the brisk tales of chivalrous adventure. We had in England, during a few generations before Dante, such literature of feigned enterprise and ad-venture, or true narrative of action by the chroniclers who waited on a race of energetic history-makers ; and to-gether with it there remains enough to show the dominant characteristic of religious earnestness marking the scanty

In England under the early Norman kings.

written utterances of the English of the people. Brother Orm's "Ormulum," a body of metrical homilies, founded on paraphrases of the Gospel for each day, designed for instruction of the congregation in the daily service of the Church, remains to us from the century before the birth of Dante. It is carefully furnished with a peculiar device of spelling, doubtless intended to secure the right pronunciation of their own words to the people by ignorant or half-Norman readers.

This being the condition of poetry among the men with whom the new kingdoms of modern Europe were rising into life, whence the sudden predominance of Dante's genius? Why should it be through a most un- *Foundations of the early influence of Italy on European Literature.* fortunate outcast from Florence in its day of utmost discord that there came suddenly the Divine Poem which first raised the literature of the moderns to a level with the highest utterances of the ancient world? The rare gift of genius in Dante really fell on the best soil in Europe when, surrounded by the warm artistic spirit of the Tuscans, it lay nurtured in the soul of a man linked to the life of the chief Tuscan city.

Florence was, in spite of its rude turmoil of independ- ence, great among cities of Europe in commerce, a resort of nations, a hive of the most active, earnest, *In activity of commerce.* enterprising life. Only in the stir of the city— where man meets man, and each man's energies are called into the fullest play; where commerce brings the world within the city's gates, and yet is not its whole life, but leaves room for all that there is in man besides and beyond the trading spirit to assert itself—can a great centre of literature be established. Such a centre Florence was in Dante's day, and after it.

To the chief discords of North Italy there was an ani- mating soul; the struggle between Guelf and Ghibelline was for a long time practically the battle of popular right

against Imperial feudalism. The Peace of Constance, in
1183, established for those Italian republics the possession
of the rights they fought for; and during another
forty years the Guelfs, who were then the Italian
party, had their way. But that grandson of Barbarossa, Frederic II., whom we have found in-
augurating in Sicily an Italian new birth, maintained again the Imperial cause in battle against North
Italian republicanism. When Dante was born, in 1265,
this conflict, not of men only, but of principle, was raging;
for Frederic's son, Manfredi, still ruled in Sicily and Naples.
During the last five years, since their triumph at the famous
battle of Mont Aperti, the Ghibellines had been enjoying
sway in Florence; and as the exiled chiefs of the Guelfs
did not return till two years after Dante's birth, when
Charles of Anjou, crowned by the Pope King of Naples,
had overcome Manfredi, we cannot suppose that the
respectable, unbanished lawyer, of whose second wife,
Donna Bella, Dante was born, though of good family, held
anything like the consideration of a party chief.

In the liberal and busy sense of individual and social rights.

The Ghibellines who left Florence when, after the arrival
of Charles of Anjou, the Guelfs returned, were restored to
their homes twelve years afterwards; and already the identification of the Guelfs with a French party was beginning
to deprive their cause of its very soul in its connection with
Italian nationality. Both parties, after the Ghibellines returned, were again combatant fellow-citizens in Florence,
from the time when Dante was a boy of thirteen, left during
the last four years, by his father's death, in charge of a most
careful mother. After four more years, when the poet was
in the first flush of manly youth, the famous Constitution of
1282, representative of the highest point of free political
strength attained by the city, was established. The soul of
liberty had animated even the licence of many a lawless
street conflict. The republican spirit, wild enough in some

of its workings, gave to the battles in North Italy against encroachment on the civil rights of men an influence far higher than that of the sentiment which prompted the Crusades. The Crusades, breeding chivalry, gave life and colour to the picturesque fictions of the minstrel, or his courtly refinements in the praise of beauty. But the Lombard cities, whether they fought against feudalism or asserted themselves against one another, were with a rude earnestness discussing at the sword's point the fundamental principles of social life. Given the apt mind, in a society so agitated its whole power could be stimulated into action. In the very focus of this movement Florence lay. The quick observation of the world, and lively sensibilities of a youth of seventeen, Dante brought to an appreciation of its newly confirmed and enlarged liberties in the Constitution of 1282. His city of a hundred thousand had, by free exercise of industry, attained the bright morning of her golden day. It was becoming the city of two hundred cloth manufacturers and a hundred banks of exchange. The Palace of Justice, and the prisons, and the Bridge of the Trinity were built less than a score of years before the poet's birth; while in Dante's own time, troubled as Florence was with civil strife, there were built the Baptistery, the Cathedral, the old Palace, the city walls.

In Dante's youth a fanciful love-poetry was still attesting, even among Florentines, the influences of Provençal song. Dante then wrote as others wrote, checking more power of song under the same restraints of artifice. The "Vita Nuova" represents the song of his youth, a string of ditties and sonnets differing in quality alone, but not in character, from a thousand other compositions of the kind. They describe his love for Beatrice, conceived when he was nine years old; its issue foreshadowed by a dream at the ninth hour before morning, never aiming at a higher reward than the exquisite

Relation to its time of Dante's "Vita Nuova."

effects of her gracious salutation. She died young, after
marrying somebody else, and died in the year when young
Dante was present, as a soldier, at the taking of Caprona.
If we are to take as it stands, quite literally, the "Vita
Nuova" as the history of Dante's early love, we can see
in it only a glorification of calf-love, much more open to
Leigh Hunt's censure than to the admiration justly claimed
for it. But it is not to be so regarded.

At the end of the "Vita Nuova" Dante celebrates his
consolation for the death of Beatrice in another love; and
in the "Convito," his next work, he explains that this maid
was Philosophy. To conquer his grief he read Cicero's
Lælius and the Consolation of Boëthius, whereby he was so
drawn to philosophy that he went to its source in Bologna
and Padua, and, after thirty months, was mastered by the
love of it, before his upward way led to the heavenly love.
Two years after the death of Beatrice, Dante was married
to a noble lady of the house of Donati. When, ten years
later, he was banished, the poet left five or six little children
in his native city with the wife who there only could shelter
and rear them, and, being allied to a house then in the
ascendant, perhaps recover for them something out of the
wreck of their father's worldly substance. The separation
was dictated strongly by prudence; and if Dante does not
mention his wife in his poetry, for good or ill, so neither
does he mention his children, his brother, his father, his
devoted mother, or anything belonging to that strictly private life which poets of his day refrained from intruding on
the public. Beatrice belonged to the public as an idealised
being, of whom what he wrote was to be read with a
mystical as well as a natural interpretation, and the natural
interpretation then was into graces of a poet's courtesy,
that were allowed freely because they were held not to
imply personal suit. Had Dante, indeed, been trained only
in studies of poetry and philosophy, he never would have

passed beyond the "Vita Nuova," and the "Convito," which, though lifted in aim, link him directly to the Provençalists on the one side and to Petrarch on the other, and by which he is more especially connected with that sequence of Italian writers through whose influence a literature marked strongly by the taste for conceits was afterwards established in this country. He would have been little more than a master in the school to which Guido Guinicelli had belonged. He might even have imitated, as at last he did, the "Tesoretto" of his old teacher, Brunetto Latini, wherein that poet—statesman as he was—coldly described how he was lost in a forest, and found Nature, who told him of many things, God, man, redemption, and the navigation beyond Spain; how in the next forest he was instructed by Philosophy, met the four Virtues, went to the abode of Love, and was led out of the wood by Ovid. But without the vigorous stirring of all his depths, by the surroundings of his life in Florence, Dante never would have, on such suggestion, yielded as he did, for the first time in all literature, the whole innermost truth of a man's soul in a poem passionate with all that was real to him, rising fearlessly to the heights and sounding the depths of an argument unequalled then in its sublimity.

I must not dwell here on the Divine Comedy. Its power is in the fulness with which it puts into fitting music a man's mind stirred to the vigorous assertion of all that was best in it. Another man might put Solinus, the geographer, in place of Virgil, and produce an exploration of the upper world in terza rima, as a "Dittamondo"; but beside such work "the Divine Comedy" was Chimborazo to a mole-hill. We skirt its base, and discuss Dante's "Vita Nuova" on our way to Petrarch and Boccaccio, when we speak of Italian literature with regard only to its influence upon old English writers.

Relation to all time of the Divine Comedy.

C

It was, then, by no abrupt transition that the strained
and fanciful love-poetry of troubadours and minnesänger
passed through the young Dante's celebration of

*Transmis-
sion of cer-
tain forms
of poetry
from the
trouba-
dours
through
Dante to
Petrarch.*
the ideal excellence of Beatrice into the sonnets of
Petrarch, from which Surrey and Wyat and the
" courtly makers" of the days of Henry VIII.
learnt to new-mould our English verse; and into
the Italian taste for conceits which exercised so
lively an influence on our Elizabethan literature.

When Dante in 1304—then thirty-nine years old—was
with the army of exiles that, by a bold stroke, almost took
Florence, the father of Petrarch, a Florentine notary, pro-
scribed with Dante, was a Ghibelline soldier in that army,
and on the night of its discomfiture, within the camp, his
wife gave birth to their son Francesco. After shifting for
seven years from town to town in Italy, the family of
Petracco, or Peterkin, settled first at and afterwards near
Avignon, where the Popes were in base exile. There the
young poet was first taught by an old exiled Italian rheto-
rician; like a whetstone, said the pupil—blunt himself, but
good to sharpen others. How the young Petracco went at
the age of fourteen to study for three years in Montpellier;
how he studied afterwards for four years in Bologna; was
then released from unwilling pursuit of the law by the death
of his parents, who left him, with a younger brother, slen-
derly provided for and in charge of thievish executors; how
he and his brother Gherardo entered the Church and looked
to Avignon, where John XXII. kept a great benefice-shop,
as the head-quarters of preferment, where he found a good
patron in the Cardinal Giovanni Colonna; this and much
more about himself and his times the poet himself has told.
He has branded also with shame the lust and licence of the
Papal capital at Avignon. He was a poet and a scholar,
half a Frenchman by residence, familiar with French as with
Italian love-poetry, with the songs of the troubadours as

with the sonnets of the "Vita Nuova." It delighted him to pore over manuscripts of Cicero and Virgil, Seneca was dear to him, and the flame of Italian patriotism, quick in him from the first, found fuel even in the Histories of Livy. If the poetry within him made his scholarship at last the mother of a Latin epic upon Africa, the same poetry wedded to love had produced his sonnets in the vulgar tongue that, copied and recopied, quoted and requoted, at once became the delight of France and Italy.

Laura, who was born at Avignon of a Provençal family, had been for two years a young wife when Petrarch, at the age of twenty-three, first saw her. She had, in addition to her husband, ten children before Petrarch had brought to an end his ideal celebration of her excellence, and her husband, Hugh de Sade, had nothing to complain of in the sonnets. Their variations of love sentiment were but the daintinesses of poetical conceit; they expressed skill in a science, the *gaye science* wherein even while Petrarch lived in France doctor-ates began to be granted, by virtue of the edict of Clementina Isaure, Countess of Toulouse, who in 1324 instituted the Floral Games. These games assembled at Toulouse the poets of France, housed them in artificial arbours dressed with flowers, and gave a violet in gold to him who produced the best poem, with the degree of doctor to him who was three times a prizeman. It was only through the affections of a doctor in gay science that Petrarch turned cold in hot weather upon seeing a country girl wash Mrs. Laura's veil, or suggested in the sonnet "quest' anima gentil," upon hearing of her illness, that on the departure of her spirit,

> " If she establish her abode between
> Mars and the planet-star of Beauty's queen,
> The sun will be obscured, so dense a cloud
> Of spirits from adjacent stars will crowd
> To gaze upon her beauty infinite

C 2

Say that she fixes on a lower sphere,
Beneath the glorious sun, her beauty soon
Will dim the splendour of inferior stars—
Of Mars, of Venus, Mercury, and the Moon."

The translation is Campbell's. Though he was constant, until her death as a middle-aged matron, to the person about whom it pleased him to weave his ideal web, in Petrarch's verse the expression of his patriotism is nobler than the ingenious and musical expression of unreal love. He sees the foreigner on native soil, and cries, of one heart with the patriots of half a thousand years later,

" Latin sangue gentile
Scombra da te queste dannose some—"

Or, as Lady Dacre rendered this part of the appeal to the princes of Italy :

" O Latin blood of old,
Arise and wrest from obloquy thy fame,
Nor bow before a name
Of hollow sound whose power no laws enforce !
For if barbarians rude
Have higher minds subdued,
Ours, ours the crime.   Not such wise Nature's course.
Ah, is not this the soil my foot first pressed ?
And here, in cradle rest,
Was I not softly hushed ? here fondly reared ?
Ah, is not this my country, so endeared
By every filial tie,
In whose lap shrouded both my parents lie?
Oh, by this tender thought,
Your torpid bosoms to compassion wrought,
Look on the people's grief,
Who, after God, of you expect relief ;
And if ye but relent,
Virtue shall rouse her in embattled might,
Against blind fury bent,

> Nor long shall doubtful hang the unequal fight ;
> For no,—the ancient flame
> Is not extinguished yet that raised the Italian name."

The fire of the poet is almost extinguished in the translation ; but it leaped high, and it still animates his country. There was in Petrarch, whose verse represents the perfection of Italian style, full measure of the earnestness that gives to a true poet permanence of fame. Truth, subtly expressed, lives in many an immortal line even of the most conceited of his Platonic love sonnets. But it was not for his patriotism or for his truth that he was made a darling poet of his age. What the troubadours had begun, he perfected. Of the two forms of his verse, he derived one—the sonnet—from the Sicilians ; the other—the canzone—from the Provençals. The recital of his verses from town to town clothed ragged men in silks, while Petrarch tells us that even the very shoemakers began to celebrate their loves in emulative rhyme.

In 1359 Dante had been dead eight-and-thirty years. Boccaccio, then a sobering man of forty-six, ten years after he had written his " Decameron," talked theology at Florence with Petrarch, nine years his senior. As Petrarch did not possess among his manuscript books the "Divine Comedy" of Dante, Boccaccio—appointed at Florence first of a line of professors to expound that poem and to glorify its author— gave him a copy, which was acknowledged in a letter from which one passage, although often quoted, is worth repetition :

Boccaccio and his " Decameron."

" Gladly do I seize this opportunity of confuting the charge made against me by my enemies of hating this great poet. Why should I hate him ? I never saw him but once, or rather he was shown to me, and that in my childhood. He lived with my father and grandfather, older than the former, younger than the latter, and the same storm

drove them all the same day from their country. This similarity of
fortune, joined by a union of tastes, united him in strict friendship with
my father ; but they took opposite courses : my father yielded to
circumstances, and occupied himself with the care of his family ; Dante,
on the contrary, resisted them, and resolutely followed the path he had
taken, thinking only of glory, and resigning everything for it. Neither
the injustice of his countrymen, nor private quarrels, nor exile, nor
poverty, nor love of children or wife,—nothing could distract him from
his studies, though poetry demands so much quiet and repose."

The seven imaginary ladies and three gentlemen whom
Boccaccio supposed to shut out the horrors of the great
plague of Florence in 1348, by enjoying themselves in a
garden with a ten-day feast of story-telling, presented—in
the best and easiest, though nearly the first, Italian prose—
among their hundred tales the choice tales of the day from
the French fabliaux, from incidents of actual life, or from
whatever source was open to the author. Even the
machinery in which the tales are set came from the East,
and had existed in a Latin form two centuries before. The
number of the stories also was perhaps determined by the
previous existence of the " Cento Novelle Antiche." Boccaccio wrote to amuse the ladies, little prizing what he
esteemed as his light labour in the vulgar tongue. But
Petrarch's love-poetry was not more to the taste of the day
than Boccaccio's tales ; the very tales of the time, in the
temper and manner of the time, perfectly expressed. Collections of stories linked together by the incidents of a slight
containing narrative, multiplied rapidly. Chaucer's masterpiece, which includes some of the " Decameron " tales, was
written upon the plan thus established, some thirty years
after the " Decameron."

Chaucer, born seven years after the death of Dante, was
twenty-four years younger than Petrarch—

" Fraunceis Petrark the laureat poete,
    Highte this clerk, whos rethorike swete
    Enlumined all Itaille of poetrie,—"

from whom he says that his Clerke took the Tale of the patient Griselda; and he was fifteen years younger than Boccaccio, from whose "Teseide" he took the Knight's Tale of Palamon and Arcite, from whose "Filostrato" he took his Troilus and Cressida, and with whose "Decameron" his Canterbury Tales have in common the Tales of the Reve, the Franklin, and the Shipman, all of which existed also among the store of French lays and fabliaux open alike to the Italian and the English poet. The complete inertness of the mere conceits of sonnet or canzone on the English mind of Chaucer is worth noting. As translator of the "Romaunt of the Rose," he recognised and shared the taste for mystical allegory. But his mind, like that of his countrymen, fastened on a poetry instinct with life and dramatic action. His wholesome sense of the ridiculous caused him to round with a shrewd English humour all the sentimental corners even of the tale of Griselda, thereby humanising it into a more sterling poetry, and doubling the force of its pathos. The influence of the French rhymers and story-tellers, and of the new classical force given in Italy by the great founders of modern literature, Dante, Petrarch, and Boccaccio, to the vulgar tongue of the land in which, of all others, the Latin had a right to be retained as its own classical language, we may trace everywhere in Chaucer; but all is digested, and serves only to feed the vigour of a most genuinely English mind. The religious heart of this country also, and its resentment of corruption and injustice both in Church and State, represented in great part by Wyclif, spoke through our great poets, and was as real in Chaucer's jests upon the greed and false pretension of the monks, and in his ideal sketch of the good Town Parson, as in the religious allegory by which the author of "The Vision of Piers Plowman" looked through the griefs of a bewildered

Italian influence on Chaucer.

The native and the foreign elements in Chaucer's verse.

and misguided people to the divine simplicities of Christian truth.

The disastrous glories of the reign of Henry V., and the still more disastrous period of the ensuing Wars of the Roses, checked the advance of our literature. Lydgate, in the fifteenth century, turned stories from Latin and Italian collections, from French fabliaux and Church legends, into prolix verse. He enforced the morals a good monk would labour to uphold, but not without admixture of the English satirical spirit, which attacked chiefly the lawyers as a class that had then taken profitable employments out of the hands of the clergy, and the women, who were in those days not more subject to a refinement of conceited praise than to the coarseness of the most damnatory jesting. Stephen Hawes's "Pastime of Pleasure" continued on French inspiration the allegorical school of romantic verse, in the style of the " Romaunt of the Rose," into the reign of Henry VII. Here the Prince Graunde Amour resolves to become worthy of La Bel Pucell by studies in the Tower of Doctrine. He is taught there by Lady Grammar and her sisters Logic, Rhetoric, Arithmetic, and Music, passes to the Towers of Geometry and Chivalry, then, being made a knight, goes forth to seek adventures ; is deceived by the dwarf False Report, kills a giant with three heads called Imagination, Falsehood, and Perjury, marries his lady, and is happy until made prisoner by Age, who gives him Avarice and Policy for companions ; he is slain by Death, buried by Mercy, and has his epitaph written by Remembrance. With Hawes we travel upon one road to the " Faery Queen."

During this long period of English social depression, by far the best part of our imaginative literature was that which the bright spirits among the people who must still be amused with songs and stories struck out for themselves, by telling the King Arthur romances and other metrical tales in plain

prose, and by turning other pleasant adventures, without a
word of waste reflection, into animated ballads ; tales and
ballads alike busy with swift action. But while
at the English Court the soldier jostled out
the poet, during the time of our worst obscurity
there was in Italy Lorenzo de' Medici, delight-
ing in the friendship of poets and scholars, and himself
poet in the Petrarchan school, enjoyer of the life of letters.
He was born in the days of our Warwick the King-maker,
and died in the year when Perkin Warbeck landed at Cork
as Richard Plantagenet. The capture of Constantinople by
the Turks in 1453 sent refugee Greeks abroad, who taught
their language at Lorenzo's Court, made Platonism (partly
sound and partly as perverted into fantastic doctrine by the
Platonists of Alexandria) nearly as popular as the ingenious
search for conceited allegory, the discovery of blemish in
the name of beauty in the verse of Petrarch. Lorenzo himself, in a love sonnet, tells how the gods made him poetical.
The rays of love from the eyes of his lady penetrating
through his eyes to the shadow of his heart as rays of the
sun enter the dark beehive by its fissure, caused the hive to
awake, and fly hither and thither in the forest sipping from
the flowers. The Florentine academicians, after the death
of Lorenzo's son, Leo X., having been caught in political
conspiracy, lost some of their number to the scaffold, and,
betaking themselves to purely literary discussion, established
in the head-quarters of Italian, that was to say of European,
literature and civilisation an idolatry of Petrarch. Each
sonnet became the text for endless lessons, dissertations,
commentaries, and allegorical interpretations. Leo died
in 1521, and it was within the next twenty years that,
as Puttenham says, in the latter end of Henry VIII.'s
reign, our courtly poets, Surrey and Wyat, "having
travelled into Italy, and there tasted the sweet and
stately measures and style of the Italian poesie," became

Spread of Petrarchan poetry, and rise of Platonism.

English Petrarchs imitating and translating from their model.

But the vigour of intellectual growth in the great centres of Italian life and commerce was not crippled by this hero-worship. A pastoral drama sprang from the seed of faith in the pre-eminent dramatic excellence of the Bucolics of Virgil. The "Orpheus" of the young Poliziano gave a strong impulse to pastoral writing, and the old Latin gods of wood and field were not fetched from afar, as when they reappeared in French or English pastoral. They were in Italy upon their native soil, belonging to a great old time of the Italian people. Of the "Arcadia" of Sanazzaro —a pastoral in prose and verse, including sonnets and canzoni of his early years, which dealt with a love begun even earlier in life than that of Dante for Beatrice—sixty editions appeared in the sixteenth century, and it suggested the "Arcadia" of Sir Philip Sidney.

Italian pastoal.

Philip Sidney is commonly remembered as the all-accomplished young Bayard of Elizabeth's Court, from whom the greatest things were hoped, but who, fatally wounded at Zutphen, died in his early manhood, was mourned as never a private man was mourned before by the whole English Court and people, and was sung in elegy by the best poets of his day. It was not for attractive graces as a courtier that he was thus loved and honoured by his Queen and country. The Queen he thwarted more than once ; the people cared little enough for Court accomplishments ; and Sidney was not alone in his time young, graceful, clever, and well born. The half-understood charm in him was that his early maturity expressed, as it were, in the flesh, the innermost soul of England, ever young, ever religiously earnest, ever busy in affairs ; though quick of fancy, more ready to act than to talk, and deeply interested in what free men knew

Influence of Petrarch and of Italian pastoral on English Literature. The English mind under the Italian manner. Philip Sidney.

to be the vital questions of the day. He was born in 1554, in the reign of Queen Mary, when the State was ill at ease. He lived in days when the strong battle for religious liberty made its sound heard in every Court of Europe. And when the battle, as it concerned England, was fought against Spain on a removed field, yet as truly and with as critical an issue as if it had been fought in Kent or Surrey, he who had in the teeth of all indifference connected championship of religious liberty with every mission that he undertook, fell in defence of it at Zutphen. This was the more than handsome Philip Sidney with whom Elizabeth could not be angry long; this was the man whom his fellow-courtiers honoured in their hearts and England loved.

At the age of seventeen Sidney was, with Sir Francis Walsingham, in Paris during the massacre of Saint Bartholomew; and it was a few months afterwards, at Frankfort, that he became the friend of Languet, whom he met as a fellow-lodger in the house of Andrew Wechel, a printer hospitable, as printers then were, to the travelling scholar. Sidney's mind ripened, and was confirmed in its endeavour towards a diffused liberty of conscience, the faster for communion with Hubert Languet, the blunt Huguenot reformer, whom he loved as he praised him afterwards,—

" For clerkly reed, and hating what is naught,
For faithful heart, clean hands, and mouth as true."

Languet was thirty-six years older than his friend, and though he died despairing of the world, yet year by year to the last he watched Philip, and openly looked to him as the youth whose earnest heart, bright genius, and strength for labour, joined to his high social position, made his future career the hope of honest men. He prepares, counsels, and cherishes him, as a lady of romance might fortify her knight who is about to go forth to battle with a dragon. He

should not eat too much fruit, or drink too much water, in
Italy, and he must avoid the July heat. "If any mischance
befall you, I should be the most wretched man in the world;
for there is nothing to give me the least pleasure save our
friendship and the hope of your manhood." And there was
the boy of nineteen with keen English soul watching the
butcheries of Alva, and discussing with a strong hope the
disastrous news from Belgium. "It is true that all that fair
region is in flames, but remember that without this the
Spaniards cannot be burnt out." In Italy, Sidney appears
especially to have studied geometry, ethics, metaphysics,
languages; accounting its poetry his relaxation, and its
luxury abomination. The Turks in 1574 thought of invasion, but said Philip—aged nineteen—"I am quite sure that
this ruinous Italy would poison the Turks themselves, would
so ensnare them in its vile allurements, that they would
soon fall without being pushed."

After his return to Ireland, Sidney was at the Kenil-
worth shows of 1575; his father, Sir Henry, being also
present there on business. Philip followed the
Queen to Chartley, where he first saw—she being
then in her thirteenth year, he in his twenty-first—
Penelope Devereux, afterwards married against her
inclinations, and, when Lady Rich, celebrated in
many sonnets as the Stella to Philip Sidney's Astrophel.
It was a poor fashion that set poets' wits at work so pertina-
ciously to refine compliments on any lady, married or un-
married, to whom they would pay honour by the dedication
of their verse. But it had come from troubadour days,
through Dante's "Vita Nuova," Petrarch's sonnets, and
many subsequent imitations of the Laura worship. It
ruffled the peace of Lady Rich no more than Petrarch's
genius suggested jealousy to the husband, or shame to the
ten children, of Laura. Sidney's sonnets are as distinctly
of the school of Petrarch, form and spirit, as his "Arcadia"

Reflection of Italian love-conceits in "Astrophel and Stella."

is, in its very manner of blending prose romance with metrical eclogue, of the school of Sanazzaro. The influence of Italian literature on Sir Philip Sidney's writings, in so far as he wrote merely for recreation, is direct and manifest.

In Elizabeth's time we find Spenser still in a few translations and in his sonnets following the lead of Petrarch, but he passed to his "Faery Queen" out of the school in which Ariosto was his best beloved master. Petrarch and Boccaccio had died within a year of one another ; and exactly a hundred years after the death of Petrarch came, in 1474, the birth of Ariosto. Ariosto died at the age of fifty-eight. Twelve years after the death of Ariosto, Tasso was born. But Tasso and Spenser were contemporaries, the Italian by nine years the elder man. The dates of their deaths lie close together, Tasso dying in 1595, Spenser in 1599. When, therefore, Spenser introduced into the closing canto of his second book a paraphrase and translation from Tasso's episode of the Garden of Armida, he expressed the exquisite enjoyment of a great poem then new to the world ; but his more frequent reproduction of matter from what he calls "that famous Tuscan pen" of Ariosto shows rather the lifelong influence of an established classic that had been singularly in harmony with the whole spirit of its time. Thus the description of the discovery of Duessa, as a "loathly wrinkled hag," is in part taken literally from Ariosto's account of Alcina. The tale of the false Philemon, in the same book, corresponding to Ariosto's tale of Geneura, and in Spenser's third book, the tale of the Squire of Dames, which is the Host's tale from the 28th Canto of Orlando, are also well-known examples of this direct testimony to Italian influence.

In nothing are the fellow-feeling of nations and the inter-dependence of men's minds more evident than in the course of the literatures which express them. The first

great Italian poets, themselves bred of their own time
under Provençal, not unmixed with Spanish and even
German, influence, were by the height of their
genius become marks for the eyes of all men who
loved poetry. They were not only making their
impulse of thought strongly felt in England, they
also were winning upon the mind of Spain so surely
that, in the very days when our "courtly makers," Surrey and
Wyat, were in the latter years of Henry VIII.'s reign bringing
the Italian form of sonnet and canzone into England, Boscan
was introducing the same sort of sonnets and canzoni into
Spanish literature, and beginning what is known as the
Italian period of Spanish poetry. Yet while Spain was
gradually being taught by Italy, Italy herself was drawing
the new life of her own literature from Spain. Spain had
been rich beyond measure in ballad and romance. Her
poems of the Cid date back to the twelfth century ; and
whatever romances of knight-errantry had been produced in
France and Spain before the opening of the fourteenth century were obscured then by the appearance of "Amadis de
Gaul," the work of the Portuguese Vasco Lobeira. That—
soon translated into French—was the great parent fiction of
the age chronicled by Froissart. Even Cervantes spared it
from his bonfire of Don Quixote's books of chivalry. How
perfect was the sympathy between the ideal and the actual
any one may judge who turns from Spanish or French-
Spanish romances of the Amadis school to Froissart's
account of the lives of the men who read and enjoyed them.
Froissart's history describes—with the same gay confusion
of fair ladies, knightly adventure, superstitious legend, pomp
of arms in jousting or in war, that we get in the romances—
the real life of the next eighty years following the appearance of "Amadis de Gaul." Long years of knightly encounter with the polished Arabs, and acquaintance with
their Oriental mind, heightened the sense of chivalry in

Marginal notes: Foreign influence upon Italy. "Amadis of Gaul."

Spanish prose romance or ballad, and introduced into their stories fairy machinery suggested by tales of the East. But the chief topic was the glory of the Empire of Charlemagne and the prowess of that great King and his Paladins. This prowess was especially displayed in the chain of songs and stories about Charlemagne that were strung together by a French monk of the eleventh century, and, ascribed to Bishop Turpin, are known as the "Magnanime Mensonge." The Italian romancers commonly amused themselves by fathering on Bishop Turpin any of their most daring inventions.

The growing taste for romance in Italy kept pace with the advance of court and camp to a social importance higher than that of the religious house. At the Court of Lorenzo de' Medici, while the scholastic conceits of Petrarch still amused the Prince himself, there were the brothers Pulci, one of whom wrote that half-mocking and half-earnest romance of Charlemagne and his Paladins, the "Morgante Maggiore," in which Roland, or Orlando, makes his bow to the Italian public as a model knight. Upon him followed, with his "Orlando Innamorato," the more seriously romantic governor of the fortress of Reggio, the Count Bojardo, who died leaving his poem unfinished, in his own opinion, and by several cantos more than finished in the opinion of others. The Count was succeeded in his command of the fortress of Reggio by Ariosto the father; and in his conduct of the story of Orlando by Ariosto the son, who took up the tale where Bojardo ought to have dropped it, not where he actually did leave off, and who surpassed it so immeasurably with his "Orlando Furioso," that although Bojardo is read now as he was improved sixty years later by Berni, there are few beyond the circle of the students who, even in Italy, read him at all. The ease and playful grace

[margin notes:] Source of the new taste for romance. The Pulci.

Bojardo.

Ariosto.

of Ariosto's masterpiece was the result of that great labour without which few masterpieces are achieved. The poet—therein a singular contrast to his successor, Tasso—was of large, robust body and healthy mind; frank, genial, and a hater of ceremonies; true to the sisters who depended upon him, moderate in all things, though tainted with the licence of his time and country. As an intent thinker and sturdy pedestrian, he found himself one day half-way to Ferrara, when he had but gone out from Carpi for a breath of morning air in dressing-gown and slippers; being so far on the road, he went on to Ferrara. From Carpi to Ferrara is a walk of rather more than thirty miles. What Ariosto did he did with determination. He pondered his "Orlando" well before a word of it was written, rejecting Cardinal Bembo's advice to make of it a Latin epic, that would now have been only as much read as Petrarch's "Africa." In writing he would often spend a day upon the polishing of a few verses written in the morning; and, having begun his "Orlando" at the age of twenty-nine, by great industry in eleven years he was able to issue the first forty cantos. Four or five editions in seventeen years testified in those days, when almost every reader was a select man, to its very great success. The central figure of the poem is not Orlando himself, but Charlemagne; the menace of whose kingdom and the siege of Paris are the events laid at the basis of the story. Six more cantos Ariosto added to the poem in his lifetime, five he left to be added after his death. A repolished edition of the "Orlando" had been issued by him almost in the last year of his life. By writing sonnets and canzoni, Ariosto connected himself with the past literature of Italy; and, by translating Spanish and French romances he showed what was most interesting to him in the present. His comedies, written in youth, were also repolished in later years, but they want original dramatic life, although they opened the way to an Italian comic drama.

Every great Italian poet studied the ancients—they were the old classics of his native land—and by right of them and of the literary pre-eminence his country had by this time regained he could still call the foreigner barbarian. Ariosto's imitation of the ancients is habitual. Distinctly and deliberately the poet turned into the romance form of his own day poets' tales of Perseus and Andromeda, of Ariadne or Polyphemus, or gave snatches of literal translation out of Ovid ; the Pallas of Virgil reappears in the young Dardinello, many romantic passages from the Latin poets, chiefly Ovid and Virgil, being reproduced by this great chief among their successors in the land. Ariosto quoted and was quoted. When we observe how all prose of his and afterwards of Spenser's time is garnished with quotation, we shall understand how the poets also, though their art forced them to assimilate their borrowings, meant by these adaptations not what we now condemn as plagiarism, but the usual homage to the cultivated reader of their day. It was a reader who delighted in such references and allusions, and almost required them of all who would prove their right to engage his attention.

The taste for quotation.

Ariosto cannot have troubled himself very much with the attachment of an allegorical sense to his poetical creations. It was found for him of course. He was soon to be read in an edition, "with the Allegories for each Canto, by Tomaso Porcacchi da Castiglione Aretino." Before Ariosto's time, a capacity for mystical interpretation was one of the acknowledged requisites of an ingenious poem. Thus the Marquis of Santillana, who died in Spain as a renowned poet about sixteen years before Ariosto's birth, in a critical letter on the history of poetry, defined the art as "an invention of useful things, which, being enveloped in a beautiful veil, are arranged, exposed, and concealed according to a certain calculation,

Growing demand for allegory. Tasso.

D

measurement, and weight." The demand for this allegorical element, strong in the days of Petrarch and Dante, set aside by Pulci and Ariosto, was again recognised by Tasso. Tasso, the son of a poet whose laborious epic of Amadis, conceived on the Spanish model, was destroyed at birth by the almost simultaneous issue of his precocious boy's "Rinaldo," inherited a highly nervous temperament, and was already touched by insanity when, after completing his "Jerusalem Delivered," he gave it up for several years to the stupidities of friendly miscellaneous criticism. The poem, at first called "Godfrey," being a somewhat regular epic, with an action occupying forty days of the first Crusade, in the year 1099, and setting forth the successful siege that made Godfrey of Boulogne (for a year) King of Jerusalem, there was no need of allegory. Nevertheless Tasso (who, as his insanity grew, nervously delivered himself to be examined and cleared with a certificate of orthodoxy by an inquisitor, and who was painfully anxious about many things) satisfied morality with an elaborate interpretation of the allegory of his own poem made after the fact.

It was not by right of their literature alone that the Italians of the sixteenth century, claiming the first rank in civilisation, spoke of the outer nations, after the old Roman fashion, as barbarians. Cardan, describing to his countrymen his visit to the Court of Edward VI., said of the English that "in dress they are like the Italians, for they are glad to boast themselves nearly allied to them, and therefore study to imitate as much as possible their manner and their clothes. Certain it is that all the barbarians of Europe love the Italians more than any race among themselves." He hinted that "perhaps these people do not know our wickedness;" but there were Englishmen then living quite ready to cry, with Roger Ascham, shame against "the enchantments of Circe, brought out of Italy to mar men's manners in

Social and literary predominance of the Italians.

England." Even our teachers themselves, we are told, certi-
fied our attainments with a proverb, saying An Italianate
Englishman is an incarnate devil.

But Italy had earned her predominance. The strong
life of commercial Florence had, in the fourteenth century,
entered into the mind of a large part of Europe. The social
Chaucer read Dante, and was influenced by influence of
Italy on
Petrarch and Boccaccio, as Spenser afterwards English
by the first masters of sustained romantic song. Literature.
The action of Italy upon old English and Elizabethan
writing was, however, of two very distinct kinds: one was
direct, the other reflex. At first, in Chaucer's time, only
the direct influence concerns our literary history. No
printing-press enticed the vacant mind to busy itself with
the blackening of paper. Foreign travel, little known as an
indulgence, took chiefly the direction of Jerusalem, and was
then undertaken rather on religious grounds than for the
mere airing of the wits. When Englishmen kept house,
only the fame of the great Italian poets reached them from
beyond the sea; but when they went, in search of good
society, to Italy itself, they were lost in the midst of the
servile drove of imitators, and became part of the herd.
When the depression of mind that accompanied our civil
wars was yielding to a new activity of thought, and the
revival of letters in Italy was making itself felt at the Court
of Henry VIII., to visit Italy was the desire alike of the
scholar and the courtier. Upon the best minds, travelled
or untravelled, the direct and wholesome influence of Italian
poetry and scholarship was still conspicuous.

But the prevalence of a poetic element in the Italian
character was of itself dangerous to foreigners Secondary
of colder blood who went to Italy for inspiration. causes of the
spread of a
In that land of song, at the beginning of the taste for
conceited
sixteenth century, there was still to be heard the writing.
complaint made by Petrarch generations earlier, Euphuism.

that the very tailors and shoemakers stitched rhymes and cobbled verse. Commentators upon Petrarch issued forth out of the printing-offices by dozens at a time, and were to be heard by thousands discoursing in society. His words were picked over for allegories, and his book of verse, weighted with fanciful interpretations, was disgraced into a pattern-book for all tailors of rhyme, a *Follet* for the literary milliner who set the fashion after which the luxury of idleness should be attired. Thus Petrarch unwittingly became a father of conceits. After the death of Leo X. the Florentine academicians, sorely punished for political conspiracy, were forced to confine their energies to literature ; verbal haggling over Petrarch became then their chief delight. Great poets were arising. The romantic epic, the pastoral, the satire, even the drama, all were dropping their first fruits upon the rich Italian soil ; but ready rhetoric, of sentiment determined to be clever and not caring to be true, still yielded the husks eaten by the mob alike of the palace and the street. It was the Altissimo Cristoforo, and it was Aretino who was the Unico, for whose sake, when he recited in Rome, shops were closed and houses blazed with light.

What had been was. Greek literature had travelled the same way. The clever but false rhetoric of Demetrius Phalereus was the hectic flush of eloquence in a decline. The later poets cut up history and science into decoration for their verses. Philetas became erudite in elegiacs, and Euphorion thought truth most acceptable when set out with fable. So it had been also in Rome. There was a thought of his time, not an original folly, in Caligula's proposal to destroy the works of Virgil, bare of ingenuity and learning, and of Livy, cold and negligent of style. Conceits were prized in Rome, and daintily-smoothed periods were admired less for their wit than for the words arranged so sweetly, that, as one boasted of his own prose works, people might sing them and dance to them. Seneca was the cause of this no more than Lyly was the cause of Euphuism. Paterculus, when he endeavoured to account for such a change, suggested that the nurse of genius, emulation, forced men who found themselves unable to pass their fore-fathers by natural walking upon the high-road of literature to quit that track "for paths hitherto unexplored, where novelty might lift them from obscurity, and make their names immortal." There is undoubted beauty in this fall of a literature. It is like that of the autumn woods, where an excessive richness and variety of colouring precedes the dreariness of winter.

There was nothing new to the world, then, in the literature of conceits that throve in Italy before Marino, as in England before Donne. Marino was, like Lyly or Donne, but a representative man. It was he, writing in the days of James I., and having no influence whatever upon Elizabethan literature, who represented the corruption of Italian taste when at its height, gave it a typical form, and therefore has been condemned to bear two centuries of censure for his "stile Marinesco," and be pilloried in dictionaries as the chief corrupter of Italian poetry.

With the spreading of the taste for rhetorical writing filled with pedantic turns of illustration, similitudes rather ingenious than natural, and the desire of writers to display above all things their skill, the fashion, of course, ran in favour of the later Latin and Greek authors. Martial and Lucan took the places of Catullus and Virgil, Juvenal super-seded Horace, and Seneca Cicero. Seneca's plays were a schoolbook for English boys of Elizabeth's time. Our first tragedies arose from imitations of them. Afterwards they were the root of the French tragic drama.

But upon the fashion of speech at Elizabeth's Court there were influences of which we have not yet taken account. Some of its peculiarities, together with the very

name that gave the term of Euphuism to its affectations, are
to be traced to the Platonists who were strong in the days
of Henry VIII. But Platonism also came to us from Italy.
It was in Florence that the refugee Greeks, after the fall of
Constantinople, were first welcomed as revealers of Plato
and Aristotle. In Italy Plato, in France Aristotle, was pre-
ferred. Neo-Platonists had given interest to the Rabbinical
doctrine of the Cabbala, then received by many a good
Christian scholar. It was joined to principles of an occult
philosophy, partly derived from the same source, but en-
riched from teaching of the Arabs ; and it was confirmed
by marvellous recitals in the Natural History of Pliny.
"The mysteries of Nature," one of her students then said,
"can no otherwise than by experience and conjecture be
inquired into by us." Until the asserted experience of
ancient naturalists had been disproved by the experience of
later times, it was not very unreasonable to assume that the
science of the ancients equalled their philosophy and poetry.
To deny virtues assigned to certain stones, plants, animals,
or stars, simply because they were wonderful, certainly would
not have been wise. Even in the magical doctrines then
widely accepted there was reasoning entitled to respect.
Their basis, it may be observed, was so far from being
diabolical, that they set out with a demand for purity of
life, and for a high spiritual adoration of the source of all
the harmony they laboured to find in the wonders of creation. It is to be remembered, therefore, that those marvellous properties of things, honestly credited and freely used
in the fashioning of ornaments of speech, had not for the
reader of their own time the inherent absurdity which now
attaches to them. It is very difficult indeed now to read in
the old sense that kind of writing in which Lyly was master,
"talking," as Drayton said,

"of stones, stars, plants, of fishes, flies,
Playing with words and idle similies.

We must not forget, then, that although Court idlers here concern us more especially, before the idlers went to Italy our scholars as well as our poets had been there. In Italy, Linacre and Grocyn, Cheke, Colet, William Lily learnt their Greek. Even after Elizabeth's day, Platonism survived to the time of the Commonwealth, in Henry More, who wrote Platonic songs of the Soul's Life and Immortality, and dedicated to his friend Cudworth a defence of the Threefold Cabbala: But Henry More's spiritual conceits have no concord with courtly affectations. "If," he says, "by thoughts rudely scattered in my verse I may lend men light till the dead night be gone,"

> " It is enough, I meant no trimmer frame,
> Nor by nice need'ework to seek a name."

To that taste for "nice needlework" Camden objected in "our sparkful youth," ready to "laugh at their great grandfathers' English, who had more care to do well than to speak minion-like."

> " I cannot quote a motte Italianate,
> Or brand my satires with a Spanish term,"

protested Marston. Bishop Hall, also, in his satirist days, endeavoured to "check the disordered world and lawless times" with very direct comment upon the fashion then prevalent in dress and speech. He decried the "words Italianate, big sounding sentences, and words of state," used by the Marlowes, whom, as tragedians, he scornfully compared with Seneca : for even the satirist himself was of his time. Seneca was his tragedian ; Juvenal and Persius were the models of his satire ; and because he was the first to imitate these writers, he supposed himself to be the earliest of English satirists. His work opens with an allusion to the pines of Ida. He was prompt as others of his day in coupling Ariosto with Du Bartas, "Salust of France and

Tuscan Ariost," and he was not without his own relish of conceits, vigorously as he attacked the fool in far-fetched livery of mind and dress.

What Hall, writing a few years after Lyly, censured in verse, Ascham's unaffected prose had censured yet more vigorously in his "Schoolmaster," a work published by his widow seven or eight years before "Euphues" appeared. There is reason for suggesting, if not for believing, that John Lyly drew from this work of Ascham's both the motive and the title of his fashionable novel. "Euphues" paints the same Italian Circe against whose snares Ascham warned his countrymen, reminding them that "if a gentleman must needs travel into Italy, he shall do well to look to the life of the wisest traveller that ever travelled thither, set out by the wisest writer that ever spake with tongue, God's doctrine only excepted, and that is Ulysses in Homer." The "Schoolmaster" observed that Ulysses "is not commended so much nor so oft in Homer, because he was πολύτροπος, that is, skilful in men's manners and fashions, as because he was πολύμητις, that is, wise in all purposes and ware in all places." Against Circe's enchantment Homer's remedy was the herb Moly, "with the black root and white flower ; sour at the first, but sweet in the end, which Hesiodus termeth the study of virtue." This was of all things most contrary to what Ascham called "the precepts of fond books of late translated out of Italian into English, sold in every shop in London. . . . Ten sermons at Paul's Cross do not so much good for moving men to true doctrine as one of these books do harm with enticing men to ill living."

Let it here be remembered that the period of English literature more directly influenced by the frivolities of Italy dates from the time of our Reformation in the Church, and runs through years in which minds engaged with intense activity upon the settlement of great religious questions

The English mind under it all. Out of decay new life.

became also more and more deeply engaged in political assertion of the rights of subjects. Throughout the days of civil war and of the Commonwealth Italian influence extends. To that part of the period thus defined, in which we find the greatest prevalence of literary affectation, belongs also the truest and most earnest work on which the pens of Englishmen have ever been engaged—our authorised translation of the Bible.

To the same period belongs the best part of our literature. High and true thoughts, with sturdy deeds, were called for by the times. Into the words of vigorous men, living energetic lives of thought or action, the demand for ingenious expression brought new force. There were men trained in this school able to satisfy to the full, out of their natural wit, at once the claims of truth in art and the popular desire for clever simile, strong line, and pithy phrase. The affectation of the weak forced into a peculiarly emphatic utterance all the originality and power of the strong. To this view of English Euphuism we shall have to recur. At present it is only necessary to remember that, by whomsoever fashions happen to be set, we must not take clothes for character.

Lyly had children, and his book shows, as we shall find, that he thought seriously for himself, and agreed with Ascham upon questions of education. He was a little man, with a wife and family ; he smoked tobacco, and was a wit in society, with a heart full of seriousness ; he was a hungry reader of good books, and to the last a hungry waiter on the Court, that repaid his honest labouring to entertain it well according to its humour, only with promise unfulfilled. "Thirteen years," he says, in a petition to the Queen, presented in or about the year when " Euphues" was published, "thirteen years your Highness's servant, but yet nothing. . . . . A thousand hopes, but all nothing; a hundred promises, but yet nothing. . . . My last will is shorter

than mine invention; but three legacies, patience to my
creditors, melancholy without measure to my friends, and
beggary without shame to my family." Surely a touching
hint—and it is all the hint we have—of the home life of the
Euphuist!

Lyly still in our own day has suffered injustice. The traditional view of his " Euphues" is represented by the saying
of Gifford, that it " did incalculable mischief by vitiating the
taste, corrupting the language, and introducing a spurious
and unnatural mode of conversation and action."

The work passed through ten editions in fifty-six years,
and then was not again reprinted. Of these editions, the
first four were issued during twenty-three years
of Elizabeth's reign, the next four appeared in
the reign of James, and the last two in the reign
of Charles I.; the latest edition before our own time
being that of the year 1636, eleven years after that
king's accession. Its readers were the men who were
discussing Hampden's stand against ship-money. During
all this time, and for some years beyond it, worship of
conceits was in this country a literary paganism, that gave
strength to the strong as well as weakness to the weak,
lasting from Surrey's days until the time when Dryden
was in his mid career. It was of this *culte* that the Euphuist
undoubtedly aspired to be the high priest, but it was not of
his establishing. Still less, of course, are we entitled to
accept the common doctrine that it had its origin in Donne's
fashionable poetry and in the pedantry of James I.

Duration of Lyly's popularity.

We may pause upon Lyly for especial illustration of the
abiding earnestness that underlies all transient fashions of
our literature. Of the treatise on education,
forming so prominent a part of " Euphues, or
the Anatomy of Wit," the main doctrines are
such as these. No youth is to be taught with stripes.
Ascham and Lyly were alone in maintaining this doctrine

Lyly himself a practical Englishman.

against the strongest contrary opinion. Life is divided into remission and study. As there is watching, so is there sleep; ease is the sauce of labour; holiday the other half of work. Children should exercise a discreet silence : " let them also be admonished, that, when they shall speak, they speak nothing but truth ; to lie is a vice most detestable, not to be suffered in a slave, much less in a son." Fathers should study to maintain by love and by example influence over their sons as they advance to manhood ; let them with mildness forgive light offences, and remember that they themselves have been young. . . . Some light faults let them dissemble as though they knew them not, and seeing them let them not seem to see them, and hearing them let them not seem to hear. We can easily forget the offences of our friends, be they never so great, and shall we not forgive the escapes of our children, be they never so small ? "

Let the body be kept in its pure strength by honest exercise, and let the mind, adds Lyly, falling again into the track of censure followed by all satirists of the day, " not be carried away with vain delights, as with travelling into far and strange countries, where you shall see more wickedness than learn virtue and wit. Neither with costly attire of the new cut, the Dutch hat, the French hose, the Spanish rapier, the Italian hilt, and I know not what." There is nothing, he reminds youth, swifter than time, and nothing sweeter. We have not, as Seneca saith, little time to live, but we lose much ; neither have we a short life by nature, but we make it shorter by naughtiness ; our life is long if we know how to use it. The greatest commodity that we can yield unto our country is with wisdom to bestow that talent which by grace was given us. Here Euphues repeats the closing sentences of the wise counsel of Eubulus, scorned by him in the days of his folly, and then passes to a direct exhortation to the study of the Bible. " Oh ! " he exclaims, " I would gentlemen would sometimes sequester themselves from their own delights, and employ their wits in searching these heavenly divine mysteries."

Advancing still in earnestness as he presents his Euphues growing in wisdom and now wholly devoting himself to the study of the highest truth, a letter to the gentlemen-scholars in Athens prefaces a dialogue between Euphues and Atheos, which is an argument against the infidelity that had crept in from Italy. It is as earnest as if Latimer himself had preached it to the courtiers of King Edward. Euphues appeals solemnly to Scripture and the voice within ourselves. In citation from the sacred text consist almost his only illustrations ; in this he abounds. Whole pages contain nothing but the words of Scripture. At a time when fanciful and mythological adornment was so common to literature that the very Bible Lyly read—the Bishops' Bible—contained woodcut initials upon subjects drawn from Ovid's "Metamorphoses," and opened the Epistle to the Hebrews with a sketch of Leda and the Swan, Lyly, in the book which has been for so many years condemned unread, does not once mingle false ornament with reasoning on sacred things. He refers to the ancients only, at the outset of his argument, to show that the heathen had acknowledged a Creator ; mentions Plato but to say that he recognised one whom we may call God omnipotent, glorious, immortal, unto whose similitude we that creep here on earth have our souls framed ; and Aristotle, only to tell how, when he could not find out by the secrecy of nature the cause of the ebbing and the flowing of the sea, he cried, with a loud voice, "O Thing of Things, have mercy upon me !" In twenty black-letter pages there are but three illustrations drawn from supposed properties of things. The single anecdote from profane history I will here quote from a discourse that introduces nearly all the texts incorporated in our Liturgy :

"I have read of Themistocles, which having offended Philip, the King of Macedonia, and could no way appease his anger, meeting his young son Alexander, took him in his arms, and met Philip in the face. Philip, seeing the smiling countenance of the child, was well pleased with Themistocles. Even so, if through thy manifold sins and heinous offences thou provoke the heavy displeasure of thy God, insomuch as thou shalt tremble for horror, take his only-begotten and well-beloved son Jesus in thine arms, and then he neither can nor will be angry with thee. If thou have denied thy God, yet if thou go out with Peter and weep bitterly, God will not deny thee. Though with the prodigal son thou wallow in thine own wilfulness, yet if thou return again sorrowful thou shalt be received. If thou be a grievous offender, yet if thou come unto Christ with the woman in Luke, and wash his feet with thy tears thou shalt obtain remission."

Surely, if Scott had read " Euphues " he could not have been satisfied to describe it through Sir Piercie Shafton as " that exquisitely-pleasant-to-be-read and inevitably-neces-sary-to-be-remembered manual of all that is worthy to be known, which indoctrinates the rude in civility, the dull in intellectuality, the heavy in jocosity, the blunt in gentility, the vulgar in nobility, and all of them in that unutterable perfection of human utterance—that eloquence which no other eloquence is sufficient to praise—that art which, when we call it by its own name of Euphuism, we bestow on it its richest panegyric."

Sir Piercie Shafton, the Euphuist, talks thus of his " Anatomy of Wit " as if it were a cookery-book of language for the use of dainty speakers. His eloquence is of the kind that calls an ass " the long-eared grazier of the common," which is hardly to be considered English Euphu-ism of the Court of Queen Elizabeth, but is the Euphuism of the Hôtel Rambouillet. There, Arthénice presided over an Arcadian academy, to which a nightcap was not a night-cap, but " *le complice innocent du mensonge.*"

Of the true form of his conceited writing, Lyly's Court-plays, some of them written earlier than his novel, furnish even better example ; and their studied prologues, the manner of which Greene exactly copied in the prefaces to his tales, are the most finished miniatures of Elizabethan Euphuism. The prologue to Campaspe will serve very well as an example. Every sentence, it will be observed, has its far-fetched similitude :

"We are ashamed that our bird, which fluttereth by twilight seeming a swan, should be proved a bat set against the sun. But as Jupiter placed Silenus' ass among the stars, and Alcibiades covered his pictures, being owls and asses, with a curtain embroidered with lions and eagles; so are we enforced upon a rough discourse to draw on a smooth excuse ; resembling lapidaries, who think to hide the crack in a stone by setting it deep in gold. The gods supped once with poor Baucis, the Persian king sometimes shaved sticks: our hope is your Highness will at this time lend an ear to an idle pastime. Appion raising Homer from hell, demanded only who was his father, and we, calling Alexander from his grave, seek only who was his love. Whatsoever we present, we wish it may be thought the dancing of Agrippa his shadows, who, in the moment they were seen, were of any shape one would conceive: or Lynces, who having a quick sight to discern, have a short memory to forget. With us it is like to fare, as with these torches, which, giving light to others, consume themselves : and we shewing delight to others shame ourselves."

In the same vein, the lover in the second part of Euphues,—"Euphues and his England"—ends the letter that declares his passion by telling Camilla that he expects her reply "either as a cullis to preserve, or as a sword to destroy ; either as Antidotum or as Aconitum ;" and when that fair lady, after supper, takes part in one of the social wit-combats to which I have referred, she begins by expressing, in this cumbrous fashion, her fear that she may be caught tripping :

"I have heard that the Tortoise in India when the sun shineth, swimmeth above the water with her back, and being delighted with the fair weather, forgetteth herself until the heat of the sun so harden her shell, that she cannot sink when she would, whereby she is caught. And so may it fare with me that in this good company displaying my mind, having more regard to my delight in talking than to the ears of the hearers, I forget what I speak, and so be taken in something I should not utter, which haply the itching ears of young gentlemen would so canvas, that when I would call it in, I cannot, and so be caught with the Tortoise when I would not."

When this clever maid's antagonist replies to her, he lauds her eloquence, and very properly observes that she brought out that Tortoise "rather to show what she should say, than to crave pardon for that she had said." There is abundant evidence that fine talkers searched books, and Lyly's books especially, for conceits and phrases to be imitated in their own discourse. It will be remembered that translations of Boccaccio and other works had in those days attractively set forth upon their title-pages that they were books in which the art of witty conversation might be studied.

Although the second part of "Euphues," designedly less serious than the first, doubtless assured to that didactic work a fashionable position, the religious earnestness of the close of the first part belonged also to the life of the nation at that time. In religion Lyly was as earnest and uncompromising as a Puritan could wish to be, and yet maintained his ground as a Court wit. In religious polemics he could not altogether avoid taking part, and there he was honestly of one mind with the bishops and the Court.

If we look from the influence of his day exerted upon Lyly to the influence exerted by him, we shall find this also blended with the common taste for wit from Italy. More prolific than Lyly, as an Elizabethan novelist, was Robert Greene. He was a close imitator at once of Lyly and of the Italians, accepting Lyly as a master in the manner of his speech, but looking more directly to Italian example for the matter of his stories. "Euphues" was a novel so much over-weighted with didactic matter that it hardly could be called a story; but Greene, if he invented any of his own plots, had un-

Influence of Lyly and the Italians on Robert Greene.

questionable genius as a story-teller. It will be remembered
that from his "Pandosto" Shakespeare took the subject of
the "Winter's Tale." The same writer, Greene, also
followed up "Pandosto," nine years after the appearance of
"Euphues," with "Menaphon," a book having for second
title "Camilla's Alarm to slumbering Euphues in his melancholy cell at Silixedra." This he described as "a work
worthy the youngest ears for pleasure, or the gravest censure
for principles;" and it is the novel furnished with that
prefatory address to the gentlemen-students of both univer-
sities commonly ascribed to Nash, which presents to us so
useful a sketch of the literary humours of the time.

The writer of the preface to "Menaphon" had a fair
sense of good literature, and a love of his own language :

"'Tut,' say our English Italians, 'the finest wits our climate sends
forth are but dry-brained dolts in comparison with other countries ;'
whom, if you interrupt with '*Redde rationem*,' they will tell you of
Petrarch, Tasso, Celiano, with an infinite more of others. To whom
if I should oppose Chaucer, Lydgate, Gower, with such like, that
lived under the tyranny of ignorance, I do think their best lovers
would be much discontented with the collation of contraries if I should
write over all their heads, Hail fellow well met ! . . . . Should the
challenge of deep conceit be intended by any foreigner to bring our
English wits to the touchstone of art, I would prefer divine Master
Spenser, the miracle of wit, to bandy line for line for my life in the
honour of England, against Spain, France, Italy, and all the world."

At the date of this writing Spenser had not yet published
the first three books of the "Faery Queen," and his fame
with the public rested on the eclogues of the "Shepherd's
Kalender," then in their third edition, vigorous with religious
feeling and so direct in sympathy with the French Hugue-
nots that two of them are direct paraphrases from Marot.
Shakespeare had not been two years in town ; and, with his
life as a dramatist yet before him, had not yet written his
delicate poetical jest upon Euphuism, putting his hook

through it as though he loved it, in "Love's Labour's Lost."

Of all quips upon ingenious emptiness, involving a firm under-suggestion of the work men live to do, that play of "Love's Labour's Lost" is the most perfect. What action we have is based entirely on the living out of a conceit. We hear affected talk in many forms :

" Love's Labour's Lost," a jest upon the fashionable style.

> " Taffata phrases, silken terms precise,
> Threepiled hyperboles, spruce affectation,
> Figures pedantical."

The King in his sonnet to his mistress foreshadows even the sublimities of Crashaw's Magdalene :

> " Thou shin'st in every tear that I do weep ;
> No drop but as a coach doth carry thee,
> So ridest thou triumphing in my woe."

But the sharpest satire is expressed in the pompous emptiness of Don Adrian Armado, by whom " our court you know is haunted : "

> " A man in all the world's new fashion planted,
> That hath a mint of phrases in his brain."

His bravery of wit is shiftlessly dependent upon that of the child Moth, whom he patronises, for it is with that as with the bravery of outside show upon his person. When he is called upon to strip and combat in his shirt, he must own that " the naked truth of it is, I have no shirt." There is schoolmaster Holofernes, too, who can tell us that "Ovidius Naso was the man, and why indeed Naso, but for smelling out the odoriferous flowers of fancy, the jerks of invention ? " The fantastical word-combats of such characters, as given by Shakespeare, have a close resemblance in spirit to some of the scenes of Lyly's plays,—to those, for

E

example, in "Endymion," which jest with Sir Tophas, the bragging soldier:

> "*Samias.*—But what is this? Call you it your sword?
>
> "*Tophas.*—No; it is my simiter, which I by construction often studying to be compendious, call my smiter.
>
> "*Dares.*—What, are you also learned, sir?
>
> "*Tophas.*—Learned? I am all Mars and Ars.
>
> "*Samias.*—Nay, you are all mass and ass.
>
> "*Tophas.*—Mock you me? You shall both suffer, yet with such weapons as you shall make choice of the weapon wherewith you shall perish. Am I all a mass or lump? Is there no proportion in me? Am I all ass? Is there no wit in me? Epi, prepare them to the slaughter.
>
> "*Samias.*—I pray, sir, hear us speak. We call you mass, which your learning doth well understand is all man, for Mas, maris is a man. The As (as you know) is a weight, and we for your virtues account you a weight.
>
> "*Tophas.*—The Latin hath saved your lives, the which a world of silver could not have ransomed. I understand you and pardon you."

It need hardly be remarked that the crowding of classical allusions into every sentence must have been, to Shakespeare's poetical sense, dull even as material for jest. He laughs at it, but does not attempt to mock it with close imitation.

While "Euphues" was thus in fashion, Shakespeare being yet young as a play-writer, at the date of the critical preface to "Menaphon," Bacon was a young barrister, part deviser of the dumb shows at Gray's Inn, and within two years of his appointment as Queen's Counsel. Sir Philip Sidney had been dead two years, and Ascham twenty years. Sackville, Lord Buckhurst, whose pen contributed to the first English tragedy, still had some twenty years of life before him. Of Marlowe's brief career only five years were yet to come; of Greene's but four, during which his overcharged confession and self-accusation of an ill-spent life would give some

Duration of Italian influence in the taste for conceits.

strain of a wild earnestness to his last novels. Ben Jonson was then but fourteen years old; Fletcher but nine;
Beaumont, Massinger, and Webster, three or four. Donne
was a youth of sixteen, and twenty years were yet to pass
before the birth of Milton, who was himself ten years older
than Cowley, and twenty-four years older than Dryden, who
was a man forty years old at the birth of Addison. Throughout the whole period thus indicated, the taste for conceited
writing, introduced from Italy in or before the first years of
the reign of Elizabeth, prevailed. It was modified by the
character of the sovereign, and influenced in some respects
by the tone of public feeling in each generation; but the
desire for constant imagery, for cunning sentences, and ingenious allusions that by display of a writer's reading
should make out his title to be read, abided by the courtiers
and scholars who were not only the chief critics but who
formed a large proportion also of the readers of a book.
The dust of Latin in the sermons of Bishop Andrewes; the
quaint wit of Fuller, which obtained for him two audiences
—one within doors and the other out of window—in his
little chapel in the Savoy; the sententious writing in the
"Enchiridion" of Quarles; manifest clearly enough their
relationship to Euphuism. Old Izaak Walton,—whose life
ran through a part of Elizabeth's reign, and extended
through the whole subsequent period even until Addison
was a boy of eleven,—becoming weary of the strain for wit,
looked back from the days of Charles I. to "'Come live with
me and be my love,' that smooth song made by Kit Marlowe, now at least fifty years ago. The milkmaid's mother
sang an answer to it, which was made by Sir Walter Raleigh
in his younger days. They were old-fashioned poetry, but
choicely good; I think," he says, "much better than the
strong lines that are in fashion in this critical age."

At what level Euphuism stood, when it came strained
out of the brains of those ordinary people who make up the

E 2

substance of polite society at court, Ben Jonson has shown, with a spice of malicious caricature, in "Cynthia's Revels."

Ridiculed by Ben Jonson in "Cynthia's Revels." The play, produced only two years before the death of Elizabeth, was wholly designed as a jest against what its chief Euphuist describes as "your shifting age for wit, when you must prove the aptitude of your genius; if you find none you must hearken out a vein and buy." It was to bid men put only to manly use the powers of their intellect—

> " And, for the practice of a forced look,
> An antic gesture, or a fustian phrase,
> Study the native frame of a true heart,
> An inward comeliness of bounty, knowledge,
> And spirit that may conform them actually
> To God's high figures, which they have in power."

We may connect the taste for conceited writing in the days of Lyly with that of the early days of Dryden, by refer-French Euphuism. The "Divine Weeks" of Du Bartas.ence to an author who is now read only by the minute student of literature – Guillaume de Saluste du Bartas. He was a French nobleman, born about the year 1544. He was educated as a soldier, shared the creed and rose with the fortunes of Henri IV., to whom he became attached as gentleman-in-ordinary of the bedchamber, and by whom he was employed as a negotiator in Denmark, Scotland, and England. He fought at Ivry, and sang of the battle, but died four months afterwards of the wounds he received in it. When not engaged in political or military duty, this worthy gentleman, who was a Euphuist of the first water, wrote poems in his château of Bartas, and his poem of "La Sepmaine" went through thirty editions in six years. It was translated into Latin, Italian, German, and English, generally more than once into each language. Its metaphors are extravagant, its classical compounds are barbarous. In France, as in England, the book is now but a curiosity of bad taste to the few who read it or know anything about it. The fate of its style has justified one of the sound maxims in Ben Jonson's " Discoveries," that body of opinion in which is to be found our first good exposition of the principles of wholesome writing—" Nothing is lasting that is feigned; it will have another face than it had ere long. As Euripides saith, no lie ever grows old."

James I., who was among his translators, sought in vain to retain the divine Du Bartas at his Court, and Sylvester became a laurelled poet mainly upon the strength of his English version of the " Divine Weeks " and the other works of the same hand. " I remember, when I was a boy," writes Dryden in his preface to the " Spanish Friar," " I thought inimitable Spenser a mean poet in comparison of Sylvester's Du Bartas, and was rapt into an ecstasy when I read these lines:

> " ' Now, when the winter's keener breath began
> To crystallize the Baltic ocean,
> To glaze the lakes, to bridle up the floods,
> And periwig with snow the bald-pate woods '—

I am much deceived if this be not abominable fustian, that is, thoughts and words ill sorted and without the least relation to each other."

We must not forget, however, that the popularity of Du Bartas in this country was due not only to the harmony of his conceited style with the prevailing fashion, but to his Protestant faith and the religious character of all his writings. The First Week of seven days, or books, sings the Birth of the World: the Chaos, the Elements, the Sea and Earth, the Heavens, Sun, Moon, &c.; the Fishes and Fowls; the Beasts and Man; the Sabbath. It is not worth while to illustrate by more citation the affectations of a book deservedly forgotten; but we may take from the Vision of

Tongues, in the poem of "Babylon," which belongs to the second day of the second week, the names of the four persons who, in Queen Elizabeth's time, had been regarded by a polished Frenchman as the chief supporters of each modern language. Of the Italian, Boccaccio, Petrarch, Ariosto, Tasso ; of the German, Peucer, Luther, Bucer, and Butric ; of the Spanish, Guevara, Granada, Boscan, and Garcilaso (the two poets last named were the chief introducers of Italian style into Castilian poetry) ; of the French, Marot, Amyot, Ronsard, and Duplessis Mornay; of the English, Sir Thomas More, Sir Nicholas Bacon, Sir Philip Sidney, and Queen Elizabeth herself, who—

> "with phrases choice,
> So on the sudden can discourse in Greek,
> French, Latin, Tuscan, Dutch, and Spanish eke,
> That Rome, Rhine, Rhone, Greece, Spain, and Italy,
> Plead all for right in her nativity."

The Queen's skill in choice phrases, and her power as a linguist, had of course favoured the growth of Euphuism at Elizabeth's Court. The character of James I. lowered the dignity, while it extended the domain, of literary affectation. A new strength of religious and political feeling caused the conceited and pedantic style to be often animated with a heat of life and passion in the days of Charles I. and of the Commonwealth. Much of the common language of the Puritans was Euphuism, cast by the fire of zeal in a religious mould. We see the grandeur of it in Cromwell's description of his victory over the Scotch at Dunbar, and the "poor, weak faith wherein, I believe, not a few amongst us shared, that, because of their numbers, because of their advantages, because of their confidence, because of our weakness, because of our strait, we were in the Mount, and in the Mount the Lord would be seen." We have it in bathos, when, after Cromwell's death, a follower "declares his steps to princely perfection, as they are drawn in lively parallels to the ascents of the great patriarch Moses, in thirty degrees to the height of Honour."

Meanwhile in France the taste for ingenious conceit and old Roman mythology, which Italian influence had made there also fashionable, was being modified by the national character. Du Bartas, when in the " Divine Weeks " he spoke of the mutability of form and constancy of matter in all things upon earth (including literature), drew from his countrymen the same example that his translator Joshua Sylvester notes parenthetically in the English,— *Italian influence in France.*

> " Here one thing springs not till another die,
> Only the matter lives immortally.
>
>   *   *   *   *   *
>
> Changeless in essence ; changeable in face,
> Much more than Proteus or the subtle race
> Of roving Polyps who (to rob the more)
> Transform them hourly on the waving shore,
> Much like the French, (or like ourselves, their apes),
> Who with strange habit do disguise their shapes ;
> Who loving novels, full of affectation,
> Receive the manners of each other nation ;
> And scarcely shift they shirts so oft as change
> Fantastic fashions of their garments strange."

Thus even in the ephemeral verse that illustrates especially a foreign influence and passing fashion of a day, we have in France, as in England, foreign influence and fashions of a day condemned. As for Italian influence in France, Petrarch himself was, by residence, a Frenchman. France looked as England never did to the Italian Popes. France also, speaking herself a language of the Latin group, as England does not, took more naturally, if not more generally than

1272

England, to enjoyment of the old classical mythology and imitation of old classical forms of speech.

There was nothing antagonist to such tendencies in the concurrent influence which her other neighbour, Spain, was exercising on the minds of France. Spain, too, spoke a Romance tongue, and early in the sixteenth century the chief poet of Spain was Boscan, who abandoned the old Gothic forms for professed imitation of Petrarch. He would replace the true Spanish ballads with his "Mar de Amor," Sea of Love, and with love "sonetos" and "canciones" that imitate Italian tenderness as well as the more fervid and sonorous Spanish voice was able to repeat its accents. That tenderness was even more closely represented by the Petrarchan writing of Boscan's friend, the soldier Garcilaso de la Vega, who sang Arcadian peace and died storming a fortress. The Spaniards, too, were looking back to Latin and Greek masterpieces with a kindred interest. Garcilaso fastened upon Virgil as well as Petrarch; Boscan translated "Hero and Leander" out of Greek; Diego de Mendoza, poet, novelist, historian, and for six years Charles V.'s Captain-General in Italy, was also a famous collector of Greek manuscripts. The studied imitation of Sallust in Mendoza's "History of the Rebellion of Granada," and the over-elaborate nicety in a rhetorical use of words, will also indicate how little of antagonism to the Italian influence France would find in the concurrent influence of Spain. Chiefly that added tendencies to a more pompous manner than Italian example warranted. A Spaniard could say of his queen entering Madrid in January, that she surpassed herself as a sun, and with the serenity of her visage gave life to the meadows and strength to the plants; or of the Spanish kings, that the sun seemed to take its course about their throne, and that their crown was the Zodiac on earth.

Spanish influence in France allied to the Italian.

The relish of such exalted nonsense was encouraged in France by the bedsides of the *Précieuses*, partly because it was the character of those ladies rather to spend thought upon words than words upon thought. As Regnier described the critics to whose school they belonged—

Tendency of French literary conceit to verbal criticism. The reason of it.

> " s'ils font quelque chose,
> C'est proser de la rime, et rimer de la prose."

Nevertheless French literature was at this time advancing to its highest point of influence, and way was being made, even by these verbal critics, towards a point at which France causes a very sharp bend in the current of our English literature. There was a reason for the minute attention that the French began to pay to the vocabulary of their language, at a time when Shakespeare proved our English capable of speaking all that man's wit can imagine or his heart can feel. North and south of the Loire there were still the Langue d'Oc and the Langue d'Oyl, in their extreme expression rather sister languages than dialects. Speech had been made unwholesome by the personal impurity of princes, and then came, in Henri IV., a king who with his Béarnois brought the Gascon dialect into familiar use at Court. The truest sense of literature would make a French writer of that day incessantly conscious of deliberation as to what should and what should not be admitted as classical French words into works for which he desired permanence. The proper and common disposition was to refer back to the parent classical tongue as a standard, and Ronsard was not alone in the desire to borrow

Ronsard.

dignity out of the Greek. He lamented in verse that he might not use the words " Ocymore, dyspotone, oligochro-nien," and he affected even a more Latinised grammar of French; such, for example, as the comparison of adjectives with "eur" and "ime." But Ronsard was in his own time the darling poet of his country. The Academy of Floral Games gave him a silver Minerva, with the name of "French poet *par excellence.*" Mary Stuart gave him a silver rock showing the spring of the Permessus, and addressed to " Ronsard, the Apollo of the spring of the Muses."

Thirty years younger than Ronsard, Malherbe during the first quarter of the seventeenth century became the most

Malherbe.

determined champion of the verbal purity of French. He was known as the tyrant of words and syllables. "This doctor in the vulgar tongue," wrote his friend Balzac, " used to say that for so many years he had been trying to de-Gasconise the Court, and that he could not do it. Death surprised him when rounding a period." " An hour before his death," says his disciple Racan, " Malherbe woke up with a start to correct his nurse for use of a word that was not good French ; and when his confessor reprimanded him for that, he said that he could not help himself, and that he would defend to the death the purity of the French language." We only understand, but Malherbe felt, the need of earnest critical attention to the unsettled language of his country as France rose in power Deliberation in the choice of words made him a slow writer. He spent three years in the composition of an ode intended to console the President of Verdun for the loss of a wife. When the ode was finished, the President had consoled himself by marrying another.

At the Hôtel Rambouillet Malherbe was the chief guest in the first years of his fame. Catherine de Vivonne de

The meetings at the Hôtel Rambouillet.

Pisani, when in 1600 she married, at the age of sixteen, the Marquis de Rambouillet, Grand Master of the Royal Wardrobe, had before her half a century of life, during which she could indulge her taste for Parisian literary conversation. Born in Rome and with Italian blood in her veins, she was skilled in Italian and Spanish and delighted in the literary spirit of her day, seasoned with the ingenious and harmless flatteries by which only an ear is tickled. Receiving company on her bed, after a fashion of the time and the manner of the whole community of *Précieuses*, who followed in her steps—so giving to fashion the phrase " courir les ruelles "—and in winter denying fire as perilous to the complexion of herself and of her delicate guests in chamber, corridor, or alcove, the Marquise de Rambouillet received princes and wits at her weekly feasts of verbal criticism. Of her indirect influence it is not easy to suggest the limits. Before her circle Corneille read his tragedies, and the youth Bossuet first displayed the genius of the preacher. Purity of speech was demanded of all who frequented the Hôtel Rambouillet. There was to be no unclean word, and much that was common it pleased the particular genius of the house to call unclean. The Marchioness disdaining her own common name of Catherine, Malherbe tortured his wit and produced for her instead of it Arthénice, its anagram. Vaugelas the grammarian ranked above princes at the Hôtel Rambouillet. " If the word *féliciter* is not yet French," wrote Balzac, "it will be so next year; M. de Vaugelas has given me his word not to oppose it." There is a playful letter of Voiture's to the Marquise de Rambouillet in which he pleads for the threatened life of the word *car*. Over-familiar words, if tolerated in the French at large, were replaced at the head-quarters of polite speech by delicately-conceited phrases. As the Marchioness saw company in her night-cap, and the idea Night-cap might have to be expressed in conversation, while the word was too coarse for choice lips, its association with sleep and dreams suggested that it might be referred to as "the innocent accomplice of falsehood." Laughter was clownish, but if mentioned it might be described as loss of seriousness. A gentleman in this assembly had once to mention hay ; *foin* happens, however, not only to mean hay

but to be also a mild French interjection. Baulked in his
attempt to find a substitute for the word, he became impatient, and for the innocent *foin* rapped out a " Devil fetch
me, there's no speaking in this house ! "

The Marquise de Rambouillet set a fashion among
ladies, and there remains a register of eight hundred she-
critics esteemed precious to France,—" Précieuses,"—as centres of refining influence. The
fashion had extended even to the provinces, when Molière
attacked it with his ridicule.

The *Pré-cieuses.*

The Hôtel Rambouillet was in the height of its credit
when, in 1635, Richelieu proposed to a weekly assembly of
male authors which met for mutual aid and discussion at the house of Conrart, one of their
number, corporate life under the protection of Louis XIV.
The offer was accepted, and the French Academy was thus
founded, with especial charge over the French language,
which the Academicians were to purify and fix by the
publication of a Dictionary and Grammar.

The French Academy.

It has been said of Dr. Johnson's English Dictionary
that he alone compiled it, while the Dictionary of the
French Academy was the work of forty men, each
subject to much feminine dictation. But between
the two works the essential difference is not to
be forgotten. The forty men in Paris had power
of life and death over the words of the French
language committed to their hands. The word they admitted into their dictionary was thereafter to be admissible
in good French literature, and the whole host of words that
they rejected were, by virtue of their rejection, to become
unlawful in polite society. It was to be a settlement of
language by a *coup d'état*. But there has been neither
need nor taste in England for that method of procedure.
Dr. Johnson might insert or omit what he pleased without
crushing a syllable of spoken English. French refinements

Settlement of
the French
language by
the forty
dictionary
makers.

tended to a tight-lacing of the language in a dictionary carefully devised as stays. Broad-chested English has allowed its lungs free play, and will be strapped up in the leather covering of no man's dictionary.

The work of the Academicians and their revision of it, with its tedious debates over the definitions of words, remained so long in hand that the first edition was not published till 1694, by which time critical France had advanced, with the help of Boileau, far ahead in a new direction. Colbert looked in upon the dictionary-makers when they had been for some years revising letter A, and found them debating on the sense of the word " Ami." " Is a friend bound by a social or emotional tie?" "Can one be called a friend where friendship is not reciprocal?" "Are men to be called friends when their warm professions of good-will are based upon self-interest?" "Who is a friend?" "Where is a friend?" The Minister, hearing such questions debated, ceased to ask when the Academicians would have talked their way down fairly into Z.

Although one would look for nothing less than strict obedience to system in the free, various utterance of the many voices that in each successive generation become fixed by the help of ink and paper, it is certain that, in the mass, men's minds obey their proper influences as the tides the moon. The moving forces lie within the mind of man himself —honour of truth and right, hope of a worthy future. Eloquent minds, in whom this honour is most active and this hope most sure, express the highest literature of each day, and their thoughts are lasting only in as far as they are true. Thus we might lay it down dogmatically as a fact that French literature advanced from the question of words and letters maintained by Ronsard and Malherbe to the larger question of forms and laws of literary composition discussed with especial power by Boileau. But they were

Advance of French writers from verbal to literary criticism.

not the devotees of choice phrases and words by whom such an advance was made, after the highest level in their former way of zeal had been attained. The larger part of the flock simply went on in the old way, and it was their aimless, down-hill wandering, as followers of a track which, for a certain distance only, took the upward way, that pro- voked from strong and honest minds a vigorous attempt to put them right. There was especial strength and honesty in the mind of Boileau, who earned a name for himself in French literature as the Poet of Good Sense, and whose good sense had in this country distinguished followers.

In our days of the Restoration and the years following the Revolution of 1688, it was Boileau, living on until his Boileau. death, aged seventy-five, in the year 1711, who gave laws on Parnassus and made critics. His father was an actuary ; his mother died in his infancy ; he was a sickly boy, subject to an unfriendly nurse ; at twenty he was an advocate unfit for the Bar, turning his mind to theology. But his place not being in the pulpit, he aban- doned the Church, and not the Church only, but also a benefice of eight hundred livres that he had been persuaded to hold at least for a certain term of years. In laying it down he gave to the poor all it had brought him. "But," said an abbé, who himself owned many benefices, "that was a good thing to live upon, M. Boileau." "Not a doubt of it," Boileau answered ; "but to die upon, Monsieur l'Abbé —to die upon !" It was his honesty that gave permanent force to this man's genius.

Resenting the degradation of taste in his day, Boileau laughed at the public that could see a rival to Corneille in Scudéri the dramatist, and could read with delight dainty romance after the manner of the Précieuses, by Scudéri's sister Madeleine, who carried to her death, at the age of ninety-four, the reputation of which she laid the foundation at the Hôtel Rambouillet. It was a reputation raised by her romances—the "Grand Cyrus," in ten volumes; "Clélie," in ten volumes—both of them first published in the name of her brother George, and many other works. Among those other works was "Almahide, or the Slave-Queen," in eight volumes, which appeared when the critic, a young man of four-and-twenty, was bent upon active war against all this emptiness that had usurped the place of honest wit. And who was then emptier than Abbé Cotin? Him Molière immortalised as the Trissotin of the "*Femmes Savantes*," and young Boileau attacked in his third satire. Chapelain, also, after thirty years' gestation, during which he was well nourished by the Duc de Longueville, had brought to light, when Boileau was a youth of twenty with a lively sense of the dull and absurd, twelve cantos of his "Pucelle." "I will make war against all this," said the young critic, three or four years later. It was urged upon him that he would bring a swarm of enemies about his ears. His answer was, "Well, I shall be an honest man, and never fear them."

Boileau declared war in his satires, whose censures are an index to the literary vices of their day. Enemies he did make, but as he had right on his side and honest sense, with ample strength of wit to make them felt, they battled with him in vain for mastery over the public mind. Cotin was dropped into obscurity. Chapelain left unpublished the remaining cantos of his "Pucelle." Molière, though by seventeen years Boileau's elder, was his companion and friend. Comrades of his, too, were La Fontaine and the pure-hearted Racine. Racine, within two or three years of equal age, was his next friend, whose death, after forty years of intimacy, caused Boileau to withdraw from Court and close his own life in retirement. In the bright hours of their life at Molière's country-house, or at Boileau's rooms in Paris, what suppers had there been, where Molière, Boileau, La Fontaine (who has described them), Chapelle, and

Racine discoursed freely, and took gaily wise counsel together ! They argued often of sound literature, and condemned each other for offences against sense to readings out of Chapelain's "Pucelle" that lay ready for the purpose. Twenty lines was the sentence for a serious offence ; but for outrages that deserved capital punishment, a page.

The literary mind, as it was cultivated at those suppers, was expressed in Boileau's poem on the "Art of Poetry."

The critical shortcomings of that work, which *Influence of Boileau on English literature.* may be said to have given the law for some years to French and English literature, nearly all proceed from a wholesome but too servile regard for the example of the ancient classic writers. The chief authors of Greece and Rome were to be as much the models of good literature as the Latin language was a standard of right speech. This led, indeed, to a sound contempt of empty trivialities, but it left the critic with faint powers of recognition for a Dante, a Shakespeare, or a Milton. Boileau was even hindered by it from perceiving how far Terence was surpassed by his friend Molière. His discipline thus tended obviously to the creation of an artificial taste for forms of correct writing excellent in themselves, but as means of perfect expression better suited to the genius of the French than of the English people. He was a true Frenchman, and English writers erred by imitation even of his excellence, in adopting too readily, for a nation Germanic in origin and language, forms that harmonised better with the mind and language of a Latin race. But, at the same time, they shared with their neighbours the benefit of assent to the appeal in his "*Art Poétique*" on behalf of plain good sense against the faded extravagances of that period of Italian influence from which life and health had departed :

> " Évitons ces excès. Laissons à l'Italie
> De tous ses faux brillans l'éclatante folie.
> Tout doit tendre au Bon Sens."

These lines declare the living spirit of the poem, in which, if we are to see only in one foremost work the altered temper of a generation, it may especially be said that the period of Italian influence ended and that of French influence began.

It was in 1672, and at the age of thirty-four, that Boileau wrote his "Art of Poetry." Dryden's age was then forty. In the previous year the Duke of Buckingham had satirised on the London stage, in his "Rehearsal," the conceits and fustian of recent English dramas, as they had been cooked by Davenant, Dryden, and others, to suit the spoiled palate of the town.

> "Spite of myself, I'll stay, fight, love, despair;
> And all this I can do because I dare,"

says one of Dryden's heroes:

> "I drink, I huff, I strut, look big, and stare;
> And all this I can do because I dare,"

mocks, in the "Rehearsal," Buckingham's Drawcansir. "Tyrannic Love" was one of Dryden's last popular plays when Boileau's "Art of Poetry" appeared in Paris. In that play a guardian angel praises his sword "all keen and ground upon the edge of day;" and a bold martyr, sentenced by the tyrant, thus defies him:—

> "Where'er thou stand'st I'll level at that place
> My gushing blood, and spout it at thy face.
> Thus, not by marriage, we our blood will join;
> Nay, more, my arms shall throw my head at thine."

And these excesses were intentional. Poets, Dryden wrote, in the Prologue to this play, misapplying Horace's "Serpit humi tutus"—

> "Poets like lovers should be bold and dare,
> They spoil their business with an overcare:
> And he who servilely creeps after sense
> Is safe, but ne'er will reach an excellence."

F

In England, then, there was as much need as in France
of Boileau's critical gospel of *Bon Sens*; and the light wits
of the day were disposed to follow for some short distance
in that direction the lead even of an earnest man, at any
rate if French.

For in those days France was strong and England weak.
The King of England was a pensioner to the French Crown.

The period of
French influ-
ence on
English
literature.

Mademoiselle de Querouaille was, as Duchess of
Portsmouth, agent of Royal France, and favourite
of Royal England, receiving an estate from the
French, and incredible sums out of the secret
service money from the pockets of the English people.
When there was no soul at Court meaner than that of the
King, capable neither of love nor of friendship, who affected
men only when they had ceased to be manly, and women
when they had become the shame of their own sex, Court
patronage of the theatre tainted the stage, and polite literature, still dependent upon courtly patronage, found no fit
audience for any song like that of Una and the Red Cross
Knight : it must needs be frivolous or censorious, critical or
satirical. But there were nevertheless great questions in
State and Church astir among the English. Vital change
was impending ; and the satire of a Dryden—since he who
could look back in his maturest day with so tender a fellow-
feeling to the purer strains of Chaucer, yet must needs be,
for the sake of bread, a dramatist in his relation to the people,
and a satirist in his relation to the Court—the satire of a
Dryden struck through the outside of things deep into the
gravest realities that then concerned his country. Therefore it is that Dryden's verse lives yet, to be read and
honoured, while the words of the light wits who played over
the mere frivolities of life belong to the antiquities of
English literature, long since dead to the English people.

But the Court and the Stage, if they were for a little
time after the Restoration the main sources of literary

repute and reward, could not claim to themselves all the nation's mind. Vigorous in the heart of the great English people there lay still the religious earnestness that gives strength to their character. In his jail there was John Bunyan writing "The Pilgrim's Progress;" and in his home sat Milton, who had as a youth dedicated his powers to God's service, and devoted himself to literature as one resolved that he would do all as in his great Taskmaster's eye. Unrecognised by fashion, Milton's "Paradise Lost" was steadily on its way to a second edition when the courtly wits of England looked to Boileau's newly-published "Art of Poetry" for help to the perception of good writing.

Boileau, in France as well as in England, gave an impetus to critical inquiry into literary styles and forms of composition. René Rapin, an elegant writer of Latin, whose treatises on polite literature were translated into English by B. Kennet; René le Bossu, Andrew Dacier and his wife, Fontenelle, and others, critics who, like Boileau, looked to the Greeks and Latins for their standard of good literature —all had their English representatives. John Sheffield, Duke of Buckingham, achieved his metrical "Essay on Poetry;" Horace's "Art of Poetry" was translated by the Earl of Roscommon, who wrote in verse also his own "Essay on Translated Verse." Horace's "Art of Poetry" was imitated by Oldham; while Boileau's "Art of Poetry," translated by Sir William Soame, a friend of Dryden's, was not published until it had received many touches from the hand of Dryden himself, who, in the prefaces to his plays, had proved himself the first of English critics. The most English and independent of the critics of his time was Dryden, yet even he cites, in the preface to his conversion of "Paradise Lost" into an opera, as authorities in literature "the greatest in this age, Boileau and Rapin; the latter of which alone is sufficient, were all

English acceptance and imitation of the French classical critics.

other critics lost, to teach anew the rules of writing." What wonder then that this allegiance to French critical taste produced for us a Rymer and a Dennis?

There can be no surer test of the quality of English fashionable and high critical taste during this period of French influence than in the slowness of our critics to perceive the marvellous success of Shakespeare as a direct student in the school of life and nature.

Pepys witnessed the performance of " Romeo and Juliet" in March, 1672, and pronounced the play to be "the worst he had ever heard." Not long after he went to the King's Theatre, where, he says, "we saw 'Midsummer Night's Dream,' which I had never seen before, nor shall ever again, for it is the most insipid, ridiculous play that ever I saw in my life." In 1676, in going to Deptford by water, he read " Othello, Moor of Venice," which, he continues, " I ever heretofore esteemed a mighty good play; but having so lately read 'The Adventures of Five Hours,' it seems a mean thing." " The Adventures of Five Hours," which made " Othello " appear " a mean thing " by comparison was a translation from a play by Calderon. In 1677 Pepys records that he " saw the ' Merry Wives of Windsor,' which did not please me at all, in no part of it;" while "Twelfth Night" he esteems " the weakest play that ever I beheld on the stage." " The Tempest " he found " full of so good variety, that I cannot," he says, " be more pleased almost in a comedy, only the seaman's part a little too tedious;" but then he adds that " the play has no great wit, yet good, above ordinary plays." With " Hamlet" he was "mightily pleased," but, "above all, with Betterton," who personated the Prince of Denmark. When he was first present at the performance of " Macbeth " in 1664, he calls it only " a pretty good play." Afterwards it rose in his favour, and in 1667 he declares it to be "a most excellent play in all

What the polite world and French polished critics said of Shakespeare.

respects, but especially in divertisement, though it be a deep tragedy, which is a strange perfection in a tragedy, it being most proper here, and suitable." It appears from a subsequent entry that the "divertisement" which he considered the especial excellence of "Macbeth," meant "the variety of dancing and music."

The professed critics were sometimes not more complimentary, as may be seen in a book published in 1721, at which date Shakespeare's works were only in their fifth edition, and the copies of that fifth edition, published by Nicholas Rowe twelve years before, were still sufficient for the public need. In this book, entitled "The Laws of Poetry, as laid down by the Duke of Buckinghamshire in his Essay on Poetry, by the Earl of Roscommon in his Essay on Translated Verse, and by the Lord Lansdowne on Unnatural Flights in Poetry, Explained and Illustrated," we are instructed that

"That famous soliloquy which has been so much cried up in 'Hamlet' has no more to do there than a description of the grove and altar of Diana mentioned by Horace. Hamlet comes in talking to himself, and very sedately and exactly weighs the several reasons or considerations mentioned in that soliloquy,

'To be, or not to be,' &c.

As soon as he has done talking to himself, he sees Ophelia, and passes to a conversation with her, entirely different to the subject he has been meditating on with that earnestness, which, as it was produced by nothing before, so has it no manner of influence on what follows after, and is therefore a perfectly detached piece, and has nothing to do in the play. The long and tedious soliloquy of the bastard Falconbridge, in the play of 'King John,' just after his being received as the natural son of Cœur de Lion, is not only impertinent to the play, but extremely ridiculous. To go through all the soliloquies of Shakespeare would be to make a volume on this single head. But this I can say in general, *that there is not one in all his works that can be excused by nature or reason.*"

The critic, however, probably Gildon, owned himself
sensible that he should raise anger of the uncultivated
English people by what he was saying, and meant further to
say, upon the faults of Shakespeare. Lucilius, he adds,
" was the incorrect idol of Roman times, Shakespeare of
ours. Both gained their reputation from a people unac-
quainted with art ; and that reputation was a sort of traditionary authority, looked upon to be so sacred, that Horace
among the Romans, in a much more polite age than that in
which Lucilius writ, could not escape their censure for at-
tacking him ; nor can Mr. Rymer, or any other just critic,
who shall presume, though with the highest justice and
reason, to find fault with Shakespeare, escape the indigna-
tion of our modern traditionary admirers of that poet.'
Rymer himself, forty years earlier, had been even more emphatic. " In the neighing of an horse, or in the growling of a
mastiff, there is a meaning, there is as lively expression, and,
may I say, more humanity than many times in the tragical
flights of Shakespeare." His own notions of a tragical
flight we may discover from his tragedy of " Edgar," where
in the first act Alfrida declares that she will, at Ethelwold's
request, discard her ornaments, and the margin directs her
to pull off her patches :—

" *Ethelw.*　Blaze on, dire comet—may thy influence be
　　　　　　To crowns and empires fatal, as to me !

　Alfr.　　Whither do your rash words and passions fly ?
　　　　　　To calm your mind, my utmost power I'll try.
　　　　　　If I receive advantage from my dress,
　　　　　　'Tis that I you might with advantage please.
　　　　　　If, wanting this, your love be not impair'd,
　　　　　　These ornaments I readily discard. [*Pulls off her patches.*"

Four years after the scholiast upon his Grace of Buckingham had spoken the opinions which prevailed among

thousands of that day, who looked upon Shakespeare as at best a rude and uncultivated genius, no less a person than Mr. Pope himself became his editor. Whatever may have been his disqualification for his task, there was no man living whose name could do so much towards securing for the dramatist the allegiance of a larger circle of admirers. Yet Shakespeare's works, even when endorsed by the name of Pope, were thought to be a doubtful venture. Only seven hundred and fifty copies were printed, and of these it may not have been the editor's fault that part could not be sold until after a reduction of the price from six guineas to sixteen shillings. It is questionable whether Theobald could have won a public, or indeed a publisher for Shakespeare, had not Pope opened the way. His edition was the first with notes, but they were few, and turned chiefly upon verbal criticism. Pope consulted many of the old copies, professed "to have a religious horror of innovation," and declared that he had not given vent to his own "private sense or conjecture." His alterations, nevertheless, were extensive, and his collation of the quartos and first folio imperfect. His text was full of the errors which had crept into the later folios; and having adopted the theory that many portions of the plays had been interpolated by the actors, and believing that he could distinguish the spurious passages from the genuine, he "degraded" the presumed additions "to the bottom of the page." His licence of conjecture was as largely exercised upon single lines and words, and his objections and emendations often show his ignorance of the manners and language of Shakespeare's times. But we gladly call to mind the finer touches of his pen. To him, for instance, we owe the reading of "Tarquin's ravishing *strides*," instead of *sides*, and it is still usual to praise him for the accepted version, which is, I think, a change for the worse—*south* for *sound*— of the lines—

Shakespeare endorsed by Pope.

> " O it came o'er my ears like the sweet sound
> That breathes upon a bank of violets."

Even Pope, then, so far failed to bring Shakespeare into immediate credit, that of the small number of copies of his edition there remained nearly a fifth part for Tonson to get rid of at less than a seventh of the published price.   No defect in the editor that could have been appreciated by the public of his own day was accountable for this.   The new spirit of French criticism was still ruling among us the taste of the polite ; and Pope himself, our English poet of good sense, was as a viceroy for Boileau in England.   Pope also had produced his metrical " Essay upon Criticism," and his mock heroic *Lutrin* in the " Rape of the Lock."   But Pope's was English wit ; and, if he saw how

> " Critic-learning flourished most in France ;
> The rules a nation born to serve obeys,
> And Boileau still in right of Horace sways,"

he at least was not born to serve.   As critic he was an emulator, not an imitator ; and he did not, like Boileau, contemplate Nature only in the mirror of the Greeks and Latins. His influence shattered the credit of

> " The bookful blockhead, ignorantly read,
> With loads of learned lumber in his head.

A Dennis feebly, but for a time successfully, maintained the literal text of French laws of criticism against the literature of his country ; although as a politician he did write on one of his title-pages " Liberty asserted against the French," and feared that peace could never be restored if he were not given up to the enemy.   He appealed, indeed, in this difficulty, to Marlborough, who said he had no influence with the ministry, but thought his own case as desperate, as he

[margin note: Under French influence, the English mind.]

had done almost as much injury to the French as Mr. Dennis himself. Dennis, inspired from such a Helicon as Pope imagined on his writing-table—"a pot of half-dead ale, covered with a Longinus,"—was an oracle no more when once he had been dragged out into the daylight. Yet even Dennis had his stronger side.

But if it was Pope, the chief of the new taste among the poets, who in 1725 first sent the English polite world to Shakespeare, thirteen years earlier it had been Addison, chief arbiter of taste among prose-writers, the same who, in a metrical account of the greatest English poets, written, according to the mind of Oxford University, in 1694, had passed from Spenser to Cowley with no mention at all of Shakespeare,—it was Addison who had in 1712 brought Milton into fashion. Yet let us not forget that Steele had in "The Tatler" shown a heart and wit keenly alive to the genius both of Milton and of Shakespeare, before Addison had criticised the one, or Pope had edited the other. Upon the independent genius of Addison, as upon that of all great English writers, the stamp of the English character is set. He reverenced the ancients, he submitted much to the French critics, and was conspicuous among apostles of the gospel of good sense. He was so well in tune with his own time that, as Swift said in his Journal to Stella, "If he had a mind to be chosen king, he would hardly be refused;" but after all, it was the earnest English mind in him that had given breadth and depth to his influence. It was this that had caused him, one January morning towards the close of the year 1712, to introduce among "The Spectator" papers that day by day so gracefully and mildly brought to the touchstone of good sense the idler follies of society, Milton himself, heralded by the motto from Propertius, "*Cedite Romani Scriptores; cedite Graii.*" During the next four months Milton was again and again his topic, "The Spectator" of eighteen

Milton endorsed by Addison.

successive Saturdays being occupied with the testimony of
Addison to the majesty of " Paradise Lost."

In bearing witness to Milton, Addison no doubt still
paid undue homage to the French lawgivers who held their
Latin
English. parliament upon Parnassus ; but his homage was
free from servility. " A few general rules ex-
tracted out of the French authors," he says in one of his
Milton papers, " with a certain cant of words, has sometimes set up an illiterate, heavy writer for a most judicious
and formidable critic." He demands of the good critic,
not, indeed, that he shall look Nature straight in the face,
but that he shall be skilled in the Greek and Latin authors ;
and adds, " There is not a Greek or Latin critic who has
not shown, even in the style of his criticisms, that he was a
master of all the elegance and delicacy of his native tongue."
For Addison also followed, with almost all other writers of
his day, the example of the French in testing the literary
worth of modern languages, whether Romance or not, by
their conformity with Latin style. Even Dryden, although
he used a less Latinised English than that which became
customary to the writers who immediately succeeded him,
declared for Latin as the pattern of good English. In
dedicating to the Earl of Sunderland his " Troilus and
Cressida," he says, " How barbarously we yet write and
speak, your Lordship knows, and I am sufficiently sensible
in my own English. For I am often put to a stand in
considering whether what I write be the idiom of the
tongue, or false grammar and nonsense couched beneath
that specious name of Anglicism ; and have no other way
to clear my doubts but by translating my English into
Latin." This of the language that had sufficed for Shakespeare ! It was not then understood that, if the English
would do as the French had done, and bring their language
into harmony with that from which it was derived, and with
the greater number of the minds that spoke it, they must

imitate French practice in the spirit, and not in the letter, by laying hold of the so-called " Anglo-Saxon " element, which is to English what the Latin is to French.

This truth is now common enough, and even liable to over-statement, for there remains justification of much study of the Latin model, in the fact that Latin was in a greater degree than First English a highly cultivated language, delicately illustrating by polished models many and very different forms of literary composition. Our vocabulary, we now know, should be taken as much as may be from the actual sources of the language : but if we look at all, as we may certainly sometimes look with advantage, to examples more than a thousand years old for help to that exact, clear, emphatic, and durable expression of our thoughts which is the whole object of writing, it is frankly to be owned that we shall get much better help from Latin than from First English authors.

At the same time let it never be forgotten that the real question for each genuine writer has been—not, Whom shall I imitate? but, How shall I give to my own mind the fullest utterance? In the distinction between perishable and imperishable reputations this is, in fact, the true form of the literary question, How shall I be saved? In Literature, as in everything else, it is the truth only that makes alive ; not the abstract, but the honest, individual truth—a man's truth to himself. No writer has ever manufactured artificially a reputation that would last.

Substance and accidents of literary style.

We have now partly seen how writers are affected by the circumstances of their time. There has been a great period of Italian influence on English literature, characterised throughout by an extravagant taste for emphasis. The demand for incessant cleverness in force of phrase and ingenuity of illustration was then so imperious, that only the most powerful minds could satisfy it without being driven into false emphasis by the equal loading of all parts of their argument with allusion, alliteration, illustration, metaphor, and everything else that should represent the seasonable outstepping of a man's free wit, not the mono-tonous briskness of a day's work on the treadmill. False emphasis, bred of ill-regulated esteem for cleverness and strength, was the characteristic fault to which the taste of the polite world tended in the period of Italian influence; but out of it came, from a few vigorous English minds, the largest and the truest utterances. Of the succeeding period of French influence critical pedantry was the prevailing bane. Even the critics who, in upholding all good sense, had an occasional approving nod for Nature, held literary good sense to consist chiefly in the imitation of Horace, carved rules of composition out of the Æneid and Odyssey, and by reference to those judged even Milton. Him, never-theless, Addison held by, even when he was an Oxford Latinist of three-and-twenty accepting generally, with little question, the decrees of the arbiters of taste acknowledged in his university. Addison was content then to excuse Milton by suggesting that " he seems above the critic's nicer laws." In that poem to which I have before referred, and which so conveniently sets forth the literary taste of good society in England under the sway of the French critics, we read of Chaucer that—

> " In vain he jests in his unpolished strain,
>   And tries to make his readers laugh in vain."

Of Spenser we learn that he " amused a barbarous age," but that his

> "mystic tale, that pleased of yore,
> Can charm an understanding age no more ;
> The long-spun allegories fulsome grow,
> While the dull moral lies too plain below."

Addison would not have had the soul in him that gives life to his name had he not grown into the perception of something higher than the dominant bad taste of the polite. In later years he spoke of Spenser as "in the same class with Milton." But because his matter was not reconcilable to any Latin formula, and his manner was not that of an Englishman ever considerate whether his English style would bear direct translation into Latin, the "understanding age" looked down from the top of its own small model of Olympus, where the Dennises and Rymers sat as gods, and spat on the ground at the name of Edmund Spenser. That "understanding age" usually now suffers undue contempt in the true heart of the young student of literature, born to the various influences of a period of popular influence in which taste is free ; and some may, at times, think that its old state of slavery has been exchanged for the mere indolence of freedom.

In generalisation upon groups or sequences of natural facts and the fruitage of men's minds under right cultivation, literature is as much in the course of nature as the fruitage of the apple-trees. We must not always forget the unity and harmony of life and thought within the small round of this world. There are no sciences in nature, no classifications, no laws, but the single Fiat of Al.-wise Beneficence. This has produced a creation of which the minutest details blend and fit together with the most intricate and surprising harmonies. All that we know points always to more forms than we have learnt to understand, of various and perfect adaptation to the single use of multiplying the great sum of happiness and beauty. But the wisdom of the one great Divine Thought would be indeed unsearchable to us if we sought, as gods ourselves, at once to grasp it all. Instead of attempting

Purpose and limits of generalisation.

that, we use, in aid of our weakness, those artificial steps of
our own making, in theories and classifications, which are as
the rounds of Jacob's ladder between earth and heaven.
It is by exercise of the power given to him of searching
the Divine Thought with some apprehension of its harmonies that man has attained whatever height of intellect
he calls his own.   There is no other way of knowledge.
And it is with the moral world as with the intellectual.
Only by battling out slowly and experimentally the moral
law can man rise even to a faint participation of the active
strength of the Divine Beneficence.   There is no other way
of right.   But as there is no battle without resistance, no
strength that is not exercised, no health in a merely passive
virtue, were all men of one right mind, uniformly good,
impeccable, untroubled, they would be happy only as the
ants and bees are happy, in a life regulated by a faultless
instinct.   All part would be denied them in the utmost
blessing of childlike participation in the sacred energy of
Him who made them in His image.   Our literature shows
one body of men in generation after generation working
onward by aid of the natural conflicts and varieties of mind.
We cannot understand our own work if we do not see also
how the minds of our neighbours have worked with us, and
our minds with theirs.   But, however far we look, the
broadest view we can take still does not, and will never,
contain the whole truth.   When, therefore, in dealing with
our own literature, we parcel it out, however aptly, into
periods of this influence and that, let us again and again
remember that all such distinctions are in their nature
arbitrary.   They are not dominant truths with which all
details must be harmonised ; they are but incidental facts, dwelt on as aids to systematic
study.   And even in this respect they are not
to be dwelt upon dogmatically. Changes of literary taste are
never so abrupt that all writing in one fashion ceases when a

The period
of popular
i..fluence.

new fashion first becomes predominant. The four periods of English literature run, more or less, into each other. The period of French influence and that of popular influence now dominant do not merely shade into each other ; they run also for some time parallel, blending together often, but not always. With Daniel Defoe this fourth period must be said to begin, but after his time the French critical school maintained its influence yet for another century over one section of English writers.

It is to be remembered also that at all times, with perhaps one doubtful exception in the " Faery Queen," it is, in England, the English people that has inspired the highest forms of English literature. In the first period of our literature the popular influence was almost throughout a marked character ; but in a merely literary classification founded upon changes in the form of writing, the fact that in this early period the language itself was being formed is, of course, more distinctive.

Afterwards, though there was no reading public outside the select circle of scholars and persons of quality, there was the English people, open-eared in the theatre, to whose natural heart Shakespeare spoke.

Milton, surrounded by the filth of fashionable wit in Charles the Second's day, remained in unison with the religious earnestness that was not gone out of the national character because a worthless court claimed momentary precedence. There was not only the one grand English poet who, from the midst of his day's licentiousness, imaged for himself and for all time a naked man and woman— Adam and Eve—in their innocence, with their pure love, human and unconcealed, yet so divine in its humanity that not even King Charles himself could have drawn a licentious thought from any line in the chaste picture. There was not only Milton then. There were also readers enough among the unfashionable men in England to consume five editions of " Paradise Lost" before Milton received the stamp of fashion.

But we come now to a period when the popular influence, always active upon the best minds, becomes with every generation more and more dominant over the small minds too. For the people at large extend their reading power into departments of knowledge formerly unsought by them, and their favour is found generally to be more remunerative than that of the most princely patron. This period should date from the day when Defoe stood in the pillory.

Daniel Defoe, a tradesman's son, born in the reign of Charles II., bred to Dissent, educated by a schoolmaster who did not account the political movements of his time an unfit study for English boys, was, even as a young hose-factor on Cornhill, zealous in the true cause of the English people. Though a Protestant in fierce anti-Popery days, he had no part in the passionate extravagance of a sectarian hatred to the Roman Catholics. But their principles, honestly carried out, were by their nature subversive of liberty of conscience. It happened that civil and religious liberty were in his time, from like causes, in equal danger; but, although a Dissenter, he could fight their battle only on the highest ground, as that of the English people, and not of the Nonconformists only. So it was that he fought, dissociated from the lesser passions of the hour, without one personal adherent. When James II. laboured openly and insidiously, by assumption of a personal supremacy over the laws, to give the Pope his own again in England, the Act of Toleration, by which he released his own church out of bondage, working under the mask of a newly-modelled comprehensiveness of charity, pleased many of the Dissenters. They were glad, by payment of a trifling fee, to open Richard Baxter's prison door. Defoe therefore was little thanked for urging that

Defoe's service of the people.

acceptance of such royal grace was an admission of the King's absolute claim to override the laws. " He that would serve men," said Defoe afterwards, "must not promise himself that he shall not anger them. I have been exercised in this usage even from a youth. I had their reproaches when I blamed their credulity and confidence in the flattery and caresses of Popery, and when I protested against addresses of thanks for an illegal liberty of conscience founded on a dispensing power." The young patriot joined Monmouth when he landed in the West, and, after the night on Sedgmoor, was an exile. But King James's turn for exile quickly followed, and, after the Revolution, William of Orange recognised in Defoe the one sound and most honest English friend. To the cry raised by the opposition that King William was no true-born Englishman, Defoe replied with his satire of "The True-born Englishman," rhymes of which 80,000 copies were sold in the streets. Among their home truths are vigorous assertions of the claims of the people against persecution in the Church, or despotism in the State. In these he finds as dangerous a thing

> " A ruling priesthood, as a priest-rid king ;
> And of all plagues with which mankind are curst,
> Ecclesiastic tyranny's the worst ; "

while of the kings false to their trust he says,—

> " When kings the sword of justice first lay down,
> They are no kings, though they possess the crown.
> Titles are shadows, crowns are empty things,
> The good of subjects is the end of kings."

Then came Queen Anne to the throne; ecclesiastic tyranny and the old doctrine of the divine right to govern ill recovered strength, and hard words hailed on the Dissenters. A substantial blow was aimed in a Bill that was to disqualify them from all civil employ-

Defoe in the pillory.

G

ments. It passed the Commons, but failed with the Lords, among whom were the foremost champions of English liberty. Bigoted preachers meanwhile lashed the populace into a heavenly mood for pulling chapels down; and Sacheverell, preaching at Oxford, had denounced him as no true son of the Church who did not raise against Dissent "the bloody flag and banner of defiance." Then it was that Defoe, a thriving citizen with much to lose, spoke boldly on behalf of liberty of conscience in his pamphlet called "The Shortest Way with the Dissenters." He wrote, as in all his controversial writing, to maintain a principle and not a party. He began his satire with a quotation from Roger l'Estrange of a fable that might have been applied to James the Second's Act of Toleration. A cock at roost in a stable, having dropped from his perch, and finding himself in much danger among restless heels, has a fair proposal to make to the horses—that we shall all of us keep our legs quiet. This fable Defoe applied to the Dissenters, who were then asking for equal treatment, although they had been intolerant enough themselves not long since, when they had the upper hand. Professing, in his assumed character of a bigoted High Churchman of the day, to show the vice of Dissent before teaching its cure, he deals, in the first place, a fair blow to his own side for past intolerance. The Dissenters ought not, perhaps, to have been blind to the irony of the second half of the pamphlet; but in the first half the irony is not all against ecclesiastical intolerance. Defoe was against all intolerance, and to the bigotry of his own party Defoe gives—I think seriously and intentionally—the first hit. The succeeding satire on the persecuting spirit of the noisy party in the Church, since it could not easily surpass the actual extravagance of party spirit, had in it nothing but the delicate sustained sharpness of ironical suggestion to reveal the author's purpose to the multitude. Several reasons, h says, are urged on behalf of the Dissenters "why we should continue and tolerate them among us," as : "They are very numerous, they say ; they are a great part of the nation, and we cannot suppress them. To this may be answered, They are not so numerous as the Protestants in France, and yet the French king effectually cleared the nation of them at once, and we don't find he misses them at home." Besides, "the more numerous the more dangerous, and therefore the more need to suppress them ; and if we are to allow them only because we cannot suppress them, then it ought to be tried whether we can or no." It is said, also, that their aid is wanted against the common enemy. This, argues Defoe, is but the same argument of inconvenience of war-time that was urged against suppressing the old money ; and the hazard, after all, proved to be small. " We can never enjoy a settled, uninterrupted union and tranquillity in this nation till the spirit of Whiggism, faction, and schism is melted down like the old money." The gist of the pamphlet, the scheme set forth on the title-page as the shortest way with the Dissenters, is propounded in this passage :—

" If one severe law were made and punctually executed, that whoever was found at a conventicle should be banished the nation and the preacher be hanged, we should soon see an end of the tale ; they would all come to church, and one age would make us one again. To talk of five shillings a month for not coming to the Sacrament, and one shilling per week for not coming to church,—this is such a way of converting people as never was known, this is selling them a liberty to transgress for so much money. If it be not a crime, why don't we give them full licence? And if it be, no price ought to compound for the committing it ; for that is selling a liberty to people to sin against God and the Government. . . . . We hang men for trifles, and banish them for things not worth naming ; but an offence against God and the Church, against the welfare of the world and the dignity of religion, shall be bought off for five shillings. This is such a shame to a Christian Government, that 'tis with regret I transmit it to posterity."

The pamphlet delighted men of the Sacheverell school. A Cambridge Fellow thanked his bookseller for having sent him so excellent a treatise—next to the Holy Bible and the Sacred Comments the most valuable he had ever seen. Great was the reaction of wrath when the pamphlet was found to be a Dissenter's satire ; nevertheless, the Dissenters held by their first outcry against the author. Defoe, aged forty-two, paid for this service to the English people in the pillory, and as a prisoner in Newgate. But his " Hymn to the Pillory," which appeared on the first of the three days of the shame of the Government in his exposure, July 29, 30, and 31, in the year 1703, turned the course of popular opinion against the men who placed him there—men, as his rhyme said, scandals to the times, who

> " Are at a loss to find his guilt,
>   And can't commit his crimes.'·

It was in the next year, as a prisoner in Newgate, that Defoe, on the 19th of February, 1704, set up his "Review," continued through nine years from 1704 to 1713.

Defoe in Newgate sets up "The Review."

With " The Review," in which Defoe addressed to the people his own earnest thoughts upon all matters that concerned the common good, begins the history of English journalism as a power in the State and a reflection of the people's influence on English literature. To much vigorous argument on grave affairs of State, Defoe united censorship of social follies by including in his plan the machinery of a supposed Scandalous Club, for hearing and deciding on domestic questions. To this part of " The Review" it will be seen that we may trace most reasonably Richard Steele's first notion of "The Tatler."

When Addison and Steele had successively passed to Oxford from the Charterhouse, where they had been school-fellows and friends together, the paths by which they took

their way into the world were widely separate. Addison
thought it best to provide for his own future
advancement by securing influential patrons.
He therefore, after the campaign of 1695, offered
to the King the homage of a paper of verses on the capture
of Namur, and presented them through Sir John Somers,
then Lord Keeper of the Great Seal. To Lord Somers he
sent with them a flattering dedicatory address. Discern-
ment of talent was at this time a merit for which more than
one political Mæcenas gladly earned credit to himself.
Preferments, lesser public trusts, and sinecures were readily
bestowed on men of letters friendly to the party of the
giver, until the accession of George I., happily for literature, removed the Court from all contact with the wit or
wisdom of the country. Somers, who was esteemed a man
of taste, was not unwilling to "receive the present of a
Muse unknown." He asked Addison to call upon him, and
became his patron. Charles Montagu, afterwards Earl of
Halifax, critic and wit himself, shone also among the states-
men who were known patrons of letters. Also to him, who
was a prince of patrons, "fed with soft dedication all day
long," Addison introduced himself. Montagu had not long
before risen to the office of Chancellor of the Exchequer ;
he had just then been busy over recoinage and the project
of the Sinking Fund ; he was a wit and patron of wits
seated in the national Tom Tidler's ground. To him, as it
was part of his public fame to be a Latin scholar, Addison,
also a skilful Latinist, addressed, in Latin, a paper of verses
on the Peace of Ryswick. With Somers and Montagu for
patrons, the young man of genius who wished to thrive
might fairly commit himself to the service of the Church,
but Addison's tact and refinement promised to be serviceable to the State ; and so it was that, as Steele tells us,
Montagu made Addison a layman. "His arguments were
founded upon the general pravity and corruption of men of

Addison in
the way of
patronage.

business, who wanted liberal education. And I remember, as if I had read the letter yesterday, that my Lord ended with a compliment, that, however he might be represented as no friend to the Church, he never would do it any other injury than keeping Mr. Addison out of it." To the good offices of Montagu and Somers Addison was indebted, therefore, for a travelling allowance of three hundred a year. The grant was for his support while qualifying himself on the Continent by study of modern languages, and otherwise, for diplomatic service. It dropped in a year or two, at the King's death, and Addison was cast upon his own resources; but he throve, and lived to become an Under-Secretary of State in days that made Prior an ambassador, and rewarded with official incomes Congreve, Rowe, Hughes, Philips, Stepney, and others. Throughout his honourable career prudence dictated to Addison more or less of dependence on the friendship of the strong. An honest friend of the popular cause, he was more ready to sell than give his pen to it; although the utmost reward would at no time have tempted him to throw his conscience into the bargain. The good word of Halifax obtained him from Godolphin the Government order for a poem on the Battle of Blenheim, with immediate earnest of payment for it in the office of a Commissioner of Appeal in the Excise, worth £200 a year. Addison wrote "The Campaign;" and upon its success he obtained the further reward of an Irish Under-Secretaryship. In his later years, when, after the Rebellion in the North, Addison fought the battle of his party as "The Freeholder," it was again not on his own free impulse that he wrote, but as the popular and discreet man of genius appointed to write by the Government, who, as it seemed to Steele, "made choice of a flute when they ought to have taken a trumpet."

Steele, on the contrary, fastened upon the duties of life with no immediate regard to patronage. He never joined

a calculation of reward to the discovering or doing of what he took to be his duty to the country. His mind belonged entirely to the English people. At Oxford his wit had shown its bent, Steele represents the people.
for he had written a comedy. But he burnt this upon being told that it had little merit. Not knowing what his words were worth, he gave himself up bodily to the service of his country, and, in days of change perilous to England at home and abroad, resolved to bear arms in her service. As a soldier he would, according to his own phrase, "plant himself behind King William against Louis XIV." True Englishman, he chose the way of life in which it seemed to him that he could best use his powers for the common good ; and this he did at the cost of a good Welsh estate, whereof he was disinherited for his patriotism by an offended relative. The same unselfish determination to give himself up to the service of his country caused him, when, fatherless as he was, he could not get a commission, to enlist as a private in the Horse Guards. Accomplished, genial, and zealous, with the soul of a gentleman, such a private as Richard Steele was soon the brother of his regiment. Its colonel made him his private secretary, gave him a cornetcy, and got him afterwards, as Captain Steele, a company of Fusileers. Among his brother soldiers, and fresh from the Oxford worship of old classical models, the religious feeling that accompanies all true refinement, and that was indeed part of the English nature in him as in Addison, prompted Steele to write, for his own private occupation, a little book upon "The Christian Hero." In it he opposed to the fashionable classicism of his day a sound reflection that the heroism of Cato or Brutus had far less in it of true strength, and far less adaptation to the needs of life, than the unfashionable Christian heroism set forth by the Sermon on the Mount. The old bent of the English mind was strong in Richard Steele, and he gave unostentatiously a lively wit

to the true service of religion, without having spoken or written to the last day of his life one word of mere religious cant. But his comrades felt, and he himself saw, that "The Christian Hero," published in 1701, was too didactic. It was indeed plain truth out of Steele's heart; but an air of superiority, freely allowed only to the professional man teaching rules of his own art, belongs to a too didactic manner. Nothing was more repugnant to Steele's nature than the sense of this. He had defined the Christian as "one who is always a benefactor, with the mien of a receiver." And that was his own character, of which the one fault was, that he was more ready to give than to receive, more prompt to ascribe honour to others than to claim it for himself. To right himself, Steele wrote a light-hearted comedy, "The Funeral, or Grief à la Mode;" but at the core even of that lay the great earnestness of his censure against the mockery and mummery of griefs that should be sacred; and he blended with this, in the character of lawyer Puzzle, a protest against mockery of truth and justice by the intricacies of the law. Of these he wrote, in his preface to the published play, "the daily villainies we see committed will also be esteemed things proper to be prosecuted by satire; nor could our ensuing legislatives do their country a more seasonable office than to look into the distresses of an unhappy people, who groan perhaps in as much misery under entangled as they could do under broken laws." The liveliness of this comedy made Steele popular with the wits; and the inevitable touches of the author's patriotism brought on him also the notice of the Whigs. Party men might, perhaps, already feel something of the unbending independence that was in Steele himself, as in this play he made old Lord Brumpton teach it to his son:—

> "But be thou honest, firm, impartial;
> Let neither love, nor hate, nor faction move thee;
> Distinguish words from things, and men from crimes."

King William perhaps, had he lived, could fairly have recognised in Steele the social form of that sound mind which, in Defoe, was solitary. In a later day it was to Steele a proud recollection that his name, to be provided for, "was in the last table-book ever worn by the glorious and immortal William III."

The stage yet represented, although less completely than it had done, the place of direct appeal by a writer to the body of the public. Shakespeare had written for the people; Congreve now wrote for the town. Players of Elizabeth's day carried *Decreased influence of the people on the stage.* their pieces out of London, even into Germany; and in London itself addressed the common heart of those who formed before their stage a natural audience, distinguished largely by some of its elements from the polite body of the arbiters of artificial taste. At the Restoration the Court patronage brought to the theatre that small circle of conventional wits who held themselves to be especially the town; and soon the lives and manners of the new order of patrons were more commonly reflected from the stage than the old large types of human character and passion. Popular interest in the stage, partly diverted from it at the same time by the growth of other influences, chiefly for this reason abated; and many who would have been good playgoers a century earlier, in Queen Anne's days, out of the same mind that would have made them so, stayed at home and read, not without approbation, Jeremy Collier's sharp attack upon stage immorality. Steele's wit took naturally the old popular course, and disported itself for a short time upon the stage ; but his comedies, with all their gaiety and humour, wanted the taint of immorality that was the game flavour then accounted necessary to the perfect relish of a play. Each comedy of Steele's was based on seriousness, as all sound English wit has been since there have been writers in England. The gay manner did not conceal all the earnest thoughts that might jar with the humour of the town; and thus Steele was able to claim, by right of his "Lying Lover"—a comedy in which the modern reader may also discover preaching—"the honour of being the only English dramatist who had had a piece damned for its piety."

With that strong regard for the drama which cannot well be wanting to the man who has an artist's vivid sense "The Tatler." of life, Steele never withdrew his good will from the players, never neglected to praise a good play, and, as we have seen, took every fair occasion of suggesting to the town the subtlety of Shakespeare's genius. But single-minded, quick-witted, and prompt to act on the first suggestion of a higher point of usefulness to which he might attain, Steele saw the mind of the people ready for a new sort of relation to its writers, and he followed the lead of Defoe. But though he turned from the more frivolous temper of the enfeebled playhouse audience to commune in free air with the country at large, he took fresh care for the restraint of his deep earnestness within the bounds of a cheerful, unpretending influence. Drop by drop it should fall, and its strength lie in its persistence. He would bring what wit he had out of the playhouse, and speak his mind, like Defoe, to the people themselves every post-day. But he would affect no pedantry of moralising, he would appeal to no passions, he would profess himself only "a Tatler." Might he not use, he thought, modestly distrustful of the charm of his own mind, some of the news obtained by virtue of the office of Gazetteer Harley had given him, to bring weight and acceptance to his writing that he valued only for the use to which it could be put. For, as he himself truly says in "The Tatler," "wit, if a man had it, unless it be directed to some useful end, is but a wanton, frivolous quality; all that one should value himself upon in this kind is that he had some honourable intention in it."

Swift, not then a writer for the Tories, was a friend of Steele's, who, when the first "Tatler" appeared, had been amusing the town at the expense of John Partridge, astrologer and almanack-maker, with "Predictions for the year 1708," professing to be written by Isaac Bickerstaff, Esq. The first prediction was of the death of Partridge, "on the 29th of March next, about eleven at night, of a raging fever." Swift answered himself, and also published in due time "The Accomplishment of the first of Mr. Bickerstaff's Predictions : being an account of the death of Mr. Partridge, the almanack-maker, upon the 29th instant." Other wits kept up the joke, and, in his next year's almanack (that for 1709), Partridge advertised that, "whereas it has been industriously given out by Isaac Bickerstaff, Esq., and others, to prevent the sale of this year's almanack, that John Partridge is dead, this may inform all his loving countrymen that he is still living, in health, and they are knaves that reported it otherwise." Steele gave additional lightness to the touch of his "Tatler," which first appeared on the 12th of April, 1709, by writing in the name of Isaac Bickerstaff, and carrying on the jest that was to his serious mind a blow dealt against prevailing superstition. Referring in his first "Tatler" to this advertisement of Partridge's, he said of it, "I have in another place, and in a paper by itself, sufficiently convinced this man that he is dead ; and if he has any shame, I do not doubt but that by this time he owns it to all his acquaintance. For though the legs and arms and whole body of that man may still appear and perform their animal functions, yet since, as I have elsewhere observed, his art is gone, the man is gone." To Steele, indeed, the truth was absolute, that a man is but what he can do.

In this spirit, then, Steele began "The Tatler," simply considering that his paper was to be published " for the use of the good people of England," and professing at the outset that he was an author writing for the public, who expected payment from the public for his work, and that he pre-

Relation of "The Tatler" to the people. ferred this course to gambling for the patronage of men in office. Having pleasantly shown the sordid spirit that underlies the mountebank's sublime professions of disinterestedness, "we have a contempt," he says, "for such paltry barterers, and have therefore all along informed the public that we intend to give them our advices for our own sakes, and are labouring to make our lucubrations come to some price in money, for our more convenient support in the service of the public. It is certain that many other schemes have been proposed to me, as a friend offered to show me in a treatise he had writ, which he called, 'The whole Art of Life; or, The Introduction to Great Men, illustrated in a Pack of Cards.' But being a novice at all manner of play, I declined the offer."

Addison took these cards, and played an honest game with them successfully. But it was only when, having laid

Addison drawn by Steele into co-operation, writes for the people, better than for patrons. "Tatler," "Spectator," "Guardian." them down for a time and bringing his sound mind and perfect humour to the aid of his friend Steele, he came with him into direct relation with the English people, that he wrote those papers in "Tatler," "Spectator," and "Guardian," wherein alone his genius abides with us, and will abide with English readers to the end. "The Tatler," "The Spectator," and "The Guardian" were, all of them, Steele's papers, begun and ended by him at his sole discretion. In these three journals Steele wrote 510 papers; Addison, 369. Swift wrote two papers, and sent about a dozen fragments. Congreve wrote one article in "The Tatler"; Pope wrote twice for "The Spectator" and eight times for "The Guardian." Addison, who was in Ireland when "The Tatler" first appeared, only guessed the authorship by an expression in an early number;

and it was not until eighty numbers had been issued, and the character of the new paper was formed and established, that Addison, on his return to London, joined the friend who, with his usual complete absence of the vanity of self-assertion, finally ascribed to the ally he dearly loved the honours of success.

It was the kind of success Steele had desired,—a widely-diffused influence for good. The "Tatlers" were penny papers published three times a week, and issued also for another halfpenny with a blank half-sheet for transmission by post, when any written scraps of the day's gossip that friend might send to friend could be included. It was through these, and the daily "Spectators" which succeeded them, that the people of England really learnt to read. The few leaves of sound reason and fancy were but a light tax on uncultivated powers of attention. Exquisite grace and true kindliness, here associated with familiar ways and common incidents of everyday life, gave many an honest man fresh sense of the best happiness that lies in common duties honestly performed, and a fresh energy, free as Christianity itself from malice : for so both Steele and Addison meant that it should be, in opposing themselves to the frivolities and small frauds on the conscience by which manliness is undermined.

There was high strife of faction, and there was real peril to the country, by a possible turn of affairs after Queen Anne's death, that another Stuart restoration, in the name of divine right of kings, would leave the rights of the people to be reconquered in civil war. The chiefs of either party were appealing to the people, and engaging all the wit they could secure to fight on their side in the war of pamphlets. Steele's heart was in the momentous issue. Both he and Addison had it in mind while they were blending their calm playfulness with all the clamour of the press. The spirit in which these friends worked, young Pope must have felt : for after Addison had helped him in his first approach to fame by giving an essay in "The Spectator" to his "Essay on Criticism," and when he was thankful for that service, the verses he contributed to "The Spectator" were "Messiah" and "The Dying Christian to his Soul." Such offerings clearly showed how Pope interpreted the labour of the essayists.

In the fens of Lincolnshire the antiquary Maurice Johnson collected his neighbours of Spalding. "Taking care," it is said, "not to alarm the country gentlemen by any premature mention of antiquities, he endeavoured at first to allure them into the more flowery paths of literature. In 1709 a few of them were brought together every post-day at the coffee-house in the Abbey Yard; and after one of the party had read aloud the last published number of 'The Tatler,' they proceeded to talk over the subject among themselves."

Even in distant Perthshire "the gentlemen met after church on Sunday to discuss the news of the week; the 'Spectators' were read as regularly as the 'Journal.'" So the political draught of bitterness came sweetened with the wisdom of good-humour. The good-humour of the essayists touched with a light and kindly hand every form of affectation, and placed everything in the light in which it would be seen by a natural and honest man. A sense of the essentials of life was assumed everywhere in the reader, who was asked only to smile charitably at its vanities. Steele looked through all shams to the natural heart of the Englishman, appealed to that, and found it easily enough, even under the disguise of the young gentleman cited in the 77th "Tatler," "so ambitious to be thought worse than he is that in his degree of understanding he sets up for a freethinker, and talks atheistically in coffee-houses all day, though every morning and evening, it can be proved upon him, he regularly at home says his prayers."

But as public events led nearer to the prospect of a Jacobite triumph that would have again brought Englishmen against each other sword to sword, there was no voice of warning more fearless than Richard Steele's. He changed "The Spectator" for "The Guardian," Steele's "Englishman." that was to be, in its plan, more free to guard the people's rights, and, standing forward more distinctly as a politician, he became member for Stockbridge. Then, when the Peace of Utrecht alarmed English patriots, Steele in a bold pamphlet on "The Crisis" expressed his dread of arbitrary power and a Jacobite succession with a boldness that cost him his seat in Parliament. For "The Guardian," which he had dropped when he felt the plan of that journal unequal to the right and full expression of his mind, Steele now took for a periodical the name of "Englishman," and under that name fought, with then unexampled abstinence from personality, against the principles upheld by Swift in "The Examiner." When the change was made, Mr. Hughes wrote on the 6th of October, 1713, to Mr. Addison a letter that begins in this way :—" Dear sir, I do not doubt but you know by this time that Mr. Steele has abruptly dropped 'The Guardian.' He has published this day a paper called 'The Englishman,' which begins with an answer to 'The Examiner,' written with great boldness and spirit, and shows that his thoughts are at present entirely on politics. Some of his friends are in pain about him, and are concerned that a paper should be discontinued which might have been generally entertaining without engaging in party matters." Mr. Hughes did not understand their friend, who, as a man of letters, in his lightest vein had never cared to be no more than "generally entertaining." Addison knew him. Steele and Addison first became friends, no doubt, through likeness of humour in diversity of character that gave to each a quality admired, but not possessed, by his companion. But the close and lasting confidence came of their common allegiance to the highest principle of action. And it may well be that Addison, with all his sense of prudence, never had a more lively honour for Steele's manliness than when he replied to the regrets of Mr. Hughes, while civilly declining the proposal to join him in an attempt to revive "The Guardian" in some other form. "In the meantime I should be glad if you would set such a project on foot, for I know nobody else capable of succeeding in it, and turning it to the good of mankind, since my friend has laid it down. I am in a thousand troubles for poor Dick, and wish that his zeal for the public may not be ruinous to himself; but he has sent me word that he is determined to go on, and that any advice I may give him in this particular will have no weight with him."

As I am here only rapidly sketching a main feature of that period of popular influence in English literature which owes so much of its health to the sound minds of Steele and Addison, I ought not perhaps now to touch upon the grounds assigned by some subsequent writers for the misplaced pity of so wholesome and true a man as Richard Steele. I will be content therefore to name them. Publication of his most sacred and private notes has proved that after marriage he remained the faithful and devoted lover of his wife, and with an exquisite gentleness bore every impatient word of hers, while yielding to every caprice that did not clash with his own liberal sense of honour. Also, he was a bad party man, who would sacrifice at any time his friends or himself to an independent sense of duty. "Principles are out of the case," said Swift; "we dispute wholly about persons." To which Steele answered, "The dispute is not about persons, but about things and causes." And so, in his steady pursuit of abstract right, he lost places that were given him, missed places that he might have had, and was, if worldly success be the aim of public life, an utterly imprudent politician. Finally and especially, he did

not become rich. Liberal always of his own to others, he
was sometimes without a guinea, and sometimes in debt.
Of which it is enough to say that he defrauded no man,
that when he followed his Prue to the grave he was in no
man's debt, though he left all his countrymen his debtors,
and that he left untouched their mother's fortune to his two
surviving children.

The influence of French literary taste on Addison had
been overcome by his own nature and the influence of
Steele, except in as far as it gave a scholarly   Pope.
accuracy and a slight dash of the Latin manner
to his English. The French influence on Pope was modified
also by his shrewd native sense. Pope sought reputation.
As a Roman Catholic he was excluded from place, and,
reputation being more to him than money, he refused a
pension. Depending on his wit to win for him a place
among their poets from the English people, as far as the
limited education of the public in his day could bring them
into relation with him he wrote under popular influence.
Faithful, therefore, to good natural sense, he in his own
way wrote as an Englishman for England, and his fame
survives. Subject and treatment differing, there is the same
war against all that is not what it pretends to be in
" Dunciad " and " Tatler."

Through " Tatler " and "Spectator" the main stream of
English literature ran in Queen Anne's reign. In the reign
of George I. the representative books were   Development
" Robinson Crusoe" and "Gulliver's Travels."   of prose
fiction—
The reading public was enlarged. From the   " Robinson
little tales and apologues interspersed by Steele   Crusoe" and
"Gulliver."
and Addison among their essays, it could pass to longer
tales if there were any it could read ; but it could not read
" Parthenissa" or the translated romances of Madame
Scudéry. No, nor, with all its appreciation of morality,
could it read Dr. Nathanael Ingelo's "Bentivoglio and

H

Urania," a book designed to turn to reasonable account one of "the impertinences of mankind, viz. the Writing and Reading of Romances," by making allegorical characters of body, soul, and their faculties, and so reviving the old stage moralities in the ten thousand times more tedious form of a long highflown romance of the school of the Précieuses. Aphra Behn had improved upon the French model in her novelets, but they had not substance of mind to contend with the imposing seriousness of " Polexander " and the " Grand Cyrus." Books of this class, therefore, were still alive to be laughed at by Steele, when in "The Tender Husband" he introduces the fair Biddy Pipkin, with her mind fed upon such meat. *She* : " I don't know how to own it, but they have called me Bridget. *He :* Bridget ? *She :* Bridget. *He :* Bridget ? *She :* Spare my confusion, I beseech you, sir ; and if you have occasion to mention me, let it be by Parthenissa, for that's the name I have assumed ever since I came to years of discretion." Alack-a-day, little Bridget ! *She :* " Alas, sir, what can be expected from an innocent virgin, that has been immured almost one-and-twenty years from the conversation of mankind, under the care of an Urganda of an aunt. *He :* Bless me, madam, how you have been abused ! Many a lady before your age has had a hundred lances broke in her service, and as many dragons cut to pieces in honour of her. *She* (aside) : Oh, the charming man ! *He* (who is playing on her weakness) : Do you believe that Pamela was one-and-twenty before she knew Musidorus ? "

In " Robinson Crusoe " Defoe gave the people such a story as they could enjoy. That tale begins the history of modern English fiction, as distinctly as Defoe's " Review " began the history of that English journalism which is the familiar expression of immediate relations between English writers and the main body of English readers. Four years earlier Defoe had parted from the political essay, and

"Robinson Crusoe" was now the first of a series of tales
that applied fancy in the most direct way to the acts and
thoughts of daily natural life. This was a wholesome reaction from the old mockery of high flown romance. It is
true that the play of Defoe's fancy was too apt at an exact
suggestion of the real to represent much that lay also within
the wide province of fiction. But there followed, four years
after "Robinson Crusoe," Swift's marvellous outpouring of
his own sense of life in the story of "Gulliver's Travels," a
satire that carries even the child's fancy captive, and that
would not win its way with children as it does if Swift had
not here, as everywhere, worked with a warm heart, ill-con-
cealed under his scornful wit.

Nevertheless, Parthenissa and Pamela and all their tribe
maintained their ground, and still, as in Steele's earlier
day, Lettice, the waiting-maid, wept as she read   <small>Richardson's</small>
by her small candle the piteous tales. "Well,   <small>"Pamela."</small>
in all these distresses and misfortunes, the faithful Argalus
was renown'd all over the plains of Arca—Arca—Arcadia—
for his loyal and true affection to his charming paramour,
Parthenia. Blessings on his heart for it! there's no such
suitors nowadays." Here Lettice weeps. But worthy,
well-meaning, ingenious Mr. Richardson, now in the reign
of George II., means to provide both Lettice and her
mistress with more honest fare. He will take that romantic
name of Pamela, will give it to a modern servant-maid, and
show for the instruction of all young ladies in something
better than romance morals, how virtuously this humble girl
of the people can resist the blandishments of her master,
and how she can be saved miraculously from all his base
plots, though certainly it is all to the end that she may have
the reward of being made a fine lady as the rascal's honest
wife. Much of the literary purpose of the novelist had been
attained far better by Defoe, but the purpose attested the
strength of the growing popular influence upon literature.

H 2

The great fault of Pamela was that, with large pretension, and especially the affectation of superior morality paraded on the title-page, and in a fine preliminary flourish, Richardson in fact exhibited only a virtue acting from low motives, under conditions more suggestive than even the old romances had been of immodest thoughts.

The true merit of "Pamela" was that it provoked Fielding, who had till then found for his sense of life and manners an imperfect expression on the stage, to begin, as Fielding. a caricature of that virtuous servant-maid Pamela, the tale of the virtuous serving-man "Joseph Andrews," which soon grew under his hand into something freer and nobler than a caricature. It appeared as his first novel, prefaced with the sound doctrine that was his literary creed, that affectation, untruth, is the only just mark for the satirist. Six years later Richardson placed himself above ridicule by his "Clarissa Harlowe"; and then, in the year following, 1749, Fielding published his "Tom Jones," assuredly the best of English novels, and a work perfect as one of Shakespeare's; as perfect in construction, and as perfect in its sense of life and character.

It may be a small matter to find good construction in "Tom Jones." a work of genius, if the author has failed in the constructor's very first requisite, the choice of a good, durable building material. A whipped syllabub may be as perfect in construction as the Parthenon, and there are doubtless people of certain taste who would prefer the syllabub. A carpenter building a pigsty may— if our criticism be confined to these particulars—be found to construct a work more perfect than St. Peter's. So there are novels and again novels. No critic has over praised the skilful construction of the story of "Tom Jones"; but the durability of the work depends on something even of more moment than its construction,—upon the imperishable character of its material, and on the security with which its foundations are laid deep in the true hearts of men.

Fielding's first novel was provoked by an affectation ; and it was prefaced with a distinct explanation of his own "idea of romance." In the first pages of his first novel he taught that "the only source of the true ridiculous is affectation." His jest was against insincerity in all its lighter forms ; his power was against untruth. In all his noveis, and in "Tom Jones" most conspicuously, a generous and penetrating mind familiar with the ways of men dealt mercifully with all honest infirmities, sympathised with human goodness, and reserved its laughter or its scorn only for what was insincere. In "Tom Jones," a work was planned upon the ample scale to which readers had become accustomed. There was room for a wide view of life. The scene was divided fairly between country and town. The story was built out of the eternal truths of human nature, and was exquisitely polished on its surface with a delicate and genial humour that suggested rather than preached censure on the follies of society in England, not unmixed with the directest Christian condemnation against crime.

The very soul of the book enters into the construction of "Tom Jones." The picture of a good man, coloured by Fielding with some of the warmth of living friendship, is presented at once in Squire Allworthy ; and there is a deep seriousness in the manner of presenting him on a May morning, walking upon the terrace before his mansion with a wide prospect around him, planning a generous action, when "in the full blaze of his majesty up rose the sun, than which one object alone in this lower creation could be more glorious, and that Mr. Allworthy himself presented—a human being replete with benevolence, meditating in what manner he might render himself most acceptable to his Creator, by doing most good to His creatures."

The two boys bred by Allworthy, Tom Jones and Blifil,

about whom the whole story revolves, are as the two poles of Fielding's mimic world. One of them is everybody's friend but his own; the other nobody's friend but his own. One is possessed of natural goodness, with all generous impulses, but with instincts, as we are once or twice distinctly reminded, wanting the control of prudence and religion. He lies open to frequent heavy blame, and yet more frequent misconstruction; yet we have faith in him because he is true, his faults are open, his affections warm. We know that time and love will make a noble man of him. The other conceals treachery under a show of righteousness and justice. His fair outside of religion and morality, the readiness with which he gives an honest colouring to all appearances, are represented wholly without caricature. His ill deeds are secret, his affections cold, and he is base to us by reason of his falsehood. Let us in mature life read the book afresh, and while we come from the work with the old admiration of the sterling English in which it is written, and of the keen but generous insight into human character that animates every page, we probably shall find that we have strengthened greatly our sense of its brave morality. It may surprise a critic who tastes evil in the scenes of incontinence which the manners of his age permitted Fielding to include among his pictures of the life about him, to be told that they were not presented as jests by their author. Fielding differs in this, as in many things, essentially from Smollett, that in his novels he has never used an unclean image for its own sake as provocative of mirth in ruder minds. In Fielding's page evil is evil. In "Tom Jones" Allworthy delivers no mock exhortations; whenever Jones falls into incontinence the purity of Sophia follows next upon the scene, a higher happiness is lost, and his true love is removed farther from his reach. And at last the youth is made to assent to Sophia, when she replies, very gravely, upon his pleading of the grossness of his

sex, the delicacy of hers, and the absence of love in amour :
" I will never marry a man who shall not learn refinement
enough to be as incapable as I am myself of making such a
distinction."

Again, what can be more determined than the purpose
underlying the invention of the theologian and the philo-
sopher Thwackum and Square, as tutors of Jones and
Blifil.

In the account given by Fielding himself of the requisite
qualities of the man who is " to invent good stories and tell
them well," we find named after genius and study "a quick
and sagacious penetration into the true essence of all the
objects of our contemplation," and, of course, conversation
with men. "Nor," he adds, "will all the qualities I have
hitherto given my historian avail him, unless he have what
is generally meant by a good heart, and be capable of
feeling."

I can only express here by a few hints the perfectness of
mind and body in this book. The episodes are as true
limbs of it. It is not merely variety that they supply. It
is completeness. In evidence of this it may be quite sufficient to refer to the one episode really open to a moment's
doubt. It is true that the Man of the Hill's story is not a
part of the direct mechanism of the plot ; but it is equally
true that it is a vital part of the whole epic history. Only
by episode could there have been interpolated between
Jones's generous and Blifil's ungenerous principle of intercourse with other men, the picture of one who has wholly
withdrawn himself from human intercourse, and dares to
solve the question of life's duties by looking from afar with
scorn upon his fellows. He had a false lover, a false
friend. "What better, my good sir," asks Jones, "could
you expect in love derived from the stews, or in friendship
first produced and nourished at the gaming-table?" And
the brave manly lesson of life taught by the whole work

closes an episode in the directest harmony with the inventor's main design.

It is a minor excellence that this part of the work has
been contrived also to supply to the large study of English
life those chapters, excluded from the main action of the
tale by the peculiar education and the characters of Jones
and Blifil, which paint the follies of youth at the university
and the life of the gambler. Partridge once breaks upon
the narrative of the Man of the Hill with a characteristic
story of his own, in which Fielding commands wise reflection on the undefended state of criminals tried for their
lives. We pass, however, from the greater to the less in
touching on these things, although they show how intimate
was here the relation of the English writer to the English
people.

The lesser critics in polite society, who applied not their
own minds, nor the minds of better thinkers, but the mere
words of those better thinkers twisted and crushed
into a critical jargon, to the estimate of works
of intellect, still held in a degenerate way to the
classicism of Paris. They decreed natural pictures of life,
and plain English, "low." Fielding was in their eyes
"low," and several times in "Tom Jones" the great
novelist takes in mockery this word out of their mouths.
Goldsmith, too, born twenty-one years later than Fielding,
we find harping on the word in playful, kindly scorn. But,
when we look back to Goldsmith, at his side we see the
figure of that elder friend, but two years younger
than Fielding—the strong, tender-hearted Samuel
Johnson. How sound a mind he kept within a body by
whose physical infirmities he should have been made
insane! Johnson was ten years old in the year of Addison's death, and twenty years old in the year of the death
of Steele. Of English writers none fought more sturdily
and honestly than he in the war of intellectual independ-

ence. He began literary life in London as what printer Bowyer called "an author of the lower class, one of those who are paid by the sheet," could subsist upon fourpence halfpenny a day, ate only what he earned. Conquering the resistance of the adverse world and of his own adverse bodily state, he fought the hard uphill fight for himself, for others with him, and for all the writers who came after him, and made himself, until his death in 1784, the worthy central figure in the literature of his country. His intellect alone would not have given him, ungainly man as he was, this rank in a day when the profession of letters was so little honoured that some such apology as the "accidental elopement of a composition" was thought necessary to excuse a gentleman for coming into print. In Johnson's days we find even the poet Gray, after his "Elegy in a Country Churchyard," much handed about over polite tea-tables, had fallen into the hands of an editor who vowed that he would print it, writing of that piece of true literature to his friend Walpole, "I have but one bad way left to escape the honour they would inflict upon me, and therefore am obliged to desire you would make Dodsley print it immediately (which may be done in less than a week's time), from your copy, but without my name;" presently suggesting also, "If he would add a line or two to say it came into his hands by accident, I should like it better." Walpole wrote an advertisement to the effect that accident only brought the poem before the public, although an apology was unnecessary to any but the author. On which Gray wrote, "I thank you for your advertisement, which saves my honour."

It was in the honour of Samuel Johnson to be absolutely free from this false pride. His wit was rooted in the highest sense of duty, and complete sincerity of thought and word. There was a true English soul in Johnson's intellect. Milton himself did not more formally dedicate his powers to the service of his great taskmaster than Johnson, who prayed for a blessing on his work when he sat down to it, habitually, but never formally, as many will pray for a blessing on their roast meat who would think it wrong, because unusual, to ask a grace upon their words. It is not the form that is here dwelt upon. Men may pray without ceasing who never kneel, and never write or whisper formal words of prayer. Johnson prayed with his heart, and with the faithful pen through which he spoke his heart, and was in all as simply true as when he pitifully carried home on his back the unhappy prostitute whom he found lying exhausted in the streets. Johnson's strength with his countrymen lay in that inner worth to which Smollett's frank eyes at once penetrated. "This," he says, "was a very grave personage, whom at some distance I took for one of the most reserved and even disagreeable figures I had seen ; but, as he approached, his appearance improved, and, when I could distinguish him thoroughly, I perceived that, in spite of the severity of his brow, he had one of the most good-natured countenances that could be imagined."

That Johnson, while drawing closer the relations between English writers and the English people, gave by his example a new life to the critical taste for sonorous Latin words not too much soiled by "low" associations, every one knows. The number of syllables in a word matters, however, infinitely less than its exact fitness to the measure of the thought it should express ; and by right of its conscientious precision Johnson's style will retain much of its power through all changes of fashion. "It would be terrible, sir," said Boswell, at Harwich, when he and Johnson were waiting for the boat to Helveotsluys that was to take young Boswell to Utrecht, "it would be terrible if you should not find a speedy opportunity of returning to London, and be confined in so dull a place." *Johnson.—*

"Don't, sir, accustom yourself to use big words for little matters. It would not be *terrible*, though I *were* to be detained some time here." Upon which passage Mr. Croker gave us his own measure as a critic, thus :—"This advice comes drolly from a writer who makes a young lady talk of 'the *cosmetic discipline*,' 'a regular *lustration* with bean-flower-water, and the use of a pomade to *discuss* pimples and clear *discoloration*' ('Rambler,' No. 130); while a young gentleman tells us of 'the *flaccid* sides of a football having swelled into stiffness and extension.'" The critic here makes the too common mistake of confounding letter with spirit. Johnson looked at the honesty of words, and Croker at the number of their syllables. The words here quoted by Croker against Johnson are, as to their sense, like all the words he used, exactly of the same size as the thought they were used to express. Bliss, although four syllables shorter, was to Johnson's mind a bigger word than satisfaction; and if his thought answered to the less word, an honest sense of literature, and of that which is the life of literature, kept his tongue and pen clear of the other. Mechanically speaking, he used big words; intellectually and morally, no English is plainer and more natural than Dr. Johnson's; and it is by the spirit rather than the letter that a writer lives.

Goethe tells us that when, aged twenty-five (and in the year of Goldsmith's death), he was a law-student at Strasburg, Herder read to him a translation of the "Vicar of Wakefield." More than half a century after Goldsmith's death, when the German poet was by many regarded as the patriarch of contemporary European literature, he ascribed, in a letter to his friend Zelter, the best influence over his mind to the spirit of that wise and wholesome story as it was made known to him "just at the critical moment of mental development." In the "Sorrows of Werther," written in the same year, 1774,

Goldsmith's influence on Goethe.

we have the record of this critical moment; and to the tone of melancholy which had deepened upon English literature Goethe partly ascribes the gathering of the clouds that Goldsmith's novel had helped to dispel.

There are moral epochs, Goethe said, under whose influence, each in his own generation, the sensitive youth falls; but the spirits of the German youth, when he himself was young, would not have tended so decidedly as they did to gloomy thought had there not been incitement from without. This came, he wrote (in Book 13 of "Aus Meinem Leben"), "through the English literature, especially its poetry, whose best features are touched with an earnest melancholy that becomes transferred to all who study it." It was in Goethe's humour then to fasten on the melancholy side of any earnest feeling. But it is also in part true that the French influence upon our literature, in the decay of merely fashionable patronage, and before there were yet established sound relations between writers and the people, had given to metrical utterance of the religious English mind a turn for didactic gloom, of which Young's "Night Thoughts" may be taken as the type. The whole literature of such a people as the English, if not of any people, must be more or less didactic; and the degree to which the inner earnestness is masked by manner of expression indicates only the wit and temper of the writer and his time. The chief causes of the gloom cast over English literature during the greater part of the eighteenth century are to be found, however, in social conditions of which we have not now to speak.

Relations between English and German literature.

In our literature following the Restoration, cultivation of Boileau's doctrine of " good sense," and gradual extension of the reading circle, helped greatly to the development of a prose literature. Fielding, in his prose novels, exercised the creative force of genius with the perfection of good sense. Goldsmith, who had a reasoning imagination, wrote the graceful and clear prose of a true poet. At the same time, aiming only at perfect clearness in expression of historical and social facts, we have such men as David Hume, but three or four years younger than Fielding, and Robertson seven, and Adam Smith five years older than Goldsmith, whom both long survived. The prose mind, dealing with simple truth, found also its way into verse, uprooting in many directions the luxuriant wild flowers of fancy, and clipping thought in the trim borders of a simply dull, didactic garden. Whole volumes of English poetry then recent could, said Goethe, be compressed into a commentary on this miserable impression of the end of man :—

> " Then Old Age and Experience, hand in hand,
> Lead him to Death, and make him understand,
> After a search so painful and so long,
> That all his life he has been in the wrong."

All that is cheerful in our literature was ascribed by Goethe to an earlier epoch ; and even here he observes that Shakespeare gave way to melancholy in his soliloquies, and that Milton could not rise, in L'Allegro, to a very moderate degree of cheerfulness until he had by a strong effort shaken off and banished his "loathed melancholy." So it is, thought Goethe, that, in the later time, even the cheerful Goldsmith sinks, as Gray does in the "Country Church-yard," into elegiac sensibility when he paints Paradise Lost in his "Deserted Village." Goethe felt strongly those points in our literature to which his own mind was most sensitive ; but he was not the only German student of the English muse. The feebler development of German literature has at several periods received a strong and usually healthy influence from the vigour of the kindred race in England that thrives under conditions very favourable to free and emphatic speech. The influence of French critical taste had been as strong in Germany as in England ; but it

had there taken a weak form. Polite personages at the
German Courts seized bodily on the French language, and
spoke it. From about the date of our Restoration till the
time when Dr. Johnson had possession of the English
public the French influence was so strong also in Germany that German writers have called this period "the
à-la-mode age." But the same tyranny of style worked in
each Germanic people towards similar results. England
took the lead. The French taste was for clearness, and a
literalness that in one form sought even to divest religion of
its sacred mystery. In Germany, as in England, the
tendency was to humanise this realism to the utmost. In
this direction, Defoe's "Robinson Crusoe" represented so delightful a success, that, while it
was reprinted and pirated at home, in Germany
it was not merely translated, it had also more than forty
imitators. There were two Westphalian Robinsons; there
was a Saxon, a Silesian, a Franconian, a Bohemian, a Jewish
Robinson, with a European Robinsonetta; there were
Robunse and Robinschen, Robinsonetta, the Moral Robinson, the Medical Robinson, the Reasoning Robinson, and
the Invisible Robinson. Such books indeed, under the
name of Robinsonades, form a distinct class in German
literary history.

Germany fastens upon "Robinson Crusoe."

Direct battle was given at the same time to the French
critical school in Germany, whereof the chief lawgiver was
Johann Christian Gottsched—whose wife translated French plays and Pope's "Rape of the
Lock"—by a party of writers who argued for
depth of feeling, truth of thought, as above the
restraints of mere formalism. Ranging themselves behind
their leader, Johann Jacob Bodmer, of Zurich, these men
raised the name of Milton for their battle-cry. For the ten
years before 1740 Gottsched, at Leipzig, a scorner of
Milton, dictated laws of taste to Germany. He did some

The spirit of Milton is abroad. Gottsched and Bodmer.

service by maintaining much that was most wholesome in the fastidiousness of French critical rule ; but he especially provoked the war in which he fell, by strong and repeated attacks on the poetry of Milton in the last three years of his reign. In 1740 Bodmer replied boldly with an essay "On the Wonderful in Poetry," and then the war began. It was not, however, until twelve years afterwards that Bodmer produced, with commentaries, his German prose translation of "Paradise Lost." In all such literary battles, victory must be in the long run on the side of full and genuine expression. Bodmer fought no battle for mere imitation of the English. He laid open to his countrymen their own old national literature ; he was the first editor of the Nibelungenlied, and of the songs of the Minnesänger. He sought only the burning of the French peruke that had been set upon the German head.

Klopstock was the foremost of young German writers who, as a type of honour to sublimest earnestness, cherished the fame of Milton. Coleridge called him "a very German Milton." The phrase is true, and Klopstock. may be taken as a compliment. In all his writings Klopstock appears as a true son of his native soil, a Christian, and a German patriot.

While this strife gave vigour to a few, there were many who shared the natural reaction of mind that was strong in France itself, and was spreading in England, from a cold, critical tone that spent itself much upon questions of style, and discouraged passionate expression of the feelings. That temper of The revolt against Despotism in Life or Literature. literature left the heart dissatisfied, and even took from the sense of religion too much of the warmth that lively exercise maintains. The chilled mind showed its gloomy discontent. Then Dr. Edward Young, singing immortal man, harped upon death, and lamentably peered through "darkness aiding intellectual light." When ancient traditions of the

Gael seized on a mind thus pining, Fionn himself became a sign of the new sickness, and the ghost of Fingal stalked through the mist of the hills protesting against periwigs. While Bodmer—who delighted also in Sir Roger de Coverley, and had himself written a sort of German "Spectator"—upheld Milton in South Germany, there was in North Germany Ebert, at Hamburg, who translated the "Night Thoughts" and "Ossian," besides the "Pamela" and "Sir Charles Grandison" of our Richardson, who was dear also to Rousseau.

The French influence of which we have been speaking was not that of France as a nation, but of France as expressed by the French Court of Louis XIV. The reaction from it was universal, and nowhere more violent in certain directions than in France itself. Klopstock, in his old age warm for human liberty, received in 1792 the diploma of citizen from the French National Assembly, and a like compliment was paid to the patriotism of Gilles, otherwise Schiller. These were both men to shrink from the last excesses of the great French Revolution; but the stir that led to it, of independent human energies shaking themselves, as they thought, free from the claws of despotism, was felt alike in Germany and France. And out of all its striving to be true came now the greatness of the German literature

The revolt most violent in France.

Goethe, the chief, although nearly the youngest, of the disciples of Bodmer, influenced deeply by the literature of this country, became by the force of his rare genius himself an influence. In his earliest notable work, "Goetz von Berlichingen," in spite of all critical dramatic canons taking Shakespeare for his guide, he dealt honestly and freely, but throughout as a true German, with a picture of old German national life. His bent was then, however, for the way of English melancholy, that enjoyed the pinch of a mind folded back upon itself. Always true to

Goethe.

his own experiences of life and his own manner of thought, he worked out the megrims of his youth in "Werther," and, to the last, struggled boldly and unsuccessfully in his writings with the problems of man's inner life.

Goethe's mind was fixed on the life of the individual—Schiller's on that of the State. His "Robbers," grappling wildly with the question of social rights; his Republican tragedy of "Fiesco;" his exaltation, *Schiller.* in "Kabale und Liebe," of the German citizen world over the Court life steeped in French frivolity and vice; the glow of humanity in Marquis Posa, planted face to face with Spanish despotism; the great human struggle in his "Wallenstein;" his choice of such subjects for dramatic handling as "Tell" and the "Maid of Orleans;"—all show how distinctly Schiller dwelt upon the rights of man as one of a community, while Goethe saw him as an individual, and dreamed or reasoned out the problem of his duties and his powers.

Of all the Germans, Goethe and those more formal thinkers who attempted to dissect the inner life of man had most influence upon the literature of England. The great German poet reflected back to us, intensified, the light, if it was light, he had received from us. In seizing upon his humour *Limits of the German influence on English Literature.* we caught, as it were, our own ball in the rebound. But there was a transmuting power where it struck; it went from us lead, and came back to us silver.

Edward Young was transmuted into William Wordsworth. What Klopstock and Kant at first hoped from the French Revolutionists, whose later friendship to himself Klopstock repelled with an abhorrent palinode— what seemed hope in them even to Alfieri, until, witness of their excesses, victim of their greed, he cursed them bitterly—stirred also in the young hearts of our own Wordsworth, Coleridge, and Southey. *Wordsworth, Coleridge, and Southey.*

I

How strongly Wordsworth himself felt we read in his
" Prelude." The spirit of many an earnest poet in that
time rises in his " Excursion " from the melancholy recollections of the solitary :—

> " Then my soul
> Turned inward, to examine of what stuff
> Time's fetters are composed ; and life was put
> To inquisition, long and profitless.
> By pain of heart, now checked and now impelled,
> The intellectual power, through words and things,
> Went sounding on, a dim and perilous way.
>
> .   .   .   .
>
> From that abstraction I was roused,—and how ?"

By the fall of the Bastile, when—

> " From the wreck
> A golden palace rose, or seemed to rise,
> The appointed seat of equitable law
> And mild paternal sway. The potent shock
> I felt : the transformation I perceived,
> As marvellously seized as in that moment
> When, from the blind mist issuing, I beheld
> Glory—beyond all glory ever seen,
> Confusion infinite of heaven and earth,
> Dazzling the soul. Meanwhile, prophetic harps
> In every grove were ringing, ' War shall cease ;
> Did ye not hear that conquest is abjured ?
> Bring garlands, bring forth choicest flowers, to deck
> The tree of Liberty.' My heart rebounded ;
> My melancholy voice the chorus joined."

Wordsworth went over to Paris, and spent a year between Paris, Orleans, and Blois. Much was said in
England on that question of the rights of man in a community, then raised with so much earnestness in France
and Germany. Coleridge and Southey were at the age of
twenty-three happy in the daydream of a life of patriarchal
innocence by the bank of the Susquehanna. Southey's verse

in those days fastened upon Joan of Arc ; and at the age of eight-and-twenty, not long after his visit to North Germany in company with Wordsworth, when the young English poet paid his visit to Klopstock, Coleridge was the translator of Schiller's "Wallenstein." The spirit of German literature attracted many to its study, and it became a concurrent influence in the literature of England. So, indeed, it has to this day continued ; but its influence has at no time been dominant.

Never perhaps was there a writer less under foreign influences than Sir Walter Scott. He had begun his career of literature in 1796, at the age of five-and-twenty, as a translator of Bürger's "Lenora" Walter Scott. and "Wild Huntsman" ; two years afterwards he translated Goethe's drama of old knightly romance, "Goetz von Ber-lichingen" ; but his pleasure in the union of strong feeling with simplicity, that characterises all good ballads and romances, was not to be satisfied alone with the romantic element in modern German literature. He went back to the Border Minstrelsy of his own country, and published his three volumes of it, which a critic said contained "the elements of a hundred historical romances." Then he grasped hands with Thomas of Ercildoune, who in the thirteenth century, was carried to her own land by the Queen of Faerie, and lived with her for three whole years. From Thomas the Rymer, Scott at once, in 1805, passed to his own bright imagining of a "Lay of the Last Minstrel," that was the first of half-a-dozen modern gleeman's songs. Speech from the heart, and freedom from conventional restraints, of which men had grown weary, these songs had to recommend them. There was then refreshment in the simple, animated flow of story, whereof every turn was warmly felt and expressed in the light, variable ballad metre. The metre itself breathed joyous defiance of the literary formalism that had delighted in trim evenness of couplet

I 2

and nice balance of antithesis.   Here were bold borderers
who never wore peruke, and could have ridden to the field
with Goetz of the Iron Hand himself :—

> " They quitted not their harness bright,
>   Neither by day, nor yet by night :
>   They lay down to rest
>   With corslet laced,
>   Pillowed on buckler cold and hard ;
>   They carved at the meal
>   With gloves of steel,
> And they drank the red wine through the helmet barred."

When these metrical tales lost influence before the growing
fame of Byron, Scott broke with rhyme, and began, in 1814,
to pour out his prose romances.   At least one, often two, in
in a year, and in one year three, appeared for the next
seventeen years without intermission, except in the single
year 1830.   Then the occasional historical and other work
for which Scott found time, in addition to that spent on
his romance-writing, had for once the whole year to itself,
and he produced only two dramas, the Letters on De-
monology, the fourth series of the " Tales of a Grandfather,"
and the second volume of the " History of Scotland."   Nowhere in print was Scott so much a poet as in the earlier of
his romances.   His bright, cheerful fancy, his quick humour,
his honest warmth of feeling, that aroused every healthy
emotion without stirring a passion, exercised, in these incessantly recurring novels, an influence as gradual, as sure,
and as well fitted to its time, as that which had been
exercised by Steele and Addison in constantly recurring
numbers of their " Tatler " and " Spectator."   There was a
wide general public now able to fasten upon entertaining
volumes.   Scott widened it, and purified its taste.   By
Fenimore Cooper, the best of his imitators, we have the
former strains caught up in a recurrence of the restless

dream of an escape from civilisation to imagined virtues of
the undrilled savage in his state of nature. In Scott there
is no form whatever of romantic discontent. His world
was the same world of genial sympathies in which, indi-
vidually at least, we may all live if we will, and do live if
we know it. He enjoyed the real, and sported with the
picturesque. As he felt he wrote, frankly and rapidly.
His kindly Toryism was a wholesome influence. The Jacob-
ites, so real to Defoe, amused the public now as the
material of pleasant dreams ; and the sunlight of Scott's
fancy glistened upon rippling waters where the storm had
menaced wreck.

Scott's novels were for seventeen years as so many
parts of a great influential family periodical, fairly punctual
to its half-yearly appearance. But a true jour-   Develop-
nalism was then being developed into adequate   ment of
expression of the English mind. To Newbery's   journalism.
" Public Ledger," started in 1760, Goldsmith contributed
his "Citizen of the World." In 1763 Wilkes, in the
"North Briton," honestly printed all the letters in the names
of persons commented upon, and suffered for his comments in No. 45 on the prorogation Speech after an un-
popular peace. Of the Letters of Junius, in the "Public
Advertiser," the first appeared in April, 1767, the last in
January, 1772, and these set an example of very bold
political newspaper criticism. In trials that arose out of
these letters Lord Mansfield sought in vain to deny to the
jury the right of deciding what was libel, and what not, by
confining its function to the question of publication. This
question was not settled properly until the passing of Mr.
Fox's Libel Bill in 1792. In 1769 the "Morning Chronicle"
was first brought out by William Woodfall, who was
especially the ear of England in the House of Commons.
Victualled with a hard-boiled egg, he could sit out the
longest debate, and next day write out for his paper, which

he both printed and edited, the pith of all that he had heard. In 1772 appeared the " Morning Post," of which the editor, in 1780, seceded to found a new paper, the " Morning Herald." At this date there were no weekly papers.

On the 13th of January, 1785, appeared a paper in four pages, " The Daily Universal Register," afterwards published, on the 1st of January, 1788, under the new name of " The Times," which, as its proprietor announced, " being a monosyllable, bids defiance to corruptors and mutilators of the language." The " Morning Advertiser " first appeared in 1794; and in the year following there were in London fourteen daily papers, ten published three times a week, two twice a week, and twelve weekly; while the distribution of newspapers throughout the country had been increased sixfold by the introduction of mail-coaches.

In 1797 Canning and his friends started, as a weekly paper, the " Anti-Jacobin," which had a brilliant career of eight months, with William Gifford, afterwards editor of the " Quarterly Review," for manager. These journals had learnt to speak boldly upon public questions, in the face of distinct peril to their writers. In the first year of " The Times," its proprietor was sentenced to fine, imprisonment, and pillory for speaking his mind out upon the Duke of York. In the year following he was again prosecuted. The English journalists were, in fact, like the poets, bent upon full natural utterance, and upon the breaking down of all undue restraints. They were all more or less in earnest, and by their variety of temper and opinion represented then, as now, though less completely, the various interests and humours that contribute their tones to the common voice.

To such continual discussion there was added the new element of a representation of the deliberate thought of the most cultivated class upon all public questions,

whether of politics or literature, by the establishment of
"The Edinburgh Review" in the year 1802, and of the
"Quarterly Review" in 1808. Truth comes only of full
argument by honest advocates of differing opinion. Of
each Review the true use was almost doubled by the
existence of the other. Their influence has been felt
throughout the whole extent of English journalism. Partly
by their example, monthly, weekly, daily writers, and as
the reading public enlarged while more interests claimed
representation, fresh groups also of good quarterly essayists,
have been taught to aim at careful, polished criticism upon
men and books. And so our English writers in a thousand
forms win for the English people liberty and full communication of thought, not by their own separate skill, but
simply by action for and with the English people, of which
they are part.

So now, and always more and more, the strongest influence on English Writers is that of the English people
which has learnt, or is learning to read. The reading is, no doubt, much larger than the think- Writers and Readers
ing public; but there is continuous advance in reading
power. The mere habit of reading that must be acquired
by the illiterate adult, or by the child, may come more
easily by the free use of a literature level to the mind whose
powers of attention are untrained. John Foster, the essayist
on "Popular Ignorance," thought it strange that any man
whilst there lay within reach of his hand treasures of wit,
should leave them untouched, and prefer to starve upon
ephemeral and worthless books. The reason is that the
worth of a book lies in original thought, in independent
play of fancy, in a delicate truth of expression that can be
fully enjoyed only by those to whom it is not more natural
to read than, when they read, to fasten upon their author
with a habit of sustained attention. Many people do not
apply such a habit even to the common occupation of their

lives. Weighty or witty thought, without a waste word in expression of it—that is to say good literature—puts on them a greater strain than they can bear. Trivial thought, diffuse in the utterance—that is to say bad literature—asks for no power of concentrated attention in its reader, and the untaught mind will read it without strain. But as, in most cases, a course of wholesome food is the best remedy for weak digestion, appetite then growing by what it feeds on, so there is little more required to give a stomach for good literature than steady application to it. Addison said that the habit of good reading was like that of smoking. There is a repugnance to get over before the taste is acquired, and great solace and enjoyment to come of the acquisition. Men who fight through their qualms to qualify as smokers, might do as much to become readers. Our English Writers should grow in power for the utterance of all good that is in us, as the day draws near when the whole nation reads ; and they who are not children read with all their minds.

> The Earth's our ancestor : from dust the grass ;
>   From herbs the herds ; and from them both the man :
> Fixed earth feeds moving earth, until it pass,
>   Dust to the dust, and end where it began.
>
> Earth, grass, ox, man, behold our pedigree.
>   Restored to earth, the meditative brain
> Takes other shape ; perchance in bud or tree
>   Earth that was part of Newton lives again.
>
> Children of Earth, we love the parent soil :
>   But whence the touch that breeds another love ?
> In the clay lamp there lies the pregnant oil
>   That gives no light till kindled from above.
>
> God, whom our fathers reverenced, and we
>   Seek as the source of all abiding strength,
> Thou art All Truth, and Thou hast made man free
>   To question, and to find All Truth at length.

By many paths we travel, and we seek
    To serve Thee, and to tread the upward way :
When, in each track, with willing steps though weak,
    We falter, guide us, that we may not stray.

Dear Earth of England, which has clothed the minds
    Of English searchers for the way of life,
Land that we love, the happy land that binds
    Us man to man in brotherhood of strife

For truth and right, and the fulfilled design
    Of our Creator ; and thou, English Soul,
One in the strength of all the souls that shine
    In English annals and with wise control,

Seek to subdue the wrong, maintain the right,—
    Breed through all time high shapers of mankind,
Till all be good in the Creator's sight,
    And God's fair Earth be Temple of His Mind.

BOOK I.

Period of the Formation of the Language.

CHAPTER I.

THE FORMING OF THE PEOPLE.

THE Literature of a People tells its life. History records its deeds; but Literature brings to us, yet warm with their first heat, the appetites and passions, the keen intellectual debate, the higher promptings of the *Life and Growth.* soul, whose blended energies produced the substance of the record. We see some part of a man's outward life and guess his character, but do not know it as we should if we heard also the debate within, loud under outward silence, and could be spectators of each conflict for which lists are set within the soul. Such witnesses we are, through English Literature, of the life of our own country. If we find in it a high spirit of freedom, let us learn through what endeavours and to what end it is free. Liberty as an abstraction is not worth a song. It is precious only for that which it enables us to be and do. Let us bring our hearts, then, to the study which we here begin, and seek through it accord with that true soul of our country by which we may be encouraged to maintain in our own day the best work of our forefathers.

The Literature of this country has for its chief mark a religious sense of duty. It represents a people striving through successive generations to find out the right and do it, to root out the wrong, and labour ever onward for the love of God. If this be really the strong spirit of her people, to show that it is so is to tell how England won, and how alone she can expect to keep, her foremost place among the nations.

Once Europe was peopled only here and there by men who beat at the doors of nature and upon the heads of one another with sharp flints. What knowledge they struck out in many years was bettered by instruction from incoming tribes who, beginning earlier or learning faster, brought higher results of experience out of some part of the region that we now call Asia. Generation after generation came and went, and then Europe was peopled by tribes different in temper : some scattered among pastures with their flocks and herds, or gathering for fight and plunder around chiefs upon whom they depended ; others drawing together on the fields they ploughed, able to win and strong to hold the good land of the plain, in battle under chiefs whose strength depended upon them. But none can distinguish surely the forefathers of these most remote forefathers of the Celt and Teuton, in whose unlike tempers lay some of the elements from which, when generations after generations more had passed away, a Shakespeare was to come.

There was a time when writers were content to mis-apply to scientific use the spiritual teaching of the book of Genesis. The nations of the world, traced back to Noah's Ark, were classed, according to the names of Noah's three sons, Japheth, Shem, and Ham the father of Canaan, into Iapetic (first so called in comparatively recent time by Rask), Semitic (first so called by Eichhorn), and Hamite (or Chamitic) families. The descendants of Japheth were said to have peopled Europe, a great part of Asia, and perhaps America, by way of Behring's Straits. To the Semitic languages belonged

Ethnology. Origin of the English.

Hebrew, Phœnician, Syriac, and Arabic, which still retain
that common name; but the Hamite were the languages of
the African tribes. Confident in this theory, the white en-
slaver of the negro sometimes fitted it comfortably for himself to the text, "God shall enlarge Japheth, and he shall
dwell in the tents of Shem; and Canaan shall be his
servant."

Our own place among the posterity of Japheth was once
defined also by acceptance of a few convenient traditions.
Gomer, we read, was the son of Japheth, Ashkenaz the son
of Gomer, and Ashkenaz, as Verstegan has it,

"According to the opinion of sundry very learned and judicial
authors, was the father of Tuisco, or Tuiscon, the father and con-
ductor of the Germans, who, after his name, even unto this day, do in
their own tongue call themselves Tuytsh, and their country of Germany,
Tuytshland; and the Netherlands, using the D for the T, do make it
Duytsh and Duytshland. Some authors, as, namely, Sebastian Munster, do report that Tuisco was the son of Noah, by his wife Araza, or
Arezia (of others called Tythea), born after the Flood; and that,
coming with his people out of Asia into Europe, he extended his
dominion from the river Tanais even unto the Rhine. Other German
authors are of opinion that he lastly made his residence and abode on
the side of the river Rhine, at a place which unto this day retaineth the
name of Duytsh, situated right over against the city of Cullin" [Deutz,
opposite Cologne]. "But now, whether Tuisco were the son of Noah,
or the son of Ashkenaz, who was grandchild unto Japheth, although
some do move question, yet surely with more likelihood of truth we
may follow the opinion of such as affirm him to have been the great-
grandchild of Japheth, and the rather in regard of the mighty and
populous offspring foretold in Holy Writ to proceed from Japheth,
which is very agreeable unto the most populous German nation, accounting all members thereof." *

As to the nation being called by the foreigner German
or Alman, Gar, says Verstegan, or Ger, has in German the
same sense as Al; "both German and Alman then is as

---

* Verstegan's "Antiquities," ed. 1628, p. 9.

much as to say, All or wholly a Man." The Germans of different provinces bore different names, and some were Saxons, thus called, some said, from *saxum*, because of their hard and stony nature. Others said they were named from one of the three princes, Saxo, Bruno, and Friso, who came from India with troops of men to serve Alexander the Great ; these settling afterwards in Germany founded Saxony, Brunswick, and Friesland. Others said they were Sac-sons, sons of the Asiatic Sacæ. But Verstegan was sure that they were Germans who received their name from their use of a weapon peculiar to themselves, called the *seax*, shaped like a scythe, just as the Scyths are named for their good shooting from the verb *scytan* to shoot. What more was wanted? There were, indeed, people even in Verstegan's time who, not content to have the Saxons come as Germans into Britain, "will needs bring them from elsewhere to come into Germany ;" but of such requirement the good anti-quary said " This seemeth to proceed of a certain kind of delight that some people take in deriving and fetching things very far off, though most commonly upon very little ground or show of certainty."

We are in our day, nevertheless, confident of success in having by comparison of languages brought our ancestors the Germans as well as the Celts out of Asia, and made a wide-spreading family tree of what Erasmus Rask grouped as the Iapetic, but we now call the Indo-European languages. John Becan, even in the sixteenth century, had pointed out many resemblances between German and Indian words; but the track of re-search upon which students of language have been active during the present century dates only from about a hundred years ago. In 1784 Sir William Jones delivered his inau-gural discourse as first President of the Asiatic Society of Bengal, and pointed out that there was in Sanskrit, the sacred language of India, "an immense mine" of informa-

The Indo-European Family.

tion. It is the mine in which nearly every subsequent philologist has speculated heavily.

Sanskrit or Aryan has not been a spoken language in India within historical times. It was a dead language more than two thousand years ago, and there is not even a record to show how it became extinct. It is the language of the four collections of the Vêdas or sacred books of the Brahmins, which seem to be the reflection of a primitive state of society in the valley of the Indus. Sanskrit is also the language of some long heroic poems. The Ramayana, next in antiquity to the Vêdas, is a sort of epic on the conquest of Ceylon by Rama, the chief of the four sons given at once to the King Dasaratha, who lived in the ancient Oude, and who had offered in his old age a horse sacrifice for children. Rama vanquished demons with celestial weapons. Rama earned Sita his wife, by not only bending but snapping her father's strong and long bow, which it took an eight-wheeled carriage to support, and which had to be drawn by a team of eight hundred men. Rama, sentenced to fourteen years' exile by his misguided father, retired with Sita to the forests of the Deccan, where, after many adventures, he was in conflict with Ravana, King of Ceylon, the demon monarch of the earth, "at whose name heaven's armies flee." Ravana, by sorcery and stratagem seizing on Rama's wife, carried her off, through the sky, to Ceylon. Rama then strengthened himself by alliance with Sugriva, King of the Monkeys; and the Monkey Monarch's monkey-general Hanuman marched with Rama, at the head of monkey soldiers, to Cape Comorin. And then they bridged the straits, overcame the demons, slew Ravana, recovered Sita, and sent her through the ordeal of a blazing fire to ascertain whether she had preserved her purity. Rama, because his fourteen years of exile were expired, returned home, where his throne was placed at his disposal, but, knowing himself to be a divine incarnation of Vishnu, instead of sitting on it he returned to heaven. Although the incidents are wild, even translation shows that there is much natural poetry in their expression, and as much may be said of the other Sanskrit epic. This is the " Mahabhárata," by interpretation the Great Battle, poetical narration of a war between the Pandus and Curus for the right to rule in Hastinapura. Krishna, an incarnation of Vishnu, fighting on the side of the Pandus, is the hero of the poem. The epic of the Great Battle contains a hundred thousand verses, but there are incorporated in it episodes, written at different times by different authors, that are in fact separate poems— the " Bhagavat Gita," for example, which is but an exposition of theology. Other notable works have been written in Sanskrit since the Sanskrit ceased to be a living language. Such are the " Hitopadesa," a book of fables, which includes nearly all that are in the ancient collection of Bidpai; and half a dozen dramas—three by Kilidasa, " Sakóntala" the most famous of them; three by Bhababhuti, who lived in the eighth century.

To Sir William Jones, Sanskrit appeared as a mine yielding only the purest virgin gold. The Sanskrit language, he said, was " more perfect than the Greek, more copious than the Latin, and more exquisitely refined than either." The mine, once struck upon, was worked with energy. In 1784 an Asiatic Society was founded. In 1785 Dr. Charles Wilkins translated the " Bhagavat Gita," to which he added in 1787 the " Hitopadesa," and this was followed two years later by Sir William Jones's translation of the " Sakóntala." Sir William himself did not regard Sanskrit as the parent language of a widely-dispersed family. Believing that Iran or Persia was the country from which all nations first migrated, he supposed " that the language of the first Persian empire was the mother of the Sanskrit, and consequently of the Zend and Parsee, as well as of Greek, Latin, and Gothic."*

* " Asiatic Researches," vol. ii., pp. 64, 65.

Sir William Jones looked rather to the Persian than to the Sanskrit as a great parent language ; but the enthusiasm fort he study of Sanskrit spread among scholars, and in 1808, when Frederick Schlegel published his work on the " Language and Wisdom of the Indians," he was considered to have discovered a new intellectual world in giving the common name of Indo-Germanic—since altered to Indo-European—to the languages of India, Persia, Greece, Rome, Germany, that he declared to be in brotherhood. In 1816 Francis Bopp published his " Conjugations System," comparing the grammar of Sanskrit with the grammars of Greek and Latin, Persian and German ; and in 1833 appeared the first volume of Bopp's " Comparative Grammar of Sanskrit, Zend, Greek, Latin, Lithuanian, Slavonic, Gothic, and German." The " Etymological Researches" of Professor Pott, which appeared in 1833 and 1836, contributed also very greatly towards the establishment of a right system of study.

The term " Aryan " (*arya*, noble) is derived from Aryana, the supposed parent country of the people who spoke Sanskrit, and the name is considered to be derived from the word *ar*, to plough or till, showing that nation to have been agricultural. Two branches of Aryans are thought to have migrated, in some far distant prehistoric time,—one to the south-east, to civilise, and even in a great measure to people, Hindostan ; the other, north-west, to perform the same services for Europe and Western Asia. Of the history of these migrations Sanskrit itself tells us nothing; the very name Sanskrit, which means " adorned, completed, perfect," is a later creation of grammarians. There is no mention of any parent country in the Sanskrit books. The names of heroes, gods, and places are those of Hindostan, and more especially of its north-western part.

The English people, in the view we have been discussing, belongs to the Teutonic " branch " of the Gothic

J

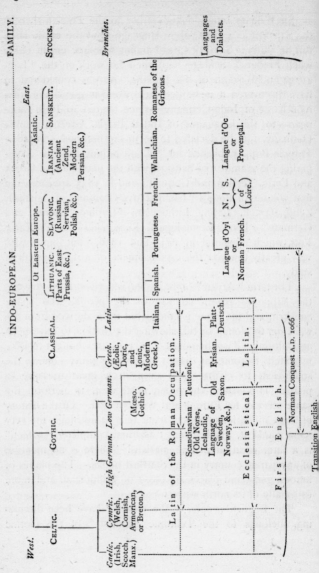

FAMILY. INDO-EUROPEAN.

STOCKS.

West. East.

CELTIC. GOTHIC. CLASSICAL. Asiatic.

BRANCHES.

Gaelic. (Irish, Scotch, Manx.)

Cymric. (Welsh, Cornish, Armorican, or Breton.)

High German. Low German. (Mœso-Gothic.) Greek. (Æolic, Doric, and Ionic, Modern Greek.) Latin.

Lithuanic. (Parts of East Prussia, &c.) Slavonic. (Russian, Servian, Polish, &c.)

Iranian (Ancient Zend, Modern Persian, &c.) Sanskrit.

Languages and Dialects.

Italian. Spanish. Portuguese. French. Wallachian. Romanese of the Grisons.

Langue d'Oyl or Norman French. N. | S. (of Loire.) Langue d'Oc or Provençal.

Scandinavian (Old Norse, Icelandic, Language of Sweden, Norway,&c.) Teutonic.

Old Frisian. Saxon. Platt-Deutsch.

Latin of the Roman Occupation.

Latin.

Ecclesiastical Latin.

First English.

Norman Conquest A.D. 1066*

Transition English.

" stock " of the Indo-European " family." Its chief con-
nexions, near and remote, will be most clearly seen when
put, as on the opposite page, in the form of a small family
tree.

Homes of our prehistoric forefathers may have been
upon the plains and in the valleys once occupied by the
Medes and Persians, and in the lands watered by those
five rivers of the Punjaub which flow into the Indus. We
may look for the first shapers of Europe westward from the
Indus to the Euphrates ; northward from the shores of the
Persian Gulf and the Arabian Sea to the Caucasus, the
Caspian and the river Oxus. But before the spreading of
the great migrations from the East there was a thinly
scattered population in Europe of a less civilised race.

Professor Huxley * holds that among the complicated
problems offered by the ethnology of the British Islands,
certain propositions rest on a secure founda- Primary,
tion, and may be taken as fixed points. There Biological Groups:
are still, as there were eighteen hundred years Fair, Dark, and Mongoloid.
ago, two types of race among us, one fair,
which he calls the Xanthochroi, and the other, which
he calls the Melanochroi, dark in hair and complexion.
Both the long and the broad skull may be found in either,
but these two stocks and one other, the Mongoloid, represent the primary biological distinction, underlying all
secondary modifications among races of the Eurasian continent. "The Mongoloids," he says, " occupy a vast triangle,
the base of which is the whole of Eastern Asia, while its
apex lies in Lapland. The Melanochroi, on the other hand,
may be represented as a broad band, stretching from Ireland
to Hindostan; while the Xanthochroic area lies between
the two, thins out, so to speak, at either end, and mingles,
at its margins, with both its neighbours." Tacitus recorded

* Critiques and Addresses, by Thomas Henry Huxley, LL.D.,
F.R.S. (1873).

J 2

the distinction between the reddish hair and large limbs of the Caledonians, and the dark complexion of the curly-haired Silurians. Language is not a sure test of race ; the language of one tribe may be taken by another. Celtic and Teutonic languages are members of the same great Aryan family, but there is evidence to show that a non-Aryan language—the Euskarian, now spoken only by the Basques—was at one time spoken over a large extent of the area occupied by the Melanochroi in Europe. The area of the language has diminished without a corresponding extirpation of the people who spoke it; so that the people of Spain must be in the present day largely Euskarian, as Cornish men are Celtic. But if there were Euskarians in Britain at the time of the Roman conquest, they had accepted, as both the dark and the fair population had accepted, Celtic speech. According to this biological view, " the name of Celtic is not properly applied to the Melanochroic or dark stocks of Europe. They are merely, so to speak, secondary Celts. The primary and aboriginal Celtic-speaking people are Xanthochroi—the typical Gauls of the ancient writers, and the close allies by blood, customs, and language of the Germans."

Antiquaries agree now in accepting the doctrine of three periods of civilisation—a Stone, a Bronze, and an Iron period, first deduced by Professor Worsaäe of Copenhagen, from an examination of the Danish barrows. From the remains in Danish bogs, it appears that the changes of climate have produced three great epochs in the vegetation of Denmark. There was first a remote epoch, when the spruce fir, now no longer a Danish tree, predominated. Upon this followed an epoch of the oak, which is now rare. After the oaks came the present period of beeches. The Danish coast is bare, but there are great beech forests in the interior. Sir Charles Lyell called attention also to the evidences of the three periods of ancient human civilisation found in the old

Stone, Bronze, and Iron Periods.

burial places by Professor Worsaäe and others, and not found in burial places only.

The earliest of these periods of civilisation is that in which men had not advanced beyond the device of tools and weapons made by chipping flint and other hard stones into axes, hammers, spear-heads. In the second period a metal easily recognised and fused, copper, hardened with a tenth part of tin into bronze, was the material chosen. In the third period civilisation had advanced to the use of iron, which is in its ores less easily distinguishable from stone, and, although more useful, less easy of extraction—an opinion which has been opposed by Dr. Percy.* Anti-quaries commonly consider that among ourselves the Teutons at their first coming used iron, but that the Celts, who preceded them, used only bronze weapons and tools. On the first coming of the Celts into Europe, says theory founded on ancient traditions and research among the tombs, they found coasts, and the patches of tolerably clear land into which men with only fire and flint to aid them could have penetrated, thinly peopled with the race or races now known as "the Stone people." Of the lan-guage of this apparently primeval population, the Basques and the Lap- or Finlanders are thought by many to be a remainder, although it is noticeable that the Basques are a freedom-loving, active, thriving race, not at all like the rem-nant of a savage people in decay. Of those most ancient occupants there was probably, as Professor Huxley argues, a disappearance of the language but not of the race. Be that as it may, man in his earliest state seems everywhere to have been ignorant of the use of metals ; hunting, fishing, fighting, labouring, by help of instruments chipped and rubbed out of stone or bone.

* For Sir Charles Lyell's views, see his " Geological Evidences of the Antiquity of Man."

How early may have been that earliest state? Underneath a fallen fir-tree of the prehistoric Danish fir epoch, The Stone Period. deep under a growth of peat that seems to be at least the accumulation of four thousand years, a flint instrument fashioned by man's hands has been found. Sir Charles Lyell calls attention also to the shell-mounds or "kitchen-middens" on all but the western coasts of the Danish Islands—masses of shells of eatable fish mixed with picked bones that, when marrow-bones, have all been broken for their marrow. Such heaps are still made on the seashore near their settlements by savage tribes of America and Australia. These ancient heaps upon the Danish shore are sometimes 1,000 feet long and nearly 200 feet wide. "Scattered all through them are flint knives, hatchets, and other instruments of stone, horn, wood, and bone, with fragments of coarse pottery, mixed with charcoal and cinders, but never any implements of bronze, still less of iron." And it is characteristic of them that the shells, although of living species, are not as they are now to be found in the brackish inland waters of the Baltic. The oyster-shells in such heaps were thrown there when the oyster attained its full size where it is now unable to live—when, therefore, the ocean had freer access, and Jutland, perhaps, was an archipelago. Cockle, mussel, and periwinkle shells are also, in these heaps, of their full natural size, as they were drawn very long since from water in which a third of that size is now the limit of their stunted growth. A few skulls, ascribed to men of this Stone age, found in the peat bogs, resemble those of the Laplanders.

To the same period belong ancient Swiss Lake-dwellings built upon piles, and Irish crannoges. Like the Pœonians of whom Herodotus tells, and like existing savages in New Guinea and elsewhere, men of the Stone period sometimes lived together for self-defence in huts built upon wooden platforms raised as islands in a lake, connected with the shore by a causeway that could be cut away in case of attack, the fish of the lake then victualling the besieged. Remains of very many such villages, with others like them of the Bronze period, have been traced in the beds of the Swiss lakes. Some of them were evidently destroyed by fire, the nature of the shelving lake-bottom having made it impossible to fix the piles and raise the wooden platform beyond reach of burning missiles.

Of the yet imperfect attempts to estimate the antiquity of these remains Sir Charles Lyell cited three,—that of M. Morlot, founded on the growth of the Delta of the Pinière, which flows into the Lake of Geneva near Villeneuve; that of M. Troyon, founded on the separation of Yverdon from the Lake of Neufchâtel; and that of M. Victor Gilliéron, founded on a calculation of the rate of separation of the old convent of St. Jean from the Lake of Brienne. These rough and insecure methods of calculation carry back the date of the Lake-villages of the Stone period some 5,000 or 7,000 years.

The wooden handles of the tools and weapons of the Stone period have only in a few instances escaped decay. A complete hatchet found in a bog near Cookstown in Tyrone showed the cutting wedge of flint thrust by its narrow and blunt end through the cleft in a sort of wooden bat. With such a hatchet a ring might be chipped round a tree-stem, into which ring fire could be put, and so by alternate chipping and charring even a large trunk might be divided. Trees so felled are, in fact, found in the peat-bogs. There has been found also in a bog a tree-boat, hollowed by stone and fire, that was made portable by means of handles like those of a butcher's tray. Even fish-hooks were shaped out of flint by this primitive people, and there are found in their tombs grooved or perforated stones that may have been used for sinking fishing-lines. The Stone people themselves have been occasionally dug up dressed in skins, sewn together merely with strips of skin, pieces of hide serving for shoes. Their trinkets, as we find them still, were knobs of bone and amber beads, sometimes formed into chains.

These people did not burn the bodies of their dead. Burial was in what are now called cromlechs (hunch-slabs),[*]

Cromlechs.

and it has been well suggested by Mr. Thoms that the word "cromlech" should be confined to the burial-place of the Stone period. A complete cromlech is, then, a slightly elevated mound of earth, surrounded at its base by a number of upright stones, and having a chamber or several chambers formed of large stones on its summit. Such burial-places abound on the eastern coasts of Jutland, Slesvig, and Holstein; on the north and west coast of Iceland; and on the coasts of Fühnen. They are rare on the west coast of Denmark, and still more rare in the interior. But we must not accept the Danish antiquary's inference of the eastern origin of the Stone people from the rarity of their remains on the west coast of Denmark without remembering that the geologists account for this by great encroachment of the sea upon those western shores since men were buried in the cromlechs. Single mounds vary in length from sixty feet or less to a hundred and twenty feet or more—one is four hundred feet long; their usual breadth is from sixteen to twenty-four feet, but the breadth of the longest is even thirty or forty feet. Sometimes there is a double enclosure of the base, with stones

---

[*] " *Crobm-lech* (as it was formerly written) signifies a crooked, flat stone. Had it been *crobn-lech* (which in pronunciation differs little or nothing from *crobm-lech*), it would have signified a round, flat stone, and been synonymous with *quoit*, the name by which these erections are here, and in some parts of Wales, most commonly known." "The Land's-End District : its Antiquities, &c." By Richard Edmonds. London, 1862. *Crob*, in Welsh, is, according to Richards's Welsh Dictionary, "a round heap or hunch ;" *llech*, " any broad flat stone, a gravestone, slate, a bakestone."

brought evidently from a distance. On the top of the mounds and sunk in them were placed the burial chambers. Each of these is six or eight feet high, and formed of several stones, rough outside and flat inside, placed close together, in a circle of from five to seven feet in diameter or in an oval of from twelve to sixteen feet long, the chinks being filled up with small stones. A great capstone, often eight or ten feet wide, smooth and flat on the under side and rough above, is its roof. The floor of such a tomb is paved partly with flat stones and partly with small flints that seem to have been strongly heated. Enclosed roofed approaches are rare, and lead only to the largest cromlechs. Generally there is an opening between two supporting stones, its place indicated by two flat stones or a row of smaller stones along the hillside. Originally covered with earth except at the top, many of these cromlech-tombs now stand fully exposed. The skeletons found in them show that, after a corpse had been deposited, the tomb was filled with clay, or earth and pebbles, in which room had to be scooped for the next person buried. Bodies seem to have been usually placed in a sitting posture in the corners. The skeleton of one has been found kneeling in the middle, because there was no corner left for it to sit in. The same arrangements are found in the small round cromlechs, consisting usually of one chamber made with a cap upon five stones. The theory that these remains are Druid or other altars, or places of justice, is as far from fact as the legend that accounts for their frequency in the south-east of Ireland. There they are called giants' beds, and said to have been made by Diarmaid O'Duibhné, when he ran away with Grainné the wife of Fionn M'Cumhail, and, being pursued by Fionn for a year and a day, never slept twice in the same bed. The simple fact that the great stones are smooth—often smoothed by artificial splitting—on the inner side, but rough and unshaped outside, shows that they were no more designed for altars than for beds. St. Iltut's Hermitage in Brecknockshire, Arthur's Stone in Glamorganshire, the Cromlechs of Anglesey, the Quoits of Cornwall, Wayland Smith's Cave at Ashbury, Berks, and Kit's Coty House on Blue Bell Hill, near Rochester, are familiar examples of these ancient burial-places.

The burial-places of the Bronze period are barrows. They have no stone chambers, but consist merely of earth with heaps of small stones. The makers of these barrows burnt their dead ; enclosed the ashes in vessels of clay within metal or small stone cysts about a foot long ; placed these in the mound, but in no defined part of it ; and covered all with stones and earth. A few of these more recent barrows were formed over cromlechs, to save labour, the urns being buried at the side. Arms and ornaments of the dead were sometimes placed among the embers of his funeral pile ; these were then covered with stones, and the barrow with the urn in it was placed over that. Sometimes burnt bones, not enclosed in an urn, but surrounded with small stones, are found at the edge of a family barrow. Sometimes a cinerary urn has been cheaply and carelessly interred without raising a barrow over it.

The Bronze Period. Barrows.

These Bronze people, who burnt their dead, are said to be the Celts, in this country the ancient Gael and Cymry, with some of whom there may have come over a certain number of the more ancient and less civilised people of the mainland ; or who found England, like the rest of Europe, thinly peopled with that earlier race of which the stones they shaped are all the traces that remain. The men who used bronze, or copper hardened with a slight mixture of tin, made axes of the shape still common, picks, sickles (that suggest corn-growing), celts (from the Latin *celtis*, a chisel), which are chisel- or axe-heads hollowed to receive their wooden handles and sometimes provided with an ear through which to pass a thong for binding them more firmly. There are found also in their tombs bronze swords about two feet and a half long, or shorter, two-edged, with the thickness in the middle of the blades, and no guards to their hilts ; the hilts, which were very small, were sometimes of wood and nails, sometimes of bronze spread over clay, sometimes even covered with gold plate or woven about with gold wire. The scabbards were of wood usually tipped with metal and sheathed with leather. These Celts had spear-heads a foot long, and there has been found the end of a battle-axe that is fifteen inches long, and weighs seven pounds. There have been found also a few large round shields in thin plates of ornamented bronze, the edges turned over a thicker frame of metal wire, the handle a crossbar within the central boss. But of the more common shields of leather-covered wood there are left only the metal borders, or the small round plates of metal with which they may have been studded and strengthened. There are dug up also the long curved lures or war trumpets of the Bronze period, which stand about three and a half feet high in their curved shape, curved for shouldering musketwise when played, with the broad round of their flat mouths by the players' knees ; they would be six feet long if straightened. Several of these old British war trumpets, blown by the antiquaries of to-day, have played a ghostly music in a tone not absolutely dull—something between a trumpet- and a bugle-note. In peace this people wore trinkets and ornaments, hair-pins a foot long, adorned and inlaid with gold, combs of bronze and bone riveted together, hair-rings, circlets, diadems, neck-rings, elastic spiral armlets like great corkscrews. These things, often adorned with characteristic spiral, ring, and wave patterns, are found in the tombs covered with a greenish rust, the bronze below, when it is got at, shining like gold. But the true gold never rusts, and this metal also was used by the Celts in bracelets, finger-rings, and even in some little cups about four inches high and seven wide across the mouth, which may possibly have been a luxurious form of cinerary urn for those whose heirs would not grudge burying their ashes in their gold.

The Bronze period was followed by that of men who had learnt to extract iron from its stone-like ore. The people The Iron of this period did not burn their dead. Their Period. barrows, often of exaggerated size, are more rare, and some of them contain wooded sepulchral chambers. The iron swords are larger than the swords of bronze, have guarded hilts, and are not usually two-edged. There is in this period less delicacy of ornamental work, and, together with the use of iron, appears for the first time evidence of the use of silver.

These men of the Iron period were the after-coming Teutons. But whence came the Celts, from whom we have the traces of an Age of Bronze, and who began the peopling of this country with offshoots of the Indo-European family of Man ? Says one, Out of Cimmerian darkness ; says another, Out of Hyperborean light.

Let us take first a theory which is based altogether upon fabulous traditions, not because it contains any historical fact, but because its traditions enter into our Were the Literature ; and, as Rome cared for Æneas, Eng-Celts Hyperland may care for a fable of the British maids boreans? who first taught to the ancient Greeks the worship of Apollo. There has been a good Celtic scholar, John Williams, Archdeacon of Cardigan, who argued that this theory, which made the Celts Hyperboreans, is true and founded upon fact. It sets out with a passage quoted by Diodorus Siculus from Hecatæus the Milesian, of whose works fragments alone remain. Hecatæus took part in the revolt of the Ionians from Darius about the year 500 B.C. An inquisitive traveller, he knew what was known among the Ionians, of whose number the Phocæans had established a commerce with Tartessus and Southern Spain. Arganthonius, a long-lived king of Tartessus, was an especial friend of the Phocæans. What, therefore, was known in Spain might become known to Hecatæus. With this preface Arch-deacon Williams requoted from Hecatæus this remarkable passage, as given by Diodorus the Sicilian :—

"Now, after describing the parts of Asia lying northward, we think it not inappropriate to narrate the mythological stories concerning the Hyperboreans. Hecataeus, and some other authors of ancient mytho-logy, say that in the regions over against ‘ Celtica,’ there is in the ocean an island, not smaller than Sicily ; that this island is situated below the constellation of the Bears, and that it is inhabited by men called Hyperboreans, because they are placed beyond the blast of Boreas. They add, that the land, being fertile and producing everything neces-sary, and enjoying a fine temperature, bears two crops in the year. Now, they mythologically state that Latona was born there, and that, on that account, Apollo is honoured by them above all other gods ; that among them there are some men priests, as it were of Apollo, and that, consequently, he is daily and continuously hymned by them with lyric songs, and exceedingly honoured ; that there is also in the island both a consecrated precinct of great magnificence, and a temple of corre-sponding beauty, adorned with numerous dedicated gifts, and in shape spherical ; that there is also a city sacred to the god, and that the majority of its inhabitants are harpers, and that these, continuously harping in the temple, sing, lyrically, hymns to the god, and greatly magnify his deeds. They also state that the Hyperboreans have a peculiar dialect, and are very kindly disposed to the Hellenes, and especially to the Athenians and Delians, and that they have inherited this friendly feeling from ancient times. They also say that some of the Hellenes have passed over to the Hyperboreans, and have left there precious dedicated gifts, bearing Hellenic inscriptions ; that in the same manner Abaris, in a former age, had passed into Hellas, and renewed with the Delians the bond of friendship and consanguinity. They also say that the moon from this island appears to be not far distant from the earth, and clearly shows certain earthly eminences. It is also said that every nineteenth year the god descends into this island. Now, every nineteenth year certain returns of the stars to fixed positions take place, and on this account a period of nineteen years is called by the Hellenes the great year ; that when the god makes his periodical appearance, he both plays the harp and dances during the night, from the vernal equinox to the rising of the Pleiades, taking great delight in his own successful efforts."

" If that information," said the Archdeacon, "was derived from Phocæans who frequented the court of Arganthonius, it is evident that these Hyperboreans were the occupants of Great Britain, which is so accurately described in the above passage, that one of the earliest editors of Diodorus could not refrain, in his index, from writing—' See whether this cannot be applied to Anglia.' " Diodorus himself did not consider that this passage referred to Britain ; yet, when he comes to describe our island, his account coincides, it is observed, curiously in several particulars with the description of the island occupied by the Hyperboreans :—

" Here are a few points in which the historian Diodorus agrees with the ancient Mythologist (book v.) :—

"For over against the Paroceanic Galatia there are in the ocean many islands, of which one, being also the greatest, is called ' Brettanica.'

"Compare the island of Mythology, ' an island off the coast of Celtica, in the ocean.'

" Again, ' the island being triangular, something like Sicily, has not its sides equally long.'

"Compare this with the expression, ' not less than Sicily.'

"Again, the Hyperborean island was ' under the Bear.'

"Compare Britannia's position, ' as it is situated under the Bears.

"Again, the Hyperboreans, from the Homeric times downward, were described as undisturbed by wars ; none of their neighbours ever molested them with the sword.

"Compare with this the following passage from the history :—' The island in ancient times was never troubled by a foreign military power. For we have not heard that Dionysus nor Heracles, nor any other hero or prince, made war against it.'

" Again, the Hyperboreans are described as innocent, prosperous, peaceful.

"Compare this description with the following account of the inhabitants of Brettanica :—' It is said that aboriginal races inhabit

Brettanica, who preserve in their habits the primitive mode of life.
For among other things they use chariots for their wars, as it is handed
down to us, the ancient heroes of the Hellenes did in the Trojan war.'
' That in their habits they are simple, and far removed from the crafti-
ness and wickedness of the present age. . . . That the island is very
populous. . . . That they have many kings and princes, and that
these for the most part are peacefully disposed towards each other.'
' That those who inhabit the western promontory of the island called
Belerium are hospitable even in an exceeding degree, and, on account
of their intercourse with foreign merchants, completely civilised in their
habits.' "

The Archdeacon quotes also, as a contemporary of
Hecatæus, Pindar,* who speaks of the "community of the
Hyperboreans, a people who are ministers of Apollo," from
which the son of Amphictyon went to the shady fountains
of the Ister. Again he says of the Hyperboreans,† that
Perseus once feasted among them, and found them sacrificing
hecatombs of asses, in which sacrifices, and in their vocal
songs, "Apollo takes incessant and most intense delight,
and laughs while he views the petulance of the restive
brutes. The Muse, moreover, is not a stranger to their
haunts: but everywhere tuneful choirs of virgins, and the
voice of harps, and the tones of pipes, are set in motion ;
and the assembly, crowned with wreaths of the golden
laurel, banquet merrily. Nor do disease nor decaying old
age affect the sacred race : and they live free from toils and
wars." Æschylus, who fought at Salamis in the year when
Pindar died, makes the Coryphæus in a chorus of the
Choephoræ allude, as if proverbially, to "the gold and great
prosperity of the Hyperboreans." So far it is argued that the
authorities lead us to look for the Hyperboreans in a country
abounding with olives, laurels, and asses ; and for the island
of Hecatæus in the ocean off the coast of 'Celtica.'" But
then comes Herodotus, of whom John Williams com-
plains, that among his crotchets was "a firm conviction,

* Olymp. Ode iii. v. 12.   † Pythian Ode x. v. 49.

that, were he on any disputed fact to procure the testimony
of one eye-witness, it was sufficient to outweigh all that
poets might imagine or mythologists enigmatically suggest;"
and Herodotus did not believe in the existence of Hyperboreans. His inquiries, it is argued, proved only that there
was no such people in the more northern parts of Asia or
Europe; but of Western Europe he confessed that he knew
little. "Now concerning the western extremities of Europe
I have no accurate account to give;" and his own statement* of a Delian report should have led him to look for
the Hyperboreans westward.

"But the Delians say much more about the Hyperboreans, as they
say that sacred gifts, bound up in wheaten straw, are regularly conveyed to the Scythians, and that the neighbours of these, receiving
them in succession, convey them to the Hadriatic, the farthest station
from the West; that thence, being conveyed southward, they are
escorted until the Dodonæans, first of Hellenes, receive them; that
from them they descend to the Malæan Gulf, and cross over into
Eubœa; and then that city sends them to another city until they reach
Carystus; but the Carystians, passing by Andros, convey them to
Tenos, and the Tenians to Delos. That in earlier times the Hyperboreans sent two virgins to bear the sacred offerings. These the
Delians name Hyperochè and Laodicè; and that as an escort they
sent with them five of their citizens, whom they now call Perpherees,
who have great honours at Delos; but that, when the men thus sent
forth never returned back, the Hyperboreans, regarding it as a great
evil that it should always be their lot never to receive back the men
deputed, conveyed on this account the sacred gifts, bound in wheaten
straw, to their next neighbours, with injunctions to escort them from
their own to another nation, and they say that the offerings, thus
escorted, reached Delos."

The later Greek authors, except Callimachus, agreed
with Herodotus in denying the existence of a nation of
Hyperboreans, or placed them in a Utopia within the arctic
circle. Zealous for the honour of the ancient Britons, Arch-

* Lib. iv. cap. 32.

deacon Williams—who would connect a hierarchy of Druids with the worship of Apollo, and of course could see only Stonehenge in the "consecrated precinct of great magnificence, and a temple of corresponding beauty, in shape spherical"—quoted further from Herodotus the Delian tradition, that Arge and Opis came to Delos from the Hyperboreans before Hyperochè and Laodicè; that they came with the deities themselves, and that their names were invoked by nations in an ancient hymn composed for them by Olen and Lycian, who lived long before Orpheus. Greek temple traditions are next quoted from Pausanias (A.D. 170). Priests of the Olympian Jupiter, in Elis, said that the wild olive was brought by Heracles from the Hyperborean land. According to a tradition of the priests of Delphi, the oracle of Apollo in Delphi was established by Hyperboreans, and by Olen, who was the first prophet of Phœbus. Having argued thus for an ancient connection of the Hyperboreans with the religious creed of Greece before Hesiod and Homer had invented the theogony of the Hellenes, the Archdeacon quoted from a fragment of Stephanus of Byzantium a passage stating that Pelmissus, who went to Caria, "where the temple of the Pelmissian Apollo now exists," was from the Hyperboreans. Now Pelmissus is at this day famous for Cyclopean ruins.

Through such reasoning the conclusion is reached, that the people called Hyperboreans inhabited the south-west of Spain, Gaul west of the Alps, and the island of Great Britain; that they were prosperous and civilised; that there was commerce and sympathy between priests of Stonehenge and those of Delphi; that prehistoric Britons were, in fact, Titan Celts, closely allied to the Pelasgians of ancient Greece; and that these people migrated by water rather than by land from Central Asia. So the young nations have also their nursery lore, and suggestive fable blends with the dim shapings of a past that lies beyond the memory

K

of man. This might become interwoven with other legends of the shaping of our people, and there is happy use made of it by Milton in his Latin verses to Count Manso.

Though still on doubtful ground, we are at least endeavouring to recover by the way of fair historical inquiry some traces of the remote past of the Celts, when we inquire into the possible relation between them and a people known to the Greeks as Cimmerians.

That the Welsh Cymry are descended from the old Cimmerians, while Scyth and Scot, Gaul and Gael, are related names, is an opinion widely held. What may perhaps be at present regarded as the strongest theory on this subject is to be found in the first Essay appended to the Fourth Book* of the annotated translation of Herodotus by Professor George Rawlinson, to which Sir Henry Rawlinson and Sir J. Gardner Wilkinson contributed their notes. Between the years B.C. 800-600 the Cimmerii, Gimiri, or Gomerim were powerful, says this authority, in Western Asia and Eastern Europe. Herodotus is confirmed as to that fact by Homer, Æschylus, Callinus, Aristotle, and by remaining names of places. The Cimmerians of Homer† dwelt "at the farthest limit of the ocean stream, immersed in darkness and beyond the ken of the light-giving sun"—a vague geographical expression, which may or may not have meant some part of the northern coast of the Black Sea. There certainly Æschylus‡ has placed Cimmeria, as neighbour to the Sea of Azov and the Bosphorus. In the seventh and eighth centuries B.C. there were Greek colonists upon the northern coast of the Black Sea from whom trustworthy information might be had. The poet Callinus§ speaks of a Cimmerian invasion, that there

Were the Celts Cimmerians?

---

* Rawlinson's "Herodotus" (London, 1859), vol. iii. pp. 183-191.
+ "Odyssey," xi. 13-22.
‡ "Prometheus Bound," 748-750. See also Strabo, vii. 309.
§ Fragment of Callinus, 2.

is reason to regard as one of a series of raids, in which this people, crossing the Danube and the Bosphorus, joined sometimes on their way by Thracian tribes, descended upon Asia Minor. The universal opinion of the Greeks was that the Cimmerians came from north of the Danube, their home lying between that river and the Don, which flows into the Sea of Azov. Making settlements in Asia Minor, they were masters of Sinope for a time, and of Antandros for a century. But of their own country modern Sebastopol was the central point ; for it was the Crimea and the coast on either side, eastward until beyond Taganrog, and to the west beyond Odessa.

Again, Ezekiel,† B.C. 600, speaks of Gomer as a nation, coupling it with Togarmah. He places it in the North Quarter (Armenia) ; and the Armenians call Gamir the ancestor of their Haichian race of kings. In the Babylonian and Assyrian inscriptions the Sacan or Scythic population, spread over the Persian empire, are called Gimiri, as if the Gimiri of one division of languages were an equivalent word to the Saka or Scyth of another. Perhaps both meant "wanderers." Festus and Plutarch say that the name of the Cimbri meant robbers ; but, in uncivilised times, "rover" and "robber" are connected terms. Identity of name and race are indeed not universal—the Persian Germanii are not Germans, the Iberi of Georgia are not related to those of Spain ; but there is at any rate a presumption raised by the close resemblance of name between the Greek *Kimmeri-oi* and the Celtic *Cymry*.

I am still giving only a digest of the able argument for this theory in Professor Rawlinson's Herodotus. When the Scythians, crossing the Don, fell on the Cimmerians from the East, the Cimmerians must, it is argued, have gone west. That has been always the course taken by Asiatic hordes pressing on Europe. But if these powerful tribes

† Ezekiel xxxviii. 6.

went west B.C. 650-600, whither did they go? Herodotus knew only, in Central and Western Europe, of the Sigynnes, the Cynetians, and the Celts. The Sigynnes and Cynetians soon disappear, and " could scarcely be the great nation of the Cimmerii, which, until driven from the Ukraine by the force of the Scythian torrent, was wont to extend its ravages over large tracts of Asia Minor." We can only find them among the Celts, who had an unvarying tradition that they came from the East, and of whom one division bears the special name of Cymry.

Celts, according to this authority, were the primitive inhabitants of Gaul, Belgium, and Britain, possibly also of Spain and Portugal. In Spain, Belgium, and North Gaul the Celts were Cimbri. In Britain Cimbric Celts occupied the south coast at the time of Cæsar's landing. Even if, as I believe, the Belgæ in South Britain were of Germanic race, it was in Britain as in Gaul the Celts whom they dis-placed. Pressed upon by the Gothic or Teutonic race, they have formed the basis of the population in several large European countries. The name of the Cimmerii and Cimbri is now shared by the Cymry of Cambria with the Crim Tartars of the Crimea, which is a portion of their ancient home.

It is probable, this theory goes on to suggest, that the Cimmerians found, when driven westward, waste land un-inhabited, or thinly peopled by a Tartar or Mongolian race, which was absorbed, causing a Tartar admixture with the Celtic blood, or, when not absorbed, was driven to the north, where it is now represented by Finns, Esths, and Lapps. Such may have been the Spanish Iberians, fore-fathers of the peculiar people of the Basque. The Cymry were first spread over central Europe by the force of Scythians from behind. It is most likely to have been the impulse of the Goths and other Teutons by which they were driven on to Gaul, and Spain, and Britain. The pressure of Iberians caused further migration of Celts across the Pyrenees to their own kinsmen in Gaul. Thence want of space forced many across the Alps to found new settlements in Italy and Hungary. Next followed a period of rest and pause in the movement; but a century later, about the year B.C. 280, hordes of Gauls from these regions entered Macedonia, and threatened Greece. Repulsed from Delphi, they went northward, invaded Asia Minor, and, when other ground was reconquered from them, still dwelt in the heart of Phrygia, giving the name "Galatia" to its northern part. At this time also they retaliated on the Scythians, inter-mixed with them, forming Celto-Scythians, and advanced as far as their old home in the Crimea, whence they were again driven by the progress of Sarmatic tribes, which then commenced. Forced along the valley of the Danube, there they left their traces in the names Wallachia and Galicia, but themselves finally sank under the antagonism of more powerful nations. From Eastern and Central Europe Celts have disappeared. In Northern Italy, in France, where their language is yet to be heard in Brittany, and among our-selves in Cornwall, Wales, the Scottish Highlands, and Ireland, their traces are distinct. In many parts of Wales, North Scotland, and Ireland the population is almost purely and entirely Celtic.

The whole body, then, of the Celtic Britons certainly did not consist of mere naked barbarians. From the remotest period to which we can look back there seem to have been more races than one in occupation *The Celtic Britons.* of our islands. That Herodotus probably meant by the Cassiterides, or Tin Islands, the same Britain which Aristotle was the first to name as "two islands, which are very large, Albion and Ierne, called the Britannic, which lie beyond the Celtæ;" that Polybius, writing 150 B.C., describes the method of obtaining and preparing tin in the Britannic Isles; that the Phœnicians, trading from their port of

Gades (now Cadiz), obtained tin from Cornwall and the Scilly Islands, keeping the source of this commerce so close a secret that, as Strabo tells, a Phœnician captain, followed and watched by Roman vessels, ran his ship ashore rather than lead to the betrayal of the mystery ; that the Phœnician trade was tracked early in Julius Cæsar's time by Publius Crassus—are the familiar and almost the only details of written British history before Cæsar's invasion. The tenth part of tin in the bronze used almost throughout Europe in the Bronze period may have come chiefly from Cornwall. Advocates of a very high previous civilisation in at least some part of Britain ascribe it occasionally to the influence of supposed Phœnician settlements.

But in Cæsar's account of Britain we find the race of the Belgæ, who, he says, were chiefly sprung from the Germans,* most powerful of all the nations west of the Rhine, in occupation of the coast of Gaul opposite South-eastern Britain, and evidently in occupation also of our own south-eastern coasts.   Cæsar notes that in language, customs, form of houses, names of towns, the South Britons agreed with the opposite Gauls ; that Divitiacus, king of the Suessones, a tribe of Belgæ, was the most powerful in Gaul, and had empire even in Britain ; that there was one name also, Cingetorix, for a king of Belgæ on the Moselle and for a king in Kent.   Cæsar speaks by report of the Northern or Celtic Britons as a pastoral people dressed in skins ; but the men of South Britain who contended with him, although in Roman phrase barbarians, had knowledge to give to the youths of Gaul, and used Greek letters in conveying it; had commerce also, accord-

The Belgæ.

---

* "Sic reperiebat plerosque Belgas esse ortos a Germanis, Rhenumque antiquitus traductos, propter loci fertilitatem ibi consedisse, Gallosque qui ea loca incolerent expulisse." "De B. G." ii. 4. Tacitus, who notes the same thing, speaks also of the language of the Æstui, a German tribe, as " Lingua Britannicæ propior." "Mor. Germ." 45.

ing to Strabo,* on the Rhine, Seine, Loire, and Garonne—
exported corn, cattle, gold, silver, iron, hides, slaves, and
dogs, and imported ivory, bracelets, necklaces, amber,
vessels of glass, and small wares. Of London, only a
hundred years after the time of Cæsar's invasion, Tacitus
says that it was chiefly noted for its gatherings of traders.†
The country to the south in Cæsar's time was cleared and
ploughed. When he first crossed he found the corn-harvest
just gathered, except one field. Without roads the British
army could not have had, as it is said to have had, its chief
strength in war-chariots. Without some political organisa-
tion the people could not have sent, as they did, a fleet
of ships in aid of the Veneti, when Cæsar made war against
them.

The Sussex iron, again, was not unknown to the South
Britons,‡ and herein also they seem to be allied to the
Germanic race. To the first advent of the "Anglo-Saxons"
it is usual (though not perhaps entirely just) to trace the
ancient remains of the "Iron period." In the subsequent
survey of Britain by Ptolemy the geographer, the Belgæ are
said to have occupied a district, including nearly the whole
of Hampshire, Wiltshire, and Somersetshire, stretching
across from the Hampshire coast to the shore of the Bristol
Channel. The people of Sussex and Surrey were then
called the Regni. "Rhegn" is "Cursed" in Cymric, as
"Belg" is a "Ravager," to which Richards's Welsh
Dictionary adds, "Belgiad, a ravager, a Belgian; Belgwys,
the ravagers, the Belgæ." Celsus, quoted by Oudendorp,
said that the Belgæ were indignant if they heard themselves
called Gauls, and it appears also that they did not speak of
themselves as Belgæ. But that name of "Ravagers" would

* Strabo, lib. iv. 5.

† Tacitus, "Ann." xiv. 33.

‡ "In maritimis ferrum, sed ejus exigua est copia : ære utuntur im-
portato." Cæsar, "De B. G." v. 12. See Mr. Lewin's Essay on "The
Invasion of Britain by Julius Cæsar." London, 1859.

naturally have been given to them by the Celtic tribes, whom, quitting the Rhine and conquering their way along the coast, they dislodged from the north-eastern shore of France, opposite Britain, and drove beyond the Seine or forced across the Channel.

It is usual to think Cæsar wrong in giving a German origin to the Belgæ, whom he places opposite to our south-eastern shores, on the coast east of the Seine, in part of Normandy, in Picardy, Flanders, and the modern Belgium and Holland. Yet Cæsar, shrewd and travelled, had personal knowledge of the difference he records between the people of the three divisions of Gaul ; Belgic, Celtic, and Aquitanian. The Aquitanians bordered on Spain. Strabo says that in language and appearance they resembled Spaniards rather than the other Gauls.* They appear, in fact, to have been Gaels, as the Iberian or Spanish Celts were. Only so could they differ in language from the Cymry of Celtic Gaul, as well as from the Belgæ, by whom some of the Cymry of the coast had been cast out of their possessions. That they did so differ is, I think, made certain when of the people of the three divisions Cæsar emphatically says that "these all differ in language, customs, and laws."† For although Cymric and Gaelic are both Celtic languages, they are as much unlike each other as Danish and German. The relationship is manifest in their vocabularies, while the difference is marked not in the vocabularies only, but still more in the inflexions and distinctive characters.

I think Cæsar was right in this matter. There can be little doubt that the first Celts who came to The Gaels. Britain were the Gaels, and that they settled in Ireland and the West of England. Irish and Spanish histories and traditions agree in asserting that the Irish Gael came from Spain. The old history ascribed to Nennius

* Lib. iv. 1-2.   † "De Bello Gallico," i. 1.

distinctly states this. From Ireland the Gael crossed to the Western Islands and Highlands of Scotland; and he crossed also into Wales. Welsh scholars have at all times observed traces of a previous Gaelic occupation of their land. They were observed in the last century by Edward Lhuyd, and more recently demonstrated by the Rev. Basil Jones in his book on "Vestiges of the Gael in Gwynedd," or North Wales. One vestige, for example, is the constant use by the Romans of "isca"—"Isca Silurum," &c.—for river or water in the West of England, the word being the Gaelic "uisge," which is not Cymric at all, and still survives in the Exe and Esk. Even the tradition of the common people in North Wales asserts that the original inhabitants were Gwythelians or Irish. The cromlechs are sometimes called Irish cots, and the foxes and polecats are said to be descended from the Irish dogs and cats.

Tacitus * says that the Silures, or people of Wales, and the Brigantes,† or people of the North of England (occupying Lancashire, Yorkshire, Westmoreland, Cumberland, and Northumberland), in his time resembled the people of Spain more than they did the other Gauls in language and appearance. The tribes on the opposite or eastern coast of Ireland were called also Brigantes, and the province of Gallicia, in Spain, where the Galliego dialect is said to contain many traces of Gaelic, has to this day the name of Brigantina. A glance at the map shows that Gaels, crossing the sea from Spain, would in fact strike most naturally upon Ireland and our western shore. Before the coming of the Cymry these Gaels were thinly scattered over England between shore and shore. Their naming of places shows this. Thus, *pen*, or

---

* "Vit. Agric." ii.

† Brigantes and Silures seem to have been names adopted by the Romans from Cymric authority, those quiet in Wales being called men of the *syl* (pl. *sylur*) or soil, those in the North of England, who battled against the gradual process of expulsion, being known as *briganted*, fighting thieves. *Brigant* is Welsh for thief and highlander.

penn, means a head in Welsh, Cornish, and Breton;
cean, *ceann*, means a head in Irish Gaelic—the *c* in all
these languages being pronounced as *k*. Now, the early
existence of the Gaelic form of *cean* for headland is traceable in the five great headlands of East Britain from Cantyre (*cean tir*, head of the land) to Kent, by the old names
of tribes—Cantii, Iceni, Cantæ; Cantabriga (Cambridge),
Canty Bay, and the Pentland Hills and Frith, where the
Cymry, next in possession, have only half transformed to
their own manner the name of Kentland. Some of the
earlier Stone people in Spain, who may or may not be
represented now by the Basques, perhaps came over with
the Spanish Gaels; and such a people, of which we find
the remains, were doubtless already existent also in this
country. In connection with this part of the subject it may
be worth while to cite the apparent connection between
Mendip Hills and Grampians, and the Basque words
Mendia, a hill, Gara, a height.

Meanwhile the Cymric Celts, traced from Cimmerians
and Cimbri, once occupied midland Gaul and
the coast opposite Britain. A people different
in language, customs, and laws, chiefly Germanic, had come
from the Rhine and had seized part of this Celtic coast,
"expelling" the previous inhabitants. These new comers
were called the "Belgæ," which means, we find, in the language of the Cymry, "ravagers." The expelled people may
have been driven partly inland, where they could only possess goods by taking those of their countrymen and neighbours, or they crossed the sea to get possession of the
thinly-peopled district of South-eastern Britain. From the
south-east the Cymry spread; the Gaels yielding before them.
But Belgæ, too, were tempted to the British shore, and had
already a firm foot in Southern England when the Romans
came to add another form of pressure.

The Gaelic aspect of the Silures in the time of Tacitus

shows that the Gael had not yet been driven back from
Wales to Ireland. The Humber, as the Chumber, was a
Cimbric river, Northumberland was called of old North
Cumri-land, and in Cumberland the last stand of the northern Cymry, themselves driven from the plains, was made
before they settled numerously in the fastnesses of Wales.
They must have spread far along our eastern coast, for even
the " aber " in Aberdeen is Welsh—that name, for the confluence of a small stream with a large being unknown in West
Scotland. The Gaelic word is " inver," as in Inverness. The
fens of Lincolnshire seem to have been retained also as a
fastness into which the agricultural invader little cared to
follow ; and among the traces of Welsh ancestry in the fen-
people was their long retention of that Celtic instrument,
the bagpipe ; " the drone of a Lincolnshire bagpipe " is one
of Falstaff's similes for melancholy. If these arguments be
sound, the admixture of Gaelic in Armorican or Breton,
which closely resembles Welsh, would result from ancient
intercourse between the Celts and Aquitanians of Gaul,
where the Breton Celts were neighbours to the dislodged
Cymry. In Ireland and the adjacent Western Islands and
Highlands of Scotland, Gaelic of Iberian origin remains ; in
the adjoining Wales only a few of the Gaels who had
original possession there, remained and united themselves
with a portion of the Cymry by whom they were dislodged ;
but there was, nevertheless, union enough to establish, by
admixture of vocabulary and of blood, a difference both in
dialect and physical appearance between the inhabitants of
North and South Wales. A Welshman and an Irishman
speaking true Cymric and Gaelic cannot understand one
another in the least, while there is Cymric enough in the
Armorican for a Welshman to understand a Breton easily,
and Gaelic enough for an Irishman to understand him,
though with difficulty.* But the main fact that we secure

* The best original argument on this subject is to be found in two essays

by not accounting ourselves more exact in our theories than so shrewd and skilled a witness as Cæsar was in evidence of what he saw and heard, is that the Belgæ in Gaul were but a tribe of the same people by whom the Frisian and Anglo-Saxon dialects of a common tongue were spoken, and that they had a firm hold in the south of Britain, even before Cæsar's time.

We find, then, in all these changes no series of sudden convulsions. By means of their small ships, slowly, and in course of years, the Spanish Gaels colonised Ireland and our western coasts. By more rapid invasion, probably, the Belgæ spread at a very remote time over the coasts opposite our south-eastern shores. The expelled Cymry must at first have crossed in large numbers, and cleared the south-east of England of the thinly-scattered Gael. Afterwards there was slow and steady migration, voluntary migration, probably, of Celts from the part of what is now called Normandy west of the Seine, and of some Bretons; voluntary migration certainly of the more thriving Belgæ, whom Cæsar found on the British shore, people of one language with those he had left in Belgic Gaul. On English soil Gael yielded ground to Cymry, Cymry to Belg, and the Belg, we shall find, must have differed little, if at all, from the people who, as the stream of colonisation and invasion still flowed in, were taken up by early chroniclers at a much later date in their history as Anglo-Saxons.

Meanwhile it was from the first the English people that was being formed. The quality of the bronze remains,

First stage in the formation of English.

read, one to the Philological Society in 1855, the other to the Ethnological Society in 1857, by the late James Kennedy, LL.B., and republished in his "Essays, Ethnological and Linguistic." London and Leipsic, 1861. Thomas Wright, whose name must always be mentioned with honour in connection with English antiquities, and who worked steadily for the diffusion of his knowledge, gave his support to the belief that Cæsar was right about the Belgæ (in "The Celt, Roman, and Saxon," ed. 1861).

the remains also of language and of literature, show that the Celts, whether Gael or Cymry, were no mere savages. They not only left the names given by them attached throughout the land to lakes, rivers, and mountains, but they perhaps contributed more than is now believed to the formation of English in its earliest stage. Such common words as gown, glove, basket — though Martial did take the Britons for rude savages, when, to bring a word into discredit, he wrote, " Barbara de pictis venit Bascauda Britannis "—even such words as hat, coat, and boots might be traced to Celtic originals. When such words are found without an etymology in Anglo-Saxon, but with an etymology in the language of the Cymry or the Gael, we may be sure that, during those centuries of contact between Celt and Teuton, it found its way from the lips of the earlier to those of the later people. Thus "hat" is connected with the German *hut* as a shelter for the head, but there is a Celtic verb *hatra* to cover, and *het* means any sort of head covering, whether a hat or a garland. This Celtic element in English might have been indicated in the Pedigree by a faint dotted line of connection through which Celtic passes into Anglo-Saxon.

The Celtic element in English.

The following list illustrates the Celtic origin of English local names. C is attached to Cymric, G to Gaelic forms :—

Celtic in local names

Aber (C.), inver (G.), confluence of small and large stream ; river mouth : as Aberdeen, formerly Aber-don, near mouth of Don ; Abergavenny, at confluence of the Usk and the Gavenny.

Ach (G.), a field : as Achniver, the Trosachs.

Argyll (G.), Arre-Gaidhel, the frontier of the Gael.

Ard, high, lofty : Ardmillan.

Afon (C.), abhan (G.), a river ; Avon. There is an Avon at Bristol, another in Northampton-shire, another in Warwickshire. Ptolemy called the Humber Αβρουτρος, which is Avon Tros (over, exceeding), an augmentative applied to the broad estuary.

Baile (G.), a town : as Ballyshannon, town on Shannon.

Bala (C.), flow of a river into a lake ; bealach (G.), a passage.

Bann (C.), high : as Bangor, the high cor, choir, or Christian college. There are hills so named in Brecknockshire, Caermarthen, and Glamorgan. Bansdown near Bath, Pan Down by Newport, I.W.

Beinn, Ben (G.), a mountain or pinnacle : Ben-Nevis (L., *nivis* of snow), or contraction of G. neambathois, cloud-browed.

Caer (C.), cathair (G.), walls of defence, castle, city : Caermarthen, city of Merlin ; Caernarvon, the stronghold yn Ar-Von, opposite Mona (or Von).

Cam (C., G.), crooked : "the crooked Cam."

Ceann (G.), a head ; ceann tire, a headland : Kent, Cantyre.

Cill (G.), kil, a hermit-cell, place of worship, burying-ground : Kilkenny, church of St. Kenny or Canice.

Carraig, craig (G.), carrick, a rock, or castle on a rock : Carrickfergus, castle of Fergus.

Cluyd (C.), a common river name in Wales, from clyd, warm, sheltered : the Clyde in Scotland was named by the Cymry.

Coed (C.), fiodh (G.), a wood : cote, in Northcote, Southcote.

Cwmm (C.), a dale, whence A.-S. comb : Wycomb, watered dale, from (C.) gwy, or wy, water ; Compton, cwmm dun, or A.-S. ton, Dale town

Din (C.), a fortified hill ; dinas, a city : the Roman dunum, dinum

in Londinum, Lugdunum, &c. Dunadh (G.) is shutting, closing ; hence some wrongly derive the A.-S. ton and English town, and, in sense of hill, sand-dunes and downs.

Dubh (G.), black : Dublin (dubh linne), black pool.

Dun (G.), a fortified hill, or town.

Dwr (C.), water : Derwent, dwr and gwen, fair ; or gwent, a fair open region ; Dart, Adour, Adur, Calder, Stour (Es Dwr). Elsewhere, the Douro, &c.

Gwy, or wy (C.), water : rivers Wye, Edwy, Llugwy, &c.

Gwysg (C.), uisge (G.), isca, a stream : Ax, Esk, Ex, Ouse, Usk, Ouse, Wisbeach (Ousebeach), Osborn (Ouse-bourn).

Llan (C.), an enclosure, churchyard, church : Lampeter (llan Bedr), church of Peter ; Llandaff, church of David ; Llanberis, church of St. Peris ; Llangollen, church of St. Collen.

Lyn (C.), lin (G.), a lake or pool : Lynn, in Norfolk, the pool ; London (lyn dun), the town of the pool, the pool of the river formerly overflowing the lowlands of the marshes.

Maen (C.), a stone : Pen-maenmawr, headland of the great stone.

Mon (C.), solitary, isolate : Mona, old name of Anglesey ; Isle of Man. Mawn, moin (G.), mountain, common, bog.

Maol (G.), mull, chief headland : Mull of Kintore.

Pen (C.), a head, summit, not confined, like ceann (G.), to sea promontories : Pendarves, head of the oakfield ; Penzance, the holy headland.

Rhos (C.), ros (G.), a mountain meadow, a moist large plain : Ross.

Tamh (G.), rest, quiet : Thama,

quiet river ; Thames (tamh uisge), quiet water.

Tref and tre (C.), a town or home : Tredegar ; Coventry, town of the Convent.

Trent (C.), from dirwyn, to wind round.

Tyne (G.), from tuinn, waves, or tuinna, water's edge.

That the Celtic element in common English speech is much larger than has been fairly recognised, nobody has shown so well as the late Mr. Garnett in his essay, read before the Philological Society, upon the languages and dialects of Britain. It was the purpose of that essay to show generally how fruitful would be the application of sound Celtic scholarship to a study of the Western languages of Europe. Mr. Garnett offered only suggestions pointing towards knowledge yet to be acquired ; but, in illustrating his case with analogies between English and Cymric, he cited a profusion of words that were, he said, but a twentieth part of those which might be quoted. Here, for example, are some English words of Celtic origin relating to the arts of life :—

The Celtic element in common English.

basgawd	basket.
botwm	button.
bràn (skin of wheat)	bran.
bwyell, hatchet ...	bill.
cab, caban, hut ...	cabin.
cae, enclosure ...	quay.
ceubal, boat ...	coble.
clwt, patch ...	clout.
cnap, button ... }	knob.
cnwb, knob ... }	
crochan, a pot ...	crock.
crog, hook ...	crook.
cwch, boat	cock-boat.
darn, a patch ...	darn.
ffynel, air-hole, chimney	funnel.
gardas (gar, shank, das, tie)	garter.
gefyn, fetter ...	gyve.
greidell, iron baking-plate ...	griddle.
gwald, hem, border	welt.
gwib, sudden course	quip.
gwibl, a turn, quirk	quibble.
gwlanen (from ... gwlan, wool).	flannel.
Heref.	flannen
gwlyb, liquor ...	flip.
gwn, robe	gown.

hob, measure	...	hoop. (quarter peck, N. Yorkshire.)	
llath, rod ...	...	lath.	
llymry, jelly of oat-meal	...	flummery.	
matog	...	mattock.	
mop, mopa	...	mop.	
paeol... ...	...	pail.	
pan, cup, bowl	...	pan.	
peg, peged, a mea-sure	...	peck.	
picyn, a small			
hooped vessel ...	piggin or biggen.		
pot (Gael. poit to drink)	pot		
potes, a cooked mess	pottage.		
rhasg, a slice	rasher.		
rhim, raised edge	rim.		
syth, stiffening, glue	size.		
tacl, instrument, tool	tackle.		
teddu, to spread ...	ted (to spread hay).		

It may be that in a few of these cases, and of those next quoted, a word has come out of English into Celtic, or has passed into English and into Celtic from a separate and common source. A large number of words have, no doubt, by Mr. Garnett and others, been derived from Celtic where there is no more than identity of origin, or there may be even a later Celtic word taken from English. But some of the words have a rational etymology in Celtic and in Celtic only; and as to others, there is the liveliest appearance of the passage of a Celtic word into vernacular English by an old familiarity of intercourse between the Celtic and Germanic tribes settled in England. In the familiarly expressive but undignified vernacular, the Celtic element is strongly marked. Thus, "bother" is good Celtic, and stands in all seriousness for tribulation in the Irish Scripture. The following analogies are among those drawn promiscuously by Mr. Garnett from the Cymric only :—

asbri, trick, mis-chief	spree.		
baldorddus, prating,	balderdash.		
bamein (Breton to bewitch, cheat)...	bam.		
bicra, to wrangle ...	bicker.		
blew, hair of ani-mals	flue (of fur).		
bwg, hobgoblin ...	bug, bugbear.		
bygylu, to threaten	bully.		
carol, movement or song or dance ...	carol.		

cic, foot, cic'an, to strike with the foot	... ... kick.	hwch, a swine	... hog.
cnoc, a rap...	.. knock.	llachiaw, a cudgel	lick.
cnòl, round summit	knoll.	llawd, youth	... lad.
cnul, passing bell ...	knell.	llodes, girl	... lass.
cocru, to indulge	cocker.	llug, partial	... } lukewarm.
cogel, short staff ...	cudgel.	llugdwy, tepid	... }
crwth, fiddle	... crowd.	llumon, chimney	... lum.
cwta, short	... cutty (pipe, &c.)	paneg, entrails	... paunch.
chwap, smart stroke	whop.	piciaw, to throw	... pitch.
dwn, dusky	... dun.	pinc, smart, gay	... pink. (to adorn).
fug, deception	... fudge.	pwmp, round mass	pimple.
glyn, valley	... glen.	tal, lofty ...	... tall.
hochi, to expectorate	... ... hawk.	tociaw, to cut short,	dock.
hoeden, a flirt	... hoyden.	tosiaw, to jerk, throw	... ... toss.
		tuig, understand	... twig

Such Celtic words as clan, tartan, plaid, kilt, and reel are clearly among those of later introduction; and some others—not only those formally recorded, as Druid and bard, but those incorporated in other Western languages as in our own—may have found their way to us from Latin or from Norman French in secondary form. There remains, however, certainly, when large allowance has been made for questionable etymologies, a Celtic element in English that indicates long habit of familiar contact in ancient time. There are more words than would have been taken in the course of conflict; and the sort of words do not belong to the language that men learn from enemies

Thus for about four hundred years from the surrender of Caractacus, A.D. 51, the Romans maintained military possession of England, and in all that time they set no mark of theirs upon the language of its people. For we can hardly account as a mark on language the inevitable attachment to the soil of four or five military words indicative of their camps

Faint traces of the Roman occupation. Latin of the First Period.

L

(castra, in Chester, Manchester); their colonies (as in Lincoln); their military roads, levelled and strewn ways, strata, streets; their harbours or ports; and perhaps their ramparts, since from the Roman vallum, a rampart, some derive the Celtic baile, whence we get the modern English bail or bailey, and the Irish bally prefixed to some names of towns. Of a really civilising intercourse evidence would have passed into the language, but there was none.

The few words of Latin origin just named are said technically to belong in English to the Latin of the First Period; those introduced afterwards, chiefly by Augustine and his successors, among the English whom Rome Christianised, being accounted Latin of the Second; those that were brought by the Normans, Latin of the Third; and lastly, those introduced for technical and scientific use, since what is called the Revival of Letters, Latin of the Fourth Period. Of these Periods, the first, second, and third contributed—the first, as we have seen, in almost no degree; the second, appreciably; and the third much, to the formation of the language.

We turn now from these earliest traces of our language to the first beginnings of our literature. Of the wisdom and splendour of the Druids wonderful things have been fabled by the later descendants of the Cymry, but in the single trustworthy account left us by Cæsar we find only the familiar sketch of a priestly class that in a rude age rises to influence by sharing, multiplying, and using to its own gain that reverent instinctive sense of unseen powers which belongs to the crude manhood of the heathen. The commonalty of Gaul, we learn from Julius Cæsar, was almost in the condition of slaves, power being in the hands of priests and warrior-chiefs. The priests, called Druids, judged and punished crimes, excommunicating those by whom their sentences were disregarded, and this excommunication was

Twilight before the Dawn of English Literature. Druids.

much dreaded by the superstitious people. The priests also controlled the education of the young. There was a fixed place for an annual assembly, to which quarrels were brought for settlement. There was a Chief Druid, who held office for life by election ; sometimes, however, in case of vacancy, the priestly candidates fought one another for supremacy. But they were militant only as a Church, and were exempt from all military service and from all payment of tribute. They had, in fact, says Cæsar, "a dispensation in all matters." This institution was supposed to have been devised in Britain, because many of those young men who were tempted by its privileges to join the priestly class went into Britain for a more accurate study of its system. Their study consisted in the learning by rote of a great number of verses, which were handed down by oral tradition, and which it was not permitted to commit to writing. What they did write on public or private matters they wrote in Greek letters for the sake of mystery. There were said to be so many verses that a man might spend, and sometimes did spend, twenty years of his life in learning them. Their traditional verse taught a cosmogony, and that there was a future life for man by transmigration of his soul out of one body into another. The gods worshipped by this priesthood Cæsar identifies with his own as Mercury, Apollo, Mars, Jupiter, and Minerva. But he tells us that their worshippers propitiated these gods with human sacrifices, using innocent persons when there were no thieves or other criminals on hand. Some of the Gauls, it is added, had "figures of vast size ; the limbs of which, formed of osiers, they fill with living men, which being set on fire, the men perish in the flames." But Cæsar does not say that they had these in Britain. The Druids, he tells us, all agreed that these people were descended from the God of Hell. "For that reason they compute the division of every season, not by the number of days, but by nights ; and they keep birthdays

and the beginnings of months and years in such an order
that the day follows the night." And so, indeed, we still
speak of a se'nnight or a fortnight. Of the producers of
our earliest literature, what else is to be learnt we gather
only from the student of the ancient records of the Gael.
The dawn of thought was represented by a search for God ;
but in a remote age there was in this country a lettered
class, apparently distinct from that of the priests, producing
a rude history and poetry for a quick-witted and imaginative
people.

We are of sundry races, but one people, within bounds

E Pluribus
Unum.
of what the world calls England. A fair sketch
of our literature must needs tell how there were
from the beginning wits at work in Ireland, Scotland, and
Wales, as well as in England east of the Severn and south
of the Tweed. The genius of a great nation is our theme,
and it is no theme to be discussed in a provincial spirit.
The name of "English" was derived from one of many
Teutonic tribes that united to become one people and
then bore a single name. In the fusion of the Teuton
with the Celt, a fusion that has brought quickening of
power to the nation ; in all fusions before and since ; and
in all putting forth of branches that have spread over the
world an English-speaking people with its centre of life in
these islands of Great Britain ; let that old tribe of Angli
still furnish the name that represents us all. Let the tribe
that was barely named by Tacitus, and from which not a
tithe of the First English were descended, still furnish the
name for our great brotherhood now spread over the world,
one in affection, one in power, one in aim.

CHAPTER II.

OLD LITERATURE OF THE GAEL.

THE story of our literature begins with the Gael ; for there is preserved in Ireland a great mass of ancient copies of more ancient writings that reproduce most interesting traces of historic tale and song in the remotest epoch of our common history. Let us at once dismiss here, as beside our purpose, the name of "Erse," derived from "Erin" or "Ierne," to distinguish Irish from Scottish Gaelic. The distinction of existing dialects does not affect the story of their ancient common literature. They were Gaedhels or Gaels, speaking Gaedhlic or Gaelic, who, coming most probably from Spain, landed in Ireland and upon the western coasts of England and Scotland, who also, as they spread themselves abroad over the new soil, crossed the narrow strait of sixteen miles dividing Ireland from Cantyre to settle also in the western islands and highlands of Scotland. Many of the Gaedhels who reached Scotland partly by land, instead of wholly by sea, no doubt sojourned a while in Ireland on their way; and in that sense most of the Scottish Gaels are said to have passed over from Ireland before the third century. But the old poems and traditions show that there was continual communication, flux and reflux, between the Gaelic chiefs in Ireland and the chiefs of Alban, the Scottish mainland, or the intervening islands.

There was no difference of nationality between the Gaels

Ancient Literature of the Gael in Britain.

of Ireland and those of the Scottish Highlands. In language, customs, and traditions they were one people until the sixteenth century, when political and religious changes parted them. Gaels on the British shores spoke to Phœnician sailors of the other land as the island "to the west": (h)èriu ; genitive, (h)erenn ; dative (h)érinn, and the name " Ierne," Erin, was adopted in that western land. Mr. Whitley Stokes connects " Erin" with an older " Everion," and the Sanskrit *avara*, posterior, western.* Erin, as the greater and more fertile possession, doubtless contained the richest chiefs ; in Erin, therefore, would be the head-quarters of song and story, and this island was also the larger stage upon which the more stirring political dramas could be enacted. Where the priests and men of letters could most readily grow fat, and where there was a court that represented the best strength of Gaelic civilisation, we should expect to find, as we do, the great mass of remaining Gaelic records. But in the beginning of our literature there was no real separation between Irish and Scottish Gael, and we dismiss, therefore, as most unprofitable, all debate as to the ancient right of Scot or Irishman to an exclusive proprietorship in any ancient worthy—to the poet Oisin, for example, of whom Scottish and Irish Gael have to this day retained equivalent traditions. Here too, then, let us avoid provincialism, and simply regard as one race, irrespective of obscure varieties of tribe, the entire body of the ancient Gaedhel.†

After the old way of inventing persons to explain the names of tribes, the name of Gaedhel was derived by the ancient Irish clergy from a Gaedhal or Gadelas who lived

* Avienus in his " Ora Maritima," which belongs to the fourth century, speaks of Ireland as the sacred island. M. H. Gaidoz in the *Revue Celtique*, Vol. II., p. 352, reasonably argues that this was his interpretation of ἱέρνη into ἱερο, suggested by old legends about Isles of the Blest.

† This doctrine is effectively sustained by Mr. J. F. Campbell, in the fourth volume of his " Popular Tales of the West Highlands, Orally Collected." Edinburgh, 1862.

in the time of Moses. His father Niul had married a daughter of that Pharaoh who, in pursuit of the Israelites, was drowned in the Red Sea, and called her Scota because he was himself a Scythian. Their son was said to have been called Gaodhal as a lover of learning, from *gaoith*, which is in Irish "learning," and *dil*, which is in Irish "love."

The first writing in this country of which there is record was by the Ogham characters, still to be seen on stone monuments and in some ancient books. The Ogham marks upon stone blocks are chiefly Irish; there are only about a dozen in Scotland. Professor Stephens, of Copenhagen, thinks them a faint and distant echo of the arrow-headed characters once used in Babylon. Taking Babylonian as one branch of the oldest stave writing, and Phœnician as the other: of the Babylonian branch the Ogham characters are the only Western representative; but the Phœnician is in the old Runic, the modern Greek, Latin, and other alphabets. Henri Martin says that the Ogham alphabet was based on the symbol of a tree. A perpendicular line represented the stem, from the two sides of which, from stem to trunk, sprang different arrangements of branches, some perpendicular and some oblique. The first letter was represented by one such bar or branch, the next by two, and so on until there were five branches on one side above the middle line. The next letters were formed by bars or branches below the middle line, and on the other side of the stem; then a third group had bars crossing the middle line perpendicularly, and in a fourth group the branches or bars crossed it obliquely. The names of the several letters were also taken throughout from trees whose names began with corresponding sounds. The first two letters, *b* and *l*, were "beith" (birch), "luis" (mountain ash), and so "beithluisnion" was the name of the Ogham alphabet. The word "ogham," in modern Irish,

The Ogham.

stands for the occult sciences; and, according to Lucian.
Oghum was painted in the second century as a Herculean
Mercury, old, in a lion's skin, with a club in his right hand
and a bent bow in his left; the ears of his worshippers
bound by a chain of gold and amber to his tongue. These
Ogham letters were cut with a knife on the staves or wands
of the poet. A copy of an ancient poem* in a manuscript
itself 850 years old, speaks more than once of an Ogham
cut in hoops or wands and placed in the path of Queen
Meav and her army. As each staff was found, it was
carried to the Queen, who sent it to the great champion
Fergus, and by him it was read. Again, in the Book of
Leinster, which contains copies made early in the twelfth
century of ancient records then existing, there is a poem
by the second daughter of King Cormac McArt, who lived
in the third century, setting forth a tradition to account for
the agglutination of two ancient Ogham tablets. This is a
tradition to which reference is made in other of the most
ancient Gaelic poems.

*The Tale of the fate of Bailé, the sweet-spoken, and the Princess Aillin
of Leinster.*

Their loves being crossed and themselves parted, this faithful pair
set out to meet each other privately on the banks of Boyne. Bailé
rested upon his way at Traighm Bailé, now Dundalk. Here he and his
people had unyoked their chariots, sent their horses out to graze, and
turned themselves to pleasure, when they saw a horrible man like a
spectre coming towards them along the shore from the south, swiftly as
a hawk darts from a cliff or as the wind rushes from off the sea.
"Let him be met," said Bailé, "to ask whither he goes, whence he
comes, and why his haste." He came from Mount Leinster, the man

---

* The Leabhar na-h-Uidre, quoted in the Second Appendix to the late
Professor Eugene O'Curry's "Lectures on the MS. Materials of Ancient
Irish History." Dublin, 1861. Professor O'Curry had unequalled knowledge of the contents of the Old Gaelic MSS. in Ireland, and, where no
other authority is named, the information on this subject given in the text
is founded upon his researches.

said, and went north. He had no news but that Aillin as she was coming to meet Bailé had been overtaken by the youths of Leinster, and was dead of the hindrance, as it was foretold by Druids that this couple would not meet in life, but would meet after death, and would not part for ever after that. The man then passed by as a blast of wind. When Bailé heard his tidings he fell dead, and Bailé's tomb-stone was set up, and a yew grew up through his grave, and the form of Bailé's head appeared on the top of it. Then the same man sped south, and passed into the sunny chamber of Aillin, and told her how he had seen the lamentation over Bailé, who died while coming to meet a favourite and beloved woman. When he had told his evil news he darted out, and Aillin fell dead, and her tombstone was set up, and an apple-tree grew through her grave, and became a great tree at the end of seven years, and the form of Aillin's head appeared on the top of it. At the end of seven years, poets, and prophets, and visioners cut down the yew which was over the grave of Bailé, and they made a Poet's Tablet of it, and they wrote the visions, and the espousals, and the loves, and the courtships of Ulster in it. The apple-tree which grew over Aillin was also cut down, and in the same way the courtships of Leinster were written in it. Long afterwards, when, on November eve, Art, the son of Conn, made festival, the poets and the professors of every art came to that feast as it was their custom, and they brought their tablets with them. And those Tablets also came there ; and Art saw them, and when he saw them he asked for them ; and the two tablets were brought, and he held them in his hands face to face. Suddenly the one tablet of them sprang upon the other, and they became united as is woodbine round a twig, so that it was not possible to separate them. And they were preserved in the Treasury at Tara, until it was burnt by Dunlang, the son of Enna, at the time he burnt the Princesses.

Another story, ascribed to the year one, tells how Cuchulain, seeking three persons who had mysteriously disappeared, was helped by a prince who inscribed an Ogham in his spear. Then he went out upon the sea, and his charm carried him straight to the island where the men he sought had been detained. Again, in a story of which the action belongs to about the year 400, a king's son of Munster, obliged to fly to the court of Feradach, King of Scotland, doubtful of his reception when there, hid in a grove near Feradach's palace, where he was recognised by the king's poet, who, having learned his history, observed an Ogham inscription in his shield. "Who was it that befriended you with the Ogham which is in your shield?" said the poet. "It was not good luck he designed for you." "What does it contain?" asked the king's son from Munster. "What it contains," said the poet, "is, that if you came by day to Feradach's court your head should be cut off before evening; and that if it were by night you came, your head should be cut off before morning." When a king's son could travel, or be supposed to travel, with an open letter like that fastened to his arm, the mystery of writing might well be associated with enchantments, and be used to magnify the power of the poet or the priest.

These were the days when poetry was first written in staves, that is to say, cut on the four sides of a square staff, or in the folds of a thick staff opening fanwise.
Poets' Staves. In the ancient Irish or Brehon laws, an article that belongs to Christian times prescribing the sort of weapon persons of each rank might carry for their defence against dogs, &c., in their usual walks, allows a slender lath or graceful crook to a priest, but assigns to a poet his tablet-staff according to the privileges of his order. Poetry was then really a staff to lean upon, and an irate bard might literally break a critic's head with a quatrain.

The primitive classification of literary men among the Gaels according to their capabilities was into the Ollamh, or perfect Doctor, who was qualified to recite at
Old Gaelic degrees in Literature. public feasts and assemblies seven fifties of historic tales; the Anroth, who could tell half as many; the Cli, who could tell a third of the number; the Cano; and so on down to the Fochlog, who told thirty; and the lowest class of literary men, the Driseg, who could relate but twenty. In the infancy of civilisation men are as children, incapable of giving their attention to a narrative

that does not appeal to curiosity and wonder. But the
stories of the Gaelic man of letters must be stories of the
right sort, told in the right words. When the visible power
of the written word was but as that of the first green sprout
from an acorn, much of intellectual care was bestowed
necessarily upon the securing of the utmost accuracy of
tradition. Of the seven times fifty tales that the Ollamh
had at his tongue's end for the instruction or amusement of
a king, five times fifty must be Prime Stories—those worth
preserving—and twice fifty, Secondary Stories; while the
Secondary Stories were permitted only to men of the four
first grades. This we read in a MS. copied into the
ancient Book of Leinster, where it is added that "these
Prime Stories are: Destructions and Preyings, Courtships, Battles, Caves, Navigations, Tragedies (or Deaths),
Expeditions, Elopements, and Conflagrations. These
following also reckon as Prime Stories: stories of Irrup-
tions, of Visions, of Loves, of Hostages, and of Migrations."

This characteristic list shows in what literary themes a
rude people delighted. There was History as well as Poetry
among our early Celtic literature, but the History
was tinged by fancy, and the Poetry was in celebration of historic incident. Again let it be
observed that in early times there was no difference of nationality between the Gaels of Ireland and those
of the Scottish highlands. From the sixth century they
remained one people, with the same language, customs, and
traditions until in the sixteenth century political and religious changes parted them. Until then there was scarcely
even a dialectic difference between their languages. We
have an example of the manner of their first historians in the
following " Prime Story " of a Battle in Erin, told in a tract
fourteen hundred years old, of which there is one ancient
copy in existence. It tells—

Of History
among the
ancient
Gaels.

Of a Battle fought on the Plain of Moytura.

The plain is still covered with cromlechs, and if the story be true in its dates, those cromlechs were raised over the slain about three thousand eight hundred years ago.

Less than two hundred and fifty years before the coming of the Milesians, the Firbolgs reached Erin. Landing at different points, they contrived to meet in the unpeopled land, and fixed their seat of government upon the green hill now called Tara. The five brothers divided the island into five parts, and ruled in peace for six and thirty years, but at the end of that time they were surprised to find that there was another people in the land, the Tuatha (that is, people) dé Danann * of whom they had known nothing. These people, after landing on the north-east coast of Erin, had destroyed their boats, slipped into fastnesses in Leitrim, and so gradually showed themselves to the Firbolg people, pretending that they had come through the air by skill in necromancy. The King of the Firbolgs sent a great warrior, named Sreng, to observe the strangers, who, seeing his approach, sent forth a champion of their own, named Breas, to meet him. The two champions approached cautiously, peeping at each other over their shields ; Breas spoke first, and Sreng was delighted to hear himself addressed in Gaedhlic. Then they conversed and found that the two nations were of one descent, the ancestors of the Tuatha dé Danann having passed into the north of Europe, when their brothers, the ancestors of the Firbolgs, went of old into Thrace. The heroes compared arms, exchanged spears for comparison of arms on either side, counselling division of the island, and mutual friendship between the two peoples. But when Sreng returned to the Firbolg King, that king and his people were bent upon giving battle. The Tuatha dé Danann, expecting attack, withdrew to Magh Tuireadh (or Moytura, near the present village of Cong, in Mayo). The Firbolgs marched upon them. The Tuatha dé Danann offered, through their bards, terms of accommodation. But the Firbolgs were resolved to fight, did fight, and were defeated with great slaughter, their numbers being brought down to three hundred after four days' battle. Sreng cut off the left arm of the King of the Tuatha dé Danann. But the maimed King had a silver arm made to replace it, and was called in story afterwards the

---

* M. Henri Martin (" D'Archeologie Celtique," Paris, 1872, p. 79) says that Tuatha dé Danann signifies People of the Gods of Dana. Dana (genitive danann), called also Anu or Ana, was, with them, he says, the Mother of the Gods.

Silver-handed. Sreng, who survived with the three hundred, still fought on, and offered to complete the battle by a series of single combats. But the Tuatha dé Danann offered him peace, and gave him one of the five divisions of the land to rule over, so that Connaught became known as Sreng's Province.

Of this most ancient piece of British history Professor O'Curry says, " I am bound to assert that I believe there is not in all Europe a tract of equal historical value yet lying in MS., considering its undoubted antiquity and authenticity."

One step more we will take in company with the most primitive of our historians.

Ancient manuscripts that contain extracts from the lost book of Drom Sneachta, written before St. Patrick's time, represent from that venerable authority what was the Prime Story of Irruption and Migration that accounted for—

The first appearance of the Gaedhels in Erin.

Before their time the Firbolgs and the Tuatha dé Danann occupied the country, and these were originally of one race with the Gaedhels in Scythia. A branch of them went to Egypt, afterwards returned to Scythia, then went to Greece, and lastly to Spain, where after a long residence they built the city of Bragantia. [Observe the perfect coincidence of this tradition with what we elsewhere learn of the Brigantes in Spain, Ireland, and England.] At last a colony of them came into Erin (about 1700 B.C.), under command of the eight sons of Galamh, who is commonly called Milesius. These Milesians landed at the mouth of the Slaney, in Wexford, unobserved by the Tuatha dé Danann, and at once marched upon Tara, the seat of government, where they called upon the three kings of the island to surrender. They replied that they were taken by surprise, and proposed to the invaders to re-embark, go out to sea a distance of nine waves, and then, if they could forcibly make good their landing, they should have the country. The Milesians agreed that this was fair, and went back to their ships ; but the Tuatha dé Danann thereupon raised a fierce magical tempest, which dispersed their fleet. The Milesians, however, had also Druids, and although five of the eight brothers were drowned, three landed, namely, Eremon, Eber Finn, and Amergen of the White Knee, the poet, chronicler, and judge, and Amergen was the first man who dispensed justice in Erin. After the landing two battles were fought and won, although in the first the Milesian brothers lost their mother Scota. The power of the Tuatha dé Danann having been thus overthrown, Eremon and Eber Finn divided the land between them. But they themselves quarrelled and fought. Afterwards Eremon was sole king, and in his reign the Cruithneans or Picts came into Erin and passed over to Alban or Scotland, where they settled.

This is the native record or tradition that corroborates the argument derived from other sources for the coming of the Gaedhels into Erin out of Spain.

Fights, courtship, and abduction ; occupation of the riches of a thinly-peopled or unpeopled soil ; combat whenever two different bodies of colonists chanced to be coveting the same broad lands, are the chief features of old Gaelic history. It represents in its details a somewhat restless pastoral people, apt to diffuse itself by great and small migrations, fierce and persistent in fight, but not cruel, and giving honour to a very chivalrous sense of fair play. There are few tales of mean espial and betrayal. More natural to the Gael was his notion that the invaders who had made good their landing unexpected, unopposed, might reasonably, at the request of the invaded people, re-embark, retire nine waves, and then let it appear whether in fair fight they could make their landing good. The half-barbarous Gael —pagan, but a gentleman in the rough—who to the best of his own way and time held women in honour, and was often gladly subject to a clever queen, delighted in rich colour (not in Macphersonian gloom), and had the taste for ornament that we find clearly displayed in the gold trinkets and the chased work of the Bronze period discovered in its tombs. He liked the joyous festival, the glad run with the hounds. He had also a religious spirit and a lively fancy, that accorded dignity to the office not of the priest only but of the man of letters. The young Gaelic civilisation showed,

even in its vanities, its follies, its misdeeds, a clever child-
ishness that might advance into maturer dignity and worth.
There are no signs of the unmanly apathy, the base animal
cunning or ferocity, that indicate a stagnant barbarism. But
barbarism undoubtedly there was. The Ulstermen were
said to mix the brains of their slain enemies with lime, form
them into hard balls, and play with them when boastfully
comparing trophies. Conchobar is said to have had his
own skull penetrated by such a brainstone, and to have
lived seven years with two brains in his head, always sitting,
for he would die were he to shake himself.

A separate piece of ancient Gaelic history records

The Origin of the Boromean Tribute,

so called from the number of cows paid in it—*bo*, being the Gaelic for a
cow. The legend is of a King of Leinster, who married the younger
daughter of the chief Sovereign at Tara, but was afterwards persuaded
by his people that he ought to have been married to the elder. He
confined his young queen in a secret chamber, gave out that she was
dead, and as a widower obtained her sister's hand in marriage. Though
he had flinched from murder, he committed bigamy. But the concealed sister, having escaped, one day appeared suddenly before her
husband and his new wife. The deceived second wife died on the spot,
of shame and horror. The first wife returned to her solitary chamber,
and died of a broken heart. Their father, who heard of the tragedy,
marched into Leinster, and compelled the King of Leinster and his
people to bind themselves and their descendants for ever to pay every
three years a tribute of 5,000 fat cows, 5,000 hogs, 5,000 fat wethers,
5,000 clocks, 5,000 ounces of silver, and 5,000 large vessels of bronze.

This penalty was evidently associated with the habits of
a people living by flocks and herds, and having among
themselves weavers and workers in metal. But there is no
mention here of iron or metallic coin. "Pecus" still represents "Pecunia." Of this Boromean or cow tribute—which is
said to have been levied until the year 680, then abolished,
and revived at the beginning of the eleventh century by

Brian the son of Cinneidigh, as a punishment for Leinster's service to the Danes—it may be here added that for reviving it Brian obtained the name, yet famous in nursery lore, of Brian Boroimhe.

The fancy of the narrator always played over the surface of an old historic tale, giving it stronger hold through curiosity and wonder on the general attention, and, through that, upon the memory of all. Sometimes the whole history was so completely interpenetrated by the workings of imagination that it became a myth. The most famous of such myths is the record of the Taîn Bo Chuailgné (Cattle-spoil of Chuailgné, a place now called Cooley, in the county Louth), through which we will pass to a consideration of old Gaelic poetry. The tale was contained in the most ancient of the lost books of the Gael, the Cuilmenn or Great Book of Skins, and it is referred to in the Book of Leinster. It was included in a MS. of the eighth century, now lost, but described less than a century ago as among the Gaelic MSS. in the possession of the Highland Society. There are venerable legends that relate the early loss of the whole story of the Tain and its recovery; but the numerous accessible copies of the tale itself are comparatively modern. About the year 580, Senchan (pronounced Shencan), who was the chief poet, called a meeting of the poets and learned men of Erin to ascertain whether any of them remembered the old tale of the Cattle-spoil of Chuail-gné, which took place about the year 39. They said that they remembered only fragments of it ; whereupon Senchan asked whether any of his pupils would go into the country Letha (Italy), to learn the tale which a learned man had taken to the East after the Cuilmenn had been carried away. The legend goes on to tell how some of those who went had proceeded no farther than Connaught, when at the cromlech of Fergus Mac Roigh, the ghost of Fergus appeared in a beautiful form. It had brown hair, and wore a collared gold-ribbed shirt, a green mantle, a gold-hilted sword, and sandals of bronze. From the ghost's dictation Saint Ciaran then wrote in its true form the Taîn Bo Chuail-gné, of which, as a most lively relic of old Gaelic civilisa-tion, I will tell briefly the substance. Heroic literature grew about it. Some ten considerable poems serve as preludes to it. What the "Argonautic Expedition," or the "Seven against Thebes," is to Grecian history, such is to Irish history—

The Tale of the Cattle-spoil of Chuailgné.

Meáv (written Meadhbh) was the daughter of that Eochaidh, King of Erin, who fought his three revolted sons, and after their defeat and death was revolted against by the men of Connaught. To keep them in order, Eochaidh made his daughter Meáv Queen of Connaught, and he gave her the powerful Connaught chief Ailill, for husband. Meáv had before then quitted Conor, King of Ulster, to whom she had been married unhappily. Ailill died, and the widowed Queen went to the Court of Leinster, there to choose for herself a third husband. Having chosen the King of Leinster's youngest son, who was named also Ailill, she married him, and brought him back as her king-consort. Many children were born of their happy marriage.

One day Queen Meáv and her husband argued with each other as to their wealth, which was the richer ; for at that time all women had their private goods secured to them in marriage. So they resolved to produce and compare treasures against each other. There were brought to them all their wooden and metal vessels, and they were found to be equal in value; their finger-rings, clasps, bracelets, thumb-rings, diadems, and necklets of gold, and they also were equal. There were brought to them their garments of crimson, and blue, and black, and green, and yellow, and mottled, and white, and streaked ; in wealth of these, too, they were equal. There were brought their flocks of sheep ; their steeds and their studs from pastures ; great herds of swine from forests, and deep glens, and solitudes ; and droves of cows from the forests and most remote solitudes of the province. Still all were equal ; but there was found among Ailill's herds a young bull calved by one of Meáv's cows, which, not deeming it honourable to be under woman's control, had gone over and attached himself to Ailill's herds.

The name of this fine animal was the White-horned, and it was found that the Queen had not one to match him.

M

She sent, therefore, for her cousin, MacRoth, and asked where, in the five provinces of Erin, she could find a bull to match the White-horned? MacRoth knew of a better bull, called the Brown Bull of Chuailgné. It belonged to Daré, son of Fachtna, of Chuailgné, of Ulster.

"Go," said the Queen, "ask Daré to lend it me for a year, and I will send him fifty heifers back with it. If the people of this district object to parting with the bull, let Daré come with it himself, and he shall have lands here of my best, equal in extent to his own, a chariot worth sixty-three cows, and my future friendship."

The courier went on his errand with nine followers, and was hospitably received by Daré, who accepted the Queen's terms. But at night-fall Meáv's messengers were chattering among themselves over their cups. One said that Daré had done well to give to nine friendly men the Brown Bull that the four provinces of Erin could not have taken by force out of Ulster. Another said that little thanks were due to him, for if he had not given the bull willingly, Queen Meáv would have forced it from him. Daré's steward happened to bring in food just at that time, and he heard the boast. Angrily throwing down the food among the messengers, he turned back and told what he had heard to his master, who swore by his gods that these unmannerly claimants should not have the Brown Bull either by consent or force.

When this was reported to Meáv, she took up the words of her boastful messenger, and raised an army to march into Ulster. The forces met at Cruachain, whence, after consulting her Druid and a Banshee that appeared to her, the Queen herself led the army of invasion, her husband and her daughter, the Fairbrowed, going with her. When the host was encamped for the night, Meáv contrived to speak privately to each of the chiefs, and promise him for his fidelity the hand of her beautiful daughter, the Fairbrowed, in marriage.

It happened that the Ulstermen lay at that time under a curse of debility, so that the only defender of their border was the youth Cuchulain, and Cuchulain's patrimony was the first to be invaded, for within it lived the owner of the Brown Bull of Chuailgné. Cuchulain, confronting the invaders, claimed of them single combat, and adjured them by the laws of war not to advance further until, in fair successive fights of man to man, he had been conquered. The demand was granted. But days passed, and Cuchulain still was victor in each combat. Meáv became therefore impatient of delay, broke compact, carried fire and sword through Ulster, and marched back to Meath with the Brown Bull.

But now also the time of the curse came to an end, and the Ulstermen, led by King Conor, Meâv's first husband, pursued the cattle-plunderers, routed them in battle, and drove them in disorder over the Shannon. Meâv, however, had despatched the bull to her own palace before the battle, so the object of the expedition was thus far attained.

But when the Brown Bull of Chuailgné found himself in a strange country among strange cattle, he set up such a bellowing as never before had been heard in Connaught. And when those sounds reached him, Ailill's bull, the White-horned, knowing that some strange foe had arrived, rushed to battle with the bellower. The sight of each other was the signal for the fight. The province, says the story, rang with the roar of the two bulls. The sky was darkened by the sods of earth they threw up with their feet, and the foam out of their mouths. Faint-hearted men, women, and children hid themselves in caves; and the most valiant dared only look on at the fight from afar on the tops of the neighbouring hills.

At last the White-horned turned and fled. He rushed through a pass where sixteen over-bold warriors were standing. These were not only killed and trampled to the ground, but buried several feet in it by the hoofs of the bull that fled and of the bull that followed. The Brown Bull at last overtook his enemy, raised him up on his horns, and so ran off with him. He ran by the gates of Meâv's palace, tossing and shaking Ailill's bull as he went, until at last he shattered him to pieces. Joint by joint he dropped him as he rushed along, and wherever a joint fell, its name remained to the spot ever after. So it is that the place formerly called Ath Môr, the Great Ford, because the loin of the White-horned Bull was dropped there has been since that time called Ath Luain, or Athlone.

The Brown Bull having shaken his enemy bit by bit from his horns, returned into his own country so furious that every one fled at his approach. He faced directly to his own home. But the people of the bailé or hamlet hid behind a great rock, which he in his madness mistook for another bull; and so butting with all his force against it, he dashed out his brains and died.

From their histories and legendary tales we now turn to the poetry of the Gaedhels, which seems to have represented always the more solemn celebration of events in the lives, deaths, and burials of chiefs. Among the poems in the Book of Leinster is a death-song, said to have been recited in the year before the birth of our Lord by a famous Queen Meâv, the Half-Red, at the placing

Old Gaelic poetry.

M 2

of the stone over the grave of her husband Cuchorb, son
of Moghcorb :—

> " Moghcorb's son conceals renown,
> He shed blood well with his spears.
> A stone over his grave ! 'Tis pity—
> He who carried battle over Cliú Mail.
> My noble king never spoke falsehood ;
> In every peril his success was sure.
> Black as the raven was his brow ;
> Sharp as a razor was his spear ;
> White as lime was his skin ;
> We used to feast together.
> High was his shield as a champion,
> Long as an oar was his arm,
> The prop against the kings of Erin,
> He maintained his shield in every cause.
> He fed with his spear countless wolves
> At the heels of our man in every battle."

The seven battles that were fought by Cuchorb are next
named in his honour, until from his death in the last rises
the wail that destruction should have come upon him.
The exercise of fancy in abundant use of simile is here as
noticeable as we shall find its absence to be in the old
heroic Anglo-Saxon verse.

But the most interesting fragments of old Gaelic verse are
those, few in number, which belong to or are connected by
remote tradition with Fionn, Oisin, and the Fenians. When
in the last century James Macpherson, after publishing some
apparently genuine "fragments of ancient poetry collected
in the Highlands of Scotland," had proceeded to the fabri-
cation of his sentimental epics Fingal and Temora, investi-
gation subsequently led a Committee of the Highland
Society of Scotland to the conclusion that there were really
a few short poems or fragments of ancient Gaelic verse,
ascribed to Oisin or relating to him, retained among the
Gaels by immemorial tradition ; and that, in some degree,

verses and legends still retained among the Gaels had been interwoven by Macpherson with his own inventions. A MS. ascribed by the Committee of the Highland Society to the eighth century, which contained the story of the "Cattle-plunder of Chuailgné" and reference to Oisin, has disappeared since it was described in 1805. Eugene O'Curry found among old Irish MSS. only eleven Ossianic poems in records earlier than the fifteenth century. Of these, seven are ascribed to Fionn, two to his son Oisin, one to Fergus Finnbheoil, and one to Caeilte. The most important authority is the Book of Leinster, containing pieces transcribed in the twelfth century. A charter of lands in Morayshire, dated 1220, refers to a "well of the Fein;"* a MS. in the Advocates' Library, at Edinburgh, dating in 1238, contains, in Irish character, the song of Deirdir, or Deardra (Macpherson's Darthula). In Barbour's Brus, 1375, the Lord of Lorn is represented quoting to his men Fionn, by the name of Fingal, in his strife against Goll Macmorna, as an example of courage. William Dunbar, in the fifteenth century, refers, in his verses, to traditions concerning "Fyn Makowle" and "Gow Macmorn." Also Gavin Douglas, Bishop of Dunkeld, inscribing a poem to James IV., tells how he saw in his Palace of Honour, among other characters familiar to the people,—

> "Greit Gowmacmorne and Fyn Ma Coul, and how
> They suld be goddis in Ireland as they say."

In this way there can be set forth a tolerably continuous chain of evidence that Fionn was in Scotland, as in Ireland, a popular hero of the Gaels; but it is not necessary to look to a later date when we have extant the collection of Highland Traditions made by Dean James M'Gregor, of Lismore,

* Campbell's "Popular Tales of the West Highlands," vol. iv., p. 45) and for the next facts.

in Argyleshire, and his brother Duncan, all of it before the
year 1550, and much of it before 1512. The volume left by
them, as "The Book of the Dean of Lismore," now forms
part of the collection of Gaelic MSS. in the Advocates'
Library at Edinburgh. * The Dean of Lismore's collection
contains twenty-eight Fenian poems, nine attributed to Oisin
(of which one only is not manifestly of the Christian period
in which Oisin was only fabled to have lived), two to Fergus
Finnbheoil, one to Caeilte M'Ronan, three to a couple of
bards not elsewhere named, and the rest to bards unnamed.

Fionn (which means the Fair-haired) was the son of
Cumhaill.

From the *Leabhar-na-h-Uidre*, or Book of the Dun
Cow, a MS. collection made in the eleventh century,
there is an old story of the Battle of Cnucha, which accounts
for the feud between Fionn McCumhaill and Goll McMorna. †

When Cathair the Great was King in Tara he had a
great Druid, named Nuadu, who asked for land in Leinster,
and chose Almu, now the hill of Allen, near Newbridge, in
Kildare. He built there a home, of which he rubbed the
walls white with *alamu* (lime), and called it Almu, which
was the name of Nuadu's wife. A son of Nuadu was also a
celebrated Druid. His name was Tadhg, and he had a
wife named Rariu. Nuadu died, and Tadhg served in his
place as Druid to the Great Cathair. Tadhg and Rariu had
a daughter, Murni of the Fair Neck, who was sought for her
beauty by the sons of kings and mighty lords. Cumhaill
was among the king's sons who sought Murni, and Tadhg
refused him. Cumhaill was serving Cond, who was his

---

* A selection of all that is most interesting in "The Dean of Lismore's
Book" has been edited, (Edinburgh, 1862) with a translation and notes,
by the Rev. Thomas MacLaughlan, and an introduction and additional
notes by William F. Skene, Esq., to whom the Faculty of Advocates was indebted for the formation of its important Gaelic collection.

† Text and translation were contributed by W. M. Hennessy to the
Revue Celtique for August, 1873 (vol. ii., p. 86).

nephew. Cumhaill carried away, by force, Murni of the Fair
Neck. Tadhg, her father, brought his complaint to Cond.
Cond bade Cumhaill restore Murni or go into banishment.
Cumhaill replied that he would give everything except
Murni. Cond sent against Cumhaill a force, in which was
Aed, afterwards called Goll, the son of Dairi, who was called
also Morna, and there was between them a great battle at
Cnucha (now Castleknock—Caislen Cnucha—on the Liffey,
near Dublin), and Aed McMorna slew, in the battle,
Cumhaill. Then Luchet struck Aed in the eye, so that it
was blinded, and thenceforth he was called Goll, which
means blind. For this reason there was blood feud between
Goll McMorna and Fionn McCumhaill. Cond, after
that, protected Murni, whom her father had cast off, and
Fionn, born after his father's death, grew up and claimed
against Tadhg battle or compensation, and Tadhg gave up,
as compensation, his house of Almu to Fionn, and went
away to dwell in Tuath Dathi, the land of his birth. But
Fionn dwelt in Almu. And the clan Morna gave compensation to Fionn for his father's death, and the feud with Goll
was at an end until there was a dispute over a slanga-pig, in
which a man was slain. A slanga-pig had the magical power
of being alive again in good condition after it had been
killed and eaten. The last slanga-pig served out to an
Irish army is said to have fed twenty-five battalions.

Fionn's pedigree is contained in the Book of Leinster,
and the date of his death is assigned in a later compilation
of authorities, the Annals of the Four Masters, to the
year 283. Oisin (which means the Little Fawn), the son of
Fionn McCumhaill, had a warrior son, Oscar, who killed
and who was killed by Cairbré, son of Cormac McArt,
King of Erin, at the battle of Gabhra, in the year 284.
Several poems assume Fionn to have survived that battle a
few years. But, as the date of St. Patrick's coming to
Ireland is 432, Oisin, who had a son killed in battle 148

years earlier, could only have survived in fable to hold
with the saint the dialogues ascribed to him by old tradition.   The battle of Gabhra in which Oisin's son was
killed, is the subject of one of the two poems ascribed to
Oisin himself in the Book of Leinster.   The other poem
ascribed to him in this ancient book is nearly eight times as
long, and written—a romantic tale—on occasion of the
ancient festival games on the Liffey, when men spoke of
the blindness of Oisin, who outlived his friends.*   Oisin
was bard and warrior.   His brother Fergus Finnbheoil
(which means the Eloquent) was chief bard, and nothing
but a bard.   Ascribed to him there is, in the Book of
the Dean of Lismore, a poem in short, smooth alliterative
lines, with vocal concords, that is said in form of language
as in matter to bear evidence of a remote antiquity.   I
quote it as a characteristic and trustworthy example of the
most polished form of ancient Gaelic poetry.   Desire to
make peace in a quarrel between his father and Goll
McMorna, chiefly by putting Goll into good-humour before
proposing terms of accommodation, is the purport of the
song.   Every stop indicates the close of a line of verse† : —

"High-minded Goll, Who combats Fionn, A hero brave, Bold in
assault, His bounty free, Fierce to destroy, Beloved of all, Goll gentle
brave, Son of great Morn, Hardy in war, His praise of old, A comely
man, King soldierly free, Of no soft speech, No lack of sense, Cheerful
as great.   In battle's day, He moved a prince ; Though soft his skin,
Not soft his deed ; Of portly mould, A fruitful branch, His heart so
pure, He trains the young.   'Bove mountains high, Rises in victory,
We ever fear, When he assails.

"I tell you Fionn, Avoid the man, Terror of Goll, Shall make you
quail.   Soothe him rather, Better than fight.   Skilful and just, He
rules his men ; His bounty wide, A bloody man, First in the schools,

* A free rhymed translation of this poem, by Dr. Anster, will be found
in the *Dublin University Magazine* for March and April, 1852.

† "B. of D. of Lismore," Tr., pp. 43-48.

Of gentle blood, And noble race, Liberal kind, Untired in fight, No prince so wise. Brown are his locks, Marble his skin, Perfect his form, All full of grace, Fierce to exact, When aught is due, In vigour great, Of fairest face, No king like Goll.

"I tell you Fionn, His strength as waves, In battle's crash; Princely his gait, Comely his form, Goll's skilled fence, No play when roused. Ready to give, Dreadful his strength, Manly his mould, Soldierly great, Ne'er could I tell, His grace and power; A fearful foe, Ready his hands, Concealed his wrath, A cheerful face. Like murmuring seas, Rushed to the fight, A lion bold, As great in deed. Powerful his arm, Choice amidst kings. Joyful his way, His teeth so white. 'Tis he that wounds, The greatest foe. His purpose firm, A victor sure, Desires the fight. In history learn'd, Warrior bold, Sharp is his sword, Contemptuous Goll, Plunders at will, A fearless man. Wrathful is he, Dreadful in look, Leopard in fight, Fierce as a hound, Of women loved. A circle true, E'er by him stood. He hurls his dart, No gentle cast. Soft are his cheeks, In blossom rich, Of beauteous form, Unchanged success, No stream so swift, As his assault, MacMorn more brave, Than any told, Of powerful speech, It far resounds. He's truly great, Liberal just, Does not despise, Yet firm resolves, Gentle yet brisk, Forsakes no friend. In fight of kings, No powerless arm; There fierce his mien, And strong his blow, When roused his wrath. He's third of the chase.

"Noble McCumhaill, Soothe and promise, Give peace to Goll, Check wrath and guile. During my day, Whate'er it be, I'd give without guile, A third of the chase.

"Let's strive no more. Soft do thou speak, Fionn's love to Goll, And third of the hounds.

"Goll leave thy wrath, With us have peace, Now without grudge, Have of Fionn's forest a third.

"That will I take, Fergus, dear friend. My wrath is gone. No more I ask.

"Friend without guile, Lips thin and red, Bounty and strength, Shall win the praise, High-minded Goll."

Ascribed to Fergus there is found in the Irish MSS. only one genuinely ancient poem. It accounts for the name of a spring by telling how Fergus's brother Oisin, when hunting, was beguiled into a cavern, and there kept by the fairies for a twelvemonth, during all which time he cut chips from the handle of his spear and cast them in the stream. His father Fionn, who was looking for him, at last came to the stream, saw a chip floating down, knew immediately that it was part of Oisin's spear, followed the stream up to its source, and saved his son.

Caeilte McRonan, the other chief poet, was Fionn's cousin, and one of his bravest warriors, fleet of foot, famous in song. Of the songs of Caeilte, the one record left in the ancient Irish MSS. is a love story, ascribed to him, which finds in the drowning of a lady named Cliodhna the local name Wave of Cliodhna for a part of the coast of county Cork. It purports to have been sung by him to St. Patrick, and must, therefore, have been composed by another poet in the early Christian times. Caeilte, like Oisin, was fabled to have survived the rest of the Fenians, till he lived to see the coming of St. Patrick and to travel with him on his missionary journeys through the country. The tale of the first labours of the priest was thus cunningly interwoven with the native poetry and legend of the Gael. With lively wit and some dramatic skill the blind old bard is represented, for example, in the Dialogue with St. Patrick—still traditional in Mayo and the Western Highlands—as expressing Pagan weariness at all the ways of that "clerk of clergy and the bells," and sighing for the old days of chase with Fionn's hounds and the lost friendship of " Fionn the hospitable, heart without malice, heart stern in defence of battle." Says Patrick—

" Now is Fionn the Whitehanded placed by God among the devils, and although once great his strength to rely upon, he is weak now in the country of pains.

" *Oisin.*—My affliction and my grief I own ! not that myself or Fionn would ever have any regard for devils, however hideous.

" *Patrick.*—It is better for thee to be with me and the clergy, as thou art, than to be with Fionn and the Fenians, for they are in hell without order of release.

" *Oisin.*—By thy book and its meaning, by thy crozier and by thy image, better were it for me to share their torments, than to be among the clergy continually talking. . . . . Son of Alphinen of the wise words, woe is me that I am near the clergy of the bells ! For a time I lived with Caeilte, and then we were not poor." *

Such conversations of Oisin and Caeilte with St. Patrick, including the accounts given by them to the saint of legend and history attached to places that he visited, form the substance of the one unquestionably ancient example of old Gaelic imaginative tales that mingled prose and verse. It is called "The Dialogue of the Ancient Men," and the oldest fragment of it occurs in the Irish "Book of Lismore," written about the year 1400. One of its incidental poems is fabled to have won the hand of Credé, a fair princess of Kerry, who had declared that she would wed none but that suitor who was so gifted in the art of poetry as to be able to write a poem in description of her house and furniture. As a lively picture of Gaelic luxury in early Christian times, at the close of the Bronze Period, I quote a passage or two from Professor Eugene O'Curry's literal translation of this poem :—

(margin note: Gaelic tales in prose and verse.)

> " Happy the house in which she is :
> Between men, and children, and women :
> Between Druids and musicians ;
> Between cupbearers and doorkeepers.
>
> *   *   *   *   *
>
> A bowl she has whence berry-juice flows,
> By which she colours her eyebrows black ;
> She has clear vessels of fermenting ale ;
> Cups she has, and beautiful goblets.
> The colour of her house is like the colour of lime ;
> Within it are couches and green rushes ;
> Within it are silks and blue mantles ;
> Within it are red, gold, and crystal cups.

* " Poems of Oisin, Bard of Erin." From the Irish. By John Hawkins Simpson. (London, 1857.) The Dialogue of St. Patrick in this volume, from a Kerry MS., and Mayo oral tradition, corresponds exactly in spirit and manner with the Ossian's Prayer in " The Book of the Dean of Lismore" (Eng. Tr., p. 17), taken from Scottish tradition.

The corner stones of its sunny chamber
Are all of silver and yellow gold ;
Its thatch in stripes of faultless order,
Of wings of brown and crimson red.
Two door-posts of green I see ;
Nor is its door without beauty,
Long renowned for its carved silver
Is the lintel that is over the door.
Credé's chair is on your right hand,
The pleasantest of the pleasant ;
All over a blaze of mountain gold,
At the foot of her beautiful couch.
A gorgeous couch in full array,
Stands directly above the chair ;
It was made by (at ?) Tuilé in the East,
Of yellow gold and precious stones.
There is another bed on your right hand,
Of gold and silver without defect,
Curtained and soft,
And with graceful rods of golden bronze.

   *   *   *   *   *

An hundred feet spans Credé's house
From one corner to the other,
And twenty feet are fully measured
In the breadth of its noble door.
Its portico is thatched
With wings of blue and yellow birds ;
Its lawn in front and its well
Of crystal and of carmogal.

   *   *   *   *   *

There is a vat of royal bronze,
Whence flows the pleasant juice of malt ;
An apple-tree overhangs the vat
With the abundance of its heavy fruit.
When Credé's goblet is filled
With the ale of the noble vat,
There drop down into the cup directly
Four apples at the same time ;
The four attendants that have been named
Arise and go to the distribution ;
They present to four of the guests around
A drink to each man and an apple."

Although Crede's bower has no doubt been partly furnished with the cheap ornaments of poetical speech, and although the picture is but of a large hut pompous with barbaric luxury, yet there is a truth to the old Gaelic character in all this glow

The Celtic influence on English literature.

of gold, chased silver, bronze, and gay colour in raiment, in the painting of the very thatch, and in the turn of fancy that suggested for the lady's porch a roofing with the blue and yellow wings of birds. The Gaels were skilful in the use of dyes, and had an Oriental taste for the enjoyment of bright colour. Thus, for example, in the famous tale of the "Cattle-plunder of Chuailgné," there is introduced a series of descriptions of the chiefs of Ulster who pursued and beat the army of Queen Meáv : it is no dingy barbarous host that rises to our view. "Another company have come to the same hill," said MacRoth, through whose eyes the army is pictured in Homeric fashion ; "it is wild, and unlike the other companies. Some are with red cloaks ; others with light-blue cloaks ; others with deep-blue cloaks ; others with green or grey, or white or yellow cloaks, bright and fluttering about them. There is a young red-freckled lad, with a crimson cloak in their midst ; a golden brooch in that cloak at his breast ; a shirt of kingly linen with fastenings of red gold at his skin ; a white shield with hooks of red gold at his shoulder, faced with gold, and with a golden rim ; a small gold-hilted sword at his side ; a light, sharp, shining spear to his shoulder." Such were the chiefs who fought with Oisin and the Fenians, and who with fancies gay as their cloaks listened to the histories, poems, and legends of the first literary men concerning whom there remains record in Britain. We shall find as this narrative advances that the main current of English literature cannot be disconnected from the lively Celtic wit in which it has one of its sources. The Celts do not form an utterly distinct part of our mixed population. But for early, frequent, and various contact with the race that in its half-barbarous days invented Oisin's dialogues with St. Patrick, and that quickened afterwards the Northmen's blood in France, Germanic England would not have produced a Shakespeare. The recollections of the past on which we are now dwelling are not to be taken as mere antiquarian details. They contribute to our full sense of more than the history of the formation of the English language. They are an essential chapter in the more interesting tale of the formation of the English character, the right reading of which is the most vital part of any study of the English written mind.

The chief exercise of the Gaelic imagination from St. Patrick's time until the year 1000 was in the repetition and invention of tales having Fionn, Oisin, Fergus, Caeilte, and the Fenians for heroes. One of the oldest and most famous of these was the tale of—

The Fenian Tales.

The Pursuit of Diarmaid and Grainné.

When Fionn went to Tara to sue Grainné, the daughter of Cormac Mac Art, he took with him his son Oisin, his grandson Oscar, and a handsome chief officer, named Diarmaid O'Duibhné. Fionn was an old, war-worn man. Oisin and Diarmaid pleased the lady more. When, therefore, she sent her cup round at the feast, selecting as was usual four chiefs at a time, each of whom passed it to four neighbours, she drugged her cup, and contrived that all should drink from it but Oisin and Diarmaid. They who drank slept. When these alone remained awake, Grainné told Oisin that she would rather marry him than the old man. Oisin would not betray his father. Then the Princess begged of Diarmaid that he would run off with her. So it was that they fled together. Fionn, when he awoke, pursued, and sent his best men out in various directions; but Diarmaid had the good will of the other Fenians, and they never came upon his traces except when Fionn himself was of the party. And then it always happened that in the moment before capture Diarmaid and Grainné, by trick or agility, contrived a wonderful escape.

The pursuit extended over all Erin, and the description of it forms a lively topographical survey of the land, with notices of its products, customs, and traditions. To this day also throughout Ireland many cromlechs are called by the country-people Beds of Diarmaid and Grainné.

In the old Gaelic battle-pieces the "badb" (royston, or hooded crow) appears frequently as a symbol of fury, and the "badb-catha" with her three sisters Neman, Macha, and Morrigau, appear as battle furies able to confound whole armies by their magic power. They play a great part in the Tain Bo Chuailgné. Neman confounds armies, and drives friends to slaughter one another; Macha revels among the slain; Morrigau nerves the arm of Cuchulain, the Hector of that old heroic song. Another superstition associates the spirit of the warrior himself with a bird, and as his rage grows his "bird of valour" rises and flutters over him. The fear excited by such fury begets *geltacht*, lunacy, which makes its victims so light that they also are blown through the air like birds. There is a glen of the lunatics twenty miles east of Ventry Harbour, to which it is said all light people would fly if they might, to cure themselves by eating the cresses of its running stream.*

Another very famous Fenian tale narrates the Battle of Finntrágha, in West Kerry, Anglicised into Ventry Harbour. The battle was fought by Fionn and his warriors against an emperor of all the world except Erin, who came to subdue Erin also. The invaders' fleet had been piloted by a traitor into the noble harbour of Finntrágha. Fionn was swimming and fishing when his warders of the coast brought the news of the invasion. Like news having been received by several chiefs and warriors of the Tuatha dé Danann, they marched also to the defence, and the enemy was beaten off after a contest of a twelvemonth and a day.

We have here the Fenians and the Tuatha dé Danann

---

* See in No. 1, the *Revue Celtique* for May, 1870, an article by Mr. W. M. Hennessy, with a postscript by Dr. C. Lottner, on "The Ancient Irish Goddess of War."

fighting as one people to drive an invader from the coast. Irish tradition says that the Fenians were an ancient militia or standing army, employed only on home service for protecting the coasts from invasion. Each of the four provinces, says the tradition, had its bard ; that of Leinster, to which Fionn and his family belonged, being called the Clanna Baoisgne. This militia is said to have been paid by the king, billeted on the people in the winter, but to have lived in summer by the chase ; and these are imagined to have been the qualifications of a Fenian :—

"Every soldier was required to swear : that, without regard to her fortune, he would choose a wife for her virtue, her courtesy, and her good manners ; that he would never offer violence to a woman ; that as far as he could he would relieve the poor ; and that he would not refuse to fight nine men of any other nation.

"No person could be received into the service unless his father and mother, and all his relatives, gave security that none of them should revenge his death upon the person who might slay him, but that they would leave the matter to his fellow-soldiers.

"The youth himself must be well acquainted with the twelve books of poetry, and be able to compose verses. He must be a perfect master of defence. To prove this he was placed in a field of sedge reaching up to his knees, having in his hands a target and a hazel stick as long as a man's arm. Nine experienced soldiers, from a distance of nine ridges of land, were to hurl their spears at him at once : if he was unhurt he was admitted, but if wounded he was sent off with a reproach.

"He must also run well and defend himself when in flight : to try his activity he was made to run through a wood, having a start of a tree's breadth, the whole of the Fenians pursuing him ; if he was overtaken or wounded in the wood he was refused, as too sluggish and unskilful to fight with honour among such valiant troops.

"Also, he must have a strong arm and be able to hold his weapon steadily.

"Also, when he ran through a wood in chase his hair should not come untied ; if it did he was rejected.

"He must be so swift and light of foot as not to break a rotten stick by standing upon it ; able also to leap over a tree as high as his forehead, and to stoop under a tree that was lower than his knees. Without stopping or lessening his speed, he must be able to draw a thorn out of his foot.

" Finally, he must take an oath of fidelity.

" The Rev. Geoffrey Keating, who wrote a history of Erin in the year 1630, gravely says, ' So long as these terms of admission were exactly insisted upon, the militia of Ireland were an invincible defence to their country, and a terror to rebels at home and enemies abroad.' "

Goll McMorna had slain Fionn's father Cumhaill in battle, and was Fionn's mortal enemy in early life. Afterwards he made a peace with him, and fought under him as chieftain of the Connaught Fenians. But the supremacy of the Clanna Baoisgne led to feuds, and at last Fionn and his clan, defying the throne itself, were attacked by all the forces of Erin except those of the King of Munster, who took part with him, and suffered carnage in that battle of Gabhra, in the flat country of Meath, wherein Oisin's son Oscar and the King fell by each other's hands. Fionn's son Cairbar was then dead, but poets feigned that he was only absent, that he arrived in time to close his grandson's eyes, and after this defeat, peace had no sweets for him and war no triumphs. Fionn died at last, it is said, by the lance of an assassin.

The following piece is from the collection of old Gaelic poems in " The Dean of Lismore's Book." The Rev. Thomas MacLauchlan, their translator, is not answerable for the attempt I have here made to represent the song of the chief bard to modern ears by a rude blending of rhyme and assonance. Fergus Finnbheoil is supposed to tell, in reply to questions from his father Fionn McCumhaill, the slaughter of his Feinn, or Fenians, at the battle of Gabhra, and the death of Oscar, Oisin's son, the old man's grandson. A Gaelic poem closes usually with repetition of its first word or phrase. That repetition here serves also to suggest the bard, who was the historian of ancient times, passing from tribe to tribe, and answering in each place the demand for full detail of the great deeds whereof it was he only who kept the record and maintained the fame :—

N

The Death of Oscar.

" Say, Bard of the Feinn of Erin,
  How fared the fight, Fergus, my son,
  In Gabhra's fierce battle day ? Say ! "

" The fight fared not well, son of Cumhaill,
  From Gabhra come tidings of ruin,
  For Oscar the fearless is slain.
  The sons of Caeilte were seven ;
  They fell with the Feinn of Alban.
  The youth of the Feinn are fallen,
  Are dead in their battle array.
  And dead on the field lies MacLuy,
  With six of the sons of thy sire.
  The young men of Alban are fallen ;
  The Feinn of Breatan are fallen.
  And dead is the king's son of Lochlan,
  Who hastened to war for our right—
  The king's son with a heart ever open,
  And arm ever strong in the fight."

" Now, O Bard—my son's son, my desire,
  My Oscar, of him, Fergus, tell
  How he hewed at the helms ere he fell."

" Hard were it, Fionn, to number,
  Heavy for me were the labour,
  To tell of the host that has fallen,
  Slain by the valour of Oscar.
  No rush of the waterfall swifter,
  No pounce of the hawk on his prey,
  No whirlpool more sweeping and deadly,
  Than Oscar in battle that day.
  And you who last saw him could see
  How he throbbed in the roar of the fray,
  As a storm-worried leaf on the tree
  Whose fellows lie fallen below,
  As an aspen will quiver and sway
  While the axe deals it blow upon blow.

  When he saw that MacArt, King of Erin,
  Still lived in the midst of the roar,

> Oscar gathered his force to roll on him
> As waves roll to break on the shore.
> The King's son, Cairbar, saw the danger,
> He shook his great hungering spear,
> Grief of griefs ! drove its point through our Oscar,
> Who braved the death-stroke without fear.
> Rushing still on MacArt, King of Erin,
> His weight on his weapon he threw,
> And smote at MacArt, and again smote
> Cairbar, whom that second blow slew.
> So died Oscar, a king in his glory.
> I, Fergus the Bard, grieve my way
> Through all lands, saying how went the story
> Of Gabhra's fierce battle-day."   "Say ! "

We have illustration here of the fact that the Fenians were not confined to Erin.   In this ancient poem on the battle of Gabhra we read of the bands of the Feinn of Alban—Alban being the old name of Scotland, north of the Firth of Forth and Clyde — and the supreme King of Breatan—Breatan being southern Scotland, of which Dunbreaton, now Dunbarton, was the chief seat—belonging to the Order of the Feinne of Alban ; and also that the Fians of Lochlan were powerful.   Now, Lochlan was an ancient name for Germany north of the Rhine ; but when the Norwegian and Danish pirates appeared in the ninth century they were called Lochlanaels, and the name of Lochlan was transferred to Norway and Denmark.   It has been argued[*] from this that the Fenians were not a militia of Gaels, but that they were a distinct Celtic race, connected with the only two races who are spoken of as having come in oldest time from Lochlan, namely, the Tuatha dé Danann and the Crúithne.   These are thought to have been some of the Celts who preceded the Germanic peoples now occupying the north German shore and Scandinavia.   The Tuatha dé

* By Mr. Skene in the Introduction to the " Book of the Dean of Lismore," pp. lxxiii.—lxxx.

Danann (people of the Dan country) landed in Scotland, and, approaching the headlands of the north-western shore, gave to the country the name of Alban (Highland or Alp-land, the words Alb and Alp being of one Celtic origin), which, as Albion, became the first native name of the whole island. The Tuatha dé Danann passed, as tradition has already told us, into Erin, and partly occupied the land before the Milesian brothers came from Spain. The Cruithne, whom some connect with the Picts, first landed from Lochlan in Erin, and migrated thence to Alba'n. To the bards, then, of these northern Celts, who had not reached our shores by way of southern Europe, the Fenians and their poets may have been allied most closely. The traditions of the Cruithne, in describing their migrations, even name as the mythic poet of their race one whom they called " Huasein."

We may only touch here on the relation of the bright heroic stories of the Pagan time among the Gaels, to the same quick artistic feeling that gave—with the zeal of which we shall find evidence hereafter— colour and form to their first Christian utterances. They showed their native genius for art even in the miniature painting that illuminates their manuscripts. The adornment of books used in the Church service, with initials carefully designed and coloured, began in Ireland in the seventh century, if not in the sixth ; the artistic spirit blending itself with the first utterances of their Christian faith. The most beautiful example known is a MS. of the Gospels which came from the Cathedral of Kells, and is in the library of Trinity College, Dublin. Next in beauty to the Kells MS. is the MS. of Saint Cuthbert, known also as the Durham MS., because it was brought from Lindisfarne to Durham at the time of transference of the See. In the north, where the Irish priests, Culdees—who received inspiration from the Eastern Church—were, before Augustine, the first bringers of

Adornment of MSS.

Christianity to Britain, their illuminators also brought their art into the first English Church. While the Irish illuminations have a common origin with other ancient examples of the art, and owed something to Byzantine influence, they have characters of their own. They are marked by an absence of decoration drawn from flowers and foliage ; a grotesque elaboration of animal forms ; and especially by the frequent use of a spiral ornament, and of an interlacement of lines, rather suggestive of basket-work, to fill up the ground of a design. These interlacements and the spiral line, like the volute of an Ionic column, single or double, are both common as ornaments of the Bronze period. But while these spiral ornaments are traceable from the earliest art of the Celts, it was in Ireland that the luxuriant and playful fancy was first applied to the treatment of animal forms in the decoration of their books. Another feature in the decoration of old Irish MSS. is a red dotted bordering to the initial letters.

A legendary tale of the Battle of Magh Rath is in a fifteenth century MS. in the library of Trinity College, Dublin, containing also other pieces. There is another MS. copy of it in the Book of Fermoy, The Battle of Magh Rath. and there was a third in the Duke of Buckingham's library at Stowe. This tale blends fable with the record of a famous battle actually fought in the year 637. It was edited for the Irish Archæological Society, with a translation and notes by a famous Irish scholar, John O'Donovan, in the year 1842, and, in the editor's opinion, the tale, as we have it, belongs to the twelfth century. If it was written to please a descendant of its hero, while his race still had power in the North of Ireland, it must have been written before the year 1197, when the last chief of the family died.

The battle upon which this tale was founded was in resistance to invasion brought on by domestic strife. A good king, Malcoba, was cut off by his successor, and the successor was cut off by his enemy, Congal Claen, a man of genius and power. Malcoba's brother, Domhnall, then became king, defeated Congal Claen in battle, and drove him to exile among the Scots in Britain. Congal's high qualities gathered to him friends among the Scots of Alban, Picts, Britons, and Saxons, and he came back with a great force to Ireland. Domhnall, King of Ireland, gathered all the forces of the country, which united for the common safety, and at Magh Rath the two great armies fought a six days' battle, ending with such defeat of the Scots of Alban as, according to Adamnan, who laboured always for accord between the brother tribes in Ireland and Britain, "to this day has obliged the Scottish nation to succumb to foreign powers, and which gives our heart grief when we consider it."

The legendary tale of the battle had soon after its production an introductory tale written for it, called—

The Banquet of Dun na n-Gedh and the Cause of the Battle of Magh Rath.

There were no eggs for that banquet of Dun na n-Gedh, and eggs were very scarce. Those sent in search of eggs carried away a tub of goose-eggs belonging to a holy saint, whose custom was to spend the day in the Boyne up to his arm-pits praying from his Psalter open on the shore before him, then to go home and dine upon an egg and a half and three cresses from the water of the Boyne. When the saint came home and found his eggs gone to the King's banquet, "he cursed the banquet as bitterly as he was able to curse it." The first person who cracked one of the saint's eggs, before the banquet had been blessed, was Congal Claen, then the provincial king of Ulster, and he did so without waiting for a blessing on the meat. Thence came the great crack in the peace of Erin, although the King said "no one else shall partake of this feast until the twelve apostles of Erin are brought to bless and consecrate it, and avert the curse if they can." The twelve apostles of Erin came, and each brought a hundred saints with him, and they must have said grace powerfully; but they could not avert the curse because Congal had tasted of the feast before it had been blest, and the venom of this they were not able to avert.

Now there had come down to the assembly before the banquet a remarkable couple—a woman and a man ; larger than the summit of a rock on a mountain was each limb of their limbs, sharper than a shaving-knife each edge of their shins ; their heels and hams in front of them ; should a sackful of apples be thrown on their heads not one of them would fall to the ground, but they would stick on the points of the strong bristly hair ; their limbs were blacker than coal, darker than smoke ; their eyes whiter than snow ; a lock of the lower beard went up over the head, and a lock of the upper beard went down over the knees ; the woman had whiskers and the man had none. They carried between them a tubfull of goose-eggs. "What is that?" said the King. "It is plain," they said, "that the men of Erin are making a banquet for you, and each brings what he can. We bring you these eggs." "I am thankful for them," said the King. So they were taken into the palace, and dinner of meat and ale for a hundred was set before them. The man ate all that, and gave none to the woman. Another dinner for a hundred was set before them. The woman ate all that and gave none to the man. Again dinner for a hundred was set before them, and they ate all that between them. "Give us food," they said, when they had finished. "You can have no more," said the King's steward, "till the men of Erin join in feast." "It shall be an evil feast for them then. They shall be quarrelsome at it, for we come from Hell." So they rushed out and vanished into nothing.

But when Congal had tasted the unblest egg of the saint, and the mighty grace had been spoken by the twelve apostles of Erin and the twelve hundred saints who came with them, they all sat to the feast, and a goose-egg was brought on a silver dish before every king in the house, and when the dish and egg were placed before Congal the silver dish changed to a wooden dish, and the goose-egg to the egg of a red-feathered hen. And a young man among his followers urged Congal to resent the insult, until his bird of valour fluttered over him and he struck out at friend and foe.

So it was that, as the tale of the battle briefly recalls, his foster-son Congal Claen, the son of Scannlan of the Broad Shield, quarrelled with long-palmed Domhnall of Derry, about the difference of the two ominous, unlucky, evil-boding eggs—namely, the egg of a blackish red-feathered hen of malediction, and the egg of a fine feathered goose, through which the destruction of Erin was wrought. And in the tale of the strife adjectives crowd as thickly as the men of the contending hosts. We have the later and more florid manner of recital, and there was terror in the grimness of the Gaels, and horrible aerial phantoms rose up, in dismal, regular, aerial, storm-shrieking, hovering fiend-like hosts constantly in motion, shrieking and howling as they hovered above the armies ; and the grey-haired Morrigu shouts victory over the head of Domhnall—

> " Over his head is shrieking
> A lean hag, quickly hopping
> Over the points of their weapons and shields
> She is the grey-haired Morrigu. "

But the touch of the Christian teacher is felt in these later tales. Apostles and saints, Church blessings and cursings enter now into the argument. Even the cowardice of the hero Suibhne, whose sudden fear is a feature in the story, and who is said in another tale to have died of the many poems made upon him, is thus moralised. It confounded him " because he had been cursed by St. Ronan, and denounced by the saints of Erin for having slain an ecclesiastical student of their people over the consecrated trench,"—that is, the clear stream over which the shrine of the Lord had been placed for worship before the battle. God before ! His blessing on the bread, His blessing on the battle, so the new note rises in the ancient song.

The chief MS. materials for a study of the old Gaelic Language and Literature are :—

Latin MSS. of the 8th or 9th Century with Gaelic Glosses.*

1. A codex of " Priscian," in the Library at St. Gall in Switzerland, crowded with Irish glosses, interlinear and marginal, as far as p. 222. (They were Irish monks who first carried Christianity to Switzerland.)

* Quoted in Zeuss's " Grammatica Celtica."

2. A codex of "St. Paul's Epistles," in the University Library at Würzburg, containing even more glosses than the St. Gall "Priscian."

3. A Latin "Commentary on the Psalms," ascribed now to St. Columbanus, in the Ambrosian Library at Milan, yet more crowded with ancient Irish glosses.

4 A codex at Carlsruhe containing *some of the works of Bede.* An entry of the death of Aed, King of Ireland, establishes the date 817.

5. A second codex of "Priscian," also at Carlsruhe, with fewer glosses than that of St. Gall.

6. A *miscellaneous* codex of St. Gall, including medical charms, in which Goibnenn the smith and Diancecht the leech of the Tuatha dé Danann are mentioned.

7. A codex at Cambray, written between the years 763 and 790, containing *canons of an Irish council* held A.D. 684, and a *fragment of an Irish sermon* containing Latin sentences.

ANNALS AND OTHER LITERATURE.—11TH CENTURY.

The "Synchronisms of Flann of Monasterboice," a monk who died in 1056, a sketch of Universal History from the remotest times.

The chronological "Poem of Gilla Caemhain," who died A.D. 1072.

The "Annals of Tighernach" (pronounced Teer-nah) *O'Braoin*, abbot of the Monasteries of Clonmacnois and Roscommon, who died A.D. 1088. Of the Annals of Tighernach there are seven MS. copies, all defective, and a vellum fragment. This is the most trustworthy of the ancient records.

The "Annals of Innisfallen," believed by Professor O'Curry to have been mainly written by Maelsuthain, a prince of the tribes of Loch Léin or Killarney, who was educated in the monastery of the lake, and died in it, retired from the world, A.D. 1009. These annals, being continued to 1215, are commonly ascribed to the 13th century.

The "Leabhar na-h-Uidre," or Book of the Dun Cow : a fragment remains of 138 folio pages, written by Maelmiore, who was killed in 1106, contains ancient poems and tales. It contains part of the Book of Genesis, part of Gilla Naemhin's translations of Nennius, part of the Taîn Bo, an account of the Pagan ceremonies of Ireland, and other tracts. It is in the library of the Royal Irish Academy.

12TH CENTURY.

The "Book of Leinster," compiled by Finn M'Gorman, Bishop of Kildare, who died A.D. 1160, for the Dermod M'Murroch who invited Strongbow into Ireland. It contains invasions, a description of

Tara, old chronicles, a fragment of Cormac's Glossary, a copy of the Dinnsenchas, genealogies, and lives of the Irish Saints. The book, now in the library of Trinity College, Dublin, contains more than 400 pages of large folio vellum.

14TH CENTURY.

The " Book of Ballymote," 502 pp. of largest folio vellum, was being written in 1391. It contains pedigrees, the adventures of Eneas, the Book of Rights, the Dinnsenchas, and several historical and mytho-logical pieces. It is in the library of the Royal Irish Academy.

The "Leabhar Breac," or Speckled Book, in the same Library.

The " Yellow Book of Lecain," historical pieces in prose and verse, also a curious law tract, copied in 1390. It is in the library of Trinity College, Dublin, where is also the " Book of Lecain," compiled in 1416 by MacFirbises, of Lecain, in Sligo.

The " Book of Lismore," written in 1400, discovered in 1814 in Lismore Castle, contains lives of Saints, dialogues of the sages, the Hill of the Bellowing Oxen, Travels of Marco Polo, and other pieces.

15TH CENTURY.

The " Annals of Ulster," so called because they were compiled in Ulster, and treat more of Ulster affairs than of those of other provinces: compiled by Cathal M'Guire, of Loch Erne, who died A.D. 1498. The annals were continued afterwards to the year 1604.

16TH CENTURY.

"Annals of Kilronan," or Loch Cé, extend to 1590.

" Annals of Connacht," a fragment detailing Connaught history from 1223 to 1562.

17TH CENTURY.

The " Annals of the Four Masters," collected from ancient MS. material by Father Michael O'Clery and his three colleagues, masters in antiquarian lore, were published in 1634.

By the same compilers, the "Succession of the Kings" and the " Book of Invasions."

CHAPTER III.

OLD LITERATURE OF THE CYMRY.

THE Cymry carry back their literature, not like the Gaels, to an Oisin, a Fergus, and a Caeilte of the third century, but to a Taliesin, a Llywarch, an Aneurin, and a Myrddin, or Merlin, of the sixth. Of the tra- *The Cymry.* ditions of an earlier date, it has been noticed * that they are connected with sites only in South Wales and the North of England. Hence it is inferred that in North Wales the Gael held ground much longer than in other parts of England. Some have considered that North Wales came for the first time under full Cymric rule when it was called Rheged (a gift), to that Urien who led the forces of the northern Cymry against Ida and his Angles, while King Arthur battled in the south. This is that Urien whose prowess Taliesin and his brethren celebrated; for in the most ancient Cymric literature we hear again the battle-cries of conflict between the resisting Celt and the advancing Teuton, and are touched with the profound melancholy of the bards who sang the death-struggle of heroes in a hopeless patriotic war. To speak, therefore, of the songs of the old Cymric bards is to speak also of the first full occupation of the plains of England by the Anglo-Saxon.

The first full occupation. Reason has been shown for belief that, after the crossing of the Cymric Celts from

* " Vestiges of the Gael in Gwynedd."

Gaul into the south-east of Britain—whence the few Gaels who had wandered so far from Erin and our western shores

Germanic settlements in Britain before A.D. 449.

were driven back on the main body of their own people—the Cymry were, in their turn, pressed by the Belgæ, a Germanic race, who partly dislodged them, first in Gaul, and afterwards in Britain. These people, as we have seen, had occupied the Frisian shore of the continent and the coast of France east of the Seine. But the ancient language of the Frisian coast is allied more closely than Old Saxon itself, or any other language, to the language of the Anglo-Saxons. Anglo-Saxon and old Frisian are, in fact, allied so closely that they seem to be only dialects of the same tongue. A dialect also of that tongue may have been the language spoken by the Belgæ who had crossed into Britain before Cæsar's time ; and the main bulk of the Anglo-Saxons may have been only Belgæ of a later date, and from another part of their long line of continental shore opposite Britain. The beginning of the Germanic immigration is, in fact, prehistoric. Speaking of Britain from direct knowledge, Cæsar said :* " The interior is inhabited by those who are traditionally said to be natives of the island itself ; the sea-coast by those who have crossed from Belgium for the sake of spoil or war, their settlements being almost all called by the names of the places whence they came. Having carried war into Britain, they remained there and began to cultivate the fields."† This process of gradual conquest and tillage led to the existence of a recognised "Saxon" fringe of

---

* Lib. v. c. 12.

† The writer of the article upon the Belgæ in Dr. William Smith's " Dictionary of Ancient Geography," believes that the Belgæ were partly Germanic and partly Celtic. " The fact," he says, " of Cæsar making such a river as the Marne a boundary between Celtic and Belgic peoples, is a proof that he saw some marked distinction between Belgæ and Celtæ. But if we exclude," he adds, " the Menapii, the savage Nervii, and the pure Germans," the rest may have been Celts.

population, Saxon being the name formerly applied from
without to the Germanic population in this country. In the
reign of Diocletian, A.D. 290, Mamertinus, the orator, in his
panegyric on Maximian, the Emperor's colleague, speaks of
a victory at London, won by the Roman provincials over
Franks (Germans), who occupied the city. In 306, Constantius dying at York, a German chief in Britain, Eroc
King of the Alemanni, helped his son Constantine to assume
the empire. Towards the close of the period of Roman
occupation, the "Notitia utriusque Imperii," compiled
between the years 369 and 408, describe the administration
of a Saxon Shore (Littus Saxonicum) in Britain and in Gaul.
The Littus Saxonicum in Britain appears from the places
named in it—our Brancaster and Burgh Castle, in Norfolk ;
Othona, in Essex, now under the sea ; Dover, Lympne,
Reculvers, and Richborough, in Kent ; Pevensey and the
River Adur, in Sussex—to have extended from the Wash to
Southampton Water. It has been argued that the Saxon
Shore, which is called also in the same record the Saxon
Boundary (Limes), meant a shore not occupied by, but liable
to attack from, a Germanic people. This, however, is only
argued to evade one of the difficulties made by rejection of
that evidence of Cæsar, Strabo, and Tacitus, with which the
appointment in Britain of a Roman Count of the Saxon
Shore is, without strain of interpretation, perfectly consistent. Eutropius, who died about the year 370, speaks *
of the Franks and Saxons who infested the sea between the
coasts of Gaul and Britain. Ammianus Marcellinus, in
whom Gibbon acknowledged an accurate and faithful guide,
and who writes of his own times, in his history which closes
with the year 378, speaks under date 364 and 368 of the
Britons or Cymry as invaded by the Picts, Scots, and
Attacots (in Erin the Aitheach Tuatha, a turbulent un-

* Lib. xii. cap. 21.

privileged class of the Gaels) ;* and the "Franks and the Saxons, who are on the frontiers of the Gauls, ravaging the country wherever they could effect an entrance." He tells, also, of the Franks and Saxons having been again fought with in London city, being attacked and beaten by Theodosius in "Londinium, an ancient town now called Augusta," as they were driving the inhabitants prisoners, in chains, with cattle before them.†

But at this time the Cymry had not yet driven the Gaels or "Scots" out of North Wales. After Britain had been relinquished by the Romans at the close of the fourth century, fresh successes of the Gaels and Picts caused aid to be invoked by the Cymry from Roman legions, by which they were helped in the year 418, only to fall again into extremity, and send by ambassadors to Rome in 446 "the Groans of the Britons." The Romans had no thought to spare from their own troubles ; and it is said to have been by the advice of Vortigern that the Cymry made common cause with the intruders from the south-east, the Saxons, against the Gaedhels and the Picts. Then, with the landing of Hengist and Horsa, ascribed to the year 449, success began to crown the work of forcing the Gaedhels in Western Britain to cross over to Erin. Very remarkable illustration of this is afforded by the recurrence five-and-twenty times in Wales, and twenty times out of the five-and-twenty in North Wales, of the name Gwyddel (for Gaedhel) attached to places which may have been remaining strongholds held by the Gaels after their main body had been cast out by the Cymry, with the added pressure of the Saxon. The old name of Holyhead was Cerrig y Gwyddel ; and there are three other Gwyddels in Anglesey, four in Caernarvon, four

Marginal note: Pressure of the Cymry and the Saxons on the Gaels in Gwynedd, or North Wales.

---

* "O'Curry MS. Mat. of Irish Hist.," p. 230.
† Ammianus Marcellinus, bk. xxvii. cap. 8.

in Merioneth, six in Cardigan—one of them, Cefn y Gwyddel (the Ridge of the Gael), having near it, not far from the sea, a farm still called Lletty 'r Cymro (the Quarters of the Cymry). All the sites indicate pressure from the east towards the sea, and are in old passes, morasses, or places at which a last stand could be made. The Anglesey "Gwyddels" are among the low grounds of the western side, intersected and partially cut off by creeks and quicksands. In Caernarvonshire, two are at the utmost point of the wild promontory of Lleyn, to which we can well imagine the Gwyddelod to have been beaten back step by step; a third is at the entrance of the wild defensible pass of Llanberis. In Merionethshire, two are at the foot of the Cader Idris chain of mountains, protected on the north by the estuary of the Mawddach, and on the west by the marshes and the sea; another is among marshes at the mouth of a valley leading to Cader Idris, the Montgomeryshire stronghold; and two others, in Cardiganshire, are on the skirts of the Plinlimmon group. That in Radnorshire, and two of those in Cardiganshire, stand at the entrance of gorges leading into the savage region of mountain and moorland, then and long afterwards clothed with impenetrable forests, between the Wye, the Tywg, and the Taifi. The Gwyddels in Cardiganshire and one in Pembrokeshire are close upon the western coast. Twll y Gwyddel, in Glamorganshire, lies also in a mountain pass.* To the list of five-and-twenty I may add one Gwyddel more, a Gwyddelwern in Denbighshire, between the hills three miles to the north of Corwen.

The names, too, are significant. The old name of Holyhead, Cerrig y Gwyddel, meant Gael Stones. There are Gael mountains, Gael Ness, Gael Moor, Gael Pass, Gael Ridge, Gael Knoll, Gael Mead, Gael Grove, Gael Alderwood, Gael Hole, Gael's Cots, Gael Church, two Gael

---

* "Vestiges of the Gael in Gwynedd." By the Rev. William Basil Jones. London and Tenby, 1857.

hamlets, a Gael town, a Gael port, and in two places the Gael's Walls.

But their German allies soon began to overwhelm the Cymry ; and after the deposition of Vortigern, the struggle of the Cymric Celts was to resist the occupation of their land by successive warrior bands of Anglo-Saxon colonists. Six settlements by invasion, spread over a period of a century, are recorded upon the authority of the Saxon Chronicle, which was not brought into its present form until after the death of Bede, and of Bede's " Ecclesiastical History," dedicated to a king who reigned in Northumberland between the years 729 and 737. Of these settlements, the first, under Hengist and Horsa, is said to have been of Jutes, the next three were of Saxons, the last two of Angles. They were settlements :—

Pressure of the Saxons on the Cymry. The record of six settlements.

1.—Of Jutes, landing A.D. 449, under Hengist and Horsa, at Ebbsfleet, in the Isle of Thanet. Six years later they established the kingdom of Kent.

2.—Of Saxons, landing A.D. 477, under Ælla, in Sussex, which they made the kingdom of the South Saxons.

3.—Of Saxons, landing A.D. 495, under Cerdic, in Hampshire, where they established the kingdom of the West Saxons (Wessex).

4.—Of Saxons, landing A.D. 530, leader unnamed, in Essex.

5.—Of Angles, who landed in Norfolk and Suffolk during Cerdic's reign in Wessex.

6.—Of Angles, landing A D. 547, under Ida, on the south-eastern coast of Scotland, between Tweed and Forth.

It is the stir of battle in the conflict of the Cymry with these last comers that animates the oldest literature of the Cymric Celts. Against Ida and his Angles Urien Rheged led the warriors of Britain, and the praise of Urien was

sung by many bards who received gifts from his hand.
Urien fought not only against Ida, but, after Ida's death,
against his sons and grandsons, and was trea- Connection of
cherously slain by Morcant, another Cymric the ancient
literature of
chief, while besieging Theodoric, the son of Ida, the Cymry
with the
on his extreme seaward border in the island of Anglo-Saxon
conquests.
Lindisfarne, which is off the coast near the mouth
of the Tweed. Ida died in 560; his son Adda, reigning
eight years, succeeded him, and then followed the four
years' reign of Ethelric, the son of Adda, before the
accession of Theodoric, the son of Ida, who reigned seven
years. Urien, therefore, did not survive the year 579. The
contest with Ida the Angle ended in the formation of the
great Anglian kingdom of Northumbria; and the original
territory of Urien probably was in the country of the
Cumbrian Britons, lying between the vale of the Clyde and
the Ribble, with the sea for western boundary, and the
eastern boundary varying with the fortune of war, since it
touched the Anglian or Saxon kingdoms of Deira and
Bernicia. These Cymry of the Scottish Lowlands, Cumberland, Westmoreland, and North Lancashire, were called also
neighbours to the Otadini, who had occupied the shores of
Northumberland from Flamborough Head to the Frith of
Forth. Overpowered by the Angles, some of the Cymry
at last withdrew from Cumberland to Wales, while others
remained, living quietly under the new rule, or maintaining
among the hills for the next century or two an acknowledged
independence.*

Urien's district of Rheged (a gift), placed by Sir Francis
Palgrave in the forests south of Scotland, is
Urien.
assigned, by traditions that make Urien a nephew
of King Arthur, to Glamorgan; and the country is said to
have been given to Urien for his valour in driving certain
Irish Gaels from Gower, in Glamorgan, back to Anglesea.

* Bede's "Hist. Eccles.," lib. v. c. 23.

He appears, accordingly, in French Arthurian romances as Sir Urience of Gore. The Cymric bards of the sixth century stand foremost in connection with the wars of Urien and of the Strathclyde Britons—Llywarch Hen, who was bard and prince ; Aneurin, who was bard and warrior ; and Taliesin, who was bard alone. To each of the latter poets has been given in posthumous honour the name " King of Bards." But if we are now to judge them by the few remains of each that are not clearly spurious, Aneurin and Taliesin were excelled by Llywarch Hen.

Taliesin (Shining Forehead) was in the highest repute in the middle of the twelfth century, and he was then and afterwards, unless we except Merlin, the hero of the greatest number of romantic legends. He is said to have been the son of Henwg the bard, or Saint Henwg, of Caerleon-upon-Usk, and to have been educated in the school of Cattwg, at Llanveithin, in Glamorgan, where the historian Gildas was his fellow pupil. Seized when a youth by Irish pirates while fishing at sea in a coracle of osier covered with leather, he is said, probably by rational interpretation of a later fable of his history, to have escaped by using a wooden buckler for a boat; so he came into the fishing weir of Elphin, one of the sons of Urien. Urien made him Elphin's instructor, and gave him an estate of land. But once introduced to the court of that great warrior-chief, Taliesin became his foremost bard, followed him in his wars, and sang his victories. He sings victories over Ida at Argoed about the year 547, at Gwenn-Estrad between that year and 560, at Menac about the year 560. After the death of Urien, Taliesin was the bard of his son Owain, by whose hand Ida fell. After the death of all Urien's sons, Taliesin mourned the past in Wales, dying, it is said, at Bangor Teivy, in Cardiganshire, and he was buried under a cairn near Aberystwith. Taliesin is named by Aneurin in the "Gododin :"—" I, Aneurin, will sing what is known to Taliesin, who communicates to me his thoughts, or a strain of Gododin before the dawn of the bright day." From this it is to be inferred that Taliesin had achieved high fame as a contemporary bard when Aneurin produced that chant of deadly conflict with the Angles. Christianity was then taking root among the Cymry. Saint David was a contemporary of Aneurin and Taliesin ; and one of the few poems ascribed to the latter bard which are not obviously of later origin, is one said to be " dedicated in praise of baptism." But the poems which seem to be most unquestionably songs of Taliesin, handed down with more or less of subsequent change or addition from the days of Urien, are those which celebrate the praise of Urien him- self and his son Owain, or describe their battles. Take for example—where Flamdwyn, the fire-bearer, is supposed to represent Ida himself—this song* of a battle fought about the year 570 :—

The Battle of Argoed Llwyfain.

" On Saturday there was a great battle,
From the rising of the sun until the setting.
Fflamdwyn hastened in four divisions,
Bent upon overwhelming Rheged.
They reached from Argoed to Arfynyd ;
They were splendid only for one day.
Fflamdwyn cried with much blustering,
' Will they give the hostages, and are they ready ? '
Owain, standing upon the rampart, answered him,
' They will not give them ; they are not, nor shall be ready ! '
Afflicted would have been the hero, Cenen, son of Coel,
If he had given hostages to any one.
Loudly Urien, the chief, proclaimed his will,—

* This and the other examples of Taliesin I take, with a few changes in the choice of words to give the sense, from " Taliesin ; or, the Bards and Druids of Britain. A Translation of the Remains of the Earliest Welsh Bards, and an Examination of the Bardic Mysteries." By D. W. Nash. London, 1858. A book based on a wholesome scepticism.

'Let my kinsmen come together,
And we will raise on the hills our banner,
And will turn against those warriors our faces,
And will lift above the heads of men our spears,
And will seek Fflamdwyn in his army,
And will slay him together with his troop.'
Because of the battle of Argoed Llwyfain
There were many dead ;
Red were the ravens through the strife of men,
And hasty men carried the news.

I will divine the year, whose life is on the wane ;
But till I fall into old age
And the painful grasp of death,
May I never smile
If I praise not Urien."

If he praised not Urien, there was neither wine nor
bread for Taliesin. He was a bard, and not a warrior, who
lived by and praised the chief's liberality, the next good
thing after the valour that gave power of gifts into his hand.
"The broad spoils of the spear," says Taliesin, in another
of these songs :—

The Spoils of Taliesin.

"The broad spoils of the spear reward my song, Delivered before
the bright, smiling hero. The most resolute of chieftains is Urien.
No peaceful trafficker is he ; Clamorous, loud-shouting, shrill, mighty,
and highly exalted. Every one knows of the extermination on the side
of Merwydd and Mordei. The chief is very swift to prepare pleasure ;
When harpers play in hall he is of peaceful cheer, A protector in Aeron ;
Excellent his wine, his poets, his musicians : He gives no rest to his
enemies ; He is the great strength of the Briton people. Like a whirling
fiery meteor across the earth, Like a wave coming from Lwyfenydd,
Like the sweet song of Gwenn and Gweithen, Like Mor, the very
courteous, is Urien. In the assembly of a hundred war-heroes He
directs and is the leader among princes, He is chief of the people of
swift horses. In the beginning of May in complete order of battle,
When his people send for him, he is coming. Eagle of the land, very
keen is thy sight. I have made a request for a mettled steed, The
price of the spoils of Taliesin.

Other of Taliesin's songs praise Urien as "the provider of wine, and meal, and mead." The issue of one of his battles is looked to as men would look to the issue of a foray, in abundance "of calves and cows—milch cows and oxen—and all good things also."

Urien.

"We should not be joyful were Urien slain. He terrifies the trembling Saxon, who, with his white hair wet, is carried away on his bier and his forehead bloody. . . . I have wine from the chief; to me wine is most agreeable. Doorkeeper, listen ! What noise is that ? Is it the earth that shakes, Or is it the sea that swells, Rolling its white head towards thy feet ? Is it above the valley ? It is Urien who thrusts. Is it above the mountain ? It is Urien who conquers. Is it beyond the slope of the hill ? It is Urien who wounds. Is it high in anger, It is Urien who shouts. Above the road, above the plain, Above all the defiles, Neither on one side nor two Is there refuge from him. But those shall not suffer hunger Who take spoil in his company, He is the provider of sustenance. With its long blue streamers His spear was the child of death In slaying his enemies. And until I fall into old age, Into the sad necessity of death, May I never smile If I praise not Urien."

In lines of two or three words each, here run together to save space, I quote from this bard of the sixth century one illustration more of the confessed dependence of the ancient poet upon the favour of a single patron in the warrior-chief whose praise he lived by singing :—

To Urien.

"In tranquil retirement I was prodigal of song; honour I obtained, and I had abundance of mead, I had abundance of mead for praising him. And fair lands I had in excess, and great feasting, and gold and silver, and gold and gifts, and plenty, and esteem, and gifts to my desire, and a desire to give in my protector. It is a blessing, it is good, it is glorious, it is glorious, it is good, it is a blessing in the presence, the presence of the bestower. The bards of the world are certainly rendering homage to thee according to thy desire. God hath subjected to thee the chiefs of the island, through fear of thy assault, provoking battle. Protector of the land, usual with thee is headlong activity and the drinking of ale, and ale for drinking, and fair dwelling, and beautiful raiment. On me he has bestowed the estate of Llwyfenydd, and all my requests, three hundred altogether, great and small. The song of Taliesin is a pleasure to thee, the greatest ever heard of ; there would be reason for anger if I did not praise thy deeds. And until I become old and in the sad necessity of death, I shall never rejoice except in praising Urien."

The fairy tales of which Taliesin afterwards became the hero, and the mythological poetry ascribed to him, belong

Llywarch Hen.

to a later chapter in this narrative. We know him here only as one of the bards of the world who found in Urien a munificent rewarder of their songs, and as the bard of the sixth century who seems to have been most careful of himself. Another poet of the same period, who gave all to his country, is Llywarch Hen (that is to say, Llywarch the Old), a warrior who sang war, and, suffering with his people, appears by his remains to have excelled chiefly in pathetic lamentation. His poems illustrate with peculiar felicity the manners and feelings of his time ; and in a happy incidental touch we learn from him how familiar was the daily contact between life and literature, when he thus pairs, as the two lights of a home, the bard's song and the household fire :

> " The hall of Cyndyllan is dark to-night—
> Without fire, without songs."

Llywarch was born about the year 490, and educated in the north of England, among the woods of Argoed, where his father, Elidir, was sovereign chief. He went when young to the court of Erbin, King of Cornwall and Devon. Traditions of the twelfth century send him to King Arthur's court, and make him for a time King Arthur's minister ; for they are the daysprings of Arthurian romance to which we are now looking back through their contemporary records.

There is no touch yet of mediæval fancy to convert them into fairy tale. Llywarch speaks incidentally of Arthur as chief of the Cymry of the south, confederate against the Saxons. When Urien was in the north, Arthur was in the south; and the young Llywarch's friend and patron, Geraint, the son of Erbin, was under King Arthur's orders. Llywarch followed Geraint to the battle in which he fell by the hands of the Saxons; and of the terrible butchery of that day thirteen times he repeats in his song that with his own eyes he saw it. Urien afterwards won the young princely warrior bard to his company, and gave him a place of honour in his halls. Llywarch was with Urien as brother in arms at Lindisfarne, where from the year 572 to the year 579 the Northumbrian chief, Theodoric, was besieged, and there again, with his own eyes, he saw the head of Urien struck off by the sword of an assassin. It was Llywarch who carried Urien's head in his mantle from that bloody field.

" *The Death of Urien.*

"I carry by my side," he sings in his chant on the death of Urien— " I carry by my side the head of him who commanded the attack between the two hosts of the son of Kenvarch, who lived great of mind. I carry by my side the head of Urien, who gently commanded the army; on his white breast a black crow. I carry in my mantle the head of Urien, who gently commanded his people; on his white breast the crow battens. I carry in my hand a head that had no rest; corruption eats into the breast of the chief. I carry by the side of my thigh a head that was a buckler for his country, a column in the fight, a war-spear for his free countrymen. I carry by my left side a head better when living than his mead; that was a citadel for the old men. . . . The head that I carry carried me; I shall find it no more; it will come no more to my succour. Woe to my hand, my happiness is lost! The head that I bear from the slope of Pennok has its mouth foaming with blood; woe to Rheged from this day! My arm is not weaker, but my rest is troubled; my heart, will you not break? The head that I carry carried me!"

After Urien's death the power of the Angles overwhelmed Llywarch's small principality of Argoed, and he sought asylum in Wales with Cyndyllan, a Prince of Powys, at his capital of Pengwern (Shrewsbury). Cyndyllan received such exiles with open arms, and maintained constant battle with the Saxons. In battle with the Saxons, fought at Tren (now Tarn), near the Wrekin, Cyndyllan and two other Cymric chiefs fell in the year 580. That is the Cyndyllan whose hall was then made dark, "without fire and without songs." His house was burnt, and his whole family was massacred. The Cymry were now being hunted from the plains, and Llywarch found no better refuge than a hut of boughs on the banks of the Dee, near Bala. He says that he had there but a cow for his companion. His four-and-twenty sons were dead. One of them had in his day rescued from prison Aneurin, who sang, "From the unpleasant prison of earth I am released, from the haunt of death and a hateful land, by Cenau, the son of Llywarch, magnanimous and bold." But of all Llywarch's sons, Gwenn was the dearest to him, and he was the first who fell under the spears of the Lloegrians. The poet grieves that he is too old and feeble to avenge him. Of Peil, his second son, "a hall," says Llywarch, "could have been built with the splinters of the bucklers he has broken." With melancholy chant the old man passes all too slowly to his grave. He sees in the night the spirit of his mother; doubts whether the God who has not heard his prayers for his sons, now listens to his grief. He turns again to his superstitions. The grey monks of the neighbouring monastery of Llanvor then afflict him. He changes his home to the valley of Aber Kioh, and sits there on the mountain-side longing for death. He calls himself the son of sorrow. But the monks of Llanvor follow him to teach him faith in one who, when on earth, was yet more a man of sorrows, and acquainted with grief. So at last in the church of their monastery Old Llywarch—Llywarch Hen—was buried. His life was one of patriotic struggle, but the temper of his mind was gentle. In a composition of the tenth century there is attributed to him the courteous precept, "Greet kindly, though there be no acquaintance." In the lament over his son, after describing the death, at the contest of the ford of Morlas, of his best beloved Gwenn, who was strong and large of stature, the old bard says—

"Llywarch's Lament for his son Gwenn.

"Let the wave break noisily; let it cover the shore when the joined lances are in battle. O Gwenn, woe to him who is too old to avenge you! Let the wave break noisily; let it cover the plain, when the lances join with a shock. O Gwenn, woe to him who is too old, since he has lost you. A man was my son, a hero, a generous warrior, and he was the nephew of Urien. Gwenn has been slain at the ford of Morlas. Here is the bier made for him by his fierce conquered enemy after he had been surrounded on all sides by the army of the Lloegrians; here is the tomb of Gwenn, the son of the Old Llywarch. Sweetly a bird sang on a pear-tree above the head of Gwenn before they covered him with a turf. That broke the heart of the Old Llywarch."*

It is a curious fact that a tumulus called Gorsedd Wen, within 150 yards of the river Morlais (which flows into a lake near Merthyr Tydfil), when opened in 1850, was found to contain the skeleton of a man six feet seven inches high— the place of the tomb, its name, and the stalwart size of the warrior there buried, testifying in favour of the belief that these were the bones of Gwenn, the son of Llywarch.

We will part with this best poet of his time at the blackened and roofless hall of Cyndyllan—in his patrimony of Tren (now at Tarn Bridge, by Wroxeter)—that he had defended in vain against the ravaging Lloegrians. The whole

* The original and translation into French of the poem from which this passage is taken, and of other poems, will be found, with much valuable information upon the whole subject, in "Les Bardes Bretons : Poëmes du VIe Siècle. Par le Vicomte Hersart de la Villemarqué. Nouvelle Edition." Paris, 1860.

poem is long; but the following passage from it sufficiently represents

"*Llywarch's Lament for Cyndyllan.*

"The hall of Cyndyllan is gloomy this night, Without fire, without bed—I must weep a while and then be silent. The hall of Cyndyllan is gloomy this night, Without fire, without candle—Except God doth, who will endue me with patience? The hall of Cyndyllan is gloomy this night, Without fire, without being lighted—Be thou encircled with spreading silence! The hall of Cyndyllan, gloomy seems its roof, Since the sweet smile of humanity is no more—Woe to him that saw it, if he neglects to do good! The hall of Cyndyllan is without love this night, Since he owned it no more—Ah Death, it will be but a short time he will leave me! The hall of Cyndyllan is not easy this night, On the top of the rock of Hydwyth, Without its lord, without company, without the circling feasts! The hall of Cyndyllan is gloomy this night, Without fire, without songs—Tears afflict the cheeks! The hall of Cyndyllan is gloomy this night, Without fire, without family—My overflowing tears gush out! The hall of Cyndyllan pierces me to see it, Roofless, fireless, My chief is dead, and I alive myself! The hall of Cyndyllan is an open waste this night, After being the contented resort of warriors; Elvan, Cyndyllan, and Caeawg. The hall of Cyndyllan is the seat of chill grief this night, After the respect I had; Without the men, without the women who there dwelt! The hall of Cyndyllan is silent this night, After losing its master.—The great, merciful God, what shall I do! The hall of Cyndyllan, gloomy seems its roof, since the Lloegrians have destroyed Cyndyllan and Elvan of Powys."*

The Lloegrians, whose victories were thus lamented by the Cymric bards, were the people of Lloegr, the part of ancient Britain occupied by the Belgæ; † but the name now applies to all England, of which, however, the people have been long called not Lloegrian, but Saxon.

---

* "The Heroic Elogies and other Pieces of Llywarç Hen, Prince of the Cambrian Britons: with a Literal Translation." By William Owen. London, 1792.

† Owen's "Llywarç Hen;" Pughe's "Welsh Dictionary," *sub voce* "Lloegr."

Myrddhin, or Merlin, is another bard of the sixth century ; but of the poems attributed to him none were written in his time.* More associated with fable than even Taliesin, the true history of Merlin seems to be that he was born between the years 470 and 480, during the invasion of the Saxon, and took the name of Ambrose, which preceded his surname of Merlin, from the successful leader of the Britons, Ambrosius Aurelianus, who was his first chief, and from whose service he passed, as bard, into that of King Arthur, the southern leader of the Britons. After he had been present in many battles, on one disastrous day between the years 560 and 574, in a field of horrible slaughter on the Solway Firth, he lost his reason, broke his sword, and forsook human society, finding peace and consolation only in his minstrelsy. He was at last found dead on the bank of a river.† Other bards of this period of active struggle were Talhaiarn, Kian, Mengant, and Kywryd. All the powers of the Cymry were knit for decisive strife. Cattle and lands were being won and lost. In the train of a strong chief there was hope of safety, hope of gain. In the arms of a strong chief there was hope of national redemption.

Merlin and other bards of the sixth century.

Our recollections of the Cymric bards of the sixth century must close with Aneurin, in whose poem entitled, "The Gododin," the whole time of struggle in Strathclyde comes back to us, and we see partly in action the last tumult of the transfer of power

Aneurin. The Gododin.

* "The Literature of the Kymry : being a Critical Essay on the History of the Language and Literature of Wales during the Twelfth and two succeeding Centuries." By Thomas Stephens. Llandovery, 1849. Second Edition, edited by the Rev. D. Silvan Evans, 1876.

† "Myrddhinn, ou l'Enchanteur Merlin, son histoire, ses œuvres, son influence. Par le Vicomte Hersart de la Villemarqué." Paris, 1862. In this volume, aiming to be popular, M. de Villemarqué is more credulous than in his former books of the antiquity ascribed to poems of a later date.

in Britain from the spear of the Celt to the plough of the Teuton. But we see in this song of the great strife, when "the men of Gododin went to Cattraeth," the tumult, without indication of the strength that was to come of it thereafter. As to Cattraeth, the poem tells us that it was a day's march from the starting-point of the Gododin, neighbours of the men of Deivyr and Bryneich, Deira and Bernicia, that is to say, Durham and Northumberland. In the adjoining county of York was a Roman town of note, called Cataractonium, now Catterick, three or four miles from Richmond, where an affluent joins the Swale, and there, perhaps, was fought the great battle celebrated in Aneurin's "Gododin." * There it may be that the three hundred and sixty-three chiefs who were at Cattraeth were all slain, except three, in battle with the Saxons. The Roman name of Cataractonium only Latinises the British word, now pronounced "Catterick," and said to be derived from "Cathairrigh," fortified city ; or "Caer-dar-ich," the camp on the water. The churchyard of the village of Catterick, a mile from the site of the Roman station and camp, is within an ancient camp of unknown origin, and ancient burial-mounds are in the neighbourhood. Aneurin, present in this battle, survived it to be killed by Eiddin, son of Einigan, with the blow of an axe, according to the Cymric Triads, one of "the three accursed deeds of Britain." In the opinion of the Rev. John Williams ab Ithel,† by whom the "Gododin" has been edited and translated, Cattraeth is identical, not with Catterick Bridge, but with the "catrail," or rampart and fosse extending across Teviotdale, for five-and-forty miles from Galashiels, southward, to Peel-fell in the Cheviots. This

---

* Stephens's "Literature of the Kymry."

† "Y Gododin : a Poem on the Battle of Cattraeth, by Aneurin, a Welsh Bard of the Sixth Century, with an English Translation and numerous Historical and Critical Annotations. By the Rev. John Williams ab Ithel, M.A., Rector of Llangmowddwy, Merionethshire." Llandovery, 1852. This book is my chief aid in describing the Gododin.

was a rampart raised to check the farther progress of the
Saxons westward ; and, if the fight was here, the word
Cattraeth may possibly mean " cad-traeth," the war-tract ; or
" cad-rhaith," the legal war-fence. But I have little
doubt that the true site of Cattraeth is the Yorkshire
Catterick.

When, in the year 547, Ida came to our northern coast
with forty ships, in aid of the Saxons combatant already with
the Cymry, the people of Gododin, Deivyr, and Bryneich
(Deira and Bernicia), on the eastern shore, bordering on
Llywarch Hen's district of Argoed, were especially liable
to depredation, and most probably already in the power of
the Saxon.

At the call of Mynyddawg, Lord of Eiddin, Cymric
chiefs formed an alliance, brought their forces to Eiddin,
and were sumptuously entertained. Eiddin is commonly
identified with Edinburgh. If so, we must look for
Cattraeth to the Catrail. Nobody, I believe, has suggested,
obvious as it seems, that the lands of the Lord of Eiddin
were on Wordsworth's " life's neighbour," the river Eden,
" whose bold rocks are worthy of their fame." The Eden,
passing through Westmoreland and Cumberland, flows
towards the north-east into the Solway Frith, and has its
source on the opposite side of the same hills from which
the Swale rises to flow by Catterick to the south-west. The
sources of the Eden and the Swale are only two or three
miles distant from each other ; and, if the fort of Eiddin
that was the gathering-point of the Cymric allies was among
the fells near the head-waters of the river, it was but a march
for the heroes of some five-and-twenty miles from thence
through Swaledale to Cattraeth. The host was large. The
larger army of the Saxons gathered in Gododin, and
marched westward to meet at Cattraeth the Britons of the
yet unconquered West. The fight began on a Tuesday,

and, like one of the great battles of the American Civil War, was maintained for a week, the last four days being most bloody. Aneurin was himself made prisoner in a panic of the men with whom he fought, and afterwards forcibly liberated by a son of Llywarch Hen. After this, at a conference during the struggle, Aneurin, as bard and herald, demanded restoration of a part of Gododin as the condition of peace. The Saxon herald answered him by killing the bard Owain, and the battle was renewed by the Cymry, and maintained so doggedly that of their three hundred and sixty-three chiefs only three, Cynon, and Cadreith, and Cadlew of Cadnant, survived with Aneurin. Allusions to protection of corn indicate that the great fight was in the harvest season, and the date usually assigned to it is the year 570.

Aneurin's poem of "The Gododin," as it remains to us, consists of ninety-seven stanzas; and with the story of the battle combines praise of ninety of the Cymric chiefs. It is considered that in the whole poem every chief had his eulogy; and that various detached pieces which are extant, and which answer to its character, are, in fact, fragments detached from this old wail over the death of Cymric heroes upon whom the Saxon set his heel. One of the ninety-seven stanzas—the twenty-first—was put into verse as "The Death of Hoel," by Gray, who had found literal translations in Evans's "Specimens of Welsh Poetry." I have followed an edition of "The Gododin" published in 1852, by the Rev. John Williams ab Ithel, with a literal prose translation, in the following attempt to give metrical form to the successive stanzas as far as the twenty-first, which is the one known to modern readers as Gray's "Death of Hoel." Here I break off, that my own ruder attempt to rhyme the Gododin may have the advantage of a poet's close.

The Gododin.

I.

A man in thought, a boy in form,
He stoutly fought, and sought the storm
Of flashing war that thundered far.
His courser, lank and swift, thick maned,
Bore on his flank, as on he strained,
The light-brown shield, as on he sped,
With golden spur, in cloak of fur,
His blue sword gleaming.   Be there said
No word of mine that does not hold thee dear !
Before thy youth had tasted bridal cheer
The red death was thy bride !   The ravens feed
On thee yet straining to the front, to lead.
Owain, the friend I loved, is dead !
Woe is it that on him the ravens feed !

II.

Wreathed he led his rustic heroes ;
In his home the friend of maidens,
Pouring out the mead before them.
When the shout of war rang out,
Spear dents were large on the front of his targe ;
He gave no quarter, chased for slaughter,
Swift to mow as grass the foe,
Unstained he disdained to return.
Of a hundred rustic heroes,
Homeward to his coast of Mordei,
To the wave-washed land that bore them,
Madog saw but one return.

III.

Wreathed, hard toiling, strength of many,
Like an eagle swooping to us
When allured to join our band.
High upraised and brave his banner ;
Higher, braver, mood and manner ;
Eagle mind that feared not any
Of the warriors trooping to us,
Flocking from Gododin land.

Manawyd, thou swift and fearless,
By no foeman's spear delayed ;
Foemen's tents through thee are cheerless,
None evade thy spearman's raid.

IV.

Wreathed the leader wolf came forth ;
Amber rings his temple twine,
Amber worth a feast of wine.
He quelled the strong of the hostile throng ;
Though his shield was shattered he shunned no man.
Mine would have been Venedot and the North,
Said the heart of the son of Ysgyran.

V.

Wreathed was the leader who, armed for the bloody strife,
Went to the battle-field noted of all.
Chief in the foremost rank, fearlessly spending life,
Sweeping battalions down, groaning they fall.
Foemen of Deivyr and foemen of Bryneich slain,
Hundreds on hundreds in one little hour.
Ever his bride-feast untasted must now remain ;
Him now the wolves and the ravens devour.
Mead in the hall, Hyveidd Hir, cost us high !
Praise shall yet live for thee till our song die !

VI.

To Gododin marched the heroes ; Gognaw laughed.
Round their flags they fiercely battled ; bore their smarts :
Few the fleeting years when pleasure's cup they quaffed ;
Strokes of Gognaw, son of Botgad, shook men's hearts.
Better penance is than laughter on the breath,
When young and old, and strong and bold,
Heroes march to meet the fated stroke of Death

VII.

To Gododin marched the heroes ; Gwanar laughed
As his shining troop went down adorned to kill.
Jest thou checkest with the gripe of thy sword-haft—
When its blade, O Death, thou wavest, we are still !

VIII.

The warriors marched to Cattraeth, full of words ;
Bright mead gave them pleasure, their bliss was their bane ;
In serried array they rushed down on the swords
With joyous outcry—then was silence again.
Better penance is than laughter on the breath,
When young and old, and strong and bold,
Heroes march to meet the fated stroke of Death.

IX.

The warriors marched to Cattraeth, full of mead ;
Drunken, but firm in array.; great the shame,
But greater the valour no bard can defame.
The war-dogs fought fiercely, red swords seemed to bleed.
Flesh and soul I had slain thee myself, had I thought,
Son of Cian, my friend, that thy faith had been bought
By a bribe from the tribe of the Bryneich ! But no ;
He scorned to take dowry from hands of the foe,
And I, all unhurt, lost a friend in the fight,
Whom the wrath of a father felled down for the slight.*

---

* Upon this verse, and the general sense of its context, Gray founded
the opening of his Ode from the Welsh, " The Death of Hoel."

> " Had I but the torrent's might
> With headlong rage and wild affright
> Upon Deira's squadrons hurl'd
> To rush and sweep them from the world.
> Too, too secure in youthful pride
> By them my friend, my Hoel, died,
> Great Cian's son : of Madoc old
> He asked no heaps of hoarded gold ;
> Alone in Nature's wealth array'd,
> He ask'd and had the lovely maid."

But the sense of the original is far more vigorous. The son of Cian had
married the daughter of one of the Bryneich. His marriage did not stay
his feud with his wife's tribe. He repudiated her family, disdained to take
her dowry, and was sought and slain in the battle by her insulted father.
The rest of Gray's Ode is a sufficiently close version of the twenty-first
stanza of the Gododin. Gray closes it like the true poet that he is ; but

P

X.

The warriors marched to Cattraeth with the dawn ;
They feared them who met them with martial uproar
A host on a handful to battle were drawn,
Broad mark for the lances that drenched them in gore.
The shock of the battle, before the brave band
Of the nobles who freely obeyed his command,
Mynyddawg, Friend of Heroes, was bold to withstand

XI.

The warriors marched to Cattraeth with the dawn ;
The loved ones lamented in masterless tents ;
A snare had the sweet yellow mead round them drawn.
That dark year full often the minstrel laments ;
Red plumes, redder swords, broken blades, helmets cleft,
Even those of the band that obeyed thy command,
Mynyddawg, Friend of Heroes, of heroes bereft.

XII.

The warriors marched to Cattraeth with the day ;
Base taunts shamed the greatest of battles. They cried
As their blades slew the baptised Gelorwydd, "Away
With your kindred the homeless, the dead, to abide !
For the Gem of the Baptised behold we provide—
We, the host of Gododin—an unction of blood ;
A last unction is due ere the last fight is fought."
Should the might of true chiefs not be mastered with thought ?

XIII.

The warrior marched to Cattraeth with the day ;
In the stillness of night he had quaffed the white mead.
He was wretched, though prophesied glory and sway
Had winged his ambition. Were none there to lead
To Cattraeth with a loftier hope in their speed.

the "diction" of the eighteenth century is answerable for his inflation of
the plain words " wine and mead" into

> " Nectar that the bees produce,
> Or the grape's ecstatic juice."

Secure in his boast, he would scatter the host,
Bold standard in hand ; no other such band
Went from Eiddin as his, that would rescue the land
From the troops of the ravagers. Far from the sight
Of home that was dear to him, ere he too perished,
Tudvwlch Hir slew the Saxons in seven days' fight.
He owed not the freedom of life to his might,
But dear is his memory where he was cherished.
When Tudvwlch amain came that post to maintain
By the son of Kilydd, the blood covered the plain.

XIV.

The warriors marched to Cattraeth with the dawn ;
Their shields were no shelter ; in shining array
They sought blood.   On their front the war thundered, its din
Crashed resounding from targets.   When he would repay
The fickle and base for their fealty withdrawn,
The mailed chief of the Mordei his high hand could slay ;
The homage they owed him his iron could win ;
For a host before Erthai would flinch in dismay.

XV.

When the bards tell the tale of the fight at Cattraeth,
The bereaved ones will sigh, as they sighed through the years
Of the mourning for warriors gone to their death,
For lands left without leaders to ruin and tears.
The fair band of his sons on his bier bore afar
Godebog, whose sword ploughed the long furrows of war
And shall Cyvwlch the Tall, and Tudvwlch, now no more,
Quaff sweet mead under torches ? Just fate we deplore :
    For the sweetness of mead,
    In the day of our need,
Is our bitterness ; blunts all our arms for the strife ;
Is a friend to the lip and a foe to the life.

XVI.

In other days he frowned on Eching fort,
To him the young and bold pressed ever near ;
In other days on Bludwe he would sport,
While his glad horn for Mordei made good cheer.

P 2

In other days he blended mead and ale ;
In other days purple and gold he wore ;
In other days Gwarthlev—" the Voice of Blame "—
Hero deserving of a truer name—
Had stall-fed steeds, who safely, swiftly bore
Their master out of peril.   These now fail.
In other days he turned the ebbing tide,
And bade the flood of war sweep high, spread wide.

XVII.

Light of lights—the sun,
Leader of the day,
First to rise and run
His appointed way,
Crowned with many a ray,
Seeks the British sky ;
Sees the flight's dismay,
Sees the Briton fly.
The horn in Eiddin's hall
Had sparkled with the wine,
And thither, at the call
To drink and be divine,
He went, to share the feast
Of reapers, wine and mead
He drank and so increased
His daring for wild deed.
The reapers sang of war
That lifts its shining wings,
Its shining wings of fire,
Its shields that flutter far.
The bards too sang of war,
Of plumed and crested war ;
The song rose ever higher.
Not a shield
Escapes the shock,
To the field
They fiercely flock,
There to fall.
But of all
Who struck on giant Gwrveling,
Whom he would he struck again,
All he struck in grave were lain

Ere the bearers came to bring
To his grave stout Gwrveling.

XVIII.

These gathered from the lands around :
Three chiefs from the Novantine ground ;
Five times five hundred men, embattled bands,
Three times three hundred levied from their lands ;
Three hundred men of battle, armed in gold,
From Eiddin ; then three cuirassed hosts enrolled
By three kings golden-chained ; three chiefs beside
With whom three hundred marched in equal pride;
Three of like mark, and jealous each of each,
Fierce in attack and dreadful in the breach,
Would strike a lion dead ; with gold they shone.
Three kings came from the Brython, Cynrig one,
And Cynon and Cynrain from Aeron,
To breast the darts the sullen Deivyr throw.
Better than Cynon came from Brython none,
He proved a deadly serpent to the foe.

XIX.

I drank the Mordei's wine and mead ;
Spears were many, men prepared
For the banquet, sadly shared,
The solemn feast where eagles feed.
When Cydywal to battle sped,
In the green dawn, he raised a shout
Triumphant over many dead.
Upon the field were strown about
The shields he splintered, tearing spears
Hewn and cast down. His were no fears ;
Son of the star-wise Syvno, he
Knew that his death that day should be
By spear or bow, not by sword-blade,
And not a sword his havoc stayed
Or could against his sword a strife sustain.
He gave his own life, took a host ;
Blaen Gwynedd knew his ancient boast
Of the brave toilers piled whom he had slain.

XX.

I drank the Mordei's wine and mead,
I drank, and now for that I bleed,
And yield me to the stroke of pain
With yearning throb of high disdain,
That upward pants to strike again.
Thee too the sword that slays me slays.
When danger threatens us, the days
Of evil-doing quail the hand :
Had we withstood we could withstand.
Presynt was bold, through war's alarm
He thrust his way with doughty arm.

XXI.

To Cattraeth's vale in glittering row
Twice two hundred warriors go ;
Every warrior's manly neck
Chains of regal honour deck,
Wreathed in many a golden link :
From the golden cup they drink
Nectar that the bees produce,
Or the grape's ecstatic juice.
Flushed with mirth and hope they burn
But none from Cattraeth's vale return,
Save Aeron brave and Conan strong,
Bursting through the bloody throng,
And he, the meanest of them all,
Who lives to weep and sing their fall.

The chiefs from the Novantine ground referred to in the eighteenth
stanza were from the opposite shore of the Solway Frith, where are now
Wigtown, Kirkcudbright, and Ayr; levies from Eiddin were from the
banks and estuary of the Eden ; three chiefs from Breitan were from the
shores of Clyde ; and Aeron may be an old form of Ayr. These completed the list of the confederate Cymric tribes on the west coast of the
Cymry who marched to Cattraeth to resist the seizure, by English invaders, of the inland region immediately behind the coasts of Deivyr
and Bryneich, romanised as the Otadini, from Ododin. Ododin,
without the prefix of an unessential "G," was the Cymric name of the

region upon which the heroes marched, full of mead, drunken, but firm in array. The ethical tone given to the whole poem by ascribing the defeat of the heroes to "the snare of the sweet yellow mead" is not to be overlooked—

> "For the sweetness of mead,
> In the day of our need
> Is our bitterness; blunts all our arms for the strife;
> Is a friend to the lip and a foe to the life."

From the twenty-first stanza to the close of the Gododin, as it has come down to us, I add now only a digest of the poem, with a few passages in prose translation :—

Motionless is the sword of Graid, the son of Hoewgi. The armour of Buddvan, the son of Bleiddvan the Bold, has been thoroughly washed in his gore. The bards at the Christmas feasts never quitted the court of Gwenabwy, the son of Gwen; "he was a mighty and fierce dragon, his land should not be ploughed though it might become wild." Swift and fierce to destroy the enemy with fire and sword was Marchten; "he would slaughter with the blade, whilst his arms were full of furze." The son of Gwddnen came from the south, having taken a strong town, "along the rampart to Offer, even to the point of Madden, there was no young offspring that he cut not to pieces, no aged man that he did not scatter about. His sword resounded on the heads of mothers; he was an ardent spirit, praise be to him." The Gododin would not be completely true without this touch in it of the ancient barbarism of war.

"When Caradawg rushed into battle, It was like the tearing onset of the woodland boar; Bull of the army in the mangling fight, He allured the wild dogs by the action of his hand; My witnesses are Owain the son of Eulat, and Gwrien, and Gwynn, and Gwriad; But from Cattraeth, and its work of carnage, From the hill of Hydwn, ere it was gained, After the clear mead was put into his hand, He saw no more the hill of his father. The warriors marched with speed, together they bounded onward; Short lived were they,—they had become drunk over the distilled mead. The retinue of Mynyddawg, renowned in the hour of need; Their life was the price of their banquet of mead. Caradawg, and Madawg, Pyll, and Ieuan, Gwgawn, and Gwiawn, Gwynn and Cynvan, Peredur with steel arms, Gwawrddur, and Aeddan; A defence were they in the tumult, though with shattered shields; When they were slain, they also slaughtered; Not one to his native home returned."

One chief of Ododin, Gwlyget, joined in the banquet of Mynyddawg, and went to his death at Cattraeth with the Cymry. "In marshalled array they went with shout of war, with powerful steeds and dark-brown harness, with shields, with uplifted javelins and piercing lances, with glittering mail and with swords." Morien fell in attack on the Saxon camp as he carried and spread fire, and as his sword resounded on the summit he was killed by a stone hurled from the wall of the fort. But the fort was taken. Terrible within it was the cry of the timid multitude; the van of the army of Gododin was scattered. Another fierce attack was made; a dwarf messenger of the Saxons hastened to the fence; the Cymry sent forward to meet him their chief counsellor, a hoary-headed man, mounted upon a piebald steed and wearing the golden chain. The dwarf proposed a compact, but the Cymry answered for themselves with a great shout, "Let heaven be our protection. Let his compact be death by the spear in battle." For this was a life-struggle in which even women of the Cymry fought among the men.

"Equal to three men, though a maid, was Bradwen; Equal to twelve was Gwenabwy, the son of Gwen. For the piercing of the skilful and most learned woman, Her servant bore a shield in the action, and with energy his sword fell upon the heads of the foe; In Lloegyr the churls cut their way before the chieftain. He who grasps the mane of a wolf, without a club in his hand, will have it gorgeously emblazoned on his robe. In the engagement of wrath and carnage, Bradwen perished,—she did not escape. Carcases of gold-mailed warriors lay upon the city walls; none of the houses or cities of Christians was any longer actively engaged in war; But one feeble man, with his shouts, kept aloof the roving birds; . . . My limbs are racked, and I am loaded, In the subterraneous house; An iron chain Passes over my two knees; Yet of the mead and of the horn, And of the host of Cattraeth, I Aneurin will sing What is known to Taliesin, Who communicates to me his thoughts, Or a strain of Gododin, Before the dawn of the bright day. The chief exploit of the North was accomplished by the hero, Of a gentle breast; a more liberal lord could not be seen; Earth does not support, nor has mother borne So illustrious and powerful a steel-clad warrior! By the force of his gleaming sword he protected me, From the cruel underground prison he brought me out, From the chamber of death, from the enemy's country; Such was Ceneu, son of Llywarch, energetic and bold."

The tide of battle turned against the Cymry. They were forced to consider terms of agreement. The demand made of the dales beyond the ridge of Essyd (perhaps Esthwaite Lake), the stabbing of Aneurin's companion by the Saxon herald, and the uprising of the Cymry to pursue the traitor, are the next incidents told.

"Together arise the expert warriors, and pursue the stranger, the man with the crimson robe; The encampment is broken down by the gorgeous pilgrim, Where the young deer" (collected as provisions for the army) "were in full melody. Amongst the spears of Brych thou couldst see no rods (white flags); With the base the worthy can have no concord; Morial in pursuit will not countenance their dishonourable deeds, with his steel blade ready for bloodshed. Together arise the confederate warriors. Strangers to the country, their deeds shall be proclaimed; There was slaughtering with axes and blades, And there was raising large cairns over the heroes of toil. The warriors arose, met together, And all with one accord sallied forth; short were their lives, long is the grief of those who loved them; Seven times their number of Lloegrians had they slain; After the conflict their wives raised a scream; And many a mother has the tear on her eyelash. . . . The soldiers celebrated the praise of the Holy One, And in their presence was kindled a fire that raged on high. On Tuesday they put on their dark-brown garments; On Wednesday they purified their enamelled armour; On Thursday their destruction was certain; On Friday was brought carnage all round; On Satnrday their joint labour was useless; On Sunday their blades assumed a ruddy hue; On Monday was seen a pool knee-deep of blood. The Gododin relates that after the toil, Before the tents of Madog, when he returned, Only one man in a hundred came with him."

At Catterick a tributary river flows into the Swale; and the next incident of the "Gododin" is that "at early dawn there was a battle at the confluence of rivers," where a fire was kindled in front of the fence, and the dwarf herald seems to have been killed treacherously in revenge for the treacherous slaying of Aneurin's companion by the Saxon herald. The rest is still celebration at length of the deeds of slaughtered chiefs, the last named being Morien and Gwenabwy.

"And Morien lifted up again his ancient lance, And, roaring, stretched out death Towards the warriors, the Gwyddyl, and the Prydyn; Whilst towards the lovely, slender, blood-stained body of Gwen, Sighed Gwenabwy, the only son of Gwen. Because of the wound of the skilful and most wise warrior Grievous and deep, when he fell prostrate upon the ground, The banner was pompously unfurled, and borne by a man at his side; A wild scene was beheld in Eiddin, and upon the battle-field. The grasp of his hand performed deeds of valour Upon the Cynt, the Gwyddyl, and the Prydyn. He who meddles with the mane of a wolf, without a club In his hand, will have it gorgeously emblazoned on his robe. Fain would I sing,—'would that Morien had not died.' I sigh for Gwenabwy, the son of Gwen."

So closes, with a sigh, the song of Aneurin. Chief after chief he has marshalled in his pride of life and flush of valour, only to weep for his death in the day when "there was slaughtering with axes and blades, and there was raising large cairns over the heroes of toil." Llywarch urged all his sons to battle for their country, and afterwards, a childless old man, he mourned them all with Gwen, the dearest, who fell by the ford at Morlas; "all slain," he wails, "by my words," for it was he who, as voice of his country, urged them to the fields of death. It was another Gwen who fell in the deadly and disastrous struggle at Cattraeth, and over whose "lovely, slender, blood-stained body" knelt Gwena-bwy, his only son—"I sigh for Gwenabwy, the son of Gwen." Merlin, scared by the horrors of the struggle, passed at last from a wild battle-field, with the light of his reason quenched in blood, to die a homeless wanderer upon a lonely river-bank. The chiefs of the Cymry may have been too ready to "quaff the white mead on serene nights," or on the eve of battles they may have been plagues to each other with disputes, forays, and petty dis-cord; it may be that among the men of Deivyr and Bryn-eich, on the eastern coast, north and south of the Humber, there were Cymry, subject to the coast-ravaging Saxons, who fought with the invaders against their own countrymen; and the peculiar bitterness with which Cymric poets speak always of the Bryneich is thought to support this opinion; but the best mind of the Cymry, as expressed by their poets, had in these grievous times assuredly the strongest influence. The seven days' battle at Cattraeth, where the Strathclyde Britons gathered their forces for a last fierce stand, and stood firm to the death, bore witness to the spirit of a generation that makes poets. Urien, chief of the confeder-ates among the hills of our Cymryland of the North—a land stretching beyond the bounds of Cumberland and Northumberland into the Scottish lowlands—had many great successes in his day. When Taliesin first sang in his halls, the struggle had not become hopeless; but Taliesin also lived and sang in the last terrible days, when war was without hope, but all the mind of the Cymry, spoken by their poets, was bent upon worthy maintenance of the disastrous strife, and Urien's camp became the centre of the nation's songs. The halls of other chiefs are visited by the bards, and named with honour. Thus we hear now and then of Arthur, who, at the head of a south-western confederacy, finally maintained ground for the Cymry amongst the hills west of the Exe, where they were the chief occupants of the five south-western counties in King Alfred's time.* Arthur, of whom there is only slight contemporary record extant, became, for reasons that will afterwards appear, the British hero of tradition. But before the Cymry of his own day, Urien was the chief warrior. In a former page it has been said that, by immigration and invasion, the Germanic races, of whose literature we shall have next to speak, had been for centuries establishing themselves upon the cultivable lands of Britain. Even now there is to be found no trace of a sweeping repulse of the whole Celtic population into Wales. In Wales the Cymry held their own to the last, and thither many probably withdrew from the dominion of the Saxon. But in Athelstane's time Britons and Saxons divided equal rule in Exeter; and to this day in the north of England, as in the south-west, the lineage of the Celt is intermixed with the type of the tall, fair-haired Germanic people, with which he is allied in ancestry. Bede, writing a century and a half after the battle of Cattraeth, speaks of the Britons of Northumberland, who were in his day partly free and partly subject to the Angles.†

* They are called in his will "Wealh Cynn."

† A little book, "Ancient Oral Records of the Cimri or Britons, in Asia and Europe, recovered through a literal Aramitic Translation of the old Welsh Bardic Relics," by G. D. Barber, A.M. (London, J. R. Smith,

The verse system of the Celts was founded, not like that of the Greeks and Romans, upon length and shortness of syllables, but upon agreements in the sounds of initial and final letters.　The old Teutonic verse, as we shall find in the case of Anglo-Saxon, was based upon alliteration of initials only.　The Gaelic and Cymric Celts used agreement not only of final consonants, the most simple and ancient form of final assonance, but also of final syllables. The Cymric verse might close two, three, or even six or more successive lines with the same syllable.　In Gaelic, a syllable ending in a vowel can assonate only with a syllable ending in a vowel.　A syllable ending in two consonants can, with a few exceptions, assonate only with a syllable ending in two consonants.　In the case of double and triple assonances, the first syllable of the first member of the set must have the acute accent, and the second syllable of the second member must have either the acute or the grave, but rather the acute. A monosyllable having the acute accent may assonate with a final syllable having only the grave.*　In assonance by repetition of the final syllable we have the germ of rhyme. It is no more true rhyme than would be the association of "ship" with "hardship" and "worship."　The Gaels used

Celtic Metres. (side note)

1855), may be named here as a curiosity of Literature.　The author takes the principal words in each line of the "Gododin," by three lines of them at a time, translates each word into Hebrew, finds all the synonyms of each Hebrew word, and then puzzles out a new sense by piecing together such synonyms as can be made to suit.　Then he tries to join his little group by twos, making in every case twenty-five experiments.　"Lastly, these double groups are to be tried with each other, and that selected which makes the most coherent whole : this result can never be mistaken"—for sense.　The process is shown in action by conversion of the "Gododin," in its Aramitic sense, into an incoherent "poem" on the game of chess.　"The heroes march to Cattraeth with the dawn," becomes "Neighbours with chess end the evening."

* Whitley Stokes on "Irish Metric." *Revue Celtique* for May, 1885 (vol. vi., p. 307).　See also R. Thurneysen on "The Irish Metre *Rinnard*," in the same Review for January, 1886 (vol. vii., p. 87).

often a two-syllabled, as *sóire, dóire* (health and misery), sometimes even a three-syllabled, assonance, as *sóinmiche, dóinmiche :* that of the Cymry was almost always one-syllabled ; and while the Cymry depended chiefly for effect upon the assonant ends of their lines, the Gaels cared more for assonant initial letters, for alliteration. The Gaels also were more careful than the Cymry to balance with a rhythmical antithesis the two halves of a verse. There was peculiar, again, to the Gaelic poetry what Dr. Zeuss—whose " Celtic Grammar " is the best authority upon this subject— calls a half-assonance, where, the vowel being the same, the consonants were only those of the same class. No distinct rule was kept as to the length of lines, but they were short, and seven—as in the first line of Gray's partly imitative " Death of Hoel, from the Welsh " *—was very commonly the number of their syllables. But much depended upon accent.

The chief MS. materials for a study of the old Cymric language and literature are :—

Latin MSS. of the 8th or 9th Centuries with Cymric Glosses.

1. The " Oxford Codex " in the Bodleian Library (Auct. F. 4-32), containing a portion of the treatise of Eutychius the grammarian, with interlinear Cymric glosses. The " Exordium of Ovid's Art of Love," with Cymric interlinear glosses from v. 31 to 370. An alphabet ascribed to Nemnivus, with letters resembling what are printed as Bardic Letters, but of different signification, and a fragment of a treatise on " Weights and Measures," partly in British, partly in Latin. These Cymric remains are of the end of the 8th or beginning of the 9th century.

2. The " Second Oxford Codex," also in the Bodleian, is theological, and contains in the middle, from p. 41 to p. 47*b*, a vocabulary of Latin words, with British interpretations written over or under them. The Cymric is of ancient form, and the following Latin entry shows

---

* Quoted on p. 225.

that it was written when the Cymry were resisting their invaders :—
' Humilibus Deus dat gratiam et victoriam. Clades magna facta est,
de Saxonibus percussi sunt multi, de Britonibus autem rari."

3. The "Lichfield" (formerly Llandaff) "Codex," or "St. Chad's
Book," contains Latin entries of donations, &c., with many words and
sentences in Cymric of the beginning of the 9th century.

4. Of the same age is *a leaf* with Cymric glosses, found by Monius,
attached to a cover of a codex in the Luxemburg Library.

5. A MS. of the Gospels paraphrased by Juvencus, in Latin hexa-
meters, contains Cymric glosses, also some verses at pp. 48, 49, 50.
The MS., of the 8th or 9th century, is in the University Library at
Cambridge (Ff. 4, 42).

ANNALS AND OTHER LITERATURE.

10TH CENTURY.

The "Laws of Howel Dda," compiled in the 10th century. The
oldest MS. is of the 12th.

12TH CENTURY.

The "Liber Landavensis," or "Book of Teilo," ancient Chartulary
of Llandaff Cathedral, published from MSS. in the libraries of Hengwrt
and of Jesus College, Oxford, by the Welsh MSS. Society, compiled
early in the 12th century.

Vellum MS. of "The Gododin," apparently of the year 1200, in
possession of Mrs. E. Powell, of Abergavenny.

The "Black Book of Caermarthen," in the library of Hengwrt, a
4to of 54 leaves, contains in the early part an elegy on the death of
Howel Dda's grandson in 1104, and later, an elegy on the death of a
Prince of Powys in 1158. This book includes the song of "The Sons
of Llywarch Hen," &c.

14TH CENTURY.

The "Llyfr Coch," or "Red Book of Hergest," in the library of
Jesus College, Oxford, a folio of 721 pp. in double columns. At p. 208
is a "Brief Chronology from Adam to A.D. 1318." At p. 499, a
"Chronological History of the Saxons to A.D. 1376." In this volume
are the oldest known copies of most of the poems ascribed to Taliesin
and Llywarch Hen, beginning at p. 513, and therefore written after the
year 1376.

OF VARIOUS DATES.

A collection of MSS. formed by Mr. Owen Jones, a furrier, in
Thames Street, at his own great expense. The contents of many of them

were published in 1801, and subsequent years, in three volumes, as the "Myvyrian Archaiology of Wales," giving, in part, the pith of Welsh literature from the 6th century to the opening of the 15th. Mr. Owen Jones was assisted in the publication by Edward Williams, of Glamorgan (otherwise Iolo Morganwg), and Dr. Owen Pughe. The first volume is a collection of 124 pieces of ancient Cymric poetry, of which 77 are ascribed to Taliesin ; the second and third volumes are in prose, and include : "The Laws of Howel Dda," "The Triads," "Proverbs," "Genealogies of Saints," "Chronicles of Tysilio and Gruffyd ab Arthur." The poetry is arranged in two parts : 1, works of the Cynveirdd, or earliest ; 2, works of the Gogynveirdd, or Bards of the Middle Ages. Besides these published pieces, the unpublished material of the Myvyrian MSS. alone, deposited in the British Museum, contain 4,700 pieces of poetry in 16,000 pages, and 15,300 pages of prose, forming of prose and verse 100 volumes. The "Iolo MSS.," or a selection from the collection made for continuation of the "Myvyrian Archaiology" by Iolo Morganwg, were published by the Welsh MS. Society, founded in 1837.

CHAPTER IV.

OLD LITERATURE OF THE TEUTONS.

GILDAS, the historian, by Anglo-Saxons called the Wise, is said to have been a Strathclyde Briton of the sixth century, a fellow-pupil of Llywarch, and a brother of Aneurin, if not Aneurin himself. Born in or soon before the beginning of the century, he was taught first by St. Iltut, and then studied for seven years in Gaul, before he dwelt near the present St. David's Head, on the coast of Pembrokeshire, and himself became a teacher. He went to Erin, and there founded monasteries among the Irish Gaels. After his return to Britain he proceeded to Rome, and on his way back, when in Brittany, founded the Monastery of St. Gildas de Ruys, where its monks say that he ended his life. Others say that he came again to England, and died in an oratory near Glastonbury.

To the Gildas of whose life these details are usually given* is ascribed a very ancient history, written in monastic Latin, " De Calamitate, Excidio, et Conquestu Britanniæ ;" or, as the text itself enlarges on the title, " about the situation of Britain, her disobedience and subjection, her rebellion, second subjection and dreadful slavery ; of her religion, persecution, holy martyrs, heresies of different kinds ; of her tyrants, her two hostile and ravaging nations ;

* The chief authority for details of the life of Gildas is a biography written in the twelfth century by Caradoc of Lancarvan.

of her first devastation, her defence, her second devastation and second taking vengeance; of her third devastation, of her famine, and the letters to Aetius; of her victory and her crimes; of the sudden rumour of enemies; of her famous pestilence; of her counsels; of her last enemy, far more cruel than the first; of the subversion of her cities and of the remnant that escaped; and finally, of the peace which, by the will of God, has been granted her in these our times." The history is very ancient, but most assuredly it was not written by a man who had in his veins the blood of Aneurin. Assuming to be one of themselves, this priest uses a tone towards the Cymry of contemptuous hostility, under the cloak of pastoral and brotherly reproof. "They are impotent," says the covert assailant, "in following the standard of peace and truth, but bold in wickedness and falsehood. . . . Britain has kings, but they are tyrants; she has judges, but unrighteous ones, generally engaged in plunder and rapine, but always preying on the innocent; whenever they exert themselves to avenge or protect, it is sure to be in favour of robbers and criminals; . . . they are ever ready to take oaths, and as often perjure themselves; they make a vow, and almost immediately act falsely; they make war, but their wars are against their countrymen, and unjust ones." This could not have been said by a Strathclyde Briton in or near the days of the battle of Cattraeth; but it might well be said by an Anglo-Saxon monk of the seventh century, who gave force to his censure by writing as one who must tell the bitter truth to his own people.

Through the equivocal Gildas, then, we pass from the Cymry to the Anglo-Saxons. Who were they? Something has been already said of their strong affinity to the Frisians, and of their probable relation to the Belgæ, who were on our southern coast in Cæsar's time. We have cited also the six recorded settle-

The Anglo-Saxon settlements.

Q

ments between the years 449 and 547, first one of Jutes, then three of Saxons, and then two of Angles. Regarding these six settlements as mainly representative of the period and character of Anglo-Saxon conquest and colonisation, we have next to ask, what is meant by the distinction between Jutes, Saxons, and Angles?

That there were such settlements we learn, on the authority of Venerable Bede, and of the Saxon Chronicle, which herein follows Bede. The statements of Bede correspond also to the brief narrative in the history of Gildas, written professedly seventeen, and at latest a hundred, years after Ida landed on our north-east coasts. Bede, born in 673, was studying history in a Northumbrian monastery only a century and a half after the landing of Ida. The information upon which he wrote was the best he could gather, chiefly by inquiry among his neighbours the monks in the north of England ; but also by collecting record and local tradition from the monasteries of the South, and consulting, in fact, every accessible record. To the best of the belief of his own day, he tells us the manner of establishing the Anglo-Saxon power in this country. Of the Saxon Chronicle the part relating to this early period was probably not put together till King Alfred's time, two centuries later than Bede. Use was then made of the existing records, the "Ecclesiastical History" of Bede being among the number. In fact, then, the account of the six settlements remains to us upon Bede's single and safe testimony to the record or tradition extant in his own day.

The chief sources of the history of the first coming of Teutonic settlers and invaders are—Gildas, who wrote perhaps early in the seventh century ; Bede, who wrote in the eighth century, finishing his history in the year 731 ; and the later history of a writer who in the twelfth century was named as Nennius, who belongs to the ninth century, and who was writing in the year 822. Of Bede and of Nennius we shall speak as we come to them in following the course of time.

There can be no doubt that the departure of the Romans who had checked descents upon the Saxon shore opened the way to the Teutons. The dam was broken and the tide poured in. But to the Romans Britain had been an outlying province little inviting and hard to subdue. Cæsar's first invasion in August, B.C. 55, lasted only for three weeks, and his second campaign not longer than two months. The invasion of Claudius, A.D. 43, carried out by his general Plautius with four legions—an army in which Vespasian and his son Titus served—was the more substantial beginning of a Roman occupation, and it has been suggested that the first occupation of the ground upon which London now stands was by a camp of Plautius in his war against Cunobeline. When Vespasian became Emperor, Rome had in military subjection Kent and Sussex, with the region to the west that had for farthest bound the estuary of the Severn, now within the shires of Gloucester, Somerset, Dorset, Wilts, and Berks. In the reign of Vespasian, Agricola, made legate of Britain about the year 78, extended the Roman power in Britain, and established civilising government. Roads were made, large tracts of the vast forest ground were cleared, Britain sent corn to Rome, and in some chief settlements there was peace and quiet payment of the tribute. But there was no intermarriage between conquerors and conquered. The occupation remained military. In the north were Picts who made invasions of their own upon the ground held by the Romans, and to repress these Hadrian built across the country between Carlisle and Newcastle eighty miles of wall.

In the time of Hadrian's successor, Antoninus Pius, a second barrier was made by connecting the forts built by Agricola between the Firth of Forth and the Clyde. On the east coast various Teutonic tribes from the opposite shores, known to the Romans generally by the name of Saxons, made fierce descents. The Roman military power spreading and strengthening, walls were built around towns even in the regions more firmly held, as protection against attack from the people of the country, and there was established a strong chain of fortresses against attack from across the sea—fortresses manned by ten thousand soldiers under a chief known as the Count of the Saxon shore. While this lasted the Teutonic invaders could gain little or no hold upon the land. But when difficulties at home obliged the Romans to withdraw their soldiers from Britain, and at last, in the year 410, Britain was required, by a letter from the Emperor, to provide for its own defence, we have a generation of confusion followed by the beginning, in the year 449 and 450, of a series of large Teutonic settlements upon our southern and eastern shores. These are represented by the six settlements that Bede describes.

Now, as to the first settlement of Jutes under Hengist and Horsa (Horse and Mare), who established themselves in Kent, Hampshire, and the Isle of Wight, and whom Bede distinctly believed to have come from Jutland,* it is to be observed that Jutland is now occupied by Danes, and that men from Jutland settling on our eastern coasts in the days of the Angles were called Danes ; but that in this case they are called "Jutes," not "Danes," and do not seem to have been Danish. Where there has been a Danish settlement, towns commonly are found with names ending in "by." Thus in Lincolnshire, within a dozen miles of Great Grimsby, there stand Foresby,

Jutes.

---

* The statement of Bede is as follows :—" De Jutarum origine sunt Cantuarii et Vectuarii, hoc est ea gens, quæ usque hodie in provincia occidentalium Saxonum Jutarum natio nominatur, posita contra ipsam insulam Vectam. . . . Porro de Anglis hoc est illa patria, quæ Angulus dicitur et ab eo tempore usque hodie manere desertus *inter provincias Jutarum et Saxonum* perhibetur."—*Eccl. Hist.*, i. 15.

Utterby, Fotherby, Ashby-cum-Fenby, Barnoldby, Irby, Laceby, Keelby, Grasby, Brocklesby, Ulceby. Yet through-out this " Jute " region of Kent, Hampshire, and the Isle of Wight there is not even one place to be found that has a name ending in " by." There is no clear ground for assert-ing, although it has been suggested as one way of conquer-ing this difficulty, that a Germanic people occupied Jutland in the middle of the fifth century. But that our invaders of A.D. 449 (or as Bede's context shows 450), called the Jutes, were Danes from Jutland, is not only against local evidence. It might be urged as against fair likelihood that the first ships from Jutland to this country, instead of crossing the North Sea, as they afterwards did, and striking on our eastern coast, should have taken the trouble to make a long voyage southward, and land nowhere until they got to Pegwell Bay, where a farmhouse, bearing the name of Ebbsfleet, now shows where the old port used to be. But to this it can be replied that they came invited as foreign auxiliaries, and came to a part of the coast appointed for them upon politic considerations. And some unknown preceding relations with their leaders, or other politic considerations, may account for their having been fetched from afar, when a like help could have been found near at hand. The Saxon Chronicle is not here a separate authority, and simply adopts the *"usque hodie"* of Bede, in testifying to " that tribe amongst the West Saxons which is yet called the Jute-kin." Again, in the Anglo-Saxon poem of Beowulf, presently to be dis-cussed, as well as in the fragment on the battle of Finnes-burgh, Hengist appears as the name of a Jute hero. It is noticeable also that with the neighbouring regions named Essex, Sussex, and Wessex, after the Saxons of the East, and South, and West, Kent kept its British name, and had a peculiar division into six nearly equal lathes, instead of the usual hundreds of the Anglo-Saxon shires ; while it has been pointed out that by Jutish law a military expedition is still called a "lething," or, in Danish, "leding" (leading). On the other hand, in support of the opinion that this first settlement was not of Jutes from Jutland, but of Goths from Gaul, Dr. R. G. Latham has observed that King Alfred, in translating Bede's "Ecclesiastical History," has dealt with Bede's recorded conquest by the three strongest of the invading peoples, "Saxonibus, Anglis, Jutis," as "that of Saxum and of Angle, and of Geatum" and of the Geats ; while the King, in whose reign the Saxon Chronicle appears to have been established, also dropped out of his version of Bede the reference to a people "yet called" Jute. Again, it is observed that Bede connects the name of the people of the Isle of Wight—Wiht-wære, *Vect*-varia—with Jutæ, as King Alfred in his day connected it with Geat. But the error here is certain ; the name being a British name, known to the Romans, and current in South Britain long before anything had been heard of Hengist and Horsa. In "The Life of King Alfred," ascribed to his Bishop Asser, Alfred himself is made by inference a Jute, his grandfather being Oslac, "a Goth by nation, for he was born of the Goths and Jutes ; that is to say, of the race of Stuf and Wihtgar, and, being made Governor of the Isle of Wight, killed in Gwitigaraburgh (Carisbrooke), their last stronghold in the island, the few native Cymry who were not already slain or exiled." Dr. Latham dwells upon this phrase "Goth and Jute," and upon Alfred's rendering of Jute by Geat, when he argues that the "Jutes" of the first settlement were, in fact, Goths ; or that, if Jutes, they were Jutes who came in company with Goths, and that they came, not out of Jutland, but only from the coast of Gaul, across the straits that divide Gaul from Britain. Thus, he argues, we may have in the names of the two Kings of Wessex, Cyneric and Cwichelm, the Goths Hunneric (Heinrich) and Wilhelm. He observes that according to this theory we have still in Kent a people that is not Saxon, to preserve the ancient name of that part

of the land; and that the division into "lathes" may be
accounted for, since Zeuss has pointed to the Lete or Lœte,
who, according to the "Notitia Utriusque Imperii," were
transplanted by the Romans in military divisions of Franks,
Teutons, Batavians, and others, into Celtic Gaul. There
were Lœts from the Batavians and Suevi, in the days of the
"Notitia," stationed at Bayeux; and Zeuss adds to the
citation of these military companies or colonies the statement of the Theodosian Code (A.D. 438), "that the lands
appointed to the Lœti, who were removed to them, were
called Terræ Lœticæ." The Lathes of Kent may, therefore,
have been "Terræ Lœticæ," held by Germanic or Gothic
military colonies from Gaul.

But while the first of the six settlements is said to have
been of Jutes, the next three are said to have been of
Saxons, who established Saxon power in the
south; and the last two of Angles, in the north
of England and the Scottish lowlands. Who were the
Saxons and the Angles? The distinction of nation between
these invaders of the South and of the North still rests on
the authority of Bede, who believed that the Angles came
from a land called Angle; in his Latin, Angulus; lying
between the countries of the Jutes and Saxons. The
region to which Bede here pointed is still to be found in a
corner of land called Angeln, in Slesvig, which lies a little
to the north of the harbour of Kiel. It forms the southern
coast at the mouth of Flensborg Fiord, includes the pro-
jection of land, thence to the mouths of the inlet of the Slie
or Schley, which runs inland to the town of Schleswig; and
if we reckon in it the marshes on the other side of the Slie
mouths, we have a district measuring at most twenty miles
by ten, which even at this day supports but half-a-dozen
villages or towns. It contained thick woods, and was in
Bede's time known to be desolate. But then the belief was
that it had been depopulated by migration of the Angles to

this country. Again, this Angulus is on the eastern, not the
western coast ; so that if their district be confined within
Bede's definition of it, the Angles when they came to Britain
either began their migration over land, or had to sail out of
the Baltic, and come round Denmark on their way. The
distance, however, is but five-and-twenty miles from the head
of the Slie to the west coast. The whole breadth of land
from the mouth of the Flensborg Fiord to the shore of the
North Sea is only forty miles ; and on that opposite shore,
among the Frisian population north of Leck, another little
district bears yet to this day the name of Angeln. If they
were in Slesvig the same Angles who proved so busy and so
strong when they reached Britain, we may be quite sure that
in Slesvig they occupied the whole breadth of the land from
coast to coast. North of the Angles, as thus placed, were
the Jutes ; and to the south, between them and the Elbe,
that is to say, in modern Holstein, were the Saxons ;
Denmark Proper in a slight measure, and Slesvig and
Holstein almost entirely, being, according to this view, the
parent country of the Anglo-Saxon race.

We have here no more than a fragment of the truth.
From the whole range of the coast opposite Britain between
Jutland and the Seine, came, reinforced by kindred tribes
that extended inland, the men who at different times took
possession of the plains of Britain. They were Frisians of
the coast, from islands over against our side of the Slesvig
shore, still called the Frisian Islands, to the border of France,
in the country that is to this day named after the Belgæ.
They were called by a name of their own as Angles ; but
the name of Saxon, like that of Welsh (foreigner) given to
the Cymry, seems to have been a name applied from
without by the Romans and the Celts ; as Welsh, meaning
foreign, was a name given by those whom they called
Saxons to the Cymry. The Angles of the North of England
were called Saxons by the bard of " The Gododin," and

were Sassenach long after to the Highland Scot. It is
therefore not improbable that the apparent difference
between Saxon and Angle has arisen from the fact that the
same people who ruled in the north under a native name,
accepted the other when establishing, among those by whom
they were called Saxon, their Angle kingdoms. If it was
Egbert, King of the West Saxons, who first gave to the
whole country the name of England—the land of the
Angles—we may consent to the opinion that he would not
have done this had it belonged to a differing race of Saxons,
he being himself a Saxon.

From the Angles of Bede we turn lastly to the Saxons,
whose land he identifies with Holstein. There is no record
of the geography of Germany within the period
of Bede's six Anglo-Saxon settlements. But
reasonable inferences can be drawn from comparison of the
latest accounts before that period with the earliest accounts
after it ; that is to say, of the accounts given by Tacitus in
the "Germania " (A.D. 100), and by Claudius Ptolemy in his
" Geography " (A.D. 161), with those of the annalists of
Charlemagne and his successors (for more than a century
after Charlemagne's accession, A.D. 768). In Tacitus there
is no Saxony ; there are no Saxons. The first mention of
Saxons is by Ptolemy, who places them on the mainland, and
in three islands adjacent to the land north of the Elbe,
from Hamburg westward to the sea, and northward to the
Eider. This is the region corresponding to the Holstein
districts of Stormar and Ditmarsh, with the (Frisian) islands,
it is supposed, of Dylt, Fohr, and Nordstrand. Both Tacitus
and Ptolemy placed on the coast south of the Elbe, between
that river and the Ems, a people called the Chauci. The
rest of the coast, north-eastern France included, was said
to be occupied by Frisians and Batavians. The Angles of
Tacitus were on the Lower Elbe, about Hamburg, Lauen-
burg, and Holstein. They were the Angles of Bede's

Saxons.

Angulus, with a wider extension to the south and west. Behind the Chauci of the coast, whose country dipped far inland, south also of the Angles, were a people called by Tacitus and Ptolemy Cherusci. Their land contained what we now call the Hartz Mountains, and included modern Saxony. South of the Cherusci were the Longobardi, and between the Cherusci and the Frisian coast were other tribes, the Angrivarii, whose district was about Engern, which is a small town between Bielefeld and Minden, and the Chamavi and Chasuarii in the province called afterwards Westphalia.

We pass now over the blank period of the six Anglo-Saxon settlements in England to the geography of Carlovingian times, two or three centuries subsequent to those events. The Franks called the parts lying to the north and east of their own frontier the four countries of the Slaves, the Danes, the Frisians, and the Saxons. The Slaves were in Eastern Europe; Dania was the country north of the Eyder, modern Jutland and Slesvig. Frisia was the coast-country between the Frank boundary and the Weser, consisting of the present Dutch provinces of Friesland and Groningen, East Friesland and a part of Oldenburg; thus including the chief part of the region formerly ascribed to the Chauci. As for the Saxony of Carlovingian days, this was a large region through which flowed the Elbe. North of the Elbe, Nordalbigian, or Transalbian Saxony, nearly corresponded to the Saxony of Ptolemy, its people being divided into Thiedmarsi (Ditmarshers), with Meldorp for their capital and Holsati (dwellers in woods, Holsteiners) separated by the river Sturia from the Stormarii, whose capital was Hamburg. South of the Elbe the Cisalbian Saxons were divided into Westphalians and Eastphalians, with the Angrarians, formerly Angrivarii, between them. The Chamavi and Chasuarii are now Westphalian (west-dwelling) Saxons; the Angles and the Cherusci, with a tribe of Fosi, who had formerly been interposed, are now called Eastphalian (east-dwelling) Saxons. Until Ptolemy (A.D. 160) there is no mention of Saxons; after the time of Claudian (A.D. 400) there is no mention of Cherusci; and, as we hear less of these people as Cheruscans, we hear more of them as Saxons. Saxon, then, was a new name among the nations, which came into use during the second century. It was applied first to the sea-faring people who had the Holstein shore north of the Elbe-mouth for the starting-point of their excursions, and who corresponded on the coasts of the North Sea to the Angles on the Baltic side of a narrow peninsula. It is at least reasonable, therefore, to believe that the adjacent tribes formed one body of Angles, occupying land with two sea-fronts, to whom on one of their fronts, early in the second century, the name of "Saxon" was applied by those among whom, by their descents upon the coast of Gaul and Britain, they were making themselves a constant subject of discussion. The name of "Saxon" was extended afterwards to the people south of the Elbe, and, supplanting other local names in the geography of the foreigner, came to be applied to the inhabitants of that large tract of land in Germany whereof a fragment remains as the modern Saxony. It is certain that these people when settled in Britain, however they may have accepted distinctions made to account for the names Angle and Saxon, all called themselves alike the English folk, and their language the "Englisce Spræc," "English." Of the word "Anglo-Saxon," it may be recorded that it was first used in the "Life of Alfred the Great" ascribed to Asser, where Alfred is called "Angul-Saxonum Rex." The term is there meant, not as an expression of union between Angles and Saxons, but to distinguish Saxons of England from those of the Continent. It was not until long afterwards that the phrase came into use as a convenient technical name for the English people and their language during the first epoch of their national life—life that has since been marked by great changes in their method of speech and their vocabulary, and by some changes of importance even in the temper of the mind that these are to express.

To the geographical details here given I add only a pertinent sentence or two from King Alfred's account of the geographical voyages of the Northmen Ohthere and Wulfstan, communicated to him by those explorers, and introduced among his numerous variations and additions to the "Geography" translated by him from Orosius. "To the north of the Thuringians," he says (*i.e.* of the district of Saxe-Gotha, Saxe-Weimar, &c.), "are the Old Saxons. To the north-west are the Frisians, and to the west of the Old Saxons is the mouth of the Elbe, as also Frisia. Hence to the west-north is that land called Angle-land, Sealand, and some part of Denmark." Again, in describing a voyage of Ohthere to Æt-Hæthum, a "port by the heaths," which is identified with Haddeby on the Slie, opposite the town of Slesvig, or, sometimes, with old Slesvig itself, Alfred says that Æt-Hæthum "stands between the Wenedæ, the Saxons, and the Angles, and is subject to the Danes. For two days before Ohthere came to Hæthum, on his right hand was Jutland, Sæland, and many islands, all which lands were inhabited by the English before they came hither." These were the lands in and about the Angulus of Bede.

To all this external evidence as to the part of the Continent from which the Anglo-Saxons came to England, there is to be added the internal evidence of community of local and personal names and close analogy of language. Thus in English names of places we have words ending in "hurst," meaning a copse or wood, and "beck," meaning a brook. Between the Lower Elbe and Weser, as well as in Holstein north of the Elbe, such horsts are numerous. Our becks we find, again, in the becks and bachs of the same

region, especially in the more inland part, where the Leine
flows towards the Aller and the Weser.

The evidence of language to the Frisian origin of the
Saxons is so strong that there is no contradiction between
the statement of Procopius in the sixth century,*   Frisians and
that Britain was inhabited by the three races of   Saxons.
Britons, Angles, and Frisians, and Bede's statement that
the inhabitants were Britons, Angles, and Saxons. Jacob
von der Marland, who in the thirteenth century produced
the first-fruits of Dutch poetry in his " Spiegel Historical,
or Mirror of History," claims Hengist himself as " a
Frisian, a Saxon," who was driven out of the land, using the
two words as synonyms :—

> " Een hiet Engistus, een Vriese, een Sas
> Die, ut en Lande verdreven was."

And Verstegan quotes, to like effect, " an old Teutonic
author, who saith thus :—

> "' Oude Boeken hoorde ic gewagen,
>   Old books heard I to mention,
>
> ' Dat al het lant beneden Nüemagen,
>   That all the land beneath Nimeguen,
>   Wylen Neder Sassen hiet,
>   Whilome Nether Saxon hight.'

Then goeth he on and telleth how the river of Scheldt was the western
limit of the Saxon country. So as accounting now for the east side of
Holsatia, which confineth on the Baltic Sea, unto this aforesaid river of
Scheldt, Saxonland, or the country of the Saxons, contained in length
more than three hundred miles. The same Teutonic author addeth
further,

> ' Die Neder Sassen hieten nu Friesen,'

that is,

> ' The Nether Saxons are hight now Frisians.' "

* " De Bello Gothico," iv. 20.

A glance at the map of Europe will soon show by what currents, in the course of nature, the tide of migration from the mainland to Britain must have sped over the dividing sea. From each region it strikes on the shore most nearly opposite, and we find accordingly to this day in our provincial speech, and in the very frames and faces of the speakers, Scandinavian in the north, to which Scandinavians would have found their way most readily, Danish types in the Midland, Frisian in the south. The great characteristic differences between a Lowland Scot or a Northumbrian dalesman, and a Sussex labourer whose forefathers have never strayed beyond the parent soil, still clearly point to difference of character in the Teutonic tribes from which they are descended.

The defeat of the Romans in the year 9 by Armin, chief of the Cherusci, had checked their successes in Germany, The Romans and won for the brave enemy a high respect. in Germany. The "Germania" of Tacitus, written in the year 100, leaves us a record of the German character as the Romans understood it, and of the divisions of their tribes. He describes them as a people of large growth, blue-eyed, and auburn-haired, who worshipped gods of war, clashed their shields to the time of war-songs, and praised in their feasts Armin, who delivered them from Rome. They reverenced women, were true to their marriage vows, and held together as a people by a strong spirit of association that would draw them readily to common action for a common good. A recent writer traces them back to the Scyths, called by the Persians Sacæ, who spread from the Aryan home to the highlands of the Scythian Imaus, and thence over large part of Asia, with an influence that imposed some of their thought on the dark-skinned Mongolian races, and levied tribute on all Asia before the time of Ninus, who freed Assyria from their yoke. The Scyths, he argues, were kin to the Thracians, and appearing first as

Germans in the Ostrogoths, spread westward, and became forefathers of the whole Germanic people.*

The earliest piece of Literature that has come down to us from a Teutonic people is a large fragment of translation from the Bible, made for a tribe of Goths known as the Mœso-Goths, by Ulfilas, its Christian guide. Of Ulfilas—whose name is written also Ulfila, Ulphilas, Ourphilas, Hulfila, Gulfilas, and Vulfilas—there are two old accounts. One is in a quotation made by Photius from Philostorgius, an Arian, who lived about the year 440.† The other is by his own pupil, Auxentius, Bishop of Dorostorus (Silistria). This account of Ulfilas was found by Professor G. Waitz,‡ written in the border of a fifth century parchment MS. in the Paris Library,§ containing treatises by Hilarius and other pieces. From these authorities we learn that Ulfilas was born in the year 311, among Goths then settled in the Dacian provinces beyond the Danube. The tribes among which he was born had made wide raids in Europe and in Asia, and had carried away with other booty many prisoners from Galatia and Cappadocia, including a few Christian priests. But these captive Christians by their way of life gained influence over their rough masters, and began their conversion. Ulfilas came of the family of one of these Cappadocian Christians, who had been brought from the village of Sadagolthina,

Ulfilas and the Mœso-Goths. Bible Translation.

---

* Die Skythen-Saken die Urväter der Germanen. Von Johannes Fressel, München, 1886.

† Auxentius writes in his Latin, Ulfila; Philostorgius, Ourphilas. The Gothic form with an initial V was used by the Goth Jornandes (c. 51), and by Cassiodorus in his "Tripartite History." The initial V sounded as w before u, easily blended with it in ears or on lips unaccustomed to the strange sound of w.

‡ "Ueber das Leben und die Lehre des Ulfilas," von G. Waitz. Hanover, 1840 ; See further Bessel "Ueber das Leben und die Lehre des Ulfilas." Hanover, 1840.

§ Supplem. Cat., No. 594. It is written round a report of the sittings of the Council of Aquileia in 381.

near the town of Parnassus. Born with the genius of a
leader, he completed the conversion of the tribe. They
sent him, about the year 328, to represent them at the
court of the Emperor Constantine, and there he was, in the
year 341, at the age of thirty, ordained bishop by Eusebius.
He returned then to his people, whose faith in him was so
complete that a saying arose among them : "All that Ulfilas
does is well done." He preached and wrote in Greek, in
Latin, and in the language of the Goths, and he began to
translate for their use the Scriptures into their own language.
That he might do this it is said that he perfected a Gothic
alphabet, with letters based on Greek rather than Latin
forms, this being done to avoid the use of heathen runes.
When he had been bishop for seven years, that is, in the
year 348, his Christian tribe had endured so much persecution from the unconverted tribes around them that he
obtained leave from the Emperor Constantius to lead them
across the Danube, and plant them at safe distance from their
persecutors in Mœsia, now known as Servia and Bulgaria.
Ulfilas having led them to the promised hills, they were
known thenceforth as the Mœso-Goths. Not counting the
seven years before their removal, Ulfilas continued to be
their teacher for thirty-three years—that is, until the year 381.
He was then summoned by Theodosius to the imperial
court at Constantinople, where he was held in high honour,
and requested as head of the Arian party which Theodosius
favoured, to dispute against certain propounders of a
doctrine that began to spread among the Goths : but when
he reached the capital he was seized with his last illness,
and died in the same year at the age of seventy. In his
last hours of life, having in mind the theological disputes
that had begun to vex his people, he dictated a declaration
of his faith. "I believe God the Father to be one only,
unbegotten and invisible, and in His only begotten Son,
our Lord and God, maker of all that is created, having none

like unto Him ; so that there is one God over all, who is also God of our God, and one Holy Spirit, an illuminating and sanctifying power, neither God, nor Lord, but the minister of Christ, obedient in all things to the Son, as the Son is obedient in all things to the Father." Philostorgius says that Ulfilas translated the whole Bible except the Books of Kings ; those he omitted because they contained histories of wars, and his Goths had a delight in war that called rather for repression than encouragement. The translation was made chiefly from Greek MSS. Copies of it were in the armies of the Goths when they invaded Italy, and many of the fragments which have furnished additions to the text of the chief copy, the famous " Silver Codex," now belonging to the University of Upsala, have been found in Italy. There remain large fragments of the four Gospels, the Epistle to the Romans, part of the First and the whole of the Second Epistle to the Corinthians,— the only complete book,—the Epistles to the Galatians and Ephesians, with a few gaps here and there in each, and fragments of Paul's other epistles. Of the Mœso-Gothic translation of the Old Testament there are only two scraps from the first and second book of Exodus.

It was at the end of the year 476 that Odoacer, at the head of his hordes of Heruli, Rugii, Scyrri, Purcilingi, and Goths, became master of Italy, and ruled in the name of the Emperor Nepos, who was murdered at Salona in May, 480. These dates belong to the history of the extinction of the Western Empire, in the next century after the death of Ulfilas. The Emperor Zeno at Constantinople had, in the year 474, ceded to the Ostrogoths the southern parts of Pannonia and Dacia, and trusted to them the de-fence of the lower Danube. In the year 475 Theodoric, who from the age of eight to the age of eighteen had lived as a friendly hostage in Constantinople, became King of the Ostrogoths. Zeno found him inconveniently vigorous

R

in the assertion of his rights, and diverted his military ardour towards Odoacer, against whom he began the march to which we owe in part the preservation of some MSS. of Ulfilas. Women and children followed with the army of the Goths, who were migrating to the fertile plains of Italy, which had been made over to Theodoric by the Emperor at Constantinople, and were to be his, if he could conquer them. Goths to the number, it is said, of two hundred thousand had crossed the Alps by the summer of the year 489, a century after the death of Ulfilas; and copies of Ulfilas's Bible were brought with them, of which fragments have since been found in Italian monasteries. Before the end of the year, Odoacer was defeated at Aquileia and at Verona. Then, after endurance of a three years' siege in Ravenna, he surrendered in 493, on condition of joint rule with Theodoric. But a few days afterwards, accused of treachery, he was murdered at a banquet to which Theodoric invited him. Theodoric then made himself master of all Italy, and, until his death in the year 526, ruled as Patricius over the Romans and as King over his own people.

The only note of old German heroic song that has come down to us is a strain from one of the heroic poems The Song of in which incidents of this great war were cele-Hildebrand. brated by the Ostrogoths. The only known MS. of it is on a piece of parchment found between the wood and leather of the binding of a Latin Prayer Book in the ancient monastery of Fulda. It is a MS. of the eighth century, now in the public library at Cassel. Theodoric, the Ostrogoth, conqueror of Italy, appears in later romance as Theodoric of Verona, Dietrich von Bern. Hildebrand, chief of his heroes, had fought in his youth in Italy, married there, and left a three-year-old son when he was driven by Odoacer to Attila, King of the Huns. After years during which the son grew up to manhood, Hildebrand

re-entered Italy as a great chief in the army of Theodoric.
His son Hadubrand was then a chief combatant in Odoacer's
army.   This is all that we have of

The Song of Hildebrand.

I have heard tell, they called each other forth,
Hildebrand, Hadubrand, among the hosts,
Son, father, made them ready for the strife,
Donned their war shirts and girded on their swords
Over ringed mail, rode, heroes, to the fight.

Hildebrand, Herbrand's son, the elder man
And wiser, spake, well skilled in questioning,
Asked in few words, who among all the folk
His father was, "or of what stock thou be?
Tell, and I'll give a mail of triple web :
Child in this realm, I knew its families."
Hadubrand spake, Hildebrand's son : "The old
And wise among our folk tell me my father
Was Hildebrand, my name is Hadubrand.
My father went to the east to fly the hate
Of Otaker, with Dietrich and his bands.
A slender bride abiding in the land
He left in bower, with an ungrown child
And weapons masterless.   Eastward he went
When sorrow came to Dietrich, friendless man,
My kinsman, Otaker became his foe.
Most famed of warriors, since Dietrich fell,
Foremost in every field, he loved the fight,
Praised by the bold, I doubt not he is dead."

"Lord God of men," spake Hildebrand, "from Heaven
Stay strife between two men so near in blood !"
Then twisted from his arm the bracelet ring
That once the King of Huns had given him,
"I give it you in token of my love."

Spake Hadubrand, the son of Hildebrand,
"At the spear's point I take of you such gifts,
Point against point.   No comrade thou, old Hun,

R 2

With sly enticing words would'st win me near :
My answer to them is with cast of spear,
Thou'rt old. This cunning out of age is bred.
Over the Midland Sea came foes who said,
'Hildebrand, son of Herbrand, he is dead.'"

Hildebrand, son of Herbrand, spake again :
"Thine arms show that in this land thou could'st not gain
A liberal leader or a royal friend.
Now wellaway, great God, Fate's evil end !
For sixty years, exile in stranger lands,
Summer and winter with spear-darting bands,
Never once legbound within city wall,
I come back by my own son's hand to fall,
Hewn by his sword, or be his murderer,—
But if thy strength hold, thou can'st readily
Win of the brave his arms, spoil of the slain,
When thine by right."   Said Hildebrand, " Now, worst
Of Ostrogoths be he who holds me back !
My heart is for the fray.
Judge, comrades who look on, which of us wins
The fame, best throws the dart, and earns the spoil ! "
The ashen spears then sped, stuck in the shields
With their keen points, and down on the white shields
The heavy axes rang with sounding blows,
Shattering their rims, the flesh behind stood firm. . . .

There is no more. Thanks to the two monks who dis-
sected the cover of a prayer-book—not the only example of
a gain to Literature from studies in the anatomy of old book-
covers—there is this one rift in the thick cloud that hides
from us the inner life of the Germans in the sixth or seventh
century ; one ray of light shoots forth, then all is dark again.
But we have seen enough to know that the old literatures of
the Scandinavians and First English pass out of ancient
times from brotherhood with Teutons of the Continent,
among whom there was not silence, though there be no
record of the song. Very noticeable in this fragment is the
sudden rise of the war spirit—of what Gaelic poets might

have called Hildebrand's " bird of valour " —at the close ;
even the strong instinct of family affection was subdued
for a time by that appetite for war which made it seem
prudent to Ulfilas to leave the record of the wars of Israel
out of his Gothic Bible.

The language of Ulfilas and of the Ostrogoths was of
the Low German type. After the death of Theodoric the
power of the Ostrogoths declined. It was finally
destroyed in Italy in the year 555, and the Dawn of
Christianity.
The
Weissen-
brunner
Prayer.
Teutonic tribes who next played a foremost
part in the shaping of the future were a confederacy known as the Franks, from whom France takes
her name. They were on both sides of the lower Rhine,
and spread their power. Meroveus, who gave the name of
" Merovingian " to the line of Frankish kings, came to his rule
in the year 448. His grandson, Clovis, succeeded in the
year of the death of Ulfilas, 481, being then only a boy of
fourteen. He succeeded to a small dominion and an army
of not more than five thousand fighting men. But it was
he who laid the foundations of the Frankish power. He
married in 493 a Christian princess, and probably through
her influence was drawn to Christianity himself and to the
Christianising of his people. Christianity thus spread
through a large population speaking a language of the
high German type, and the earliest traces of high German
literature are a few Frankish pieces of Church writing :
portions of catechism, promises at baptism, confessions of
faith, and the Lord's Prayer—instruments in the work of
conversion. There is also one small piece of original verse,
which is known as

The Weissenbrunner Prayer.

I sought out and heard among men
The greatest of wonders.

Earth was not, nor heavens bright,
There was not hill or tree,

No sun shone, no moon gave light,
    There was not the sea.
There was nothing, so no end,
    Beginning, bounds, were there :
Only God, man's tenderest friend,
    And His angels fair.
Holy God, Almighty God,
    That madest sky and land,
That givest man so many a good,
    Give me to understand
Thy grace, in right belief and will,
    In wisdom and in strength,
To fight against the powers of ill,
    And come to Thee at length.

This prayer, which I have ventured to turn from the old unrhymed alliterative measure into modern rhyme without one change in the sequence of its thought—unless it be a change to treat in the last line " coming to God," as equivalent to the "doing of God's will"—is the oldest attempt at Christian song that has come down to us from our Teutonic forefathers upon the Continent.   It was discovered in the Benedictine monastery at Weissenbrunn in Bavaria, set among Latin pieces, and having a Latin inscription over it, " De Poeta."*   Its author probably lived after our English Cædmon, but his date cannot be later than the eighth century, and it was followed in the ninth century by a far more important work, the " Heliand" (modern German "Heiland," Saviour), a detailed poem on the Messiah, in about six thousand lines of Low German—with only two High German forms—composed by a Saxon priest about the year

* I have taken my versions of the "Hildebrand's Lied" and " Weissenbrunner Gebet " from the study of them by the Brothers Grimm : " Die beiden ältesten deutschen Gedichte aus dem achten Jahrhundert : Das Lied von Hildebrand und Hadubrand und das Weissenbrunner Gebet, zum erstenmal in ihrem Metrum dargestellt und herausgegeben durch die Brüder Grimm." Cassel, 1812.

830. This will be afterwards referred to in connection with our first English paraphrase of Cædmon.

The eastern members of the Indo-European family took no direct part in the shaping of English; but it may be said that the Slavonic tribes date the beginning of all utterance that has come down to us from their conversion to Christianity in the ninth century by Cyril and Methodus. Cyril, who died in the year 868, was their Ulfilas, and, like Ulfilas, he shaped an alphabet for his translation of Scripture.

CHAPTER V.

SCANDINAVIA.

PYTHEAS, a Greek navigator who lived in the time of Alexander the Great, sailed from the port of Massilia, now

Ultima Thule. Marseilles, on a voyage of inquiry to Thule, which he made to be six days' sail beyond Britain. He brought home reports concerning lands which must have been a part of Scandinavia, but his reports were treated as untrustworthy by Polybius and Strabo. For the next twelve hundred years, until the time of King Alfred, little was known of the lands whence the ships of the Northmen came with crews of plunderers or settlers to the British shores. Those were the lands of Low German tribes quickened to energy by soil and climate, and by battle with the wild Atlantic in their search for bread.

With high, free spirits, the Scandinavians were bold also in invention; long winter nights much favoured story-telling, and none but the old Greeks excelled them in the number and the beauty of their legendary tales. They personified the great forces of Nature until they had framed a wide and beautiful mythology; they developed their chief heroes into mythical forms, half human, half divine; they preserved the glory of the deeds of their forefathers in family traditions that were cherished in the settlements of every valley.

They shaped at last their god Odin, or Woden (after whom we name our Wednesday) into an historical myth that

accounted in their own way for the division of their tribes
into Norwegians, Swedes, and Danes. When Pompey defeated Mithridates (B.C. 66), he overcame also Scythian
tribes that Mithridates had armed against Rome. One of
these tribes was said to have been headed by Sigga, son of
Fridulf, who fled from the Romans to the north of Europe,
and took the name of Odin, the chief god of the Teutons.
His tribe had been the Æsir, between the Black Sea and
the Caspian, and the chief city of the Æsir was Asgard, a
famous centre of worship. These were names of the gods
and of their home, borrowed from myth for the making of
history. Odin led his followers to northern conquest, and
gave sons to rule kingdoms that he founded. Staying
long in the pleasant island of Fünen, he there built the
town of Odensee. Subduing the rest of Denmark, he
made his son Skjöld its king. He passed to Sweden,
where Gylfi, its king, paid him worship. There he established his authority, and left his son Yngvi as king,
whence kings of Sweden were said to be of the race of the
Ynglingar. Odin established in Sweden his form of worship, and went on to Norway, over which he gave the rule
to his son Sæming. Then, assembling his friends, he gave
himself nine lance-wounds in form of a circle, and many
sword-cuts, whereof he died, declaring that he so returned
to Asgard to sit at eternal banquet with the other gods,
where he would receive with great honour all those who
should die bravely, sword in hand. The northern chroniclers make this Odin the most persuasive of men, first
teacher of poetry to the Scandinavians, and inventor of
runes. His skill in magic helped him to pass as a god, and
his singing was so sweet that mountains opened with delight
and ghosts were drawn out of their caves. In war he was
as a wild wolf, biting his shield with rage, so that his
enemies, by terror of his aspect, were struck blind and
deaf.

Runes were the letters of the alphabets used by all the old Teutonic tribes. When the art of conveying sound by sight was new, it was a great marvel and a mystery known to few. This we have seen in the Gaelic Ogham letters; and among Germans and Scandinavians Rune was at once used as another word for secret conversation, private council. The letters were even considered magical, and cast into the air written separately upon chips or spills of wood, to fall as fate determined on a cloth, and then be read by the interpreters. So in our First English, "runian" was to whisper or speak secretly, runing was dealing in secrets, and, with the phonetic addition of a d after the n, (like that in "sound" and "thunder"), remained as "round" even to Shakespeare's time.* The writing of the runes was upon slips of wood, or upon stone when permanence was sought; they were set as charms also upon weapons, and the first sense of the word "write" was to cut or carve. In our First English Beowulf, the hero, in mortal battle with the dragon, *wrote* him in the middle with his deadly knife. The association of the runic letters with heathen mysteries and superstition caused the first Christian teachers to discourage, and, indeed, as far as possible, suppress their use. They were, therefore, superseded by the Latin alphabet, which in First English was supplemented by retention of two of the runes, named "thorn" and "wen," to represent sounds of "th" and "w," for which the Latin alphabet had no letters provided. Each rune was named after some object whose name began with the sound represented. The first letter was F, Feoh, money; the second U, Ur, a bull; the third Th, Thorn, a thorn; the fourth O, Os, the mouth; the fifth R, Rad, a saddle; the sixth C, Cen, a torch; and the six

Runes.

---

* "rounded in the ear
By that same purpose changer."—*King John.*

sounds being joined together make Futhorc, which is the name given to the runic A B C.

On the 20th of July, 1639, a poor girl found in a field near Gallehus, in Denmark, a golden horn, apparently of the fourth century, with runes upon it signifying "Echlew made this horn for the most dread forest god." On the 21st of April, 1734, a second and shorter horn was found in the earth only a few paces from the spot where the first had been found. Its weight was eight pounds. Its finder was a poor cottier who was digging clay. He gave it to his lord, who gave it to the king, and the king sent two hundred dollars to the peasant. These golden horns of Gallehus were double horns, each with an outer case of purest gold over an inner horn made of silver and gold in equal parts. The larger horn had animal figures on it. Two casts had been made of them, but the casts were lost, and the mould had been destroyed as useless to those who had the very horns in their own keeping. But on the 4th of May, 1802, both horns were stolen from the Danish Museum, and they were, no doubt, finally sacrificed to the wood gods in a crucible over a charcoal fire.

Professor George Stephens, of Copenhagen, the chief student of Scandinavian and English runes, argues from their nature and distribution that there began Scandinavian with the first incoming of the Teutons a wide England settlement of Scandinavians in this country, between Thames and Tweed. Indian gravemounds, from the iron age, have weapons, horse harness, and ornaments like those in barrows of the North. Tradition associates the first use of runes with iron-wielding clans of cavalry that swarmed over Scandinavia from the East. Did they bring them from India, or shape them first in Scandinavia? The intervening steppes are without stone; runes upon wood or iron would wear out. However that may be, the traces of the older futhorc, more copious and complex than the later, are to be found scattered about England and the northern lands. As old buildings are taken down and various diggings are made, runic stones are continually being found, but not one ever comes to light in any Saxon or German territory. Of the thousands of inscribed remains dug up in Germany, says Professor George Stephens, all are Roman tiles, altars and funeral stones, or other such. The region within which these runes are found, he says, is all Scandinavia from Lapland to the Eider, and all England from Kent to the Firth of Forth, and to his mind "there is no longer doubt that the old population of Danish, South and North Jutland, the old outflowing Anglic and Jutish and Frisic settlers, mixed with Norsk and Swensk adventurers who flocked to England in the third, fourth, and fifth, and following centuries, were chiefly Scandinavians, Northmen, not Saxons, still less Germans." That is to say, the North furnished the dominant type of the Low German people who united to make England. The north of England was chiefly peopled by the Northern Scandinavians who were most nearly opposite to them, the Midland by the Danes, and the energetic North had touched also and left its mark upon the Southern Frisians. "This runic brand," adds Professor Stephens, "this Broad Arrow, this outstanding mark of a peculiar culture and nationality, is not confined to one particular spot in each northern land. . . . . The runes meet us in Sweden from the north to the south, in Norway from the north to the south, in Denmark from the north to the south, in England from the north to the south; and everywhere from the oldest Northern days, and at one common period." But over all this common ground there were diversities of tribe and speech, dialects that ran into each other, and under different conditions were subjected to different degrees and rates of change.

For record of the life and literature of our Scandinavian forefathers before they became Christians, as aid to the study of our own earliest heroic poem, Beowulf, we are indebted chiefly to the northern colonists of Iceland. Iceland.

Iceland, touching the Arctic circle on the north, is a fifth larger than Ireland. It is volcanic, and deeply indented with fiords on all sides except the south. The chief mountains are in the south. In the south-east is a mass of glacier, covering an area of 3,500 square miles, the Vatna-Jökull * Westward, between this and Bláfell,† Hekla, Torfa Jökull, is ground rising in sweeps towards the glaciers. North of this, on the eastern half of the island, is a desert plain crossed by three tracks, the routes being marked by stone pyramids or heaps of turf. These regions include 20,000 square miles of barren country, imperfectly explored. Ice, desert, geysers, and volcanoes, swamps, lakes, and chasms in the earth, leave in the whole island about 4,000 square miles of habitable ground. At Reykjavik, on the south-west peninsula, the mean temperature of the year is 39° 2′; at Akureyri, in the north, it is 32°. In winter there is the aurora, there are electric flames about metals, and streams from the heads of men like glories of saints. There are mock suns—sometimes nine at once, storm-rings about the moon, meteors ; also fierce hurricanes and whirlwinds.

Iceland was discovered in the year 860 by Naddothr, a Norwegian Vikingr,‡ who was voyaging to the Faroe Islands.

---

* *Vatn,* water ; *jökull,* an icicle, a glacier ; First English *gicel,* whence *is-gicel,* icicle.

† *Blá,* blue of waves or horizon, but in the east of Iceland it means a meadow covered with half-melted snow. *Fell,* a single wild hill, in plural a range of hills. *Hekla-fjall,* abridged to Hekla, so called from its cowl of snow, *hekla* being the name of a sort of cowled or hooded frock. *Torfa,* turf, or a green spot, or a place where many farms are built together.

‡ *Vikingr* was the man who went on a *viking.* *Viking* was a free-booting voyage, named from the *vik,* or small bay, out of which the pirate vessel ran, or within which it lurked. But free-booting was so far from

He looked out on it from a hill on the east coast, and called it Snjá-land, Snow-land. In the year 864, Garthr, a Swede, went round Iceland in his ship and called it Garthr-hólm.* In 868 Floki Rafn, another Norwegian, explored the south and west of the island, and it was he who called it Ís-land, Iceland.

Soon afterwards, when Harold Harfagr (Fairhaired) had been crushing the petty chiefs of Norway, Ingolfr and Hjorleifr were the first to seek independent life in Iceland. They were followed by bands of such exiles, with their servants, cattle, household goods, their national traditions, and their spirit of freedom. Ingolfr had killed his adversary on a small barren island, whither they had gone to fight alone together to the death, after the way known as a "holmgang." As Harold would make him answerable, he sailed away with all his household and his household goods, and with the door-posts of his Norwegian home, which he cast into the sea near Iceland, that he might establish his new home wherever they were cast ashore. But this was in the ninth century, in the days when our Alfred succeeded to a kingdom which he had to save from ruin by the Danes.

The earliest piece of Icelandic literature, the "Íslendiga Bók," is ascribed to Ari Fróthi,† who was not born until the year after the Norman Conquest of England. He gathered into this book, as accurately as he could, the traditions of the island. He cites various people, upon whose testimony he gives facts and dates, but only once quotes written authority, that being for the year 870,

The Íslen-diga Bók.

being regarded as discreditable, that an old Scandinavian scarcely had social position until he had distinguished himself in a bold raid by land or sea.

* *Hólmr* an islet, whence the name of Holms in the Orkneys and the Bristol Channel.

† *Ari,* an old Norse word for Eagle. *Fróthi,* learned. The most thorough account of Ari and his writings was by Professor Werlauf, who published, at Copenhagen in 1808, a Dissertation "De Ario Multiscio."

the date of the death of St. Edmund, after whom, as his place of interment, Bury St. Edmunds is named. Ari's book is a plain chronicle of facts which it was desired to put accurately upon record. It is the most ancient piece of Scandinavian history, and filled only twenty-six quarto pages when first printed at Skalholt in 1688.

The "Landnama Bók" was a development from the work of the priest Ari Fróthi, the son of Thorgil, and from another of the same kind. Its author was Sturla The Land- Thortharson, a judge in the Higher Court, who nama Bók. died in 1284, aged seventy. His work was edited by Hauk Erlendsen, who was himself a judge in the Higher Court from 1294 to 1334, and his "Landnama Bók" is Thorthar-son's with addition of facts from a history by Styrmer the Learned, wherever Styrmer had anything to add. This "Landnama Bók" (Book of the Taking of the Land), the fullest of the old Icelandic chronicles, is in five parts. The first treats of the discovery and settlement of the island, and the other four are given to a description of its several quarters, including detail as to the families by which each was settled. This record is of great value for the verifica-tion of the Sagas.*

The first emigrants found on the shores of Iceland a few hermit settlers, whom they called Papar. These deserted the island, not wishing to live among Irish hermits heathen, and they left Irish books, bells, and in Iceland. croziers behind them. The Irish monk, Dicuil, hereafter to be spoken of, who wrote in the earlier part of the ninth century, says that he had spoken with priests who had visited Ultima Thule, and describes the place in a way that points only to Iceland. There remained also records in names of places, Patreksfjord, Papey, Papyli, and Erlendr-ey, "ey" meaning island.

* The "Landnama Bók" was first printed in 1638. There were more elaborate editions in 1774 and 1843.

For sixty years after the arrival of the first emigrants
there was a constant influx of settlers. Celts came some-

Iceland
peopled. times, and some were brought home as prisoners
of the vikings. By the year 930 the land was
as fully peopled as ever afterwards, and a code of laws was
then adopted. An annual meeting was appointed on the
plain of Thingvöllr. This meeting, which established the
government as a commonwealth, was called the Althing.*
The Althing met by the river Öxará, near Armansfell ; an
assembly had before been held at Kjalarnes. The time of
meeting was about the last fortnight in June. The Althing,
instituted in the year 930, was reformed in 964 ; and in the
year 1000 it resolved upon the establishment of Christianity
as the religion of the land.

The colony had been formed as a place of refuge for
men who were among the foremost of their land, who took
with them their families, their household goods, their old
religion, customs, and traditions, and transmitted them to
their children's children. Although the actual literature of
these Northmen is all later than that year 1000, in which
Christianity was adopted as the national faith, the established families in Iceland that had preserved their traditions
and advanced their culture were able to furnish to the new
church their own bishops and priests, borrowing little from
abroad after the consecration of their first native bishop,
Isleif, in 1056. To these native priests and bishops the
traditions of the faith of their forefathers were of the deepest
interest. From life to life, through successive generations,
tales and songs had passed for the lightening of time

---

* *Völlr* meant a field or plain ; Thingvöllr was, therefore, the Parliament Field. *Thing* meant thing, as in English, but as a law-phrase meant
also any public meeting, especially for legislation or administration of the
law. *Al*, as a prefix, meant quite—thoroughly—completely ; so that
Althing meant the supreme or absolute Assembly, as distinguished from
such assemblies as that of the hús (or house) thing,—whence our word
" hustings,"—to which a chief summoned his people or guardsmen.

through the long northern winters, among men whose home-
steads were thinly scattered in valleys parted by wide
solitudes of rock and glacier from nearest settlements outside their own.

From the end of the thirteenth century comes the
earliest known copy of a collection, begun about the year
1240, of old mythical, religious, and heroic songs
and tales, then chanted and told by the grand-
mothers throughout the land. That earliest copy of them
was a parchment book ("Codex Regius," No. 2,365, in
Copenhagen), which was sent in 1662 from Iceland, as a
present from the Bishop Brynjulfr Sveinsson, of Skalholt,
to King Frederick III. of Denmark. The bishop had discovered it in a farmhouse in 1643. This work was ascribed
to Sæmund Sigfusson, who was priest, poet, and historian,
had a share in forming the ecclesiastical code in Iceland,
and died in the year 1135, a hundred years before the
collection was made. It has been known, therefore, as
Sæmund's Edda, or the Elder, or the Poetical Edda.

The Younger or Prose Edda—Snorri's Edda—was the book
to which the name Edda was first attached, and the author of
this was Snorri Sturluson. Snorri Sturluson, poet
and historian, was born in 1178, rose to high
office in Iceland, and was murdered in 1241. His
book called "Edda" was an Ars Poetica, containing the old
rules for verse-making and poetic diction; but as the
diction included a large number of allusions and phrases
derived from the old Northern mythology, a summary was
also given of the myths from which they all were drawn.
First came two sections, Gylfaginning (the Delusion of
Gylfi) and Bragaraedur (Bragi's Tales), which gave larger
and smaller sketches of the old mythology; then came a
third section called Skáldskaparmál (the Ars Poetica),
which described the conventional circumlocutions and the
other devices of the skalds, or Northern poets; the fourth

s

and last section was called Háttatal (Counting of Metres), which was a Prosody ingeniously set forth by help of a Song of Praise in a hundred and two lines, contrived as examples of all verse-measures in use. Four grammatical and historical treatises were appended to Snorri's work. The oldest of these grammatical treatises is ascribed to a Thorodd, called the Runemaster, who lived in the middle of the twelfth century, and the third treatise was by Olaf Thordarson Hvita Skáld, a nephew of Snorri's. The discovery of this work was due to Arngrim Jonas, an Icelandic clergyman, who sent it, in 1628, to Ole Worm, the Danish antiquary, with whom he was corresponding about runes. The book was called "Edda" from its great-grandmother's tales of a dead faith that had become living poetry. But, as the whole work was designed to teach the rules of poetry, Edda, and rules of Edda, would be often used as a name for the poet's craft. Some have derived "Edda" from Odde, the home of Sæmund. Professor Rhys has suggested,[*] Aideadh, a Celtic name given to old Irish tragic tales concerned with "aitte," death. There will be need to refer to the rules of Snorri when discussing our own early forms of verse.

The oldest of the Edda poems date no farther back than the ninth century. They reproduce the old faith of the

Relation of England to the Edda myths.

people, but with touches of life and action in myths and heroic tales, with a wealth of fresh and vigorous imagination, for which there was no parallel except in ancient Greece. Professor Sophus Bugge, of Christiania, in a study of the origin of the old myths and tales,[†] has pointed to words in the Edda poems, as well as to

---

[*] In the *Academy* for January 31, 1880.

[†] "Studien über die Entstehung der nordischen Götterund Heldensagen" von Sophus Bugge, Professor der Universität Christiania. Vom Verfasser autorisierte und durchgesehene Uebersetzung von Dr. Oscar Brenner, Privatdocent der Universität München. Munich 1881–82.

matter that must have been carried home from England and Ireland in the energetic viking days, to which this intellectual activity is traced, and he suggests that even the word viking was accepted from the speech of England, where it was formed from the Latin "vicus," which could mean a camp. From Celtic and English Christians, Sophus Bugge suggests that the Northmen carried home pieces of Christian faith and legend, with tales from the Greek literature that was familiar especially to Celtic priests, who drew their inspiration from the Eastern Church. Thus he shows traces of the legendary tales of Christ in the story of Balder, and associates Loki with Lucifer, while in some parts of the Balder myth he finds adaptations from the story of Achilles, and generally a fantastic use of incidents from the Siege of Troy, as told in the history ascribed to Dares the Phrygian. When darkness gathered over all the rest of western Europe, the churches and monasteries of the British island, first among the Celts and afterwards among the English, supplied, says the Danish scholar, in and after the seventh century, the only shelter and home to the higher studies. The British clergy travelled far in search of books, until in the time of Charlemagne it was from the Church in Britain that the clearest light shone through the western world.

CHAPTER VI.

BEOWULF.

BASED on historical events earlier, perhaps, in date than those which have given rise to any heroic tale among the Scandinavians, we have at the beginning of First English Literature the great poem entitled BEOWULF. It shows the touches of a Christian hand, but it preserves, with the fidelity of one who took an artist's pleasure in the work, a picture of the Northern life and tone of thought in days before the spread of Christianity. Grundtvig's clear identification of Hygelac, a chief in the story, with a Chocilaicus who fell in battle in the year 520, fixes a time for the historical events that were transformed into the fables of the poem. The poem extends, as we have it, to 6356 of the short First-English lines, or half lines, as they are usually printed in England. The only existing MS. is in the Cotton Library in the British Museum ;* it is full of inaccuracy, and, the

Beowulf. The Poem and the Manuscript.

---

* MS. Cott. Vitellius, A. 15. Dr. Matthew Parker, Archbishop of Canterbury (b. 1504 ; d. 1575) rescued many Anglo-Saxon MSS. from among the ruins of the dissolved monasteries. They were bequeathed by him to his own University and College, where they are among the Parkerian MSS. of Corpus Christi College, Cambridge. Sir Robert Cotton (b. 1570 ; d. 1631) rescued many more of the Anglo-Saxon MSS. newly scattered abroad, beginning to collect at the age of 18. By the fire, in 1731, in Little Dean's Yard, Westminster, 111 MSS. were lost, burnt, or entirely defaced, and 99, including the Beowulf, made imperfect. The collection was removed to the Old Dormitory at Westminster, and then, in 1753, to the British Museum.

change beginning at line 1940, was written by two copyists, probably in the first half of the eleventh century. It was also much injured by the fire at Cotton House. We must think of it, however, not as a tindery manuscript, but as a bright gleam of human light and life from the far past. The greater part of Beowulf belongs at latest to the seventh or eighth century, and ranks as the oldest heroic poem extant not only in English but in any Germanic tongue.

And now is to be asked, what is the substance of this ancient tale? For we must know something of the text itself before we turn to its interpreters. We enter one of the great festive halls to join at the ale-drinking and hear the gleeman's song. The Sub-stance of the Tale. The hall is long and wide, say 200 feet by 40, with a high roof and curved gables. There is at each extremity an entrance in the middle of the wall, protected by a porch, that is continued at its farther end to form cellar and pantry. We pass into the hall, a spacious nave with narrow side aisles. Pillars, dividing aisles from nave, sup-port the central roof. The nave is the great hall itself, and down the middle of its floor run the stone hearths, upon which blaze great timber fires. At the upper end is the raised seat of the chief, at a cross-bench, where his wife, who fills the cups of the guests, and his familiar thanes, or those whom he distinguishes, sit with him. On each side of the long hearth there runs a line of tables, flanked with benches and stools, at which sit the people who are the chief's " hearth-sharers." At the lower end, in the space corresponding to the daïs, is a table for the drinking-cups. Between the rows of pillars and the outer walls spaces are parted off within the narrow aisles for sleeping-benches of the warriors. In some of the spaces are the gilded vats of liquor into which the pails of the cup-bearers are dipped. If women sleep in the hall, the recesses of the pillars behind the daïs are kept sacred to them, and there are in the aisles, if the hall be the chief's dwelling, as that in Beowulf was not, distinct enclosures for the occupation of the family. The sleeping space behind the pillars might, perhaps, be parted from the hall by panelling and tapestry. In such a hall the gleeman often chanted to his harp now one adventure now another, as the guests or their lord might call for this or that favourite incident, from the long rhythmical, alliterative poem that contains the tale of

BEOWULF.

An elder Beowulf was for a long time the beloved king of the Scyldings, and from his root grew forth at last the lofty Healfdene. Old and war-fierce, he gave to the world four children, heads of hosts : Heorogar, and Hrothgar, and Halga the good, and Ela.

> Then was to Hrothgar given speed in war,
> Honour in battle ; his dear kinsmen then
> Obeyed him gladly, till the youth grew up,
> A numerous band of kindred. In his mind
> It ran that he would bid a court be built—
> A mead-hall greater than had yet been known
> By talk among the sons of men, therein
> Would deal to young and old what God made his,
> Except the people's share, and lives of men.
> Then was I told that among many tribes
> Wide went the call over the earth, to work
> To adorn this home of the people. Time went by
> Among men swiftly, till the chief of halls
> Was all prepared, and Heorot was the name
> That he, whose word had power, shaped for it ;
> He was not false to his promise, rings he gave
> And treasure at the feast. There rose the hall
> High crested ; waiting to be tried by heat
> Of hateful fire.

Then the grim foe came, Grendel, he that held the moors, the fen, and fastness. Forbidden the homes of

mankind, the daughters of Cain brought forth in darkness
misshapen giants, elves, and orkens, such giants as long
warred with God, and he was one of these.

> He, when the night had come, went forth to see
> The high hall, how the Ring Danes housed in it
> After the beer-drinking. He found therein
> A band of lords asleep after the feast,
> Knowing no care that pales the lives of men.
> Then, grim and greedy, the malignant wight,
> Rugged and wroth, was ready soon, and took
> Thirty thanes as they rested, thence again
> Turned to go home with shout over his prey,
> With the death-stricken seek his own abode.
> Then before sunrise, with the early day
> Was Grendel's craft in war disclosed to men.
> Then after feasting was a wail upraised,
> A great cry in the morning. The high chief,
> Good honourable lord, sat cheerlessly,
> Suffered sharp grief, sorrow the thane endured,
> After they saw the track of the loathed foe,
> The accursèd spirit. That strife was for them
> Too strong, sustained and loathsome. No more pause
> Than for a night, and then again he shaped
> More deadly bale, and for no feud and crime
> Made moan, he was too firmly set on them.
> 'Twas easy then to find those who elsewhere
> Sought distant beds, whom the clear token showed
> The hall thane's hate: he who escaped the fiend
> Held himself after that safest afar.
> So Grendel ruled, one against many, warred
> Against the right, until the best of halls
> Stood empty. For long time, a twelve years' space,
> The Scyldings' gentle lord endured his wrath,
> With every woe, and sorrows limitless.

In the morning a whoop was upraised; the strong in war
suffered; the thanes sat in sadness when they saw the
track of the accursed sprite. With Grendel, strife would be
too strong, too long, and loathsome. In the night following, Grendel again had sway, and so often as the darkness

came he warred against right, one against all, till empty
stood the best of houses. Twelve winters' tide was his rage
borne, and it became openly known in sad songs that
Grendel warred then against Hrothgar, would have peace
of no Dane, was not to be met with money. The high and
young he sought and snared. In lasting night he held the
misty moors. Heorot he held in the swart night, with its
seats richly stained, but the gift-stool [the chief's seat,
whence gifts were distributed] he might not touch. Hrothgar, the Scyldings' friend, broken in mind, sat many a time
in thought. Sometimes they worshipped at the holy places,
prayed in words for help from the Ghost-slayer.

> When from his home Hygelac's thane had heard,
> Good among Goths, of Grendel's deeds, he then,
> The strongest of the living race of man,
> Noble and prosperous, he bade prepare
> A good sea traverser, said he would seek
> Over the swan road the brave king, great prince,
> Because he was in need of men. That voyage
> The wise blamed little, though they loved him much,
> But whetted his keen mind, foretold good end.
> Fifteen, the bravest warriors he could find
> Among the Goths, the good chief chose, with them
> He sought the floating wood. A warrior skilled
> In shallow seas made known the bounds of land.
> A space of time passed on, afloat on waves
> The boat lay by the hill, the ready men
> Mounted the prow ; the shallow waters rolled
> Upon the sand ; the warriors bore bright arms
> Into the bark's hold, war gear well prepared.
> Upon the chosen path the men shoved out
> The banded wood. On waves of the deep sea
> The floater, foamy necked, departed then,
> Speeded by wind, and most like to a bird,
> Until the twisted prow had run for an hour
> Of the second day, and then the voyagers
> Saw land, the sea cliffs glitter, the steep hills,
> The broad sea nesses. Then in shallower sea
> The sailors' voyage ended. Quickly thence

Up stepped the Weder's people on the plain,
Bound the sea wood, shook war-shirts, and thanked God,
Who eased for them their way across the waves.

When the Scyldings' warder who had to keep the sea-
shores saw from the wall bright shields borne over the
bulwark of the ship, he asked in his mind what men those
were. Then went to the shore Hrothgar's thane; the
mighty spear quaked in his hand; and he asked, "What
weapon-bearers are ye, wearing war-shirts, who thus come
hither leading over the water-street a foamy keel? I hold
ward that to the Dane's land no foe may bring war by sea.
Never have I seen a greater earl on earth than is one of
you; he is a man worthy with his weapons, if his face tell
true. Now ye far-dwellers,—quickly tell me whence ye
come?"

The leader of the band unlocked his word-hoard: "We
are of the Goths' kind, Hygelac's hearth-sharers; my father
was known widely, a high-born lord hight Ecgtheow; he
abode in his house many winters ere he went on his way,
almost all the wise throughout the wide earth keep him in
mind. We have come through kindness to help thy lord.
We have heard say that a wretch, I know not who, does to
the Scyldings hurt in the dark nights. I may teach Hrothgar how to overcome the foe."

The fearless warder, seated on his horse, then said: "A
sharp shield warrior knows words from works. I hear that
this is a band friendly to the Scyldings. Bear weapons
forth; I show the way; I will bid also my fellow thanes to
hold against every foe your new-tarred ship until it bear
back to the Weder marches those to whom it shall be given
to come whole out of the rush of war."

They went therefore; the wide-bosomed ship stood fast
at anchor, heavy in the mud.

Enwreathed with gold, over their faces rose
A boar-like crest, fire-hardened, many-hued,

It held the life in guard.   Warlike and fierce
The men pressed on, together they went down,
Till gay and golden, rich in timber work,
They saw that greatest house under the sun,
The king's house, whose light lighted many lands.

Of the warriors, one turned his horse, and said, "Now is my time to go ; may the all-wielding Father hold you safe in your undertaking : I will back to the sea to hold ward against foemen."

The street was made handsome with stones, it showed the path to the men.   The war-shirt shone, hard, hand-locked, the bright ringed-iron sang as they came walking to the hall in gruesome gear. Sea-weary, they set broad shields, round and stone hard, against the house-wall ; then, stooping to a bench, placed in a ring their war-shirts, garb of men ; the darts, the seamen's weapons, stood together, with the ash-wood grey above.   Then Wulfgar, a proud warrior, asked the sons of strife : "Whence bear ye your stout shields, grey shirts, fierce helms, and heaps of war-shafts ? "

The proud lord of the Weders answered him from beneath his helmet : "We are Hygelac's board-sharers, BEOWULF is my name.   I will make known my errand to the lord, thy master, if he grant us that we give good greeting to him."   Wulfgar said, " I, then, the Danes' friend, will speak to the lord of the Scyldings, the sharer of rings, and I will soon make known the answer he thinks fit to give." He then turned to where Hrothgar, old and hairless, sat among his earls.   He went so that he stood before the shoulders of the Danes' lord, for he knew the ways of a king's house.   Wulfgar spake to his friendly lord : " Hither are come Goths from afar, the leader these sons of strife name Beowulf ; they beg, my lord, to talk with you ; do not deny them.   They seem worthy to be gladdened with your speech and mix with earls ; at least, he seems so who has led hither the men of war."   Hrothgar, helm of the

Scyldings, said : " I knew him when a boy. His old father was named Ecgtheow, to whom Hrethel, lord of the Goths, gave his only daughter. The seamen, who brought gifts for the Goths, said that he has in his hand-gripe the might of thirty men. Him holy God hath in His kindness sent to us West Danes ; therefore I have hope against Grendel. I shall bestow gifts on my good friend for his daring. Speed thou to bid him in, see the band gathered together as our kindred, say to them that they are welcome to the Danes." Wulfgar bore the bidding : " My doughty lord, King of the East Danes, bids me say that he knows your worth ; that ye come, welcome guests, over the sea. Now go in your war-dress to see Hrothgar, but let the war-boards and the deadly shafts abide here the bargain of words."

Then arose the mighty lord and his brave band of thanes, they hastened together, hard under helm, until they stood at the king's hearth ; then Beowulf spake, on him the war-shirt shone, the war-net sewed by the smith's cunning : —" Be thou, Hrothgar, hail ! I am Hygelac's kinsman and fellow-warrior. I have undertaken many great deeds in my youth. The thing done by Grendel became known to me on my own turf ; seafarers say that this hall, this best of houses, stands empty and good for nought after the evening light is gone. I beseech thee now, lord of the bright Danes, shielder of the Scyldings, that I alone may with this bold band cleanse Heorot. I have heard also that the wretched Grendel recks not of weapons ; I will scorn then to bear sword or the yellow round of a wide shield into the strife ; but with grasp I shall grapple at the fiend, and foe to foe struggle for life. It is the lord's doom whom death shall take. I ween that he will, if he win, fearlessly eat the Goths in the war hall. Thou wilt not need to hide my head, for he will bear my flesh away to eat it in his lonely den. Care for me then no more. Send to Hygelac, if I die in the strife, the best of war-shrouds that wards my breast. That

Hrædla left me, it is Weland's work. What is to be goes ever as it must." Hrothgar, helm of the Scyldings, said : " For fights, friend Beowulf, and for high praise thou hast sought us. Thy father quelled for me the greatest feud, coming over the waves to the Scyldings, when I in my youth first ruled the Danes. Sorrow is me to say why Grendel shames me thus in Heorot. Full often have sons of strife, drunken with beer, said over the ale-cup that they in the beer-hall would bide Grendel's onslaught with sharp edges ; then always in the morning was this mead-hall stained with gore ; when the day dawned all the bench-floor was besteamed with blood of faithful men. Sit now to the board and unseal with mead thy breast among my warriors." Then was a bench cleared in the beer-hall for the sons of the Goths. The thane who bare in his hand the bravely-beset ale-cup, minded his work, poured out the bright, sweet ale ; at times the glee-man sang, peaceful in Heorot : there was gladness of warriors, of men great among Danes and Weders.

Hunferth spake ; Ecglaf's son, who sat at the feet of the Scyldings' lord. To him was the coming of Beowulf, the bold sea-farer, most irksome, because he grudged that any other man ever won more praise than himself : " Art thou the Beowulf who strove with Breca on the sea, when ye from pride tried the fords and for foolish boast risked life in the deep water?" [More, also, in this wise said Hunferth] : " He overcame thee in swimming. He had more strength. Now I look for worse things, though thou shine ever in war, if thou durst bide a night near Grendel." Beowulf replied : " Well, thou a great deal, my friend Hunferth, drunken with beer, hast spoken about Breca. I say truly, that I had greater strength at sea than any other man. We agreed, being striplings, that we would risk our lives on the flood, and we did thus : We had a naked sword in hand when we rowed on the deep, meant for our war against the

whale fishes. He could not swim away from me, nor I
from him ; we were together in the sea five nights till the
flood drove us asunder ; the boiling fords, the coldest of
weather, cloudy night, and the north wind deadly grim
threw up rough billows : roused was the rage of the sea-
fishes. There my body-shirt, hard, hand-locked, gave me
help against the foes ; my braided war-rail lay upon my
breast, handsome with gold. A painted foe drew me to the
ground, a grim one had me in his grasp, yet it was granted
me to reach the wretched being with the point of my war-
blade. Thus often my foes threatened me. I paid them
as was fit with my dear sword. In the morning wounded
with thrusts they lay, put to sleep in shoals, so that they
have not afterwards been any let to the sea-farers. Light
came from the east, the seas were still, so that I might see the
headland's windy walls. The Must Be often helps an undoomed man when he is brave. Yet it was my lot to slay
nine nickers. I have not heard of harder fight by night
under heaven's round. Breca never yet, nor any of you, at
the game of war did such great deeds. Of this I boast not.
Though thou hast been the slayer of thy brothers, for which
thou shalt pay in Hell, Grendel would not have done such
gruesome deeds in Heorot, if thy mind were as war-fierce as
thou tellest of thyself. He has found that he cares not for
the strength of your folk, he slays and shends you, and
expects not strife from the Gar Danes. But a Goth shall
show him fight, and afterwards he shall go to the mead who
may, in peace and gladness "

Glad then was the bright Danes' lord, hoary-locked and
war-praised, trusting in help when he heard Beowulf. There
was laughter of men, the din rose, words were winsome.
Wealtheow, Hrothgar's queen, went forth. Mindful of their
rank, the cheerful wife, gold-decked, greeted the men in hall,
first gave the cup to the lord of the Danes, bade him, dear

to his land, be blithe at the beer-drinking. He gladly
shared the meal and hall-cup. Then she went round, and
gave on every side rich vessels to old and young, until she
bore the mead-cup, bracelet-covered queen, to Beowulf.
She greeted the Goths' lord, thanking God that the will had
befallen her to trust in any earl for help. He, the fierce
warrior, drank of the cup from Wealtheow, and then

> Beowulf, the son of Ecgtheow, spake : " I meant,
> When in the boat set with my warrior band
> I mounted the deep sea, that I alone
> Would work your people's will, or yield my life,
> Fast bound in the foe's grip. I shall use strength
> Nobly, or in this mead-hall bide my end."
> Those words, the Goth's proud speech, well pleased the woman.
> The people's joyful queen, adorned with gold,
> Went to her lord, she sat. Then as before
> Bold words were spoken in the hall with joy,
> The people raised the cry of victory.
> Till suddenly the son of Healfdené
> Prepared to seek his rest. Strife was ordained,
> He knew, against the wretch, in the high hall,
> After the sunlight left them, and dusk night,
> The shadow-helm of all created things,
> Came rolling onward, wan, beneath the clouds.
> The whole band rose, men greeted one another,
> Hrothgar so greeted Beowulf, bade him Hail,
> Gave power over the wine-hall, said thereto :
> " Never before, since I raised hand or shield,
> Gave I to any man the Dane's strong hall
> As now to thee. Have thou and hold thou now
> The best of houses, have thy fame in mind,
> Show thy great strength, keep watch against the foes.
> Thou shall not want all things to thy desire
> If thou complete this work of strength and live."
> Then the defence of Scyldings, Hrothgar, went
> With all his warriors, from the hall, would seek
> Wealtheow, the queen, his bedfellow. Men say
> The glory of kings had against Grendel set
> A guard over the hall, about the chief of Danes

This was his separate office, to keep watch
Against the eoten.* But the chief of Goths
Gladly put trust in his great might alone,
In the Creator's favour. Then he doffed
His iron coat of mail, helm from his head ;
His well-forged sword, choicest of blades, he gave
To an attendant thane, bade him take charge
Over the war gear. Then Beowulf the Goth
Spake a few words of boast ere on his bed
The good chief stept : " I do not count myself
Feebler than Grendel for the toils of war.
Therefore not with my sword, though easily
I may, will I put him to sleep, deprive
Of life. He knows not of that way of war,
To strike at me again, hew on my shield,
Though great his fame for deeds of enmity.
But we two shall to-night do without swords,
If he dare seek war weaponless, and then
Wise God give glory as seems meet to him."

The warrior bowed him, to the bolster laid
His cheek, the earl's face, and in the hall around
Many an eager seaman bowed to rest.
Not one thought he should ever seek again
The home he loved, his people, the free borough
Where he was fostered, for they had heard tell
How in that wine-hall bloody death had seized
On former nights too many of the Danes.
But to the Weder's people the Lord gave
The woof of battle-speed, comfort and aid,
So that by strength of one, his single powers,
All overcame their foe. Sooth is it shown
That mighty God has ever ruled mankind.

In the wan night the shadow-walker came.
The guards who should defend that pinnacled hall
Slept, all but one. For it was known to men

---

* *Eoten.* This is the First-English form of the Scandinavian jötunn,
giant, a word common in the old Norse poetry. The mountains were
"giants' ways," jötna vegir ; the vault of heaven was "the giant's skull,"
jötuns hauss ; and gold, for its large power of persuasion, was called "the
speech of giants."

That the foul spoiler might not drag them forth,-
Since the Lord willed not,—under shade of night,
But he in wrath was watching for attack,
Waited with swelling heart the strife's ordeal.

Then from the moor, under the shroud of mist,
Came Grendel striding. Wrath of God he bare.
Scather of men, he thought in the high hall
To snare one of man's race. Shrouded he went
Till he saw clearly the gold-hall of men,
The wine-house, gay with cups ; nor then first sought
The home of Hrothgar. But in his life-days
Never before or since a bolder man
He found, or hall thanes. Journeying to the house
Came then the man divided from all joys ;
Quickly he rushed upon the door made fast
With bands fire-hardened ; with his hands broke through,
For he was swollen with rage, the house's mouth.
Then soon upon the many-coloured floor
The foe trod ; on he went with ireful mood,
Came from his eyes a fierce light likest fire.
He saw within the hall a kindred band
Of many men asleep, a company
Of comrades, all together ; then he laughed :
For the dire monster thought before day came
To part life from the body of each one.
Hope of a glut of food had grown in him,
Yet it was not his fate that he should eat
After that night more of the race of men.
Hygelac's strong kinsman saw how the foul foe
Would make his sudden grasps ; nor meant the wretch
Delay, for at the first he swiftly seized
A sleeper, slit him unaware, bit through
His bone-case, from his veins drank blood, and soon,
Swallowing in large lumps, had eaten all
The dead man, feet and hands. Then nearer, forth
He stepped, laid hands on the stout-hearted chief
Upon his couch. But he against the foe
Stretched out a hand, soon knew his foul intent,
And fastened on his arm. Herdsman of mischiefs,
Soon he found that on earth in all its parts
A stronger hand-grip never had he felt.

Fearful in mind and soul, he sought escape,
But not for that came he the sooner thence.
He to his lurking-place would fly, would seek
The wild throng of the devils ; his life-days
Had known before no tug so sharp as this.
Then Hygelac's good kinsman bore in mind
His evening speech, stood upright, grasped him hard ;
His fingers burst, outward the eoten was.
The earl advanced more. The bold champion thought
Whether he might not so get room to escape,
Fly to his fen pool, but his fingers' strength,
In the fierce grip, he knew. The harmful spoiler
Found that his path to Heorot led to grief.
The great hall thundered, for all Danes who dwelt
There fortified, for all the brave men, earls,
The ale was spilt ; that the wine-hall withstood,
The fair house of the world, the shock of war,
That it fell not in ruin, was great wonder.
But it was strengthened against that with bands,
Within, without, of iron, cunning work
Of smiths. There many a mead-bench, gold adorned,
Was tilted from its sill, as I've heard tell ;
Old counsellors of the Scyldings never thought
That any man in hate and slaughter stained
Could break it or unclose it by his craft,
But only by the hot embrace of fire.

Uprose a cry, new, urgent ; a dire fear
Fell on the North Danes, on each one of those
Who from the wall heard the wild whoop, the chant
Of horror sung by God's antagonist,
Song of no victory, the thrall of hell
Wailing in pain ; too tightly he was held
By him then strongest of all living men.
The help of earls would not for anything
Let go that deadly guest while living, thought
His life-days of no use to any man.
Then many an earl of Beowulf's drew his sword,
His ancient heritage, and would defend,
If so he might, the prince's life. They knew not,
These eager sons of battle, when they joined
The strife, and sought to hew on every side,

T

To seek his soul, that no sword upon earth,
Choicest of blades, could touch the wicked fiend.
But he all martial weapons had forsworn,
Every edged blade. And he was wretchedly
On that day of this life of men to die,
His ghost far journeying to serve the fiends.
Then he who erst against the race of man
In mirthful mood had wrought out many crimes,
He was God's foe, found that his body failed
To serve him, because Hygelac's bold kinsman
Had him in hand. The other's life to each
Was hateful ; the fell wretch endured sore pain,
A wide wound on his shoulder could be seen ;
The sinews snapped, the bone enclosures burst,
Glory of battle was to Beowulf given ;
To his fen shades, death-struck, must Grendel flee,
Seek a sad home, well knowing that life's end
Was come, the number of his days was past.

So he who had come from afar fulfilled
In deadly fight the will of all the Danes ;
Wise and stout-hearted, had cleansed Hrothgar s hall,
Saved it from malice. Glad in his night's work,
His fame for strength, the chieftain of the Goths
Had served the Danes according to his boast,
Healing the deep-set griefs they had endured,
No slight affliction, borne through hardest need.
Clear was the token of this, when the stout chief
Laid down hand, arm, and shoulder, there was all
The grip of Grendel under that great roof.

Then came in the morning, as I have heard tell, many a warrior about the gift-hall from far and near, to see the wonder. The foe left his track as he fled, death-doomed and weary, to the nickers' mere. There was the surge boiling with blood, the waves welled hot with clotted gore. Grendel had dyed it after he laid down his life in shelter of the fen. From the mere again went the glad fellow-warriors proudly to ride on horses. Beowulf's praise was sung, nor blamed any the glad Hrothgar, for that was a good king.

At times the war-men ran their fallow steeds in trial of the race, where the earthways were smooth. At times a king's thane, a boast-laden man, mindful of songs, knowing full many an old saga, found another high tale that had truth in it. Then he began with skill to tell of Beowulf's undertaking, well he told of Sigemund, of the Wælsings' wars and wide wayfarings—men knew not his wars and works save Fitela, who went with him. The king, also, warden of ring hoards, with a throng about him, stept from his bride-bower; and his queen with him measured the meadow-path, begirt by her maidens. Hrothgar spake (he went to the hall, stood in the forecourt, and saw Grendel's hand), "For this sight give thanks forthwith to the Almighty. Lo, whatsoever mother brought this son forth, if she yet lives, let her say that the great Maker was good in her child-bearing. Now I will love thee, Beowulf, best of warriors, as a son in my heart ; henceforth hold our new kinship well. There shall be no lack to thee of wealth that I can give. Often have I held worthy of part in my hoard for a less help a weaker warrior. May the All-wielder pay thee with good as He yet has done." Then was Ecglaf's boasting son quieter, after the Athelings had seen over the high roof the foe's fingers. Each had before it hand-spurs, most like steel, instead of nails. The best of iron would not bite into that bloody hand.

Then was Heorot bidden to be made fresh, many men and women worked at the wine-house, the golden webs shone on the walls full of sights wondrous to the gazer. That bright dwelling, fast with bands of iron, was much broken, the hinges were rent, the roof only was sound when the wretch turned to flight. Then came the time when Healfdene's son should go to the hall, the king himself would share many a mead-cup with his warriors. Heorot was full of friends. Then the son of Healfdene gave to Beowulf a gold flag with rich hilt, a helm and war-shirt, a

T 2

sword of great worth many saw borne before the warrior.
Beowulf shared the cup in the court. The shelter of earls
then bade eight steeds be led into the court; on one of
them stood a saddle cunningly worked; that was the war-
seat of the high king when the son of Healfdene played the
game of swords. To Beowulf he gave all,—horses and
weapons. Also, the lord of warriors gave to each of those
on the mead-bench who came the sea-way with Beowulf a
gift, an heirloom; and bade that the one whom Grendel
slew should be paid for with gold. Before Healfdene's
war-leaders the glee-wood was touched, and Hrothgar's
gleemen, gladdeners of the hall, told of the works of Fin's
offspring, the tale of Fin Folcwalding, of Hnæf and Hengest,
and the sons of Hildeburh burnt by their mother at Hnæf's
pile. The lay was sung, the gleeman's song, games were
begun again, the noise was loud, the cup-bearers gave wine
from wondrous cups. Then Wealtheow, wearing a golden
crown, came forth to where the two good kinsmen sat.
There also sat Hunferth, the spokesman, at the feet of the
Scyldings' lord. The Queen said: "Take this cup, dear
lord, and be thou happy, golden friend of men, speak to the
Goths kindly. Heorot, bright hall of rings, is cleansed.
Enjoy the mead of the many, and leave to thy sons folk
and land when thou must forth to behold God." Then she
turned towards the bench where her sons were, Hrethric
and Hrothmund, where Beowulf the Goth sat by the two
brethren. To him the cup was borne and friendly bidding
done, and twisted gold, two sleeves, a cloak and rings were
given, the largest I have heard tell of on earth since Hama
bore off the Brosings neck-ring. Wealtheow said: "Wear
this ring, dear Beowulf, O youth, with all hail! and with
this cloak, these riches, thrive; enliven thyself with strength,
and be to these boys a kind helper. Thou hast done that
which shall beget praise throughout all time as widely as the
water girds the windy walls of land. Live thou a thriving

Atheling, and be kind to my sons. Here all are friends."
She then went to her seat. The meat was choice, the men
drank wine, they knew not of a grim hereafter. When
evening came and Hrothgar had gone to his rest, many
earls guarded the house, as often they had done. They
bared the bench floor, it was overspread with beds and
bolsters. Filled with beer, ready for sleep, they bowed ;
they set at their heads the round, bright shields. There,
on the bench, was to be seen over each Atheling his high
war-helm, his ringed shirt, and stout war-wood. It was
their way to be ready for war at home and in the host;
when need came to their lord their help was near.

But Grendel's mother, wretched woman—she who dwells
in gruesome waters, the cold streams—came on a path of
sorrow to wreak wrath for her dead son. She came to
Heorot, where the Ring-Danes were all sleeping through
the hall. When in rushed Grendel's mother, the hard edge
was drawn, many a broad shield lifted. She was in haste,
would save herself, being thus found, and quickly seized
one of the Athelings as she went to the fen. He whom she
killed was Hrothgar's counsellor, his dearest friend between
the seas. Beowulf was not there, for another abode had
been fixed for him after the gifts to the great Goth. There
was a din in Heorot. She took away the kindred hand
clotted with gore.

Then was the wise king, the hoar warrior, wroth when
he knew his chief thane, his dearest, to be dead. Quickly
to his bower was Beowulf fetched. Hrothgar, helm of the
Scyldings, spake : "Æschere is dead, Yrmenlaf's elder
brother, who knows my runes, my counsellor. For that
thou killedst Grendel yesternight, there is now come another
mighty man-scather to avenge her son.

> " The country people talking in my hall
> I have heard say, that they upon the moor
> Have seen two striders of the border-land,

Strange beings, of which one, as they could tell
Most nearly, was in woman's likeness, one
A wandering man, larger than other men,
Whom the old dwellers on the land named Grendel.
They know not of a father, whether more
Had been of those dark spirits. They inhabit
The dim land that gives shelter to the wolf,
The windy headlands, perilous fen paths,
Where, under mountain mist, the stream flows down
And floods the ground. Not far hence, but a mile,
The mere stands, over which hang death-chill groves,
A wood fast-rooted overshades the flood ;
There every night a ghastly miracle
Is seen, fire in the water. No man knows,
Not the most wise, the bottom of that mere.
The firm-horned heath-stalker, the hart, when pressed,
Wearied by hounds, and hunted from afar,
Will rather die of thirst upon its bank
Than bend his head to it. It is unholy.
Dark to the clouds its yeasty waves mount up
When wind stirs hateful tempest, till the air
Grows dreary, and the heavens pour down tears.
Again now counsel is with thee alone,
Thou knowest not yet the spot, the place of daring
Where thou may'st find this wicked being. Seek it :
If thou be bold, I recompense the strife
With gifts, old treasures, as I did before,
If thou return to us."
           Then Ecgtheow's son,
Beowulf, replied to him, " Wise man, sorrow not,
Better for each to avenge his friend than mourn.
An end to this world's life awaits us all ;
Let him who can, do high deeds ere he die,
So will be happiest when the warrior's dead.
Guard of the helm arise, and let us go
Quickly upon the track of Grendel's kin,
I promise thee that not in the deep sea
Shall she escape, nor in embrace of earth,
Nor in the wood upon the mountain-side,
Nor on the sea's broad bed, go where she will.
Have patience for to-day, in all thy woes,
This I expect of thee."

Then the old chief
Leapt up, gave thanks to God, the mighty lord,
For what the man had said.   For Hrothgar then
A horse was bitted——

[But the next passage in the poem I translate into a
measure that repeats the form of the original.   First-English
was written to be chanted to a rude stringed instrument,
and transmitted from lip to lip by memory.   There was no
rhyme, or equal numbering of syllables, but accent suited
to the thought, and alliteration, through two half-lines, of
the consonant at the beginning of three words of chief
importance.   In the first of the two half-lines there were
two words with the repeated initial letter, and in the
second half-line there was one.   Alliteration of a word
with a prefix to it was on the main word, not on the prefix,
as is shown in the lines :—

An un*w*insome *w*ood,
*W*ater stood under it.

In the case of vowels the alliteration was obtained, not
by repeating, but by varying them.   Thus, then, the old
song runs on :—]

A horse bitted
With curling crest.
The careful prince
Went worthily ;
Warriors marched also
Shining with shields.
Then there were shown
Tracks of the troubler,
Telling plainly
Her way through the waste,—
As they went forward
On the murky moor,—
With the murdered thane
Of Hrothgar's heroes,
Home defenders,

Best and bravest
Brought to his end.
Then they threaded,
Athelings' sons,
Steep, stony gorges,
A strait road,
Weird, narrow way,
Wastes unknown,
Naked, high nesses,
Nicker houses many.
Before all Beowulf
And some of the bravest
Went on the way,
Wise men,
To explore the plain,
Till, planted leaning
Over the rough rock,
He reached suddenly
An unwinsome wood.
Water stood under it
Ghastly with gore ;
It was grief for all Danes,
A sight of sorrow
For the Scylding's friends,
A horror for heroes,
When the head of Æschere
Was found by the steep flood
Floated ashore.
The water welled blood,
The warriors gazed
On the hot heart's blood,
While the horn sang
A doleful death-note.

The band all sat. They saw along the water many of
the worm kind, strange sea dragons ; also in clefts of the
nesses Nickers lying. These hurried away, bitter and angry,
as soon as they heard the war horn. One the Goth's lord
killed with an arrow. Quickly on the wave he was, with
boar-spears, sharply hooked and drawn on the ness.

Beowulf clad himself in weeds of a chief. His warbyrnie, twisted with hands, wide and cunningly dyed, must know the deeps. But the white helm guarded his head, made worthy with riches, girt with lordly links, beset with the likeness of swine, that no brand might bite into it. Nor least of aids was the hafted sword, Hrunting its name, lent him by Hrothgar's speaker. Its edge was iron, tainted with poison twigs, hardened with warriors' blood. Ecglaf's son bore not in mind what he had said drunken with wine, when he lent the weapon to a better sword-wielder. Himself durst not meet death under the stir of waters. Beowulf spake, " Gold-friend of men, I am ready. If I die for thy need, be a helper to my fellow-thanes, and send, dear Hrothgar, to Hygelac the gold thou hast given me, that the Goth's lord may know I found a good bestower of rings. And let the far-famed man have my sword Hunferth, the old relic. I will with Hrunting work my doom." He awaited no answer, the sea-wave took the warlike man.

It was a day's space ere he sank to ground. Then she who had dwelt in the flood, grim and greedy, for a hundred years, saw a man coming from above into the land of wonders, grasped at him and clutched the warrior. But she could not break his ring mail with her fingers. The sea-wolf bore the prince of rings to her dwelling, many a sea-beast with its war tusks broke his mail. Then the warrior found himself in a roofed hall, where was no water. A pale beam of firelight shone, and then he saw the ground wolf, the mighty mere wife. He struck hard with his war-sword. The edge failed. The angry fighter cast upon the earth the twisted brand and trusted in his strength, the might of his hand-grip. So shall a man do when he thinks to gain in battle lasting praise, nor careth for his life. Then Grendel's mother seized the Goth's lord by the shoulder. Fearless he dragged her till she bowed. She caught him quickly with fierce grasps, and threw him weary, pressed him down, and drew her seax, broad, brown-edged. She would avenge her son. The braided breast-net on his shoulder withstood point and edge.

He saw among the weapons a huge bill, an old sword of the Eotens, work of giants, greater than any other man might bear forth to the game of war. The Scyldings' warrior stood up and seized the knotted hilt, fast and fierce he struck with the brand upon her neck, her bone rings brake, the bill went through her flesh, she sank on the ground. The sword was gory, the beam still shone, mild as the light from heaven's candle. He looked through that dwelling and saw Grendel lying lifeless. His huge trunk sprang far away, when he cut off the head. But then behold ! that sword melted away as ice in the hot venomous blood ; there was left only the hilt. Beowulf took none of the wealth that he saw ; he took only the giant's head and the rich sword hilt.

The men who were with Hrothgar looking on the water saw it mixed with new blood. They said this was a warning that the Atheling was slain. Then came the noon of day, and the bold Scyldings left the headland, sick of mood, gazing upon the mere, wishing, not weening, to see their dear lord. Forthwith he was afloat ; he dived up through the water, came swimming to land, glad in the burthen he brought with him. The stout band of thanes loosed quickly his helm and war-shirt, the stream trickled down of water stained with gore. When they went forth from the sea-shore four men could hardly bear upon the deadly stake the head of Grendel.

So they came to the hall, fourteen brave Goths, marching with their lord over the meadows. The worthiest of thanes came to greet Hrothgar ; then Grendel's head was borne by the hair into the place where men were drinking, and the head of the woman also. Beowulf said, " Behold, these tokens from the sea we bring with gladness to thee, son of Healfdene, lord of Scyldings. Now may'st thou with thy warriors in Heorot sleep free from sorrow." The golden hilt, the giant's work of old, was given to the hoar war-leader. Hrothgar gazed on the hilt; in Runic signs the tale of its birth was told upon it. Then spake the son of Healfdene; all were silent: "Thy glory is upreared now through wide ways, Beowulf, my friend. Long shalt thou be a blessing to thy people." Many words spake Hrothgar, for he spoke of the past and of its warnings to his friend and to the folk around him. The Goth, glad of mood, went to his seat; there was a new feast made. The helm of night grew murky, the aged Scylding sought his bed, and the Goth wished for rest. The guest slept till the black raven, gladdener of heaven, blithe of heart, announced the coming of the light.

The Athelings then wished to go to their own land, and Beowulf bade the son of Ecglaf take again his sword; gave for the lending thanks, said that he held Hrunting to be good, he would not with blame hurt pride in its good edge; that was a high-souled warrior. Hrothgar said, "Peace be to the Goths and the Gar Danes; wealth in common. Over the gannet's bath the ringed bark shall bring gifts and love-tokens. Each folk I know, fast friend, fast foe, and in the old way stainless always." Twelve gifts also gave to Beowulf the son of Healfdene, bade him go and quickly come again. The good king kissed the best of thanes, and tears fell as he took him round the neck.

The bright warriors went to the ship, laden with weapons, steeds, and gold; the mast rose over Hrothgar's hoards. Beowulf gave to the boat-guard a sword bound with gold, and on the mead-bench he was afterwards the worthier for that heir-loom. They sailed away, and the known headlands of the Goths were reached. The hithe-guard, who had seen them when afar, was ready; he bound the ship to the sand and bade men bear to the hall

of Hygelac, who dwelt by the sea-wall, the wealth of the
Athelings.   Kinsman faced kinsman ; Hæreth's daughter,
gentle of mood, bare the wine-cup to the high chief's hand.

Hæreth's daughter, who poured wine for her lord when
Beowulf returned, was Hygd, the second wife of Hygelac.
Second wife, because she is described as very young, and
Hygelac had already, when he came to the gift-stool, a
marriageable daughter.   Hygd seems in the poem to be
first described as young, wise, well-bred, and generous, and
then held up to scorn for cruelty and murder, and spoken
of as a wife of Offa.   Dr. Grein has suggested that, in
fact, the word translated violent is a proper name, applied
to a half-mythical she-monster, whose character is contrasted
with the mildness of Queen Hygd, as in an earlier part of
the poem the praise of a good king had been enforced
immediately by contrast with a bad one.

Hygd had a young son, Heardred.   When Beowulf returned afterwards from the expedition in which Hygelac
was slain, Hygd believed that her child was too young to
succeed his father, and offered the chief rule to Beowulf.
But Beowulf sustained the boy in his hereditary rank, and
served him as protector.   Onela, the son of Ongetheow,
was then ruling in Sweden, and two of his nephews, sons of
a younger brother, having rebelled against him, came as
exiles, Eánmund and Eadgils, to young Heardred's court.
Heardred received them hospitably.   His land was therefore
invaded by Onela, he was besieged in his high wall, and
killed in battle.   Eánmund also was then slain.   Onela
returned to his own land, and Beowulf then became king of
the Goths, keeping Eadgils at his court, and helping him
afterwards to his revenge upon Onela, who was attacked in
his turn and killed.   Beowulf was Goth only on his mother's
side.   His father, Ecgtheow, was of another race.

We may now go back to the old poem and tell its story
to the end.   Beowulf, returned from his adventures among

the Danes, had landed in Gothland. He went with his
chosen band along the sands, treading the sea-plain, the
wide shores.

> Quickly to Hygelac was Beowulf's voyage
> Made known, that there was come into the place,
> The warriors' shelter, his shield-friend, alive,
> Sound from the war-play, coming to his house.
> Quickly the hall was cleared for them,
> As the king bade. Then facing him who came
> Safe from the conflict, kin looked upon kin.
> After his lord had greeted with loud voice
> The faithful friend, went Hæreth's daughter, she
> Who loved the people, through the hall, poured mead,
> And bare the wine-cup to the high chief's hand.
> Then in the high-hall Hygelac began
> Kind question with his guest, eager desire
> Urged him to know how the sea-Goths had fared.

Hygelac asked, and Beowulf answered, adding to his
recital of the greatness of Heorot, that at times he had
seen the daughter of Hrothgar, whom he heard called
Freaware, bear the ale-cup to the earls.

Freaware married Ingeld, son of Froda, king of the
Heathobards, between whom and the Danes there had been
long feud, in the course of which Ingeld's father, Froda,
had been slain. When Freaware was taken to her husband's
court, one of her Danish followers wore as a trophy Froda's
sword. This was noticed, and the old feud, which the
marriage was to have ended, broke out again fiercely.
"Then," said Beowulf, finishing that episode in his narrative :—

> "Then on both sides the oaths of warriors break.
> In Ingeld deadly hate boils, for his wife
> Love cools after the burning of his care.
> Therefore I do not count the Heathobards
> As having love, or part in fellowship,
> Or any settled friendship to the Danes.
> But now of Grendel I speak on, that thou,
> Giver of gifts, may'st know how went the fight

> Of warriors hand to hand.   When heaven's gem
> Had glided over earth, in anger came
> The guest, the giant, grim at eve,
> To visit us who safely kept the hall.
> There was his glove, deadly in war, life bale
> To the doomed.   He who lay first, girt champion,
> To him, the brave thane of our blood, became
> Grendel mouth-murderer, the body, all,
> Of the beloved man, he swallowed.   Yet
> For that no sooner went the murderer
> With bloody tooth and evil in his mind,
> From that gold hall, but trial made of me,
> Proud of his might, grasped with a ready hand,
> His glove, broad, wondrous, with strange fastenings,
> All cunningly prepared with devil's crafts
> And skins of dragons.   Shaper of ill deeds,
> He thought to make me, unoffending, one
> Of many victims.   But that might not be,
> When I in wrath stood upright.   Long ɔ tell,
> O prince, how I repaid the miscreant's wrongs,
> What I did there set forth thy people's worth."

Beowulf proceeds in this manner to recount how Grendel fled to his mere, leaving his arm in Heorot ; how Hrothgar rewarded his champion ; how Grendel's mother came and snatched away Æschere ; how he descended to the bottom of the mere and overcame that monster also.

> "Not easily I brought my life away,
> I was not fated yet.   The shield of earls,
> Healfdené's son, again gave many gifts.
> So the great king lived as he should, rewards,
> The meed of strength, have not been lost to me,
> For he, Healfdené's son, put in my power
> Treasures that I will bring, O warrior king,
> To thee, with joy prepare for thee.   Of thee
> Are all my satisfactions.   For I have
> Few kinsmen near me, Hygelac, save thee."

Then Beowulf bade them bear in the boar-head ensign, the helmet, corslet, and rich sword, and said, " These

Hrothgar gave me, and bade me say that they had come down to him from King Heorogar, but he gave them to Beowulf rather than his own son, Heoroweard, whom he loved." With these, Beowulf gave to Hygelac four steeds; and the necklet that Wealtheow had given him he gave to Hygd, with three black horses brightly saddled. Thus flourished Ecgtheow's son, a warrior known for good deeds, thoughtful and gentle, no rugged soul, though God had given him strength above other men. He had long been despised, and made of small account on the mead-bench. Now came a reverse to every grief. Then Hygelac commanded the rich sword bequeathed by Hrethel to be brought in, and laid it on Beowulf's lap; gave him too seven thousand pieces, a manor, and a princely seat.

But in the crash of war in after-days
When Hygelac lay dead, and to the heart
Of Heardred were swords stabbing under shields,
When Scyldings, hardy warriors, triumphing,
Attacked Hereric's nephew.*
              After that
The broad realm came next under Beowulf's hand.
For fifty years he ruled, was the wise king,
The land's old guardian, till one began,
A dragon, who kept watch over a hoard
In a high heap, began to spread his sway.
Beneath a rocky hill there lay a path
Unknown to men. And one once entered there,
I know not who——

At this point some words and lines of the MS. can no longer be deciphered; but the story is being told of one who had seen the treasures hidden there of yore, within a mound near the waves of the sea below the headland.

---

* Hereric, here called the uncle of Hygelac's son Heardred, must have been Hygd's brother. These lines dispose of the succession of Heardred, and the poem passes on to the days when Beowulf was king.

The earl who heaped it there had spoken his farewell to the helmets that had fallen from the fated, the swords that should moulder after the warrior. There was no joy to him in music, no hawk in the hall or steed in the city. Death had brought desolation ; let earth hold the treasures of the dead. The burier of the treasure died.

The burning scather of the twilight, who seeks out the mounds, the naked envious dragon who flies by night girt with fire, found the hoard. For three hundred years he held the hoard in the earth, until one man enraged him, who took a cup from the hoard to his liege lord as a peace-offering. Then the hoard was plundered, the hoard of rings borne off, the prayer of the poor man was granted. The lord saw for the first time the ancient work of men. When the dragon awoke, the deed had been renewed. Then he smelt along the rock, the strong-hearted found the foot-trace of the foe. He had stepped forth by secret craft, near to the dragon's head. Thus may an undoomed man escape from woe when the Almighty favours him. The dragon sought, and found no man in the surrounding desert. He returned sometimes to his hoard, and found it plundered. It was hard for him to wait till evening came, then he would requite the wrong with fire. When the day was ended to his wish, he would abide no longer in his mound, but carried fire over the land. He vomited fire over the bright dwellings, the scather of the Goths would leave nothing alive. He had wrapped the land in flame with fire and burning. He trusted in his mount, his war, and his wall. That hope deceived him.

It was made known to Beowulf that his own home, the best of houses, was burnt, with the gift-stool of the Goths. The wise chief weened that he had angered the Almighty. The fire-dragon had wasted with fire an island without, the country's safeguard. Then the warlike king bade fashion for himself a wondrous shield, all iron, for he knew that wood of the forest would not help him against fire. Life's miseries must end for the prince, and for the worm with him, though he long had held the hoard-wealth.

The giver of rings disdained to seek the highflier with a host of men, he dreaded not the battle for himself. Rashly daring, he had escaped from many strifes since he had cleansed Hrothgar's hall and taken Grendel in his grasp. That was not the least of conflicts when Hygelac was slain, lordly friend of the peoples, in the Frieslands. Thence Beowulf escaped by his own power. He had need to swim. He had on his arm thirty war-coats, spoils of the slain, when he went down to the sea. The Hetwaras who bore spears against him in that battle had no need of boast; few who met him saw their homes again.

[Here follows in the poem the reference to the events following Beowulf's return, to the death of Heardred and his own coming to the throne.]

Thus Ecgtheow's son had outlived all conflicts till the day came when he must go forth against the dragon. A man who had visited the hoard and stolen from it a cup must show the path to the mound under the rock by the near stir and strife of waves.

> Then on the headland sat the warrior-king,
> Gold-friend of Goths, and there he bade farewell
> To his hearth companions. He was sad of mind,
> Wavering, ready to depart, the fate
> Most near which now must meet him in his age,
> Seek his soul treasure, part his limbs from life ;
> Not long was flesh to enwrap the prince's soul.
> The son of Ecgtheow, Beowulf, spake : " In youth
> I have out-battled many a rush of war.
> Seven years I had seen when Hrethel, people's friend,
> The king, received me from my father, kept me,
> Gave me good gifts and feasts, mindful of kin.
> I was not in his courts a whit less loved
> Than any of his children, Herebeald,
> Or Heathcyn, or my Hygelac. For one

U

The eldest, by his brother's deed the bier
Was strewn.   He missed his mark, and shot
His kinsman, brother, not to be avenged,
When Heathcyn with an arrow from his bow
Laid low his lord and friend.   So sad it is
For an old father to await the death
Of his young child upon the gallows.   Then
Rises his song of sorrow, when his son
Hangs to delight the raven, and he, old
And feeble, has no help that he can bring :
With every morning will come memory
Of his boy's death ; he cares not to await
Another heir within his gates, when one
Has died for his life's deeds.   In his son's hall
Wind whistles, and he sees the wine-bench empty,
Reft of its cheer ; sleeps hanging in the dark
The warrior ; there is no sound of harp,
Mirth in his homestead, as there was of old.
Then passes he to songs, lay after lay
Of sorrow, all around him desolate ;
The home, the world is empty."   Thus then mourned
The prince for Herebeald, and bore heart's pain.

And he told more of the past to his surrounding followers, sadly recalling life, with the foreshadowing of death
upon him.   He told of the invasion by Ongetheow, the
death of Hrethel, the succession of Heathcyn, the return
attack upon Ongetheow, in which Ongetheow was slain, of
his slaying of Dæghrefn, the Haga's champion, not with
sword, but by a hand-grasp in the fight.

" Now shall the falchion's edge, hand and hard sword
   Do battle for the hoard."   Then Beowulf spake
And uttered for the last time words of threat :
" Yet will I, a wise guardian of my land,
Seek conflict, do great deeds, if the vile scather
Will from his cavern seek me."   Helmeted
And bold, for the last time he greeted dear companions
" I would not bear a weapon if I knew
How I might grapple with this evil one,
As once with Grendel.   But now I expect

Fire, hot, fierce, poisonous ; for this I bear
The shield and buckler. Not by a foot's step
Will I allow the guardian of the mount
To take his flight from me. Here at the mound
As Fate wills shall it be to one of us."

Beowulf bade his companions, protected by corslets, await on the hill the end of the adventure. Then he arose, and, with his shield, went down in helmet and buckler, under the crags ; he trusted in his single strength.

He saw where a stream broke from the hill and passed out hot with fierce fires from under a stone arch. For the dragon's flame, he could not dive under it unburnt. Then his voice stormed in loud rage ; the dragon heard the voice of man, and first there came his breath out of the rock, hot sweat of battle. The rock resounded with the roar of fire. Beowulf turned his shield against the enemy ; already his sword was drawn. Each feared the other. The stroke of Beowulf's sword bit less deep than there was need. The dragon threw his deadly fire. Again they met. The dragon breathed with new force ; Beowulf, encompassed by flame, was in sore need.

His companions had turned to the wood to save their lives, but in one of them, Wiglaf, Wexstan's son, there was grief for the suffering of his liege lord. He remembered the rich dwelling-place of the Wægmundings that Beowulf had given him, and all the rights. He grasped his shield, drew his old sword, which had belonged to Eanmund, Ohthere's son, whom Wexstan slew, taking his helm and sword. To Wiglaf, his son, he had left the relic, and now was the first time that the young champion should brave death for his chief. Wiglaf reminded his comrades of what the band of followers owed to its chief. Now is the day come when they could help him. Then he waded through the deadly smoke, encouraged Beowulf to fight as he had fought in the days of youth—" I will support thee."

U 2

Then came again the angry dragon; the waves of his
fire burnt the youth's shield, but he defended himself boldly
behind the iron shield of his kinsman. Again Beowulf recalled his past prowess, and struck with his main force upon
the dragon's head. His good sword, Nægling, snapped
asunder with the stroke. It was not granted to Beowulf to
prevail with edge of the sword. His hand-stroke was too
strong. It broke every blade.

A third time the dragon rushed on the great chief.
Then Beowulf fiercely grasped his neck with its horrid
bones. Blood bubbled forth in waves, staining him with
the life-gore.

Then Wiglaf sought to aid his kinsman, heeded not the
head, struck lower. The sword went deep; the fire began
then to abate. The protector of the Goths drew then the
deadly knife that he bore on his corslet, and stabbed the
dragon in the midst. Then the kindred chiefs had destroyed the foe. There was to the prince a pause of victory.

But the wound given at first by the dragon then began to
burn and swell; the poison worked within him. The prince
sat on a seat by the mound, looked on the giant's work,
saw how the stone arches, firm on their pillars, held for ever
the cave within. Then the thane laved with water the
wound of his prince. Beowulf spake of the deadly livid
wound, knew that his joy of earth was ended.

"I have ruled," he said, "fifty winters, and had I a
son of my own would now bequeath to him my arms. I
have held my own well, sought no treachery, sworn no
false oath; though wounded to death, I have joy, for I
have done no wrong to my kinsmen. Now go, dear
Wiglaf, to see the hoard under the rock; let me behold the
treasure of the past before I resign life and kingdom."

The poem then tells of the treasures seen by Wiglaf in
the cavern. With treasure for his prince to see he hurried
out, lest when he returned he should find life at end. The

aged man looked at the gold with sorrow, and thanked the
glory king that he had been able before death to acquire
this riches for his people.

> " My life is well paid for this hoard ; and now
> Care for the people's needs, I may no more
> Be with them.   Bid the warriors raise a barrow
> After the burning, on the ness by the sea,
> On Hronesness, which shall rise high and be
> For a remembrance to my people.   Seafarers
> Who from afar over the mists of waters
> Drive foamy keels may call it Beowulf's Mount
> Hereafter."   Then the hero from his neck
> Put off a golden collar ; to his thane,
> To the young warrior, gave it with his helm,
> Armlet, and corslet, bade him use them well.
> " Thou art the last Wægmunding of our race,
> For fate has swept my kinsmen all away.
> Earls in their strength are to their Maker gone,
> And I must follow them."   The aged chief
> Spake not again.   This was his latest word.

The ten who had fled to the wood came now with
shields and arms to where the dying champion lay with his
face turned to Wiglaf.   He sat, wearied, by the shoulders
of his lord, laving him with water.   But there was no power
on earth to revive the chieftain.   Then easily came a fierce
answer from the youth to those who had lost courage.   For
every earl, he told them, death is better than a life of
reproach.

Then a messenger was sent to the dwellings, where the
return of Beowulf was in vain expected, with news that
Wiglaf sat over Beowulf, the living over the lifeless.   The
poem following the news of the death of Beowulf to surrounding nations again falls into an episode of retrospect.
Then is told the coming out of the people to bring Beowulf's
body with all honour to the burning on the funeral pile.

They went sad and tearful to the rocks under the eagle's
ness, and found the good chief soulless on the sands.   The

fire-dragon lay near, fifty feet of measure ; by him were
rich cups and bowls, dishes and costly swords, with rust as
of a thousand years upon them.   Wiglaf told with lament
the prince's wish that a lofty mound should be raised over
his ashes.   The bier was made ready.   Wood was brought
from afar for the funeral pile.   Seven men entered the
cavern with Wiglaf, one carrying a torch, to bring out the
treasures.   The dragon's body was rolled over the cliff into
the sea.   Twisted gold was drawn, heaped in a wain, to
Hronesness.

> Then the Goth's people reared a mighty pile
> With shields and armour hung, as he had asked,
> And in the midst the warriors laid their lord,
> Lamenting.   Then the warriors on the mount
> Kindled a mighty bale fire ; the smoke rose
> Black from the Swedish pine, the sound of flame
> Mingled with sound of weeping ; the wind fell ;
> Until hot on the breast the bone-case burst.
> Sadly they waited their lord's death, while smoke
> Spread over heaven.   Then upon the hill
> The people of the Weders wrought a mound,
> High, broad, and to be seen far out at sea.
> In ten days they had built and walled it in
> As the wise thought most worthy, placed in it
> Rings, jewels, other treasures from the hoard.
> They left the riches, golden joy of earls,
> In dust, for earth to hold ; where yet it lies,
> Useless as ever.   Then about the mound
> The warriors rode, and raised a mournful song
> For their dead king, exalted his brave deeds,
> Holding it fit men honour their liege lord,
> Praise him and love him when his soul is fled.
> Thus the Goth's people, sharers of his hearth,
> Mourned their chief's fall, praised him, of kings, of men,
> The mildest and the kindest, and to all
> His people gentlest, yearning for their praise.

So ends the most ancient heroic song, not only in English
literature, but in the literature of any Teutonic language.

And now, how much is history, how much romance, in the old poem of Beowulf? It contains historical episodes and allusions on which scholars have exercised their ingenuity with various effect since the text was first printed by the learned Icelander, Grim J. Thorkelin, in the year 1815. Attention was first called to the MS. by Humfrey Wanley in his catalogue of old Northern books, printed in 1705 with Hickes's "Thesaurus." He called it "Tractatus Nobilissimus Poetice Scriptus," gave a faulty transcript of its opening lines, and added a guess at the subject of the poem. Sharon Turner gave some extracts and translations in his "History of the Anglo-Saxons," of which the four volumes were first published in the years from 1799 to 1805. In his account of the work he was misled by a transposed page of the MS. into regarding Beowulf as the enemy of Hrothgar. Thorkelin, in 1815, gave with the text an interpretation of his own. The incidents of Grendel and the Dragon he considered to be Scandinavian myths, originally connected with Boe or Boav, called in Latin Bo-us, the son of Odin. The short history of this hero is told by Saxo Grammaticus in the third book of the "History of the Danes." It contains nothing like the story of Beowulf, except that it is there said of Bo, as of Beowulf, that he was buried under a great and famous barrow.* Thorkelin, having identified Beowulf with a Bo,

Interpretations of Beowulf.

Thorkelin.

---

* Bo's barrow has been sought by antiquaries, and said to be at Horlef, near Tryggeveld in Iceland, where there was a corroborative inscription which the late Dr. Peter Erasmus Müller, Bishop of Iceland, and editor of Saxo Grammaticus (his work having been completed since his death by Dr. J. M. Velschow), declares to have been written certainly not before the 14th century. Dr. Müller notices a Jutland hill called Bui, at Lynge, in the district of Skanderburg, with a royal barrow (Köngs-hoe) near it. But he warns his readers that there are 600 barrows scattered about Denmark, called for their size royal. Bui may, he thinks, answer to the Icelandic Bua-stein, a hill haunted by spectres. The only kings with a name like

afterwards, as Mr. Conybeare observes,* identifies him with the second syllable in Hroth-wulf, being equally glad to take the wolf without a bo. Mr. Conybeare himself gives in his " Illustrations of Anglo-Saxon Poetry " the first complete English account of the poem, with numerous specimens of the original, to which he supplies translations into English blank verse and literal Latin, adding to his account a list of Thorkelin's misreadings, from collation of the Copenhagen edition of Beowulf with the original MS. at the British Museum. Thorkelin, however, is perhaps less to blame than Admiral Nelson. He had made his transcript in the year 1786, and had it ready for press, with a translation, when his literary work of thirty years was destroyed by the bombardment of Copenhagen. He was urged by the liberality of the Danish Privy Councillor, Johan Bülow, of Sanderumgaard, to begin afresh ; and his edition of Beowulf, published in 1815, was the result.

It was at the cost of the same nobleman that the Danish scholar Nik. Fred. Sev. Grundtvig published in 1820 his free Danish translation of Beowulf. The same scholar dedicated to the same patron an edition of the text, which he had studied in the original MS. when in England between 1829—31.†

Grundtvig.

In the year 1833, a new edition of the text of Beowulf

Bui are a Bögi (bogie), and an avaricious Bökus, who was consumed by Rolvo. (Saxo Gramm. " Hist. Dan." Ed. Müller et Velschow (Havniæ, 1858), Vol. II., Proleg. et Not. p. 124.) The best suggestion is Grein's, which we will follow when we take his reading of the historical element in " Beowulf."

* " Illustrations of Anglo-Saxon Poetry," by John Josias Conybeare, M.A., &c., successively Professor of Anglo-Saxon and of Poetry in the University of Oxford. Edited by his brother, William Daniel Conybeare, M.A., &c. London, 1826.

† "Beowulfes Beorhaeller Bjovulfs-Drapen, det Old-Angelske Heltedight, paa Grunds-proget, ved Nik. Fred. Sev. Grundtvig." Kjöbenhavn, 186ʟ

was published by Mr. John M. Kemble.* A prose translation, with a glossary, was published four years
afterwards in a companion volume ; and this contained, in a postscript to the original preface and
in the appendix, Mr. Kemble's latest and fullest opinion of
the meaning of the poem. He considered Beowulf to belong
essentially to the poetical cycle of the Angles, and to be
founded on legends which existed previous to the Angle
conquest. Beowulf himself he presumed to be originally
the name not of a man but of a god, one of Woden's ancestors, represented throughout in this poem " as a defender,
a protecting and redeeming being." The relationships
given to him are accounted for " by the necessity of bringing him into the legend." Beowulf belongs to the Geáts
or Goths, but Geát or Gaut was the parent of a tribe called
by Procopius Γαυτοί. A Gothic verb gives the præt. gáut ;
the Anglo-Saxon geótan gives geát; both words with the
sense of pouring. Was not Geát, then, the god of abundance, Odin? For the Edda says that Gàutr was Odin's
name among the gods. Hrothgar and Halga Mr. Kemble
identifies with Hroar and Helgi, Danish kings actually
reigning in the fifth century. But in his second preface
the same scholar says, " Although I will not raise Hrothgar
and his brother to the rank of gods . . . yet I must observe
that any attempt to assign historical dates to these, or almost
any other princes, before the introduction of Christianity . . .
leads to nothing but confusion. . . . All that part of my
preface which assigns dates to one prince or to another, or

John
Mitchell
Kemble.

---

* "The Anglo-Saxon Poems of Beowulf—the Traveller's Song and the
Battle of Finnes-burh—edited, together with a glossary of the more difficult words, and an historical preface," by John M. Kemble, Esq., M.A.,
of Trinity College, Cambridge. London, 1833. The volume is a delightful little 12mo, printed by Whittingham and published by the late Mr.
Pickering, of which, according to a bad fashion among antiquarians for
the creation of an artificial rarity, there were only one hundred copies
printed.

which attempts to draw any conclusions from dates so assigned, I declare to be null and void, upon whatsoever authority those dates may pretend to rest." Mr. Kemble's arguments would, in fact, go far to transport Beowulf altogether to the land of dreams.

Next there appeared, in 1839, and of the same school of criticism, without text, a mythological, historical German analysis of Beowulf by H. Leo. The first German translator of Beowulf, Ludwig Ettmüller,* who ascribes the work on his title-page to the eighth century, proposes also to show that the legend of Beowulf was originally a myth, and says of himself, " In general I follow Kemble." He places the Geáts in Sweden, and considers the term Weder Goths, which occurs often in Beowulf, to be equivalent to Weather Goths, meaning Northern Goths, because out of the north came the bad weather. This critic is, I think, the first who observes, what is worth observing, that neither the name Angle nor the name Saxon occurs once in the whole poem. In 1849 a translation of Beowulf into English verse by A. Diedrich Wackerbarth † was prefaced by another argument upon the meaning of the poem, in which, after describing the first Beowulf as a son of Odin, if not Odin himself, the writer says, " I believe with Kemble that he is really the same mythical person."

In 1855 appeared Benjamin Thorpe's edition of Beowulf, text and translation, with a short introduction and a glossary ; and this is the very serviceable edition which was used for many years by English students. Thorpe's opinion here expressed is that the poem is "not an original production of the Anglo-Saxon muse, but a

Leo.

Ettmüller.

Wacker-barth.

Thorpe.

---

* "Beowulf : Heldengedicht des Achten Jahrhunderts." Zurich, 1840.
† "Beowulf : an Epic Poem, translated from the Anglo-Saxon into English verse, by A. Diedrich Wackerbarth, A.B., Professor of Anglo-Saxon at the College of Our Ladye of Oscott." London, 1849.

metrical paraphrase of an heroic Saga composed in the south-west of Sweden, in the old common language of the North, and brought to this country during the sway of the Danish dynasty."

In 1859 Dr. Karl Simrock appended a claim for Beowulf as a German Mythus to his German translation of the work. Dr. Simrock says that if Mr. Thorpe gives Beowulf to the Swedes, he must give them also, as he does not, the "Traveller's Song" and the "Fight at Finnesburg." Simrock.

The next interpreters of Beowulf—Dr. Grein and Mr. Haigh, a German and an Englishman—discovered in the poem more evidence of an historical foundation than had usually been admitted. Dr. C. W. M. Grein, of Grein. Cassel, was editor of the completest and compactest body of Anglo-Saxon poetry that has hitherto been published, a "Library" in two volumes, to which he added an Anglo-Saxon and Latin Glossary.* In a German quarterly devoted to the

---

* "Bibliothek der Angelsächsischen Poesie in kritisch bearbeiteten Texten und mit vollständigem Glossar, herausgegeben von C. W. M. Grein." Cassel and Göttingen, 1857—61. Text, 2 vols. Glossary, 2 vols. (1861—64). Dr. Grein also, in a separate work, translated the chief remains of Anglo-Saxon poetry into German alliterative verse, in two volumes, entitled, "Dichtungen der Angelsachsen stabreimend übersetzt." Göttingen, 1857—59. The student who does not desire English translation with his texts, may, at no great cost, set up a library of Anglo-Saxon poetry in Grein's two volumes, which are being re-edited with exemplary thoroughness by Dr. Richard Paul Wülcker, Professor in the University of Leipzig. Professor Wülcker, as a faithful guide to students of Anglo-Saxon, occupies the place left vacant by the lamented death of Dr. Grein. Of the Anglo-Saxon text of Beowulf alone, Grundtvig's Danish edition (Copenhagen, 1861) ought not to be overlooked. The texts most used are an edition by Grein, and an edition by Dr. Moritz Heyne, Professor in the University of Basel, each furnished with glossary and apparatus of study, cheap and thorough. Heyne's edition is much used in England as well as in Germany. It first appeared in 1863, and there were new editions in 1868, 1873, 1879. The edition of 1879 was benefited by including results of fresh collations of the text with the MS., such fresh collations having been published by Dr. Eugen Kölbing, Professor at the University of Breslau, in 1876, and by Sophus

study of literature in the Romance languages and English,* there was in the year 1862 an article by Dr. Grein on the historical element in the poem of Beowulf, which he agreed with others in considering to have been written in the beginning of the eighth century at latest. Dr. Grein thought that the mythical adventures were ascribed to an historical person. The two populations mentioned in the poem are the Danes, over whom Hrothgar ruled, and the Geâts or Goths, who were ruled by Hygelac, and from among whom Beowulf came to Hrothgar's help. The Danes are called in the poem, without apparent distinction, Sea Danes, East, West, South, and North Danes ; also, from their armour, they are previously called Ring Danes from their ring-mail, Gar Danes from their spears, or Bright Danes from their shining panoply.

The Danes also are called Scyldings, from the founder

Bugge, in 1868—69—73. Grein's edition was published in 1867. In 1876 there was published in London an edition of Beowulf with a translation, Notes, and Appendix, by Thomas Arnold. In 1883 there was published at Boston an edition of Beowulf and the Fight at Finnes-burh, with text and a glossary based upon Heyne's edition. In the same year, also, there was a carefully re-edited text of Beowulf in Professor Richard Wülcker's new edition of Grein's " Bibliothek der Angelsächsischen Poesie." In the next year, 1884, Beowulf was edited with the text and a glossary by A. Holder, as No. 12 of the "Germanische Bücherschatz." An Autotype Facsimile of the Unique MS. of Beowulf, in the Cotton Collection (Vitellius A xv.), was published by the Early English Text society in 1882, with a Translation and Notes by an excellent English scholar, Dr. Julius Zupitza, Professor of the English Language and Literature in the University of Berlin. There was published in London, in 1881, an English metrical translation by Lieut.-Col. H. W. Lumsden ; and at Boston, in 1882, an English prose translation by James M. Garnett.

* " Jahrbuch für Romanische und Englische Litteratur unter besonderer Mitwirkung von Ferdinand Wolf, herausgegeben von Dr. Adolf Ebert, Professor an der Universität Leipzig." (Leipzig.) Vierter Band, Drittes Heft. April to June, 1862. This valuable journal was brought to an end with a twelfth volume in 1871. A new series, edited by Dr. Ludwig Lemcke, Professor at the University of Giessen, was begun in 1874, but ended with the third volume in 1876.

of their dynasty Scyld Scefing, or Scyld the Son of the Skiff. The old myth was, that on a boat laden with arms and treasure a child was floated to the Danish coast, and the Danes, being then in great trouble, accepted the boy as sent them by the gods, made him their king, and under his lead established and extended their power. When after a long reign Scyld died, his body, placed again on a ship laden with arms and treasure, was set adrift upon the sea ; and no man ever heard or knew whither that vessel went. Scyld may have been a real warrior, who brought help to the Danes against their tyrant Heremod, established his own dynasty among them, and left his son, the elder Beowulf—not him of the poem—to succeed him.

Dr. Grein considered that the poem treats of actions done among the Danes in Denmark. Mr. Haigh, we shall find, places the scene wholly in England. Each writer identifies Heorot (which means a hart) with a place so called on a spot tallying exactly with his theory. The true seat of the Danish kingdom, says Dr. Grein, was the island of Sæland, on which in fact, at this day, Copenhagen stands. Now on the east coast of Sæland, over against Sweden, not far to the south of Helsingor, and opposite the Island of Hveen, there is a town about two miles from the sea called Hjortholm, or in German Hirschholm—Hartholm ; that might be Heorot ; and a little more inland there is a lake, the Siæl Lake, that might be Grendel's Lake ; from which a stream flows by Hjortholm to the sea. Here, then, Dr. Grein fixes the site of Heorot. Where does he find the shore of Hygelac, King of the Geáts or Goths, whence Beowulf came to Hrothgar's aid ? This he agreed with Thorpe in finding on the opposite coast of the mainland, and a little to the north, in Swedish Gothland, and he indicates as the probable neighbourhood of Beowulf's grave the ruined castle of Bóhûs, Bo-house, built in 1308 upon a rock, where the mouth of the Gotha divides, to enclose

the island of Hisingen. This Bôhûs gives to its township
the name of Bohuslæn ; upon the island also is a Biörlanda;
but Biarr, says Dr. Grein, is an old northern form connected with the name of the Scylding Beowulf. The
identification of this continental Gothland and the neighbourhood of the River Gotha with Hygelac's kingdom is
partly supported by the fact mentioned in the poem—that
Hygelac's predecessor and brother Heathcyn was engaged
in a desperate war with the King of the Svéons in
Sveorice, now Svearice, or Svealand, lying immediately to
the north of Gothland. We have also, apparently, one tan-
gible corroborated fact to give us a date for the reign of
Hygelac. In four passages of Beowulf * there is mention
of an expedition of plunder made by Hygelac with Beowulf
in his train against the Frisians, when Hygelac, being opposed by the Hetware, the Hugas, and the Frisians, fell in
battle, and "the king's life departed into the grasp of the
Franks," Beowulf and the rest of the Geáts only saving
themselves by swimming to their ships. Can this be any
other than the descent recorded by Gregory of Tours and
the Gesta Regum Francorum, as having been made in the
year 520 by the Dane Chocilagus upon the coast of the
Frankish Hattuarii, whose allies and neighbours were the
West Frieslanders as far south as the mouth of the Maas?
There is record also from the tenth century of a tradition
then ascribing immense bones on an island at the mouth of
the Rhine to "Huiglaucus, King of the Geti," who was there
slain by the Franks. This historical parallel had been
pointed out by Leo and Ettmüller. Conceding mythical
origin to the stories of Grendel, of the swimming match
with Breca, and of Beowulf's battle with the dragon, Dr.
Grein argues that such myths are attached to persons who
were really living in the early years of the sixth century,

* Grein's edition, lines 1202—1214, 2354—2372, 2497—2508, 2910—
2921.

and that, besides the few traces of fact that have been in
the main story overlaid by fable, there are in the episodes
distinct and not unfaithful records of fragments of history,
that were brought into this country from Danish Sæland
and from Gothland, on the neighbouring coast of the
Swedish continent.

On the other hand, thus runs the substance of the argument of the Rev. Daniel H. Haigh, who has claimed for Beowulf a purely English origin,* as the composition Rev. D. H.
of a Northumbrian Scóp familiar with the scenes Haigh.
described, and acquainted with men who had known the
heroes of his story.   Mr. Haigh also accepts the coincidence
between the poem of Beowulf and Gregory of Tours'
"History of the Franks" on the subject of the death of
Hygelac, as evidence for the historic character of that
ancient heroic song.   Sceafa, Scyld, Beowa, and other
names, were not confined to single persons.   There are
several Scylds in the Scandinavian genealogy, and it may
be that they all, including the Scyld of the poem, derived
their name from the popularity of the original hero.
Beowulf is not necessarily Beowa; but if Scyld and
Beowulf did repeat Sceldwa and Beowa, that is not more
remarkable than that there should have been in the eighth
century two contemporary Eadberhts, each the son of an
Eata.   That Scyld, Beowulf the first, and Healfdene
reigned in Northumbria, as, it is argued, Hrothgar certainly
did, is not improbable.   Reckoning the generations back,
Scyld must have been living about the time when there is
known to have been an immigration of Saxons.   Simeon of
Durham speaks of a Scythles-cestre, Roger of Howden of
a Scylte-cestre, by the Wall, a name that seems to contain

---

* "The Anglo-Saxon Sagas; an Examination of their value as Aids to
History ; a Sequel to the History of the Conquest of Britain by the Saxons."
By Daniel H. Haigh. London, 1861.

that of Scyld, which we have to this day in the neighbouring North and South Shields. North of the Wall again,
in the same neighbourhood, is Shilbottle—Scyldes-botl—the
palace of Scyld; near at hand also is Bolton on the Alne,
the Bolvelaunio of Ravennas, which seems to contain the
names of Beowulf and Alauna. Hrothgar's mead-hall Heorot,
Mr. Haigh fixes at Hart, in Durham. Its situation, two
miles from the coast, agrees (like that of the Sæland Hjortholm) with the distance of Heorot from the shore, as indicated by the description of the march to it after Beowulf's
landing. But that is not all. Grendel's mere, to be found
"by the way where the hill-stream goes under the shade of
the cliffs," was said by Hrothgar, speaking at Heorot, to
be a mile thence, overshaded with bushy groves : "there
liveth none so wise who knows its bottom." Just a mile
from Hart there once was a large pool, called the
Bottomless Carr, now turned like the fens into arable land,
from which a stream, still called How (mountain) Beck,
flows through the parish of Hart into the slake of Hartlepool. In the following lines concerning the mere, "although
the heath-stalker wearied by hounds, the hart firm of horns,
seeking that holt-wood, driven from afar, will not drink
of it ere he dies," there seems also to be a reference to the
story from which the name of Hartlepool arose, as represented on the common seal of the borough, a hart standing
in water, attacked by a hound. Then as we read on of
the "naked high nesses, nicker-houses many," we are reminded of the coast of Hartlepool and its wave-worn caves.

The scenery, however, of the poem is to be looked for
south of Hartlepool, between Bowlby Cliff and Whitby.
Such a glen as that which runs up from the sea at Staithes
into the high moorland with the nicker-houses in the lias
rocks by the sea-shore, reproduces more exactly than any
coast scenery in England or Sæland the aspects of nature
described in the poem. There is nothing at Hart nearer to

this than a smooth and shallow dip in cultivated ground, and sand-hills are the chief feature of the shore below. It may be that Beowulf, though a Danish tale, was made English by a poet who lived in the Whitby district, and when he described or suggested scenery, produced impressions from the only scenery he knew. That is my own thought. I return now to the argument of Mr. Haigh.

At Hart there are traces of an ancient fort, and near it is an enclosure called the Palace Garths. There is no record of any residence at Hart by the historic kings of Northumbria. But the Palace Garths near the old fort would answer to the site of Heorot by Hrothgar's fortress. There is reference, moreover, in Beowulf and in the " Traveller's Song," for which also an English origin is argued, to an attack on Heorot by the Beards under Wythergild, Frode, and Ingeld, his son. In the neighbourhood of Hart traces of such a battle have been found. Near the north-western end of the slake of Hartlepool a number of graves, eight feet square, have been found filled with human bones. In one grave were the bones of a hundred and fifty men of tall stature. Again, we may have trace of Ingeld's principality in the three Inglebys, the Ingleton, and Ingleborough of the neighbouring county of York, and of the Wycings and Beards in Wycliffe, Bartin, and Barforth. As for the destroying chief who is represented by the monster Grendel, he also has left the mark of his name behind him. It is certainly the name of a man. There is a Grendlesmere in Wiltshire, and a Grindelespytt in Worcestershire, a Grindleton in Yorkshire, and Crindale dykes on the Roman wall, near which are Grindon loch and Grandy's knowe. Near Hart there is a parish named Grandon and Grandy's Close, with, close to Grandy's Close, Thrum's Hill, the Giant's Hill.

Beowulf the Scylding is said in the poem to have reigned in the Scedelands, at Scedenig, which Dr. Grein identifies with the Scandinavia of old geographers, Schonen, the southernmost part of the Scandinavian peninsula. But Mr. Haigh observes that Mr. Kemble has rightly translated " Scedelandum," " the divided lands," Sceadan and Sundrian having the same meaning, to divide or sunder, and these Scedelands appear to be represented by the modern Sunderlands, of which one is on the coast of Northumberland, north of Shilbottle.

Then if we look for the kingdom of Hygelac, the son of Hrethel, who ruled over the Weder Goths, we find, perhaps, traces of the Suffolk Weders in two Suffolk Wetherdens, and Wetherheath, Wetherup, and Wetheringsett, with a Wetherby hundred in the adjoining county of Cambridge. We may suspect Hrethel's family name in the Suffolk Redling-field, and traces of himself at Rattlesden and Rattlerow Hill (Hrædlan hræw, Hrethel's corpse), which may have been his place of burial. A mile distant from one of the Wetherdens is an ancient Anglo-Saxon fortress called Haughley, in which are at least the H, g, l, of Hygelac. There is also a Hoxne, which has been called Hoxton, and Eglesdon, which is called by Leland, quoting a life of St. Eadmund, Hegilesdune—*quasi* Hygelácesdune—and this place is only four miles from Redlingfield and not far from Uggeshall, perhaps once Hygdeshall, Hygd being either another name of Hygelac, or the name of his queen. Even details of the deadly war of Hygelac with Ongen-theow, King of the Sweofolk, may be faintly traced in local names on our own soil. The first battle was fought at Raven Wood. There is a Ravenhill near Whitby, on the coast of Yorkshire, and the adjacent Robin Hood's Bay may be a corruption of Raven Wood. There are remains of entrenchments to the south of this neighbourhood called War Dyke, and to the east called Green Dyke ; six miles to the north-west is a village of Ugglebarnby, which seems to contain the name of Hygelac, and may mark the scene

of the second battle; close to it has been a place called by
the name of Breca, one of Hygelac's neighbours, and
twenty miles farther to the west is Roseberry Topping, a
lofty hill, with a complete circle of large pits around its
conical summit, which may recall the name of the fortress
of Hreosnabeorh, in which Ongentheow defended himself
after his battle with Hygelac and in defence of which he
died.

That Ongentheow is called King of the Sweos does
not decide whether his people were a Swedish settlement
in England, or were still inhabitants of Sweden.

The period was the close of the fifth century or beginning of the sixth, and if Hygelac was confederate then with
Garmund in war against the Britons, we might have, as we
do, on the scene of that war a Hygeláce's git* near Clifton,
in Somersetshire, a Hucklecote, near Gloucester, and
Hugglescote, near Chorley, in Leicestershire. Even that
descent of Hygelac, A.D. 520, on the island at the Rhine
mouth is quite as traceable to the Suffolk Hygelac as to a
Dane from the continent of Scandinavia. Hygelac's son
is called Hereric's nephew. Chararic, who might be
Hereric, and the brother of Hygelac's queen, was
a Frank king, who had been treacherously slain by
Chlodovech, who then reigned in his stead. The Garmund
just mentioned made, therefore, with Isambard an expedition against Chlodovech, and Hygelac's descent on
Theodoric's adjacent territory may have been a detached
part of the same unsuccessful enterprise of vengeance. Mr.
Haigh's ingenuity goes yet farther. Hygelac's wife is said
in the poem of Beowulf to have been the wife of that Offa
whom Matthew of Paris, writing in the thirteenth century,
makes in England the son of Warmund, King of the West
Angles, who repaired and gave his name to Warwick. To

* Cod. diplom. 566.

the theory which places the scene of the poem in Denmark and Sweden it is necessary, he says, that this Offa should be carried off to the original home of the Angles. But the story of Offa, as told in the poem of "Beowulf" and the "Traveller's Tale," has also its strong confirmation attached to our English soil. The fabled history tells that Offa was blind till his seventh year, and deaf and dumb till his thirtieth, when he recovered all his faculties under the pressure of danger from the chief Alewih, who sought to usurp his right of succession. The forces of Offa and Alewih met on the opposite banks of a river named Avene, and fought by missiles till Offa crossed, and the enemy suffered a great defeat, according to the "Traveller's Song," by the border of Fifield. There was honourable burial given to the nobles, and the rest of the slain were buried under a great heap of stones, which received, there-fore, the name of Qualmhul (Slaughter Hill). The battle-field was called afterwards Blodewald. Now Fifield, in Oxfordshire, is separated from Gloucestershire by the river Evenlode (Avene of the poem); there is no Blodewald, but the parish next Fifield, on the other side of the river, is Bledington, and three miles west of Bledington there is to this day Slaughter Hill, giving its name to two neigh-bouring parishes as well as to the hundred. The bodies of the nobles were buried apart. In the immediate neigh-bourhood are two parishes, called Upper and Lower Swell. Swell means a burning, a funeral pile. The name occurs only in one other part of England, in Somersetshire, also near an ancient battle-field. In digging foundations for enlargement of the church of Lower Swell, a long deep bed of ashes was discovered in the churchyard, and of eleven barrows in the parish the largest is called Picked Morden—selected slain. The field in which it stands is called Camp-ground. History records no battle but that of Offa on this spot. Overcome in this battle, Offa's opponent fled and was pursued, and, after a second fight, perished in the Riganburn. A stream flowing into the Stour near its junction with the Avon was afterwards known as Rugganbróc, and nearly in direct line between Fifield and Rugganbróc, near Chipping Campden, we have a place called Battle Bridges. Alewih's name is in the Warwickshire Alveston, a place directly north of the stream in which he perished, which may, therefore, have been the fort of his own to which he was flying; there is also an Alveston in Gloucestershire, and in Oxfordshire an Alvescott. This, in corroboration of the written record, Mr. Haigh considers to be strong evidence against taking the first husband of Hygelac's wife out of England.

We return now to Beowulf, at the court of Hygelac. Let us assume that the great swimming-match with Breca, Prince of the Brondings, was a rowing-match, in which Beowulf was victor. Beowulf is said to have reached the shore of the land of the Fins, Breca to have landed at Hæthoræmis, whence he sought his dear territory, the land of the Brondings. Beowulf and Breca, then, must have been neighbours. About ten miles from Hrethel's abode, or Rattlesden, we have Breckley, bearing, perhaps, the name of Breca, and in the same county, Bransfield, Brandeston, Brantham, and Brandon may indicate settlements of the Brondings, or clans of Brand or Brond. Of the Fins there is no trace on the coast; but two Finboroughs, not far from Rattlesden, appear to show that there were Fins here, neighbours, if not subjects, of Hrethel.

From the descriptions given in the poem of Beowulf's voyage out and home to Heorot, Mr. Haigh suggests that Uggeshall in Suffolk, about five miles inland, was Hygelac's royal residence, and Covehithe, of which the name indicates an ancient harbour, Beowulf's place of embarkation. Thence to Hartlepool the distance is about two hundred and twenty miles, a distance that might be accomplished in the specified time, the adventurers reaching the court of Hrothgar on the second day. At six miles an hour, rather below the speed of the fishing cobles on the Yorkshire coast, Beowulf and his companions would, at seven or eight o'clock in the morning of the second day, be opposite Cromer; and then steering direct for Hart, within sight of Flamborough Head, they would make their way to the cliffs of Hartlepool, on which Hrothgar's coastguard was stationed, disembark on the sands, and march two miles on the road to Hart or Heorot. On their home voyage they would descry the well-known cliffs of the Geats in the highlands between Lowestoft and Southwold.

After Hygelac's fall we are told in the poem that Beowulf's reign was disturbed by war with the Mere-Wiowings, or Sea Wiwings, people of Wiwa, whose name occurs at Wiveton in Norfolk, and who founded the kingdom of the East Angles early in the sixth century. Recently arrived, and settled at first on the coast, they were Beowulf's neighbours, and the contest with them ended in their absorption of his little state. He then went to the scene of his old fight with Grendel, and ruled over the Scyldings, dying in an encounter which, whatever its nature, is said to have taken place on Earna Næs, Eagle's Cliff. There is a promontory so named south of Hartlepool, about fifty feet high, nearly surrounded by the Tees. Finally, if the barrow raised over the dead hero on the sea headland called Hronesnæs was to be known by seamen as Beowulf's Mount, it looks something like identification that Hron's name may be preserved in Runswick, a village near Whitby, having four miles to the north of it a lofty sea headland, that may well have been Hronesnæs, for on it is the village of Bowlby, an easy contraction for Beowulfes-beorh.

The latest theory that assigns an English origin to

Beowulf is that of a very genial scholar, who has often put freshness of thought into old English studies, the Rev. John Earle, professor of Anglo-Saxon in the University of Oxford.* He says that early in 1884 he received from the Commendatore di Rossi a copy of his pamphlet on a discovery of Anglo-Saxon coins at Rome in 1883. This caused him to observe the singular beauty of Offa's coinage in the midst of the long series of Saxon coins, and it occurred to him that the reign which produced that coinage might well have produced the Beowulf. At Easter in the same year, being for some days in a Hampshire rectory, he found in it the whole series of the Folk-lore Society's publications. Examination of this series having led to a conviction of the great historical importance of oral tradition, and of its continuity with the earlier efforts of written literature, Professor Earle came to the conclusion that Beowulf itself is a piece of folk-lore, and that evidences may still be found of its prehistoric pedigree. In October, 1884, Professor Freeman lectured at Oxford on the "Historia Francorum" of Gregory of Tours. "The prolonged contemplation of Gregory's pages, which I owe to Mr. Freeman's lectures," says Professor Earle, "had the effect of convincing me that the Beowulf has some affinity with that sixth-century narrative literature of which Gregory is our chief representative." These were the three ideas that put the Oxford Professor of Anglo-Saxon on the track he desired to find, and he added, "By help of these new lights I hope to construct a probable history of the antecedents of the Beowulf from its earliest stage in the radical myth down to the time when it came forth as an epic poem from the hand of the English poet." Accordingly, in his second letter, Professor Earle argued

Prof. John Earle.

---

* Professor Earle's theory was first published in two communications to the *Times* newspaper for September 30 and October 29, 1885.

that he might rely especially on the dragon story in Basile's "Pentamerone," a book of tales in the Neapolitan dialect, which was published in the middle of the seventeenth century, for evidence that folk-lore tales included killing of dragons. But in Beowulf a tale of going out on adventure, achieving, and returning home, has been grafted on the dragon story. In further evidence of origin in folk-lore, Professor Earle cites the gibing at Odysseus by Alcinous, who sees reason to change his opinion, and offers in return a valuable sword, as Hunferth does to Beowulf. That the tale was recast in the Merovingian age Professor Earle infers from the fact that the kings in Beowulf are very like the kings of the "Historia Francorum" in the prominence given to goldsmiths' work and to precious jewels and decorations of apparel. Again, in Gregory of Tours the warriors immediately about a prince are called "leudes," and the word "leód," for lord, occurs repeatedly in Beowulf.* Again, Gregory of Tours tells of a bishop who found his church at nights full of fiends, and the archfiend himself in the episcopal throne. This forcibly recalls to Professor Earle the passage in the Beowulf where it is said that though Grendel had Heorot all to himself, yet divine power permitted him not to touch the royal seat.

Having satisfied himself with these arguments, Professor Earle proceeds to say that "from Gaul, the dragon tale in its new Frankish dress passed into Scandinavia, and obtained a local settlement there. . . . At the back of the northern sagas, as of all European romance, lies the grand narrative era of the sixth century." The geography of the poem is consistently Scandinavian. "This alone affords strong presumption that the Beowulf has been based on a

* It occurs also in Cædmon : "Leód Ebrea," *Genesis*, line 2,835, line 2,163 ; *Exodus*, line 277. The name " leudes " for the *comites* of a chief is known to most readers of early history. It is enough to refer to Montesquieu, " De l'Esprit des Lois," liv. xxx., ch. 16, Des Leudes ou Vassaux.

Scandinavian saga. This was the saga of Gretti." Grettir's
contest with Glam is, he says, substantially the same as that
of Beowulf with Grendel. Also there occurs in the poem
of Beowulf, and in no other known piece of Anglo-Saxon
literature, the word " hæft-mece," and there occurs in the
Grettis saga the word "hepti-sax." ‡ It was Dr. Gudbrand
Vigfusson who first pointed this out. Then follows the
particular suggestion. John Mitchell Kemble had inferred
nearly forty years ago from a passage in praise of the
mythic Offa, a reputed ancestor of Offa, King of Mercia,
that the poem was Anglian. Professor Earle now sees in
this fact evidence that the poem was written in the reign
of Offa, King of Mercia, between the years 755 and 794.
" The aim of the poem as a whole is to set up an heroic
example, as if to kindle admiration in a young prince, and
every occasion is seized for illustrating the relations of
king and subject, and especially as regards those military
subjects who immediately surround the person of a king.
The poem is, in short, the institution of a prince ; and that
prince can be no other than Ecgferth, the son of Offa."
The mythic Beowulf is in all things exemplary. Beowulf
particularly resembles Offa, King of Mercia, in that " having

‡ " Hæft-mege," hafted sword, in combination, happens to occur only
once in Beowulf, but " hæft " is used elsewhere as expression of the sway
and power of the sword or spear. It occurs in other poems, and " hapti " is
common in Scandinavian for a haft or hilt. The saga of Grettir the
Strong was developed from the history of an Icelandic hero who lived about
two centuries after Charlemagne, in the beginning of the eleventh century.
The legendary tale of him is ascribed to the end of the thirteenth century.
" In historia Gretteri Robusti, qui sæculo undecimo floruit in Islandia . . .
Primus Islandus ferrum candens gestasse perhibetur Grettir Robustus cui id
a rege Olavo in Norvegia est injunctum, anno circiter 1017." Müller and
Velschow's notes to Saxo Grammaticus. There may be, and is, question
of the influence of Beowulf on the Grettis saga, but argument of influence
the other way is like arguing about the influence of Thackeray on Fielding.
Grettir was a hero of North Iceland, and Iceland was not even colonised
until more than fifty years after the death of Charlemagne.

been a youth of no promise, an incapable, he suddenly, when occasion called for a hero, broke out and became great." "If the poem was written for the benefit of the king's son, what treatment more pleasing to the father or more attractive for the youth than that which identified heroic virtues with incidents in his father's career and with the hereditary temperament of his family!" Ecgferth was consecrated king nine years before the death of his father. "He was consecrated manifestly by Higebryht, the new Archbishop of Mercia. This," says Professor Earle, "is the occasion with which I connect the production of our poem." He finds Hygebriht under the name of Eomær, who is said to have been born in the mythic Offa's house, and "the story of Thrytho the virago, who was tamed by the mythic Offa, is in direct praise of the reigning Offa, with covert admonition of Cynebriht, the Queen Consort. I feel confident," says Professor Earle, "that the whole of Hygelac's court and nation was first introduced in the English poem, and was never in the saga." Offa was in correspondence with Charlemagne, who was no despiser of old songs and tales. He caused them to be written down. "By this channel," Professor Earle says, "I imagine the saga came out of Frankland to the hand of the poet, and probably it was written in Latin." It suggests a Latin association, has its scene in Scandinavia, and has no Scandinavian words, but an occasional untranslatable word, like "hæft-mece," may have been embodied in the context. As a Frankish scholar may be supposed more likely than a poet in England to be acquainted with the "Historia Francorum," from which part of the story of Hygelac was borrowed, it might seem easier to lay this part of the work at the door of the Frank. But there are stronger reasons for crediting it to the English poet. "What are they? If the above reasonings be true, the poet must have been a person who could speak with

weight and authority to the highest personages. There is
one name of such eminence, that of Higeberht, Offa's
prime adviser, whom he made Archbishop of Lichfield.
The poet, whoever he was, took Hygelac and his disastrous
fate out of the 'Historia Francorum,' and he changed the
form of his name from Chocilaicus to Hygelac." "Now,
though it is not clear what Chochi means, it is pretty safe
to say that it does not mean 'hige,' mind, reflection, understanding, and that Hygelac is not a true equivalent for
Chocilaicus, but an arbitrary adaptation for the poet's
purpose. That purpose was to leave in the poem the
mark of his own name, Higeberht, and in the same spirit
he gave Hygelac's queen the name of Hygd, a word which
is one of the same group, an abstract substantive to signify
the very qualities with which he has adorned her, namely,
good sense and discretion."

Gregory of Tours, to whom there has been frequent
reference by students of Beowulf, died at Tours, aged fifty-
one, in November of the year 595. He was of a
rich and noble family, that included men distinguished in the story of the early Church. He
studied at Clermont under Saint Gall and his successor in the bishopric, who regarded grammar as a
Pagan study, and trained him only in the Latin of the
Vulgate. At the age of twenty-nine, in the year 573, he
was consecrated Archbishop of Tours, a see in which most
of the preceding archbishops had been of his kin. In
the year 567, Northern Gaul had been divided into the
three Frankish kingdoms of Austrasia, Neustria, and
Burgundy. Gregory went to his archbishopric from the
court of Sigebert, King of Austrasia. They were rough times.
Feuds were fierce and murders frequent. Gregory held his
own at Tours with a rare vigour, even against the violence
of Fredegond, the lawless queen of Chilperic, King of
Neustria. At the close of his life Gregory of Tours was

The Historical Hygelac.

active ambassador in the affairs of Sigebert's son, Childebert, who became, in 593, King of Austrasia and of Burgundy. Not long before his death, in 595, the great Archbishop Gregory travelled to Rome to visit the great Pope Gregory, who expected to see in him a creature of heroic mould, and was surprised to find that in body he was but a weak, mean-looking little man. This was the same Pope Gregory who, in the year after the death of Gregory of Tours, sent Augustine to preach Christianity in England. The ten books of "Historia Francorum," by Gregory of Tours, are of the greatest value for their free and fearless telling of the wild history in which he himself had part. They give the fullest and the truest record of events of his own time in Gaul.

It was Nikolas Grundtvig who, in the "Dannewirke," published in 1817, and in his "Bjowulfs Drapen," published at Copenhagen in 1820,* first directed attention to the passage in Gregory of Tours by which the historical element in the legend was made clear. Heinrich Leo, in 1838, regarded this identification as established ; and the reader who will now follow the argument can have no reasonable doubt upon the point.

Gregory of Tours wrote, " After this the Danes, with their King Chocilaicus, seek Gaul with a fleet across the sea, and, having landed, devastate and take prisoners in a part of the kingdom of Theodoric. Having loaded their ships with slaves and spoil, they desired to return to their country. But their king waited on shore till all his ships were on the high sea, when he would follow. When it was told to Theodoric that a region of his had been laid waste by foreigners, he sent Theodobert, his son, to those parts with a strong army and great store of arms. Theodobert

---

* A translation into Danish followed in 1861 by a text, "Beowulfes Beorhaeller Bjovulfs-Drapen, det Old-Angelske Heltedight, paa Grunds-proget, ved Nik. Fred. Sev. Grundtvig." Kjöbenhavn, 1861.

having killed the king, subdued the enemy in a sea fight, and restored all the plunder to the land."*

The same incident is thus recorded in another chronicle, the "Gesta regum Francorum." "The Danes, with their king named Chocilagus, seek Gaul over the sea with a fleet, devastating and taking prisoners, in Theudoric's dominion, the Attuarii or others; having their ships full of captives, while they embarked on the high sea, their king remained ashore." † Here there is mention of a tribe, the Attuarii, who are called Hetware in the poem.

A tenth-century MS. of Phædrus at Wolfenbüttel has appended matter of the same date, which includes note of a King Hunglacus, who was an example of the wonderful size to which men attained. He ruled, it is said, over the Goths, and was killed by the Franks. After he had reached his twelfth year he was so big that no horse could bear him, and his bones, found in an island at the mouth of the Rhine, are shown as a miracle to people coming from afar.‡

* "His ita gestis Dani cum rege suo Chocilaico evectu navali per mare Gallias appetunt, egressique ad terras pagum unum de regno Theodorici devastant atque captivant; oneratisque navibus tam de captivis quam de reliquis spoliis reverti ad patriam cupiunt: sed rex eorum ad littus residebat, donec naves altum mare comprehenderunt, ipse deinceps secuturus. Quod cum Theodorico nuntiatum fuisset, quod scilicet regio ejus fuerit ab extraneis devastata, Theodobertum, filium suum, in illas partes cum valido exercitu ac magno armorum apparatu, direxit ; qui, interfecto rege, hostes navali prœlio superatos opprimit, omnemque rapinam terræ restituit."—Hist. Franc., iii. 3.

† "Dani cum rege suo, nomine Chocilago, cum navale hoste per altum mare Gallias appetunt, Theuderico pagum Attuarios vel alios devastantes atque captivantes, plenas naves de captivis habentes, alto mare intrantes, rex eorum ad littus maris residit."—Gesta Reg. Franc., c. xix.

‡ "De Hunglaco Magno.—Et fiunt monstra miræ magnitudinis ut rex Hunglacus, qui enim imperavit gentes (Getis) et a Francis occisus est, quem equus a duodecimo ætatis anno portare non potuit, cujus ossa in Reni fluminis insula, ubi in oceano prorumpit, reservata sunt et de longinco venientibus pro miraculo ostenduntur." Quoted from Müllenhoff through Hermann Dederich's "Historische und Geographische Studien

In the name Chocilaicus the Ch, of course, corresponds to the old sound of the letter H, which was
equivalent to the Hebrew letter *cheth,* and had originally
a strong guttural sound. This is represented by the *g* or *c*
before it in a word like English *laugh,* and German *lachen ;*
so also Ham, the son of Noah, was called Chem.* This
Hygelac of old chronicle was, then, a Danish king of
Goths (the Swedish Gothland), who made an attack upon
the Attuarii (Hetware) in a part of north-east Gaul, under
the rule of Theodoric I., King of Metz between the years
511 and 534, and who, as he was about to depart, rich in
plunder, was attacked by Theodebert, the son of Theodoric,
who was afterwards King of Austrasia, in the years from
534 to 548. The evidence that this was the Hygelac of
the old heroic poem does not rest upon one passage. In
Beowulf† there is an episode mentioning a jewelled neck
ornament equalled only by that which Hama took from
the Brosings ; and this ring or circlet, it is said, "had Hygelac
the Goth, the nephew of Swerting, when he went for the
last time under the banner to lay hold on treasure, to
defend spoils of the slain. Fate snatched him away when
through pride he sought sorrow in feud against the Frisians.
The mighty king carried the ornament with him, the precious
stones over the cup of the waves. He fell under his shield.
The life of the king then passed into the grasp of the Franks,

zum angel-sächsischen Beowulf-liede." Köln, 1877. This excellent mono-
graph, by a young scholar, put together very clearly some of the chief results of recent criticism.

* Relying upon common knowledge of this fact, Mr. G. W. Kitchin,
in his " History of France," has spelt the names, usually written Clothaire
and Chilperic, as Hlothair and Hilperic. In the vowel of Huglekr, or
Huglek, as the name stands in three old Danish records, the *u* weakens to
o, and, later, to *i,* the successive vowels in Hygelac becoming *i, e* by the
usual action of the umlaut. Huglatus is the name in Saxo Grammaticus
of a very rich king in Ireland, who was so avaricious that when he gave
away boots he kept their laces.

† Beowulf, ll. 1,202—1,214.

breast armour and jewel together." Here there is reference to Frisians, as well as to the power of the Franks, and the Hatuarii were on a Frisian shore.

Again,* in the account of Beowulf's enterprise against the dragon, there is reference to the fall of Hygelac, the offspring of Hrethel, in battle with the Hatuarii, in the land of the Frisians, a battle from which Beowulf came away by swimming, and carrying as he swam the spoils of thirty men whom he had slain on the field. He swam over to where Queen Hygd awaited him, and offered him the throne of Hygelac, not trusting that her child would have force to resist assaults of foreign foes.

Again,† before his fight with the dragon, Beowulf recalls at length his past life and his services to Hygelac as warrior, and among others how he slew with his fist, not with his sword, Dæghræfn, the banner-bearer of the Hugas, so that he could not take the jewelled breast ornament (of Hygelac) to the Frisian king.

The Hugas are again ‡ associated with the Franks and Frisians when Beowulf's death is lamented by his followers, as he lies by the dragon he has slain. They may expect war when the Franks and Frisians shall hear that Beowulf is no more. Strong feud was raised with the Hugas when Hygelac went with his navy to the Frisians, and was over-whelmed by the force of the Hetware (Hatuarii). Ever since then, says the song, we have been denied the friend-ship of the Merovingians.

The Hugas, whom the poem cites as fellow-combatants with Hatuarii in this battle on a coast near to the left bank of the Rhine, are not named in the Frankish chronicles. Hermann Dederich suggests § that they were

* Beowulf, ll. 2,354—2,372.
† Beowulf, ll. 2,497—2,508.
‡ Beowulf, ll. 2,910—2,921.
§ "Historische und Geographische Studien zum Beovulf-liede." Köln, 1877.

the tribe called by Tacitus the Gugurni and Cugurni, who were named also by Pliny as neighbours to the Batavians, and those who lived on islands of the Rhine. If the second syllable represent the old Gothic ending in -airns, we have only to allow for the guttural sound of the letter *h* to identify Huga with Guga. But the Quedlinburg chronicle says that once all Franks were called Hugos, from their chief Hugo ; and Widukind speaks of a Huga, King of the Franks, who was succeeded by his son Theodoric. But this was (the son of Chlodowic) Theodoric, King of Metz, upon whose shore Hygelac made his descent, and in the Quedlinburg chronicle he is distinguished from Theodoric the Ostrogoth as the Frankish Hugo Theodoric. He is the Hug-Dietrich of old German romance. The historical references, then, to the battle in which Hygelac fell are perfectly consistent. They clearly identify the Hygelac of the poem with the Chocilaicus of Gregory of Tours and of the " Gesta Regum Francorum," who fell in battle in the year 520.

Let us now turn to the shrew whose character is contrasted with the mildness of Hygelac's young Queen Hygd, An episode in the account of the feast welcoming Beowulf of a Shrew. on his return to the court of Hygelac. Her name, Modthrytho, or rather Thrytho, has been misread into an adjective joining passionate temper and all the vices of the bad woman to the virtues of Hygd, with whom she is contrasted and who is praised as one who loved * the people. Thrytho is described as so violent that no one dared to look in her eyes except her husband, who looked on her daily, and to him she decreed fetters and death. The kinsman of Heming reproached her over the ale-drinking, and said that it was not womanly for a peace-weaver, though beautiful beyond compare, to practise the death of

* Beowulf, ll. 1,931—1,962.

a husband. Others said that she was less wicked after she had, by her father's counsel, crossed the sea to be joined to the young Offa, that she was happy on the throne, and had high love for her husband, the best of men for war and wisdom. His son was Eomer, kinsman of Heming, nephew of Garmund, great in fight. The passage, of which this is the text, was formerly read into the life of Hygd, who was therefore supposed to have been married to Offa after the death of Hygelac. Taken now, as it has been read by Grein * and others after him, it is an episodical remembrance of a fierce woman in contrast to the gentleness of Hygd. The Offa here referred to is named in the " Traveller's Song," hereafter to be described, as King of the Angles, and is the elder of the two Offas whose lives were recorded in the thirteenth century by Matthew Paris. Matthew Paris calls the elder Offa son of Warmund, and in Saxo Grammaticus † he is ca'led Uffo the son of Vermund, who was son to the King of Denmark by whom Hamlet's usurping uncle was succeeded. Uffo, large and strong, broke through all armour of other men that he might try

---

* " Die Historischen Verhältnisse des Beowulfliedes " in Ebert's "Jahrbuch fur Romanische und Englische Literatur, unter besonderer Mitwirkung von Ferdinand Wolf," vol. iv., pp. 260—285.

† Saxo Lange, Latinised Saxo Longus, and styled, for the good Latin he wrote, " Grammaticus," was a friend and companion of Svend Aagesön, whose " Compendiosa Historia Regum Daniæ " was the first attempt at a continuous history of Denmark. Aagesön said himself that his record was the shorter because he knew that his friend Saxo was engaged on a more detailed history of his time. They were both ecclesiastics, but Aagesön certainly, and Saxo probably, went with Archbishop Absolon to war against the Wends. Saxo's father and grandfather were soldiers under Waldemar the Great. Saxo was private secretary to Archbishop Absolon, whom he survived, inscribing to Absolon's successor his famous chronicle of Denmark, " Gesta Danorum," or " Historia Danica." Saxo died in or after the year 1208. His book is a grand store-house of the legend and history of Denmark, as they were collected in the Middle Ages by a skilful writer who had the touch of an artist with the grasp of an historian.

w

to wear, and could break a sword by the force with which he slashed it through the air. He fought a memorable duel on an island of the Eider—the Fifeldor referred to in the "Traveller's Song"—upon which now stands the citadel of Rendsburg. The Saxon Chronicle, under the year 755, in tracing the descent of the Mercian Offa who ruled over the Angles of the continent, makes him twelfth in descent, ascending from Eomær the son of Angeltheow to Angeltheow the son of Offa, Offa the son of Wærmund. Sequence here of the names of Wermund, Offa, Eomær agrees with what we find said of the Offa mentioned in Beowulf, with addition to his other triumphs, that he tamed a shrew. This mythical Offa, so far as he can be dated, must have lived in the middle of the fourth century—it has been suggested that he was born about the year 336—and Hygelac was killed in the year 520. The reference therefore to King Offa and his ill-tempered wife was parenthetical use of a tradition which added a crowning triumph to the fables of the prowess of Offa ; Hygd's kindness in her husband's home and kingdom suggesting contrast with the shrew whom only an Offa had the power to tame. Matthew Paris gives us the very name now disentangled from misreading in the text of Beowulf. He calls her Drida, and says she was of wondrous beauty, but with a temper so intolerable that at last, after some act especially atrocious, she was condemned to death, but so far reprieved that she was only cast adrift upon the sea. The waves tossed her to King Offa's shore. By her beauty and her distress Offa was drawn to love and pity. He placed her under the care of his own mother, and she soon recovered health with the full sway of her beauty, but, at the same time, she regained also the full swing of her temper. Nevertheless, Offa was won by the beauty, and married her. Matthew Paris, living in the thirteenth century, confuses here the two Offas, and makes the Mercian the man who married

Drida.* But she evidently is the Thrytho who took in old northern tales the part played afterwards by Baptista's daughter Katherine, and she had the old mythical King Offa for Petruchio.

In another episode use is made of Heremod, a device of contrast exactly corresponding to the contrast between Hygd and Drida. When Beowulf had returned victorious and presented to Hrothgar the heads of Grendel and Grendel's mother, with the rune-marked golden hilt of the sword of the eoten, Hrothgar says of him that he was a true guardian of his country, supporting all with patience, might, and prudence, one who would long be a comfort to his people, and then proceeds at once to a contrast.† Not so was Heremod a blessing to the Scyldings, to Ecgwela's children. He grew not to the desire, but to the death of the Danes. In his mood, swollen with anger, he killed his hearth-sharers, his nearest friends, till the great chief, to whom God gave above all men vigour and the joy of power, came to a joyless death. His heart was blood-thirsty, he gave no rings. He was a long evil to the people. Let this teach Beowulf to be liberal. There is another passage ‡ that tells more of Heremod. Among the rejoicings after the victory of Beowulf over Grendel himself, it is said that at times a king's thane mindful of songs, who remembered many an old saga, found an apt theme to bind with the truth, and joined the praise of Beowulf to the tale of Sigmund and his son Fitela (who is called Sinfiotli in the Scandinavian Völsunga saga), and the glory also of Sigmund is then contrasted with the shame

---

Heremod.

* The confusion arose very easily. The Mercian Offa's wife was a bad woman named Cynedrid, and Matthew Paris says that Drida, after her marriage with the King of Mercia, was called Cwendrida (Queen-drida), a name not far from Cynedrid.

† Beowulf, ll. 1,709—1,722.

‡ Beowulf, ll. 900—913.

of Heremod, who, when his strength diminished, was betrayed into the power of his enemies and cast out of the land. There is some reason to think that the tyrant Heremod was the last sovereign of a dynasty overthrown by his people with aid from a leader who became the founder of the next dynasty, that of the Scyldings.

The dynasty of the Scyldings is said to have been founded by a Scyld who came as a child on a ship laden with arms and treasure to the coast of Denmark at a time when the country was in great distress. The Danes received the child as a gift from heaven, and in good time they made Scyld king. He reigned long and prosperously, subjecting many of the surrounding nations, founded the dynasty of the Scyldings, and was after death, by his own direction, put into a ship again with treasure and arms, and cast adrift. No man ever heard whither that ship went. "This," says Grein, "may be a legend framed from the name of the Sceáfa, who is said, in the 'Traveller's Song,' to have ruled over the Lombards. Scyld, son of Sceáfa—Scyld Sceafing—may have been an adventurous son of the Lombard chief, may have gone out in the usual way in search of profitable adventure, and may have founded a dynasty on the ruins of that which had Heremod for its last representative." The poem makes a Beowulf to be the son of Scyld and the father of Healfdene. In the tables of descent of the Sverris saga, the son of Skialdi was Biarr. In the Saxon chronicle Scealdva was the father of Beao. Healfdene's eldest son was Heorogar, who succeeded him, but did not reign long. He had a son, Heoroweard, who died, probably, before his father The succession passed therefore to Heorogar's next brother, Hrothgar, at a time when Hrothgar must have been a young man, since he had reigned fifty years at the time when the poem opens. The next brother was Hela, and then came Ela, who married a king of the Swedish race

Marginal note: Scyld Scefing.

of the Scylfings; probably, as Grundtvig suggested, Ongetheow, King of Sweden, who was contemporary with
Hygelac and with the sons of Healfdene.

The episode of the fight at Finnesburg requires also
some separate attention, but that will be most conveniently
given when we discuss, in the next chapter, a distinct fragment of verse on the same subject.

In the twenty-ninth number of the Journal of Philology
(that for July, 1886), the Cambridge Professor of Anglo-
Saxon, the Rev. Walter W. Skeat, has a paper
on "The Monster Grendel in Beowulf," which
was read before the Cambridge Philological Society on the
3rd of December, 1885. It assumes that Beowulf was a
real man, one of whose exploits was the slaying of Grendel,
who was not a man at all, but a bear. Grendel's name,
derived as Ettmüller derived it, means that he is the
grinder; that he is carnivorous, a grinder of bones. He
was fierce and furious, he "used to prowl round the great
hall every night just like Horace's ' vespertinus ursus '
(Epod. xvi. 51), and caught and carried off so many men
that at last the great hall was deserted at night."

"Grendel," Professor Skeat observes, "never used
weapons, but trusted solely to the strength of his grip, *i.e.*
the well-known bear's hug." When he seized a sleeping
warrior, tore him unresisting, bit his bone-frame, drank
blood from his veins, and, in great bites, swallowed him,
"this," says Professor Skeat, "is obviously the mode of
procedure of a carnivorous beast."

It is further argued that Grendel was, as bears are, a
solitary animal, and an excellent swimmer. The bear, like
Grendel, seeks its food at night, and never fails to return to
its own district. When Beowulf had slain Grendel, he had
a harder task with Grendel's mother. "This," says Professor Skeat, "might easily happen in the case of an old
she-bear, especially if angered by the loss of her whelp.

Prof. Skeat on Grendel.

' Let a bear robbed of her whelp meet a man rather than a fool in his folly' (Prov. xvii. 12). We know of two Asiatic she-bears that 'tare forty and two children' at one time (2 Kings, ii. 24).'' Beowulf's dive to reach Grendel's mother was his swim across to the bear's cave. Grendel's mother, being a she-bear, had no weapon but her grip, she was, like Grendel, carnivorous, and she came also by night when she seized Æschere. Again, it is suggested that Grendel and his mother were both dumb beasts. There is no hint of their use of speech; but Grendel uttered a terrible cry or howl when he lost his arm. The name of Beo-wulf, bee-wolf, means bear, and the hero was so named for his achievements, and for that also he was credited with the strength of thirty men. Of the bear, the Norwegians had a proverb that he has the strength of ten men and the sense of twelve. Finally, Professor Skeat pays special attention to the wording of the passages that speak of Grendel's hand. He finds the bear's claw in its hard nails, and the bear's furry paw in its glove or handsceo. The lines 2,076—2,100 Professor Skeat translates :—

"There was the glove, *i.e.* paw, ready to descend in conflict, a life bale [was it] to the doomed man ; he lay the nearest, a girded warrior ; to him was Grendel ; viz., to that great warthane, a slayer with his mouth."

And at lines 2,085—2,088 Professor Skeat translates : "But he, strong in might, made trial of me, groped (after me) with ready palm. His glove (or paw) hung suspended," etc.

Professor Skeat points out that his readings of Grendel's hand into a paw remain the same, even if Grendel be not a bear. "All uncouth monsters," he says, "must be treated as having something in the way of hands, which a poet would more naturally liken to the paws of a beast than to the wonderful hands of man. I merely throw out the suggestion that Beowulf's feats may have been founded upon

some actual encounter between two bears and a hero of
antiquity who was remarkable for his strength of grip, and
who was delivered, like David, 'out of the paw of the
bear.'"

Professor Skeat's arguments in support of his suggestion
are admirably well put, and his philology is sound ; but I do
not believe Grendel was a beast, except in his behaviour.

In the poem of Beowulf, more or less blended with
ideas of those unseen forces which surround and
press into man's battle with the elements and
with his fellow man, we have mythical history
of the simplest kind. A chief's power in battle
is poetically typified by putting the force of thirty men
into his hand grip. A Danish chief, whose praise is
to pass from sire to son, is overmastered by an enemy.
The praise of the chief, Hrothgar, lives, and he belongs to
history. But for the foe who prevailed over him in
frequent expeditions of attack and plunder, the poet
refuses to transmit to future generations knowledge of
his name and power. He is lost under the image of a
superhuman monster, Grendel. The attacks were from over
sea, for which reason Grendel was a water fiend, who came
from the bottom of a mere. In the wrestle with Grendel,
Beowulf defended Hrothgar upon his own ground, in a
successful battle. The second attack, represented mythically
as made in revenge by Grendel's mother, was replied to
by carrying the war home to the enemy, and this is represented by Beowulf's plunge into the mere, tempting the
deep—" Brimwylm onfeng hilderince."

The ocean surge received the warrior, and it was the
space of a day before he saw the plain below. This trans-
forms clearly enough into mythical history an expedition by
sea to stay ravages of an enemy whom the poet, in shaping
his song of victory, commits to oblivion under the mythical
form of a strong evil power. In Beowulf's fight, at the

(margin: Beowulf as mythical history.)

close ot his lite, with the dragon that laid waste his own
dominions, there is the same common poetical device.
Some enemy provoked by petty plunderings upon his own
domain harries Gothland—

> ne on wealle leng
> Bidan wolde, ac mid bæle fór
> Fyre gefysed.

He would stay no more in his own stronghold, but went
forth with flames, prompt with his fire, and presently afterwards we are told that as he flew he poured out fire and
burnt the dwellings of the land. Again Beowulf battles
with a dangerous invader, and while the poet sings the glory
of the chief, he denies fame to the strong antagonist, and
fashions a more welcome and wondrous tale by fabling him
into a fire-breathing dragon.

Before any clue had been found to the historical element
in the accounts of Hygelac, all Beowulf was read into myth,
and harmonised with the legends of nature that
form part of the old northern mythology, as set
forth in the Eddas. Jacob Grimm * identified
Grendel with Loki, the malicious god of the
Scandinavians, and found in the monster's home under the
water a resemblance to Œgir's dwelling. Beowulf, said
Jacob Grimm, means Bee-wolf, name for the Woodpecker,
a bird greedy for bees; and this pie (Picumnus) is placed
by classical mythology in the race of Kronos, Zeus, and
Hermes, and interwoven by the old Bohemian mythology
with the race of Sitivrat, Kirt, and Radigost, as Beowulf
with Geát and Woden. It may be asked, however, whether
(since "beado" is an Anglo-Saxon prefix, meaning "war")
War-wolf is not a simpler reading than Bee-wolf for the
hero's name.

Marginal note: Of other myths in Beowulf. Jacob Grimm.

* "Deutsche Mythologie," 1835.

Mr. J. M. Kemble, in a paper on West - Saxon genealogies, suggested that the old Saxon "beo," "bewod," a
knife, was in the first part of the name, making J. M.
Beowulf a god of the harvest. In the comments Kemble.
joined to his translation of Beowulf, he identified Beowulf
with Beaw or Beawa, and he also saw in his fight with
Grendel a reflection of the struggle of Thor with the
Midgard serpent.

Kemble did not believe that in England the woodpecker
was ever called "bee-wolf," and opposed the woodpecker
theory.* Ettmüller argued that the names of L. Ett-
mythical heroes or demigods are compound, those müller.
of the greater god simple, and that the name of Beowulf,
therefore, ought not to be read as Beowa. He adopted the
interpretation of the name into Bee-wolf, the woodpecker.

Müllenhoff pronounced it to be only a guess that the old
Germans called the woodpecker Beewolf, and says it is
not clear that they accounted the bird sacred. Karl Mül-
He agrees with Kemble that the name is Beaw, lenhoff.
which he allies with bauen, to build; and he sees a
myth of the coming - in of civilisation when peaceful
Sceaf, who first brings the culture of the earth and
the full Sheaf of corn, has for his son Scyld, Shield,
the defending warrior, who shaped the young community
into a state, and gave security to those who ploughed
and sowed : their descendants were then called Beav and
Tætwa, because tillage and building on the settled soil had
made life pleasant to the ancient Germans. But Müllenhoff
held that Sceaf, Scyld, Beáw, and Tætwa were all to be
taken as Freyr, god of the fields and of the sea. Müllenhoff
finds Freyr not only in the Beowulf who was Hrothgar's
ancestor, but also in the hero of the poem, Beowulf son of
Ecgtheow. For the swimming race with Breca, he finds

---

* Kemble's "Saxons in England."

parallel in Freyr's contest against storm, personified by the Giant Beli ; Beowulf and Breca swam towards the Polar seas, and the swords they carried signified that they went to subdue the rigour of the northern blast. Grendel is the god of the wild sea in storm at the time of the spring equinox. Beowulf's contest with Grendel typifies, says Müllenhoff, the checking of the fury of the waves that threaten to flood the flats of the low German shore. As Grendel represents the sea under the equinoctial gales of spring, the Dragon represents the gales of the other equinox, and the wild sea and the storms that bring winter. Beowulf has become an old man (that means, it is autumn) ; he knows that his death is near (winter is coming) ; but the winter storms are not to overwhelm all life, and Beowulf dies victorious. His heroic life of action is the Summer between the victory over the storms of early spring, beyond which he lives in summer glory, and over the autumn storms that leave him dead, with the land saved from lasting ruin.

Uhland saw in Grendel a pestiferous marsh on a low shore; and Laistner has carried out this idea by

Uhland. seeing in the assaults of Grendel, that bring
Laistner. death to the dwellers in Heorot, the entrance
of malaria into the house, and a highly increased death rate. He traces the Beo of Beowulf to the Mæsogothic " bangjan," to cleanse, whence Beawa, the cleanser. Wolf he explains into mist, and thus makes Beowulf the cleanser from mist. If, therefore, Grendel be mist, Beowulf is the wind that blows the mist away. The Dragon also is interpreted by Laistner into mist. When Beowulf swam with Breca, they were, according to Laistner, wind and sun, armed against ice of the north ; for Beowulf was wind, and Breca, the breaker, ruled over the Brondings firebrands, hot rays of the summer. Here let us pause. Enough of wind and mist. One more of these ingenious turns of the mythologic screw might convert Beowulf into

the myth of a mining engineer, if not of a drainpipe. One of the twelve labours of Hercules has been interpreted, rightly perhaps, into the draining of a swamp.

Karl Müllenhoff has given us the best reading of the Beowulf tale into that play of the forces of nature which was no doubt, reflected from the minds of the first shapers of faith in the working of an unseen power. He is the author also of the boldest attempt at a literary criticism that shall resolve the authorship of the work into various constituent elements. There is a delusive air of accuracy in this kind of criticism that has helped to bring it into favour. Courage is all that is wanted to make any one great as an analyst in the new speculative chemistry applied to books. There are two separate main stories in Beowulf, that of the fight with Grendel and that of the fight with the Dragon. Say, then, that they were originally separate. That is a first piece of discrimination. In the Grendel story there are two parts, one of the fight with Grendel, one of the fight with Grendel's mother. Say that they were originally separate. That is a second piece of discrimination. Now look to the poem and fix lines of demarcation. The first old song, say, of the fight with Grendel, extends from line 194 to line 836—call that (I). Somebody added to (I) the lines from 837 to 1,628, the second old song—call that (II). As the introduction is not part of the direct story of Grendel, and now lies outside the analysis, say that somebody next added that. As there is connecting matter between the Grendel story (I) and the dragon story (II), ascribe that to somebody else, and call him Reviser A. Say that he put poetical touches into the whole, and added the account of Beowulf's return to the court of Hygelac. Ascribe to him conspicuous little passages here and there, always knowing precisely to a line or word where a touch of Interpolator A. is to be found, since nobody has any direct evidence to prove you wrong. There remains

Who wrote Beowulf?

then the Dragon story (II); give this to another man, whom you call Interpolator B. He revises everything that has been done before, is the monk who puts in the Christian touches, edits the whole vigorously (show exactly where and how; never doubt that you know all about it), and he introduces the little historical episodes. This describes, exactly enough, the theory of Karl Müllenhoff, one of the ablest of the modern workers upon Beowulf, and may serve as a key to the last new method of criticism in our early literature. The method is not itself so exceptionable as the delusive air of exactness with which it is applied. This gives to mere guesses an air of positiveness unfavourable to the growth of that sound critical judgment which never forgets the boundaries between known, probable, and possible. As there are some evident touches from a Christian hand in a poem which, in other respects, is body and soul pagan, and as we have it in the language here formed by a fusion of dialects, a language spoken only in this country, we know it to have been shaped by a Christian in England, and reasonably accept it as his faithful revision of a legend brought from over sea.

Müllenhoff's view of the poem, as composed of parts once separate, has been adopted and confirmed by Her-

Hermann Möller s argument from the analysis of metre.

mann Möller in a book which seeks to procure a strophic arrangement of the poem into four-lined ballad stanzas. By throwing out whatever interferes with an arrangement of the narrative into four-lined stanzas, each of them closed with a full stop, and with aid here and there only of a little reasonable ingenuity, Hermann Möller shows that he can leave the two main stories clearly told through in such ballad form. But he finds only fragments of this arrangement in the parts believed to be interpolated. The theory of strophic arrangement will be discussed when we come to a consideration of First English Metre; only its use in support of the theory of Müllenhoff concerns us now.

CHAPTER VII.

THE FIGHT AT FINNESBURG.

A FRAGMENT of heroic Anglo-Saxon poetry, containing part of a description of the fight at Finnesburg, was found in the seventeenth century by Dr. George Hickes on the cover of a MS. of Homilies in the library at Lambeth Palace. The volume has been, doubt- The fight at Fin- nesburg. less, since rebound and the old cover destroyed, in ignor- ance of its great value. The fragment was published by Hickes in his "Thesaurus of old Northern Languages" * (1703–5), and is part of a poem on the same "peril of Fin's offspring" which forms an episode of the tale told at the feast after Beowulf's conquest of Grendel. Fin was a prince of the Frisians ; and the rush and stir of the life of the past that aroused a quiet antiquary by its cry from the cover of a sober book of early Homilies in an old library, was this :—

" . . . . never burn. Then cried aloud the warlike young king, 'This dawns not from the East, nor flies a dragon here, nor are the horns of this hall burning ; but here it blazes forth. The birds sing, the crickets chirp, the warwood resounds, shield answers to shaft. Now shines the moon wandering among clouds. Now arise deeds of woe that the hatred of this people will do. But wake up now, my warriors, hold your lands, remember your valour, march in rank, be one of

* Hickes's " Thesaurus Linguarum Septentrionalium," i. 192.

heart." Then arose many a gold-decked thane, girded him with his sword. Noble warriors went to the door ; Sigeferth and Eaha drew their swords, and at the other doors Ordlaf and Guthlaf and Hengist himself turned on their track. Then yet Garulf reproached Guthhere, that he, so joyous a soul, bore not arms to the hall's door at the first instant, now that a fierce enemy would take it. But above all, the fierce warrior asked openly, ' Who held the door ? ' ' Sigeferth is my name,' quoth he ; ' I am the Secga's lord, a warrior widely known. I have suffered many woes, hard battles. Whichever thou wilt seek from me, is here decreed for thee ! ' Then was the din of slaughter in the hall. The keeled board should * * (the sword) they took in hand to break the bone helm. The burg floor resounded until Garulf, Guthhere's son, fell first of earth-dwellers in the fight. The corpses of many good foes were about him. The raven wandered, swart and sallow brown. The sword-gleam stood as if all Fin's burg were on fire. Never have I heard of sixty conquering heroes who better bore them at a conflict of men, nor ever requited song or bright mead better than his young warriors requited Hnæf. They fought five days, so that none of them, of the noble comrades, fell, but they held the door. Then the wounded hero went walking away. He said that his byrnie was broken, his war dress weak, and also that his helm was pierced. Then the guardian of his people quickly asked him how the warriors had recovered from their wounds, or whether of the young men——? "

The Fin-
nesburg
Episode in
Beowulf.
The same struggle is the subject of an episode in Beowulf.* At the feast in Heorot after the victory over Grendel—

" There was song joined with the sound of music, the gleewood was welcomed, the song frequent, when Hrothgar's scóp, the joy of the hall, told after the sitting at mead of Fin's offspring seized by sudden danger when Healfdene's hero, Hnæf of the Scyldings, fell in Friesland.

" Not Hildeburh, indeed, could praise the faith of Jutes. At the shield - play she, sinless, was deprived of her dear ones, children and brothers : their fate was to fall pierced by the spear. Not without cause Hoce's daughter mourned her doom when, in the morning, she might see under the sky the baleful murder of her kindred, wherein she before had most of the world's joy.

* Beowulf, ll. 1,068—1,159.

" War snatched away all but a few of the thanes of Fin, so that he might not fight against Hengest on the place of slaughter, nor protect the sad remains from the king's thane. But they offered to prepare for him another dwelling, hall, and high seat, so that they should have power over half, possess it with the sons of the Jutes, and every day at the distributing of gifts Folcwalda's son (Fin) should honour the Danes, serve Hengest's band with rings, with treasures of gold, even as much as ne would furnish in the beer hall to the Frisians. Then they plighted troth on the two sides to a firm agreement of peace. Fin earnestly and peacefully declared with oaths to Hengest that he would maintain in honour the sad remnant according to the decree of the counsellors, so that no man should break the conditions by word or deed, nor injure any one by craft, though now without a lord they followed, as need was, the slayer of their own ring-giver. But if any one of the Frisians, by bold speech, recalled to mind the death-feud, then he should atone for that at the sword's edge. The oath was taken and treasure of gold raised from the hoard.

" The best of the warrior Scyldings (Hnæf) was made ready for the bale fire. There was easily seen on the funeral pile the bloodstained war shirt, the boar iron hard. Many an atheling, wounded to death, lay in the field of slaughter. Then Hildeburh caused the bodies of her own sons to be fastened to Hnæf's funeral pile to be burnt to ashes. The wife mourned, moaned in song, the warrior rose winding to the clouds, the greatest of bale fires roared before the barrow, the heads were consumed, the wounds burst and their blood sprang forth ; flame, greediest of ghosts, devoured all whom the fight had snatched from both the folks. They flourished no more.

" Then the warriors departed to visit the homes bereft of friends, to see Friesland, its homes, and its high burg.

" Hengest yet dwelt at peace with Fin through the pale winter, mindful of home, though he could not urge his ringed prow over the sea. The deep sea boiled with storm, warred with the wind, winter bound up the waters with a lock of ice, until there came next year into the dwellings, as still it does when it provides a happy time and weather gloriously bright. Then winter was gone, fair was earth's breast ; then the stranger, the guest, sought to quit the dwellings.

" He thought more of vengeance than of the voyage, if he could bring about a conflict, because he had in mind the sons of the Jutes ; so he did not oppose fate when Hunlafing set to his bosom the best of falchions, the flame of war. With the Jutes were men famed for the cutting of the sword.

" Hapless sword-bale came afterwards upon Fin in his own home, when Guthlaf and Oslaf in fierce attack, after sea voyage, were mindful of sorrow, and avenged their share of woes; the wavering courage stayed not in his breast. Then was the hall beset with enemies, Fin also was slain, the king in the throng and the queen taken. The warriors of the Scyldings carried to their ships all the goods of the king of the land, such as they might find in Fin's home of jewels and rare gems. They carried away with them the royal woman, took her to their people.

"The lay was sung, the song of the gleeman; uprose again the sound of sport, and noise was loud upon the benches."

The Frisians of this song, who had Fin for their leader, were the North Frisians on the west coast of Schleswig and in the islands of the North Sea, not the West Frisians by the Rhinebank, who shared the fight in which Hygelac fell. Fin was the son of Folc-walda. Folcwalda means ruler of the people, and the name of Fin has been derived from the Gothic "fani," old High German "fanni" or "fenni," a fen, his people having their homes among broad lakes and fens.

From the lines which say that after the funeral of Hnæf the warriors departed to visit the homes bereft of friends, to see Friesland, its homes, and its high burg, Grein inferred that Finnesburg was a hall of Fin's in Jutland, not his chief seat of government. As Grein read these fragments of an old heroic song, Hnæf, of the race of the Hocings, a thane of the Danish king Healfdene, father of Hrothgar, was staying at Finnesburg as a guest, with sixty men; one of the sixty being Hengest, who is no way to be regarded as the Hengest who came to England with his brother Horsa. Fin's men treacherously attacked these guests one night. It is a suggestion of Ettmüller's that the attack came of a fresh outbreak of old tribal feuds that had been imperfectly stayed by marriage between Fin and Hildeburh. Hermann Möller adds that the giving of Hnæf's sister as wife to Fin would, according to the old laws for the staying of blood-feud, be in atonement for the killing of Fin's father, Folcwalda, by Hnæf or by Hnæf's father, Hoca. The Danes defended themselves for five days within Finnesburg, killing many of their assailants, and with little loss among themselves. At the end of the fifth day Hnæf was killed. Hengest then took his place as leader of the defence. Fin, seeing that nearly all his men were killed, stayed the attack, and offered terms of peace. He promised Hengest and his men another hall, with equal share of gifts to Danes and Frisians. There followed the burning and burial of the body of Hnæf by Hildeburh, daughter of Hoca, who seems to have been Hnæf's sister and the wife of Fin. Then Fin went to his chief royal seat, his high burg in Friesland. The winter seas delayed Hengest's return to Denmark ; and either before or after his return, Hunlafing killed him with the sword. Another reading, however, makes Hunlafing the name of his own sword, which he simply fastened to his bosom. If before he could sail away, he fell when attempting a revenge upon the treachery of Fin, as the context makes probable (" he thought more of vengeance than of the voyage "), then the revenge followed his death. The Danes returned in force under Guthlaf and Oslaf, and made fierce attack upon Finnesburg. The hall was filled with the slain, Fin himself fell in the throng, and his queen Hildeburh was carried back to her own people.

Joseph Mone has called attention to clear traces in the fight at Finnesburg of correspondence with some points in the story of Gudrun and the story of the Nibelungen. Mr. Haigh, who makes England itself the scene of all these heroic tales in the first English speech, argues ingeniously that the site of Finnesburg is to be found at Finnsham in Norfolk.

There remain to us fragments of Waldhere, a first English poem upon the tale of Walter of Aquitaine—Waltharius Manufortis. Two parchment leaves of Waldhere, each containing thirty-one lines, were *Waldhere.* discovered by Professor E. C. Werlauff, chief librarian of

x

the King's Library at Copenhagen, among MSS. that had belonged to Thorkelin, and they were published by Professor George Stephens, of Copenhagen, in the year 1860. These fragments probably represent a version of that heroic tale nearly two centuries earlier than the Latin metrical version made by Ekkehart, who died Abbot of St. Gall, in the year 973. Ekkehart preserved in his Latin verse an old heroic tale then current among the people. But there is much yet to be told of myths and sagas of the north and of the kindred life across the sea, old tales that touched us and were touched by us as English Literature grew from infancy to youth.

There is a Traveller's Song also—the traveller a Scóp who calls himself Widsith, Farway, and whose wandering is through many lands in the old days on which we have been dwelling. But he was a Scóp, a great chief's poet, and so also was Deor, from whom we have lament that he had been supplanted by a rival. We pass next with them into the old Teutonic song world, and learn something of the art by which rough warriors were stirred, through which also by Christian guides rough passions were set at rest.

Widsith.
Deor.

> Red-handed, panting, slaying through the night,
>   Man scatters death and gluts the mortal brand;
> Red flames the sky, dead faces are alight
>   With fire not kindled by a foeman's hand.
>
> Dawn brings a blush upon the dead cold face;
>   A morning breeze moves in the matted hair:
> Here hope, here hate; man's ruin, Heaven's grace
>   Bathing in light the wreckage of despair.
>
> Hnæf is no more; a new chief in his stead
>   Battles against the spirits who betray.
> The Word made Flesh lifts from the field of dead
>   Our eyes towards the springing of the day.

BIBLIOGRAPHY OF BEOWULF.

———◦⋄◦———

1705.—Humfrey Wanley, in *Catalogus Librorum Veterum Septen-trionalium*, IX., fol. 130, cites the MS. of Beowulf as "Tractatus nobilissimus poetice scriptus. Præfationis hoc est initium . . ." and adds, "In hoc libro, qui poeseos Anglo-Saxonicæ egregium est exemplum, descripta videntur bella quæ Beowulfus quidam Danus, et Regis Scyldingorum stirpe ortus, gessit contra Sueciæ Regulos."

1787.—Grim Johnson Thorkelin, who came to London in 1786, returned to Denmark with two transcripts of Beowulf made in 1787 :—

"Poema Anglosaxonicum de Rebus Gestis Danorum, ex mem-brana Bibliothecæ Cottonianæ. . . . fecit exscribi Londini, A.D. MDCCLXXXVII, Grimus Johannis Thorkelin, LL.D."

"Poema Anglosaxonicum de Danorum Rebus Gestis . . . ex membranaceo codice . . . in Bibliotheca Cottoniana . . . exscripsit Grimus Johannis Thorkelin, LL.D., Londini, anno MDCCLXXXVII."

1805.—Sharon Turner, in "The History of the Anglo-Saxons," 4 Vols., 1799—1805, gives the first account of the contents of Beowulf. He described the first part of the poem, with inter-spersed passages of translation, and added a few lines on the rest of the poem.

1815.—Grim Johnson Thorkelin, "De Danorum Rebus Gestis Secul. iii. et iv. Poëma Danicum Dialecto Anglosaxonica. Ex Biblio-theca Cottoniana Musæi Britannici edidit versione lat. et indicibus auxit Grim Johnson Thorkelin. Dr.J.U." He dedicated his volume to the patron who enabled him to print it, the royal councillor John de Bülow of Sanderamgaard. Thorkelin believed that Beowulf was a Dane who fell in Jutland in the year 340, that the poem was by one of his contemporaries, and conjectured that it was King Alfred who caused it to be translated out of Danish into Anglo-Saxon.

1815-16.—Thorkelin's Latin Translation given with the text caused this first printed edition of the Poem to be discussed, in 1815, in Denmark, in the " Literatur-Tidendi," and the " Nyeste Skilderei at Kjöbenhavn," where Grundtvig was the critic ; in Germany, in 1816, " Jena Lit. Zeitung," and the " Kieler Blätter " ; in England, in " The Monthly Review," Vol. 81, also for 1816 ; [in 1817, by Grundtvig in the " Danne-Virke ; " and by the Swedes, at Stockholm, in " Iduna." In 1818, the poem was also discussed in the " Gelehrte Anzeigen " of Gött ngen]. In 1816 Grundtvig proposed to Erasmus Rask, who then returned from a visit to Iceland, that they should join forces in an edition of Beowulf, which Rask had begun to work at when he set out on the long journey to the East from which he came home to die.

1817.—Rask printed a specimen of Beowulf in the Reading Book added to his " Angelsaksik Sproglære."

1820.—Nik. Fred. Sev. Grundtvig. " Bjowulf's Drape. Et Gothisk Helte Digt fra forrige Aar Tasinde af Angel-Saxisk paa Danske Riim." A free rhymed translation into Danish.

1826.—John Josias Conybeare. "Illustrations of Anglo-Saxon Poetry. Edited, together with additional Notes, Introductory Notices, &c., by W. D. Conybeare, M.A., London. Published by the Society of Antiquaries." This contains a full description of Beowulf, with passages in metrical translation and some pieces of the Anglo-Saxon.

1833.—" The Anglo-Saxon Poems of Beowulf, the Traveller's Song, and the Battle of Finnesburh." Edited, together with a Glossary of the more difficult words, and an Historical Preface, by John M. Kemble. London : W. Pickering. Edition of 100 copies all sold in three weeks.

1835.—A second edition of Kemble's " Beowulf."

1837.—" A Translation of the Anglo-Saxon Poem of Beowulf," with a copious Glossary, Preface, and Philological Notes, by John M. Kemble.

1839.—Heinrich Leo. " Beowulf, dasz älteste deutsche, in angelsächsischer Mundart erhaltene, Heldengedicht, nach seinem Inhalte und nach seinen historischen und mythologischen Beziehungen betrachtet. Ein Beitrag zur Geschichte alter deutscher Geistes Zustaende." Published at Halle.

1840.—Ludwig Ettmüller. " Beowulf. Heldengedicht des achten Jahrhunderts. Zum ersten Male aus dem Angelsächsischen in das

Neuhochdeutsche stabreimend übersetzt und mit Einleitung und
Anmerkungen versehen." A translation into alliterative verse,
published at Zurich.

1847.—Frederik Schaldemose. "Beo-Wulf og Scopes Widsith, to angel-
saxiske Digte, med Oversættelse og oplysende Anmærkninger."
Text, with translation into Danish, of which there was another
edition published also at Copenhagen in 1851.

1849.—A. Diedrich Wackerbarth. "Beowulf, an Epic Poem translated from the Anglo-Saxon into English Verse." London : W.
Pickering.

1855.—Benjamin Thorpe. "The Anglo-Saxon Poems of Beowulf, the
Scóp or Gleeman's Tale, and the Fight at Finnesburg," with a
Literal Translation. Published at Oxford by J. A. Parker.

1857.—C. W. M. Grein. Beowulf in the "Bibliothek der angelsächsischen Poesie." Published at Göttingen.

Also in the same year, a translation into alliterative German
verse, in Grein's "Dichtungen der Angelsachsen, stabreimend
übersetzt."

1859.—Karl Simrock. "Beowulf. Das älteste Deutsche Epos. Ueber-
setzt und erläutert." Stuttgart and Augsburg.

1861.—N. F. S. Grundtvig. "Beowulfes Beorhaeller Bjovulfs-Drajen,
det Old-Angelske Heltedigt, paa Grunds-proget." Copenhagen.

1863.—Moritz Heyne. "Beowulf. Mit ausführlichem Glossar."
Published at Paderborn ; and, in the same year, with Heyne's
Text, his Translation, "Beowulf. Angelsächsisches Heldengedicht
übersetzt von Moritz Heyne."

1867.—C. W. M. Grein. "Beovulf nebst den Fragmenten Finnsburg
und Valdere in kritisch bearbeiteten Texten neu herausgeben, mit
Wörterbuch." Cassel and Göttingen.

1872.—Hans von Wolzogen. "Beovulf (Bärwelf) Das älteste deutsche
Heldengedicht. Aus dem Angelsächsischen." Published at
Leipzig.

1876.—Thomas Arnold. "Beowulf," a Heroic Poem of the Eighth
Century, with a Translation, Notes, and Appendix. London :
Longmans.

1877.—L. Botkine. "Beowulf, Epopée Anglo-Saxonne." Traduite en
Français pour la première fois. Preceded in 1876 by "Beo-
wulf, Analyse historique et géographique." Both published at
Havre.

1881.—Richard Wülcker. A Text of Beowulf, newly collated with
the MS. in the second edition of Grein's "Biblothek der Angelsächsischen Poesie," edited by R. Wülcker.

Lieut.-Col. H. W. Lumsden. "Beowulf, an English Poem, translated into Modern Rhymes." London.

1882.—A. Holder. "Beowulf. Abdrück der Handschrift im British Museum." Freiburg and Tübingen.

Julius Zupitza. "Beowulf." Autotypes of the Unique Cotton MS. Vitellius A. xv in the British Museum.

1883.—James M. Garnett, "Beowulf, an Anglo-Saxon Poem, and the Fight at Finnesburg, Translated." Boston : Ginn, Heath, and Co.

James A. Harrison and Robert Sharp, "I. Beowulf : An Anglo-Saxon Poem. II. The Fight at Finnsburh. A Fragment. With Text and Glossary on the basis of M. Heyne. Edited, corrected, and enlarged, by James A. Harrison, Profe or of English and Modern Languages, Washington and Lee University ; and Robert Sharp (Ph. D. Lips.), Professor of Greek and English, University of Louisiana." Boston : Ginn, Heath, and Co.

1884.—Holder's text was republished by J. C. B. Mohr at Freiburg and Tübingen as No. 7 of the "Germanische Bücherschatz."

1885.—By Friedrich Ramhorst, in a Dissertation upon Cynewulf's "Andreas" (published at Berlin) ; and by

1886.—Dr. G. Sarrazin, of the University of Kiel, in an article in the ninth volume of "Anglia" (pp. 515—550) has called special attention to many correspondences of phrase between the poem of "Beowulf" and Cynewulf's "Elene" and "Andreas"—the "Andreas" especially. The question thus raised as to the authorship of "Beowulf" will presently be considered in the chapter upon Cynewulf.

INDEXES.

— ✦ —

INDEX TO THE INTRODUCTION.

A

Academy, The French, 60, 61
Addison, Joseph, 51, 73, 74, 76, 77, 85, 86
"Adventures of Five Hours, The," 68
"Africa," Petrarch's, 19, 32
Alcamo, Ciullo of, 10
Allegory, 24, 33, 34
"Almahide," Madeleine Scudéri's, 63
Alva, The Duke of, 28
Amadis of Gaul, 30
Amyot, Jaques, 54
Andrewes, Lancelot, 51
Anjou, Charles of, 14
"Anti-Jacobin," Canning's, 118
Arabs, Influence of the, 9, 10
"Arcadia," Sanazzaro's, Sydney's, 26
Ariosto, 29, 31—33, 54
Aristotle, 38
Armida, Garden of, Tasso's, in Spenser, 29
"Art Poétique," Boileau's, 64, 65
Ascham's "Schoolmaster," 40
Astrophel and Stella, 28, 29
Avignon, The Popes at, 18

B

Bacon, Sir Nicolas, 54
Barbarossa, Emperor, 11, 12
Bartas, Guillaume de Saluste Du, 52—55
Beatrice, Dante's, 15, 16
Bede, 7
Bembo, Cardinal, 32
"Bentivoglio and Urania," 97
Bickerstaff, Isaac, 91
Boccaccio, 21, 22, 54
Bodmer, Johann Jacob, 110 112
Boileau, Nicolas Despréaux, 61—68, 108
Bojardo, Matteo Maria, 31
Boscan, Juan, 56
Bossu, Réné le, 67
Boswell, James, 106, 107
Brittany, Early romance in, 12

Bucer, Martin, 54
Buckingham, George Villiers, Duke of, 65
Buckingham, John Sheffield, Duke of, 69
Bunyan, John, 67
Butric, 54

C

Cædmon, 7
Cabbala, The, 38
Camden, William, 39
"Campaign," Addison's, 86
Canterbury Tales, Chaucer's, 23
Cardan's Description of the English, 34
"Cento Novelle Antiche," 22
Cervantes Saavedra, Miguel de, 30
Chapelain's "Pucelle," 63
Chapelle, Claude E. L., 63
Charlemagne, 7
Chaucer, Geoffrey, 22, 23
Cheke, John, 39
"Christian Hero," Steele's, 87, 88
Christian Literature, Our Early, 7, 8
Chronicles, Our Early, 12
Cid, Spanish Poems of the, 10, 30
"Clélie," Madeleine Scudéri's, 63
Colbert, 61
Colet, John, 39
Collier, Jeremy, 89
Conceited Writing, 46—51
Congreve, William, 89
Constance, The Peace of, 14
Constantinople, Capture of, by the Turks, 38
"Convit," Dante's, 16, 17
Cotin, Charles, 63
Criticism, French-Classical, 67—77, 97, 104, 105
Crusades, Influence of the, 11, 15
Croker, John Wilson, 107

D

"Daily Universal Register, The," 118
Dante Alighieri, 13—18

Decameron, Boccaccio's, 22
Defoe, Daniel, 80—84, 97
Dennis, John 72, 73
Devereux, Penelope, 28
Dictionary of the French Academy,
    61
"Divine Comedy," Dante's. 17
"Divine Weeks," of Du Bartas, 53.
    54
Donne, John, 37, 51
Drawcansir, 65
Dryden, John, 53, 65, 67

E

"Edgar," Rymer's Tragedy of, 70
"Edinburgh Review, The," 119
"Elegy in a Country Churchyard,"
    Gray's, 105
Elizabeth, Queen, 54
"Englishman, The," Steele's Paper,
    95
Euphuism, 36—54

F

Fielding, Henry, 100—104
Fletcher, John, 51
Florence, Early Growth of, 13—15
Floral Games of Toulouse, 19
Folcacchiero de' Folcacchieri, 10
Formation of the Language, Period
    of the, 6—9
Frederick II., Emperor, 10, 11
"Freeholder," Addison's, 16
French Influence, Period of, 55—77
Fuller, Thomas, 51
"Funeral, The," Steele's Comedy, 88

G

Gai Saber, 11
Garcilaso de la Vega, 56
Generalisation, 7, 77
Germany and England, Influences of
    one on the other, 108—110, 112
Gifford, William, 118
Gildon, Charles, 69, 70
Goethe, Johann Wolfgang von, 107—
    110, 112, 113
"Götz von Berlichingen, 115
Goldsmith, Oliver, 104, 107, 108, 117
Gottsched, Johann Christoph, 110,
    111
Gray, Thomas, 105
"Grand Cyrus," Madeleine Scudéri's,
    63
Greek Studies, Introduction of, 38, 39
Greene, Robert, Novels of, 47, 48
Grocyn, William, 39
"Guardian, The," Steele's Paper, 95
Guelf and Ghibelline, 13, 14
Guinicello, Guido, 17
"Gulliver's Travels," Swift's, 97, 98

H

Hall, Joseph, 39

Hawes, Stephen, 24
History of Literature, 1—4
Horace's "Art of Poetry," 67
Hughes, John, 95

I

Ingelo, Nathanael, 97
Isaure, Clementina, Countess of Tou-
    louse, 19
Italian Influence, Period of, 9—55
Italianate Englishman, The, 34, 35

J

"Jerusalem Delivered," Tasso's, 34
Johnson, Samuel, 104—107
Jonson, Ben, 51—53
Journalism, Development of, 117—119
Junius, Letters of, 117

K

Klopstock, 111

L

La Fontaine, Jean de, 63
"L'Allegro," Goethe on Milton's, 109
Languet, Hubert, 27, 28
Lansdowne, George Granville, Lord,
    69
Latin, Petrarch's Study of, 19
    — Authors Preferred under Eliza-
        beth, 36, 37
Latini, Brunetto
Laura, Petrarch's, 19
"Lay of the Last Minstrel," Scott's
    115, 116
Leo X., Pope, 25
Libel, Laws of, 117
Lilly, William, 39
Linacre, Thomas, 39
Lorenzo de' Medici, 25, 31
"Love's Labour's Lost," 49, 50
Luther, Martin, 54
Lydgate, John, 24
"Lying Lover, The," Steele's Comedy,
    90
Lyly, John, 40—50

M

Manfredi, 10, 11
Marino, Gianbatista, 37
Marlowe, Christopher, 50, 58, 61
Marston, John, 39
Marot, Clement, 54
Medici, The, 25
Mendoza, Diego de, 56
Milton, John, 73—77, 79, 80, 110, 111
Minnesänger, The Suabian, 11
Molière, 63
Montagu, Charles, Earl of Halifax
    85, 86
More, Henry, 39
    — , Sir Thomas, 54
"Morgante Maggiore," 31
Mornay, Philip du Plessis, 54

"Morning Advertiser," 118
" — Chronicle," 117
" — Herald," 118
" — Post," 118

N

Neo Platonists, 38
Nibelungen Lied, The, 11
Normans, The Early, 8, 12
"North Briton," Wilkes's, 117

O

"Orlando Innamorato," Boiardo's. 31
" — Furioso," Ariosto's, 31, 32
"Ormulum," The, 13
"Ossian," Macpherson's, 112

P

"Pamela," Richardson's, 99
Partridge's Almanack, 91
"Pastime of Pleasure," Stephen
  Hawes's, 24
Pepys, Samuel, on Shakespeare, 68,
  69
Period of the Formation of the Lan-
  guage, 6—9
Period of Italian Influence, 9—55
  — — French —, 55—77
  — — Popular —, 77—119
Periods of English Literature, The
  Four, 4—9
Petrarch, Francis, 18—21, 54
Peucer, Caspar, 54
Platonism, 38
Poliziano, Agnolo, his "Orpheus," 26
Précieuses, The, 45, 57—60
"Public Ledger," Newbery's. 117
" — Advertiser," The, 117
Pulci, Luigi, 31
Puritan Euphuism, 54

Q

Quarles, Francis, 51
"Quarterly Review, The," 118, 119
Quotation, The Taste for, 33

R

Racine, Jean, 63
Rambouillet, Hôtel, Dainty Speech at
  the, 45, 58—60
Rapin, René, 67
Regnier, Mathurin, 57
"Rehearsal," the Duke of Bucking-
  ham's, 65
"Review," Defoe's, 84
Revolution, The French, 113, 114
Richardson, Samuel, 99, 100
Richelieu, 60
"Rinaldo," Tasso's, 34
"Robinson Crusoe," 97—99, 110
Ronsard, Pierre de, 54, 57, 58, 61
Roscommon, Wentworth Dillon, Earl
  of, 67
Rymer, Thomas, 70

S

Sanazzaro, Jacopo, 26, 29
Santillana, Marquis of, 33, 34
Schiller, Friedrich von, 112, 113
Scott, Sir Walter, 45. 115—117
Scudéri, George and Madeleine, 62
  63, 97
Shakespeare, William, 49, 50, 57, 69,
  70, 71, 72
"Shortest Way with the Dissenters,"
  Defoe's, 82—84
Sicilian Language, The, 10
Sidney, Sir Philip, 26—28, 54
Soame, Sir William, 67
Somers, John, Lord. 85, 86
Sonnets, 10, 15, 16, 19, 28
Spain, Influence of, 10, 11, 30, 56
"Spectator," Steele and Addison's,
  92, 94
Spenser, Edmund, 29, 47
Squire of Dames, The, in Ariosto and
  Spenser, 29
Steele, Richard, 87—97
Suabian Minnesänger, 11
Surrey, Henry Howard, Earl of, 25
  26
Swift, Jonathan, 91, 96
Sylvester, Joshua, 55

T

Taliesin, 6
Tasso, Torquato, 19, 34, 54
"Tatler," Steele's, 90—93
"Tender Husband, The," Steele's
  Comedy, 98, 99
Theobald, Lewis, 71
"Times, The," Origin of, 118
"Tom Jones," Fielding's, 100—104
Troubadours, 10—12
"Tyrannic Love," Dryden s, 65

U

Urien, 6

V

Ventadorn, Bernard de, 11
"Vicar of Wakefield, The," its In-
  fluence on Goethe, 107
"Vita Nuova," Dante's, 15—17

W

Walton, Isaac, 51
Wars under Henry V. and VI., 24
Wechsel, Andrew, Printer, 27
Woodfall, William, 117
Wordsworth, William, 113—115
Writers and Readers, 119, 120
Wyat, Sir Thomas, 25, 26

Y

Young, Edward, 108, 109, 111

INDEX TO BOOK I.

A

Aber, 155
Aberystwith, Merlin's Grave at, 210
Adornments of Old Gaelic MSS., 196
Adur, The River, in Sussex, 205
Advocates'Library,Edinburgh,181,182
Aed (afterwards Goll) MacMorna, 183
Ælla, 208
Æschylus, Hyperboreans referred to by, 143
— , Cimmerians of, 146
Æsir, 265
Agricola, 243
Aillin, the Princess, Tale of Bailé and, 168, 169
Alban, 165, 195, 196
Albion, 149, 165
Alexander the Great, 126
Alfred, King, 246, 264
Alliteration, 295, 296
Alman, 125, 126
Althing, The, 272
Ammianus Marcellinus, 205
Aneurin, 210, 219—235
Angles, 164, 208, 247—249
Anglesey, 138
Anglo-Saxon, The Name, 251
— Settlements, 208, 241—253
Annals of Connaught, 202
— — the Four Masters, 202
— — Innisfallen, 201
— — Kilronan, 202
— — Tighernach, 201
— — Ulster, 202
Anroth, The, 170
Antoninus Pius, 243
Apollo, Supposed worship of, in Ancient Britain, 141—144
Argè and Opis, 145
Argoed Llwyfain, The Battle of, 211, 212
Arians, Ulfilas and the, 256, 257
Aristotle's Britannic Islands, 149
Arminius, 254
Armorican, 155
Arnold, Thomas, 316
Arthur, King, 209, 215, 235
Arthur's Stone, 138
Artistic Genius of the Celts, 189, 190
Aryans, 127, 129
Ashkenaz, 125
Attacots, 205
Augusta (London), 206
Auxentius, 255

B

Badb-catha, The, 191
Bailé, the Sweet-spoken, Tale of 168, 169
Ballymote, The Book of, 202
Bangor Tewy, 210
Bards, Cymric, 208—237
Barker, G. D., 235
Barrows, 132, 138—140, 309, 312
Basques, 132, 154
Becan, John, 126
Bede, 242, 246
Belgæ, 150—152, 154, 156, 204
Beowulf, 273—348
Bernicia and Deira, 209, 220, 221, 224, 225
"Bhagavat Gita," 128
Bible, Translation of the, by Ulfilas, 256, 257
Bird of Valour, The, 191, 199
Bôhus, The Castle of, 317
Book of Ballymote, 202
— — the Dean of Lismore, 181, 182, 184, 187
— — the Dun Cow, 201
— — Leinster, 176, 179, 181, 183, 201, 202
—, The Red, of Hergest, 238
—, The Speckled, 202
—, The Yellow, 202
Bopp, Franz, 129
Boromean Tribute, Origin of the, 175
Boyne, The, 168
Bragaraedur, 273
Brancaster, 205
Breatan, 195
Breca, Beowulf's Swimming Match with, 318
Brehon Laws, 170
Brian Boroihme, 176
Brigantes, 153, 173
Brittany, 155
Bruno, Brunswick, 126
Bryneach, 209, 220, 221, 224, 225
Bugge, Sophus, 274, 275
Bülow, Johann, 312
Burgh Castle, 205

C

Caeilte, McRonan, 186, 187
Caerleon upon Usk, 210
Caermarthen, The Black Book of, 236
Cæsar, Julius, 150, 151, 204, 243

Callinus, 146
Cambridge, 154
Cano, The, 170
Cantyre, 154
Cassiterides, 149
Castle Knock on the Liffey, 182, 183
Catrail, The, 220
Catterick Bridge, 220, 233
Cattle Spoil of Chuailgné, Tale of the,
    177—179
Cattraeth, The Battle of, 220—224
Celtic Stock, The, 130
— Element in English, The, 157—
    161
Celts, Ancestry of the, 142—150
—, Influence of, on English, 189,
    190
Cerdic, 208
Chamitic Families of Man, 124, 125
Chauci, 249—251
Cherusci, 250, 251, 254
Chocilagus, 318, 331—336
Christianity, First Dawn of, 186, 187,
    200
— Established in Ireland, 272
— in Early Britain, 275
Cimmerians and Celts, 146—150
Claudius, Invasion of, 243
Cli, The, 170
Cnúcha, The Battle of, 182, 183
Conchobar, 175
Cong in Mayo, 172
Congal Claen, 198, 199
Constantine, Emperor, 256
Conybeare, John Josias, 312
Cooley in Louth, 176
Covehithe in Suffolk, 325
Crannoges, 134
Credé's Bower, 187, 188
Crimea, 148
Cromlechs, 136—138
Crow, The Hooded, 191
Cruithne, 195, 196
Cuchorb, Queen Meav's Lament for,
    180
Cuchulain, 169, 178, 191
Cuilmenn, or Great Book of Skins, 176
Cumhail, Father of Fionn, Death of,
    183
Cyndillan, 214, 216, 217
—, Llywarch Hen's Lament for, 218
Cyril, 263

D

David, Saint, 211
Dean of Lismore's Book, The, 181,
    182, 184, 187
Death Song, 180
Dederich, Hermann, 333, 334, 335
Deivyr and Bryneich (Deira and Ber-
    nicia), 209, 220, 221, 224, 225
Deor, 354
Dialogue with St. Patrick, Oisin's, 186,
    187
— of the Ancient Men, 187

Diarmaid and Grainné, 137, 190
Dicuil, 271
Diodorus Siculus, 141
Domhnall, King of Ireland, 198, 199
Dover, 205
Dragon, The, in Beowulf, 342—344
Drida, 337—339
Driseg, The, 170
Druids, 145, 162—164
Dundalk, 168

E

Earle, Prof. John, 326—331
Ebert, Adolf, 316
Eddas, The, 273, 274
Eichhorn, Johann Gottfried, 124
Eiddin, 221, 222
Ekkehart, 354
Elidir, 214
Elphin, Son of Urien, 210
English, The Name, 164
Erbin, 214
Erin, 166
Erse, 165
Essex, 208
Ettmüller, Ludwig, 314, 318, 345
Euskarian, 132
Ezekiel's Reference to Gomer, 147

F

Fenians, The, 180—195
—, as a militia, 192, 193
Feradach, King of Scotland, 196, 318,
    334, 335
Fergus Finnbheoil, 184
— —, his Soothing of Goll Mac
    Morna, 184, 185
— —, his Death of Oscar, 193
Fiann of Monasterboice, Synchron-
    isms of, 201
Fifeldor, 338
Fin Folcwalda, 345, 352—354
Fingal in Barbour's Bruce, 181
Finnesburg, The Fight at, 292, 349—
    354
Finntragha, The Battle of, 191
Fionn, Mac Cumhaill, 137, 180, 183—
    185
Firbolgs, The, 172, 173
Fitela, 339
Floki Rafn, 270
Fochlog, The, 170
Freaware, 301
Fressel, Johannes, 255
Freyr, 343
Friesland, 126
Frisians, 249—253, 130, 204, 248
Friso, 126
Froda, 301, 302
Furies, The Gaelic, 191
Futhorc, The, 267

G

Gabhra, The Battle of, 193—196
Gadelas, 166, 167
Gaedhels (See also Gaels), 166, 173, 174
Gaels, First Settlements of the, 130, 152—154
— in North Wales, 206—208
—, Old Literature of the, 165—202
Gallehus, The Golden Horns of, 267
Gallicia, 153
Garnett, Richard, 160
Garthr, 270
Gaul, Movements of the Celts in, 148, 149
Geraint, 215
Germanic Settlements in Britain, 204—206
Gesta Regum Francorum, 318—333
Gildas, 240, 242
Gilla Caemhain, Poem of, 201
Gimiri, 146
Gododin, The, 219—233
Goll Mac Morna, 183—185
Gomer, 125, 147
Gotha, The Swedish River, 318
Grace before Meat, 198, 199
Grampian Hills, 154
Gray's "Death of Hoel," 222, 225 230
Gregory of Tours, 318, 327, 330—333
Grein, C. W. M., 315—319, 340, 341, 352
Grendel, 341—347
Grettis Saga, 329
Grimm, Jacob, 344
Grundtvig, Nic. Fred. Sev., 312
Gwenn, Llywarch's Lament for his Son, 217
— Estrad, Battle of, 210
Gwyddel, Significance of, in Local Names of North Wales, 206—208
Gwynedd, The Gael in, 153, 206—208
Gylfa-ginning, 273

H

Hadrian's Wall, 243
Haigh, Rev. Daniel H., 319—326, 353
Hamite Families of Man, 124, 125
Hampshire, 151
Harold Harfagr, 270
Hart, and Hartlepool, 320
Háttatal, 274
Heardred, 301, 303, 305
Heathcynn, 318
Hecatæus, the Milesian, 140—143
Hengest of Finnesburg, 352, 353
Hengist and Horsa, 208, 244
Hengwrt, 238
Henwg, the Bard, 210
Heremod, 339, 340
Hereric, 303
Hergest, The Red Book of, 238
Herodotus on the Hyperboreans, 144

Herodotus on the Cimmerians, 146
— — — Celts, 148
Hetware, The, 318, 333—335
Heyne, Moritz, 315, 316
Hickes, George, 311, 349
Hildebrand and Hadubrand, 258—261
Hildeburh at Finnesburg, 353
History, Old Gaelic, 171—179
Hitopadesa, 128
Hjortholm, 317
Hnæf, 352, 353
Holyhead, 207
Howel Dda, The Laws of, 238
Huasein (Oisin), 190
Hugas, The, 318, 335, 336
Humber, The, 155
Huxley, Thomas Henry, 131, 132
Hygd, Wife of Hygelac, 300, 336—339
Hygebriht, 330, 331
Hygelac, 318, 332—335
Hyperboreans, Celts and, 140—146
Hyperochè, 144

I

Iapetic Families of Man, 124—126
Iberians, 148
Iceland, 269—276
Ida, The English Settlement under, 208, 209, 211
Ierne, 145, 165, 166
Illuminations, Character of, in Old Gaelic MSS., 196, 197
Indo-European Family, The, 129—131
Influence of the Celts on English Literature, 189, 190
Ingeld, 301
Innesfallen, Annals of, 201
Inver, 155
Iolo Morganwg, 239
Iran, 128
Irish Hermits in Ireland, 271
Iron Period, 140
Isca, 153
Islendinga Bók, 270, 271

J

Jones, Rev. Basil, 153
—, Owen, his Myvyrian Archæology 239
—, Sir William, 126, 128
Jutes, 208, 244—247

K

Keating, Rev. Geoffrey, 193
Kemble, John Mitchell, 312, 345
Kent, 154, 208
Kian, 219
King Arthur, 209, 219, 235
Kitchen-middens, Danish, 134
Kit's Coty House, 138
Kölbing, Eugen, 316
Kywryd, 219

L

Laistner, L., 346
Lake Dwellings of the Stone Period, 134, 135
Landnamabók, The, 271
Laodicè, 144
Latham, Dr. R. G., 246
Lathes of Kent, 247
Latin, Periods of the Introduction of, into English, 162
Leabhar Breac, 202
— na-h-Uidre, 182, 201
Lecain, The Yellow Book of, 202
Leinster, 168, 169, 175
— , The Book of, 176, 179, 181, 183, 201, 202
Leitrim, 172
Lemcke, Ludwig, 316
Leo, Heinrich, 314, 318
Lhuyd, Edward, 153
Liber Landavensis, 238
Lincolnshire, 155
Lindisfarne, 215
Lismore, 181, 182
Literature of People 123
— — the English People, 124
— , Old Gaelic Degrees in, 170, 171
Littus Saxonicum, 205
Llandaff, 238
Lloegrians, 218
Llyfr Coch, 238
Llywarch Hen, 210, 214—218
Local Names, Celtic, 157—159
Lochlan, 195
London, 151, 206
Lycian and Olen, 145
Lyell, Sir Charles, 134, 135
Lympne, 205

M

MacGregor, James, Dean of Lismore, his Book, 181, 182
Macpherson, James, 180, 181
Magh Rath, Legend of the Battle of, 197—200
Mahábhárata, 128
Mailand, Jacob van der, 253
Manuscript Materials for Study of Gaelic Language and Literature, 200—202
— — — — Cymric Language and Literature, 237—239
Matthew Paris, 337, 338
Meav, Queen, her Lament for Cuchorb, 179, 180
Melanochroi, 131, 132
Mendip Hills, 154
Mengant, 219
Merlin, 219
Merovingians, 261, 335
Methodus, 263
Metres, Celtic, 236, 237
— , Scandinavian, 273, 274
— , Anglo-Saxon, 295, 296, 345, 346

Milesians, 172, 173
Mithridates, 265
Modthrytho, 336— 339
Möller, Hermann, 348, 352, 353
Mœsogoths, 130—255—258
Mone, Joseph, 351
Mongoloids, 131, 132
Morlais, the River, 217
Morrigau, the Battle Fury, 191, 200
Moytura, Battle on the Plain of, 172, 173
Müllenhoff, Karl, 345, 348
Müller, Peter Erasmus, 311
Munster, 169, 170
Mynyddawg, 221
Myrddhin, 219
Myths, Early, 141—144
— suggested in Beowulf, 343—347
Myvyrian Archæology of Wales, 238, 239

N

Naddothr, 269
Neman, Macha, and Morrigau, old Irish Battle Furies, 191
Nennius, 242
Norfolk, 208
Northumbria, 155, 209

O

O'Curry, Eugene, 173, 181, 187
Odin, 264, 265, 313, 344
Odoacer, 257—259
O'Donovan, John, 197
Offas, The Two, 327—330, 337—339
Ogham Letters, 167—170
Oisin, 166, 180—186
Olen, 145
Ollamh, 170
Onela, 300
Ongetheow, 300—306
Opis and Argè, 145
Oral Tradition, Accuracy in, 170, 171, 176, 177
Oscar, son of Oisin, 183, 184
— , Poem on the death of, 194, 195
Ostrogoths, 257—261
Otadini, 209
Othona, 205
Oudendorp (or Oldendorp), Johann, 151
Owen, William, 218

P

Palgrave, Sir Francis, 209
Patrick, Saint, and Oisin, 186, 187
Pegwell Bay, 245
Pelnissus, 145
Pentland Hills, 154
Percy, Dr. John, 133
Pevensey, 205
Philostorgius, 255

Pindar, his reference to Hyperboreans, 143
Poets' Staves, 170
Pompey, 265
Pott, August Friedrich, 129
Prime Stories, Gaelic, 171
Priscian, MS. of, with Gaelic Glosses, 200
Procopius, 253
Ptolemy, Claudius, 249
Pursuit of Diarmaid and Grainné, 190
Pytheas, 264

Q

Quoits, the Cornish, 138

R

Ramáyana, The, 127
Rask, Erasmus, 124, 126
Rawlinson Prof. George, 146
— , Sir Henry 146
Reculvers, 205
Red Book of Hergest, 238
Regni, 151
Rheged, 203—209
Richborough, 205
Roman Occupation of Britain, 161,162, 243, 244
Romans in Germany, 254
Runes, 266—268

S

Sacæ, 126, 147, 254
Sæmund Sigfusson, 273
Saint Iltut's Hermitage, 138
Sakóntala, 128
Sanskrit, 127—130
Saxo, A Mythical, 126
— Grammaticus, 311, 337
Saxons, 126, 208, 249—254
Scandinavia, 130, 264 275
Scota, Mother of the Milesians, 167, 174
Scyld Scefing, 317, 340, 341
Schlegel, Friedrich, 129
Scyths, 126,147 167, 254
Semitic Families of Man, 124
Senchan, Gaelic chief poet, 176
Settlements, The Six Teutonic, in England, 208, 241—253
Siæl Lake, 317
Sigmund, 339
Silures, 153
Silver Codex at Upsala, 257
Simrock, Karl, 315
Sinfiolli, 339
Skáldskaparmál, 273
Skeat, Prof. W. W., 341—343
Slanga pig, 318
Slavonians, 130, 263
Snorri Sturluson, 273
Somersetshire, 151

Spoils of Taliesin, The, 212
Stephanus of Byzantium, 145
Stephens, Prof. George, 267, 268, 354
— , Thomas, 219
Stokes, Whitley, 236
Stone Period, The, 132—138
Strabo, 205
Styrmer the Learned, 271
Suffolk, 208, 325
Suibhne, The Cowardice of, 200
Surrey, 151
Sussex, 151, 208
Swaledale, 221

T

Tacitus, 150, 151, 153, 205, 249
Tain Bo Chuailgné, 176—179
Tales Classified for Recitation, 171
Talhaiarn, 219
Taliesin, 210, 214
Tara, 173, 175
Teilo, The Book of, 238
Teviotdale, 220
Theodoric, the Ostrogoth, 257—261
— I , King of Metz, 332, 335
— , Son of Ida, 209, 215
Theodosius, Emperor, 256
Thingvöllr, Plain of, 272
Thorkelin, Grim Johnson, 311, 312, 352
Thorpe, Benjamin, 314, 315
Thortharson, Sturla, 271
Thule, 264, 271
Tighernach, Annals of, 201
Tin from Britain, 149, 150
Tuisco, 125

U

Uffo, 337, 338
Uggeshall in Suffolk, 325
Uhland, Ludwig, 346
Ulfilas, 255—258
Ulster, 175
— , Annals of, 202
Upsala, Silver Codex at, 257
Urien; 203, 209—217
— , Taliesin's Songs of, 213—214
— , Llywarch Hen on the Death of, 215

V

Vedas, The, 127
Velschow, Dr. J. M., 311
Ventry Harbour, 191
Verstegan, Richard, 125
Vespasian, 243
Villemarqué, Vicomte Hersart de la, 217, 219
Völsunga-saga, 339
Vulfilas, 255—258

W

Wackerbarth, A. Diedrich, 314
Wægmundings, 309
Waitz, G., 255
Waldhere, 353, 354
Wanley, Humfrey, 311
Wayland Smith's Cave, 138
Weissenbrunner Prayer, The, 261, 262
Wessex, 208
Widsith, 354
Wight, Isle of, 245
Wilkins, Charles, 128
Wilkinson, Sir J. Gardner, 146
Williams, Edward, of Glamorgan, 239
— , John, Archdeacon of Cardigan, 140
— ab Ithel, Rev. John, 220
Wiltshire, 151

Woden, 264, 265, 313, 344
Wolf, Ferdinand, 316
Woodpecker, The mythical, 344, 345
Wülcker, Richard Paul, 315, 316

X

Xanthochroi, 131, 132

Y

Ynglingar, 265

Z

Zeno, Emperor, 257
Zupitza, Julius, 316

PRINTED BY CASSELL & COMPANY LIMITED, LA BELLE SAUVAGE, LONDON, E.C.
5.998.